A HISTORICAL END

GLOBAL PERSPECTIVES ON
CHINA'S POVERTY ALLEVIATION AND WORLD DEVELOPMENT

历史性句号

全球发展视野下的中国脱贫与世界发展

中国日报社中国观察智库 主编
Edited by China Daily China Watch Institute

SPM
南方出版传媒
广东人民出版社
·广州·

图书在版编目（CIP）数据

历史性句号：全球发展视野下的中国脱贫与世界发展：汉英对照 / 中国日报社中国观察智库主编 . -- 广州：广东人民出版社 ，2020.12
ISBN 978-7-218-14915-8

Ⅰ．①历… Ⅱ．①中… Ⅲ．①扶贫－研究－中国－汉、英
Ⅳ．①F126

中国版本图书馆 CIP 数据核字（2020）第 255938 号

LISHIXING JUHAO

历史性句号

中国日报社中国观察智库　主编

出 版 人：肖风华

出版统筹：肖风华
策划编辑：黄洁华
策划顾问：付　敬
责任编辑：黄洁华　李丽珊　张　芳
责任校对：梁敏岚　胡艺超
责任技编：吴彦斌　周星奎

出版发行：广东人民出版社
地　　址：广东省广州市海珠区新港西路204号2号楼（邮政编码：510300）
电　　话：（020）85716809（总编室）
传　　真：（020）85716872
网　　址：http://www.gdpph.com
印　　刷：雅昌文化（集团）有限公司
开　　本：787毫米×1092毫米　　1/16
印　　张：28　　字　　数：380千
印　　数：2020年12月第1版
版　　次：2020年12月第1次印刷
定　　价：118.00元

如发现印装质量问题，影响阅读，请与出版社（020-85716809）联系调换。

策划编辑团队

王　浩　拉维·香卡　高大伟　宋　平
朱启文　肖风华　黄洁华　刘　毅
张　钊　辛　欣　李丽珊　布英娜
刘　夏　王　哲　章　婷

Editorial and Production Team

Wang Hao　Ravi Shankar　David Gosset　Song Ping
Zhu Qiwen　Xiao Fenghua　Huang Jiehua　Liu Yi
Zhang Zhao　Xin Xin　Li Lishan　Bu Yingna
Liu Xia　Wang Zhe　Zhang Ting

编 写 说 明

　　"70年来，中国人民发愤图强、艰苦创业，创造了'当惊世界殊'的发展成就，千百年来困扰中华民族的绝对贫困问题即将历史性地划上句号，书写了人类发展史上的伟大传奇！"这句话出自习近平总书记在庆祝中华人民共和国成立70周年招待会上的讲话，充分表达了对决战决胜脱贫攻坚的必胜信心和坚定决心。在中国共产党的坚强领导下，中国人民创造了人类历史上前所未有的脱贫奇迹。2020年，中国消除了绝对贫困，逐步实现了全面建成小康社会的目标，提前10年率先实现联合国《2030年可持续发展议程》的第一目标，谱写人类减贫史上的壮丽篇章。本书阐述了中国减贫对全球贫困治理的积极意义，充分展现了中国脱贫为推动人类发展事业作出的巨大贡献，从国际视角出发，多维度探索中国精准扶贫方略在经济、社会等领域的宝贵经验和启示，向世界分享中国经验、中国智慧、中国方案，秉持构建人类命运共同体的崇高理念，与世界各国一道，共同促进全球减贫。

　　本书从国际视野审视中国脱贫攻坚战，结合统计数据和典型案例，论述中国脱贫和全面建成小康社会的世界价值和意义。全书共分为四篇：第一篇主要围绕中国脱贫和全面建成小康社会的世界意义，探讨中国经济社会高速发展、成功摆脱贫困的深层次原因，以及中国脱贫这一标志性成就带给世界其他发展中国家的启迪和希望。第二篇从微观的角度，对中国在摸索脱贫致富方方面面的举措进行梳理和分析，意在总结有益实践，为更高效推广经验和巩固成果提供参考。第三篇从国际扶贫合作与经验交流的维度，不仅记录了国际力量助力中国脱贫的举措，同时还侧重中国如何开展国际互助，把先进技术和经验以可持续发展的思路推广给其他地区，有力推动实现联合国《2030年可持续发展议程》目标。第四篇围绕中国迈向下一个百年目标和巩固脱贫成果这两个关键议题，对防止返贫、全面建成小康社会的挑战、如何保持可持续发展等一些国内外都非常关心的话题展开了讨论。

本书撰稿人均为全球从事扶贫事业知名机构的代表、相关领域的权威学者。同时，还有一些国内的知名专家、有国际影响力的资深学者和政商界精英。采用中英文对照，一是基于本书的特殊性，很多内容是外国专业人士用英文所撰，以保持原貌；二是兼顾相关人群，除了中国读者，还有外国专家和外籍在华人士；三是便于该书迅速"走出去"。相信通过汇辑这些对中国扶贫探索的前瞻性分析和研究，将能让国内读者了解外部世界如何看待中国脱贫，还能带给海内外从事中国发展研究的人士更多的线索和灵感，为全球减贫治理添砖加瓦。

本书编写组

2020年12月

Introduction

"Seventy years, Chinese people have worked hard and strived for a better life, and have made historic achievements that have greatly shaked the world! China will soon put an end to extreme poverty that has plagued Chinese nation for thousands of years, making a legendary success in human history." These words are from President Xi Jinping's speech at the reception in celebration of the 70th Anniversary of the Founding of the People's Republic of China, which has expressed firm confidence and determination to win the battle against poverty. Under the leadership of the Communist Party of China, China has made a miracle in human history by realizing the largest scale of poverty alleviation. China will eliminate extreme poverty by 2020 and build a moderately prosperous society in all respects soon after, taking the lead of achieving the first goal of the United Nations 2030 Sustainable Development Goals 10 years in advance, penning a glorious chapter in the history of humanity's fight against poverty. This book interprets the positive significance of China's poverty alleviation to global poverty governance, and fully demonstrates China's great contribution in promoting human development. From a global vision, it explores the valuable experience of China's targeted poverty alleviation measures in economic, social and other fields. It endeavors to share China experience, China wisdom and China solutions with the world. Bearing the notion of building a community with shared future for mankind, this book will tell you how China will work with other countries around the world to address the issue of global poverty.

This book looks into China's battle against poverty from a global perspective and elaborates the significance of China's poverty alleviation as well as building a moderately prosperous society in all respects through statistics and typical cases. This book has four chapters, namely, "The great legend", "The journey", "Joint effort" and "The way forward", in which topics including the witness of breathtaking speed and scale of China's poverty reduction, the value of China's poverty alleviation for world development, introducing China's geographical targeting of its poverty reduction programs and other solutions, the inspiration and examining specific programs to tackle poverty, the global impacts of the experiments, China's determination to sharing the fruits of development with the world and the approaches and measures to handle challenges and risks in the future.

The contributors of this book include numerous numbers of foreign well-known scholars and influential representatives as well as some Chinese leading experts and elites working on poverty eradication in various fields. The contents are in both Chinese and English since most texts are originally written in English, and it can be introduced to not only Chinese but also foreigner readers. Through this book, readers can understand how the outside world consider China's poverty alleviation and also find more inspiration and hints for global poverty governance.

The editorial team

December 2020

序　言

这部减贫作品的出版意义重大。

中国日报旗下传播型智库中国观察与广东人民出版社展开了富有成效的合作，并积极出版了这部减贫图书，对此，本人表示衷心祝贺。无论是对于中国还是对于世界，减贫这个主题都可谓影响深远。在这本书中，中国和国外作者就这一问题各抒己见、畅所欲言。毋庸置疑，这一问题理应成为全球促进可持续发展和"尊重人的尊严"的核心。

2015年通过的联合国《2030年可持续发展议程》将"消除贫穷"作为首要目标，即"在2030年以前消除全世界一切形式的贫穷"，这并不是偶然。如果想要实现"不让任何人掉队"，这是根本性的使命，也是《2030年可持续发展议程》的基本目标。

中国改革开放40多年来，经过不懈努力，到2015年，有7.3亿多贫困人口成功脱贫，占同期全球减贫人口总数的70%以上。中国经济奇迹中，有一点值得注意：中国政府已将人的发展作为其政策的重点。中国实行有针对性的、强有力的经济和社会政策，确保没有一个人掉队。

为响应联合国《2030年可持续发展议程》，中国实施了令人印象深刻的政策——精准扶贫，目标是到2020年，全面消除中国农村极端贫困，提前10年实现联合国《2030年可持续发展议程》中的"消除贫困"目标。

习近平主席已将脱贫定为2017年至2020年的"三大战役"之一，由此发起了"有史以来规模最大的一次脱贫攻坚战"。可谓成果斐然，举世瞩目。

2019年，适值中华人民共和国成立70周年，联合国发布了最新《人类发展报告》。该报告认识到中国发生的重大变化，不仅在经济增长方面，更重要的是，在人类可持续发展进程的各个方面。

中国在这方面的进步可谓举世瞩目。自1990年引入人类发展指数以来，中国是世界上唯一一个从"低人类发展水平"跃升至"高人类发展水平"的国家。

2005年，伟大的反种族隔离斗士、南非前总统纳尔逊·曼德拉发表了一篇载入史册的著名演讲《让贫困成为历史》。曼德拉在演讲中说："消除贫困并非做慈善，而是事关正义。消除贫困就是保护基本人权，拥有尊严和体面的生活。只要存在贫困，就谈不上真正的自由。"

如今，中国已经取得了非凡的成就。在减贫方面，中国创造了历史。

当然，今年，世界各国面临全球性公共卫生危机。我们需要强有力的国际合作和政治承诺，从而让全人类携起手来，共同战胜新冠病毒。

但是，与贫困的斗争还应该不断继续，甚至应该加快减贫步伐。许多国家，贫困根深蒂固、积重难返，贫困剥夺了亿万人的尊严与发展。中国已经逐渐步入小康社会，与此同时，世界许多地区的贫困问题依然形势严峻。

中国在经济和社会发展方面的经验不仅造福了中国人民，并且在多个领域为互联互通的世界带来了进步。

本书内容丰富翔实，希望它能够成为一个助推器，加快实现联合国可持续发展的首要目标——消除贫穷。

中国提出了"构建人类命运共同体"的宏伟愿景，正是提醒我们，开放包容始终是世界的重中之重。

伊琳娜·博科娃

联合国教科文组织前总干事（2009—2017）

2020年4月4日

Preface

The publication of this collection of essays on poverty alleviation is of the highest significance.

I would like to congratulate China Daily's think tank China Watch and the Guangdong People's Publishing House for their fruitful cooperation and for taking the initiative of publishing this collection of essays on a topic of huge importance for China and for the world —the eradication of poverty. Let me commend also all the contributors from China and abroad for sharing their reflections on an issue which should be at the center of our actions for sustainable development and respect for human dignity.

It is not by chance that the United Nations 2030 Agenda for Sustainable Development, adopted in 2015, put "No Poverty" as the first goal—"To end poverty in all its forms everywhere by 2030". This is fundamental, if we want to "leave no one behind", which is the underlying ambition of the Agenda 2030.

Since the beginning of the reforms in China, a little more than four decades ago, China has lifted more than 730 million people out of poverty by the year 2015, accounting for over 70 percent of global poverty reduction accomplishments. What is remarkable in the Chinese economic miracle is that the government has made human development the focus of its policy. It has implemented strong and targeted economic and social policy to ensure that no one is left behind.

In response to the adoption of the UN Agenda for Sustainable Development (SDGs), China launched an impressive policy campaign called "the targeted poverty alleviation", aiming at the complete elimination of extreme poverty in rural China by 2020, 10 years ahead of the agenda of SDGs.

President Xi Jinping has identified anti-poverty as one of three "tough battles" for the period from 2017 to 2020, launching thus "the largest poverty alleviation campaign in history". And it has given astounding results.

The last *Human Development Report*, issued by the United Nations in 2019, which coincided with the 70th anniversary of the People's Republic of China, recognizes the remarkable changes that have taken place in China—not only in terms of economic growth, but more importantly, the wider range of sustainable human development progress.

China's advances in this regard have been uniquely impressive—it is the only country in the world that progressed from a "low human development country" in 1990 to a "high human development country" today.

In his well-known speech "Make Poverty History" in 2005, the great fighter against apartheid in South Africa Nelson Mandela famously said: "Overcoming poverty is not a gesture of charity. It is the protection of a fundamental human right, the right to dignity and a decent life. While poverty persists, there is no true freedom."

Today, China has made an extraordinary achievement—it has made poverty history.

Of course, this year is marked by a tragic global public health crisis. We need strong international cooperation and political commitment so that mankind declares victory over COVID-19.

However, the fight against poverty should continue and it should even be accelerated. There are many countries where poverty is enduring and where it deprives hundreds of millions of people of dignity and development. While China becomes a "moderately prosperous society", the issue of poverty remains acute in many regions of the world.

The Chinese experience in terms of economic and social development has not only benefited the Chinese people, but it has also brought progress in many areas of our globalized and interconnected world.

I hope that the rich content of this book serves as a catalyst for a more rapid achievement of goal number one of the UN Sustainable Development Goals—the eradication of poverty.

By putting forward the great vision of a community of shared future for mankind, China rightfully reminds us that inclusiveness should always be a strategic priority.

Irina Bokova

Director General UNESCO 2009–2017

April 4, 2020

前　言

中华人民共和国成立70年来，中国在脱贫方面取得的成就举世瞩目。2020年，尽管面对新冠肺炎疫情这道难度空前的"加试题"，中国仍以更加坚定的信心，排除万难，在毫不放松抓好常态化疫情防控的同时，不断加大脱贫攻坚力度。

在决战决胜脱贫攻坚的关键时刻，习近平总书记指出，脱贫攻坚不仅要做得好，而且要讲得好。一个14亿人口的大国消除绝对贫困，是人类发展史上的壮举。怎样呈现这一波澜壮阔的历史画卷，是摆在我们面前的重大课题。我们要站在时代高度，面向世界讲好中国脱贫攻坚故事，让世界读懂中国脱贫攻坚的伟大实践。

20年前，联合国千年首脑会议通过了以减贫为首要目标的"千年发展目标"。经过不懈努力，全球减贫事业取得重大进展，同时各国继续为实现2030年可持续发展目标而奋斗。作为世界第一人口大国，中国在5年前就基本实现"千年发展目标"，成为全球最早实现"千年发展目标"中减贫目标的发展中国家。

2018年，联合国秘书长安东尼奥·古特雷斯在出席中非合作论坛北京峰会时，在采访中提到："过去10年，中国是为全球减贫作出最大贡献的国家。"很多国际人士也深信，中国将如期实现消除绝对贫困的目标，中国的减贫成绩为全球减贫作出了重要贡献，中国的扶贫脱贫经验对世界各国的减贫事业意义非凡。

在习近平主席亲自指挥部署下，走在中国特色减贫道路上的14亿中国人民，即将实现第一个百年奋斗目标——全面建成小康社会。这将给长时间困扰中华民族的绝对贫困问题历史性地画上句号，也必然具有更广泛的世界意义。

在这样的背景下，中国日报旗下中国观察智库和广东人民出版社合作出版了这本有关中国扶贫经验及其对世界意义的评论集《历史性句号：全球发展视野下的中国脱贫与世界发展》。上海合作组织秘书长弗拉基米尔·诺罗夫、英国财政部前商务大臣吉姆·奥尼尔、世界银行前副行长伊恩·高登、国务院扶贫开发领导小组专家咨询委员会委员李小云、中国国际扶贫中心主任刘俊文等40多位国际知名人士应邀写作。他们或根据自己的学术研究，或结合亲身经历，详细介绍了中国扶贫减贫的方法，生动描绘了中国建设小康社会带来的巨变，并高度赞扬了中国脱贫攻坚的非凡成就。

刘俊文提到："党的十八大以来，以习近平同志为核心的党中央把脱贫攻坚摆到治国理政的突出位置，实施精准扶贫精准脱贫方略，创造了中国减贫史上的最好成绩。精准扶贫成为推动全球减贫进程的重要经验，为实现联合国《2030年可持续发展议程》目标贡献了中国智慧和中国方案。"

弗拉基米尔·诺罗夫在书中写道："自1978年中国实行改革开放以来，中国累计已有近8亿贫困人口脱贫，占同期全球减贫人口总数的70%以上。放在世界范围内看，这一减贫数据甚至超过了今天拉丁美洲的人口总数。"

吉姆·奥尼尔在文章中赞叹："中国不仅使数亿人摆脱了贫

困，而且使大约一半人口的生活水平达到了七国集团主要经济体的标准。"

通过几十位作者从不同角度对中国减贫成就的剖析，本书深刻揭示了中国减贫成功背后的深层次原因，这也将进一步启发读者去探索中国减贫奇迹对全球发展的重要意义。

中国是世界减贫的最大贡献者。中国反贫困完成的是历史性跨越。作为曾经最贫穷的国家之一，中国是世界现代史上无可争辩的"减贫巨人"。20世纪80年代后的30多年，中国累计减贫8亿多人，以占世界五分之一的人口贡献了全球七成以上的减贫总量。同时，中国扶贫攻坚的难度之大非同寻常。国际经验表明，最后10%的贫困人口是"贫中之贫""困中之困"，是减贫脱贫的"难中之难"。2012年底以来，中国减贫9000多万人，贫困发生率从10.3%降至0.6%。今年完成脱贫攻坚任务，中国将提前10年实现联合国《2030年可持续发展议程》的减贫目标。这么短时间实现这么多人口脱贫，是新时代中国发展进步的最鲜明标志。

"以人民为中心"是中国共产党最深入人心的执政理念。"脱贫攻坚"是"瓦解关于中国的偏见、改变对中国认知的最强有力叙事"。世界上没有任何其他国家的领导人，把一个基于"确切时间表"的减贫目标作为自己的施政纲领并作出郑重承诺。美国库恩基金会主席罗伯特·劳伦斯·库恩在文章中感叹道："我们惊讶地发现，中国为每个贫困户都完成了建档立卡工作，并制定了与之相对应的精准脱贫计划。"

"人民"二字是中国扶贫故事的灵魂。彻底改变亿万贫困人口的命运，就是把"人民对美好生活的向往"作为奋斗目标的最生动实践。同时，如习近平总书记所指出的，"脱贫致富终究要靠贫困群众用自己的辛勤劳动来实现"。我们要始终把人民作为脱贫攻坚故事的主角，书写人民创造历史的时代记录。

扶贫成绩打造了新时代贫困治理的中国话语。消除贫困是人类面临的历史任务，也是困扰世界的现实话题。长期以来，从"什么是贫困"到"怎么消除贫困"，西方形成一套占据主导地位的话语体系。全球减贫格局的演变将推动构建新的反贫困理论。中国减贫扶贫脱贫的实践创新，蕴含着丰富的贫困治理话语资源。我们要围绕"精准扶贫"这一新型贫困治理模式和科学理论体系，在讲好中国脱贫攻坚故事的过程中，构建面向世界的中国特色扶贫话语体系，不断提升贫困治理国际话语权。

周树春

中国日报社总编辑

2020年10月

Foreword

Since the founding of the People's Republic of China seven decades ago, the country has made stunning progress in poverty reduction. Despite the difficulties caused by the COVID-19 pandemic this year, China has remained committed to its target of eradicating extreme poverty by the year's end and has doubled efforts in poverty relief while ensuring pandemic prevention and containment.

President Xi Jinping has said: "We should not only fulfill the mission of poverty alleviation successfully, but also share the experience with the rest of the world." It is an unparalleled feat in human history for a country of 1.4 billion people to eliminate absolute poverty. How to explain and present this magnificent achievement, and how to tell China's poverty reduction story and make its practices in poverty relief understandable to the rest of the world is the essence of this book.

Poverty reduction is at the top of the agenda of the United Nations Millennium Development Goals (MDGs) set 20 years ago. The world has achieved major progress since then, and countries around the world are endeavoring to meet the 2030 Sustainable Development Goals. As the world's most populous nation, China essentially achieved the MDGs on poverty reduction as early as in 2015, making it the first developing nation to reach the target.

In 2018, when attending the Beijing summit of the Forum on China-Africa Cooperation (FOCAC), UN Secretary-General Antonio Guterres said in an interview that in the previous 10 years, China was the country that contributed most to global poverty reduction. Many people in the international community also believe that China will realize the goal of eradicating absolute poverty in 2020 and recognize the great contributions it has made to global poverty alleviation, and the great significance its practices hold to other countries.

Under the leadership of President Xi, China is poised to reach its first "Centennial Goal" of building a moderately prosperous (xiaokang) society. This will mark an end to the perennial problem of absolute poverty that has plagued the Chinese nation in its long history, and has great significance for the entire world.

In this context, China Daily's think tank China Watch, in collaboration with Guangdong People's Publishing House, has published *A Historical End: Global Perspectives on China's Poverty Alleviation and World Development*, a collection of commentaries on China's poverty alleviation efforts and its international significance. The authors include Vladimir Norov, Secretary-General of the Shanghai Cooperation Organization (SCO); Jim O'Neill, former commercial secretary to the UK Treasury; Ian Goldin, former vice-president of the World Bank; Li Xiaoyun, member of the Advisory Committee of the State Council Leading Group Office of Poverty Alleviation and Development; Liu Junwen, director of the International Poverty Reduction Center in China, and etc. Based on their academic studies or personal experiences, they depict China's poverty reduction efforts and achievements of building a moderately prosperous society.

Liu Junwen wrote in his article: "Since the 18th National Congress of the Communist Party of China, the Party Central Committee, with Xi Jinping at the core, has made poverty elimination a priority in national governance and has implemented the strategy of targeted poverty alleviation. Targeted poverty alleviation has become an important example for the global poverty reduction process and has contributed Chinese wisdom and solutions to the achievement of the goals of the Untied Nations 2030 Agenda for Sustainable Development."

Vladimir Norov said: "After launching the reform and opening-up in 1978, China pulled nearly 800 million people, or 70 percent of the world's total, out of poverty. In global terms, this figure exceeds the total population of Latin America."

Jim O'Neill commented: "Not only has China lifted hundreds of millions of people out of basic poverty; but it has also succeeded for probably around half the same number, achieving the living standards of a major G7 economy.

The book reveals the profound reasons behind China's poverty relief accomplishments through analyses made by the authors from different angles, inspiring readers to explore the great significance China's poverty reduction miracle has to the world.

As the largest contributor to global poverty reduction, China has made a historic leap forward in the fight against poverty. One of the world's poorest nations in the past, China is now a "giant" in poverty alleviation. Since the 1980s, China has lifted more than 800 million people out of poverty, accounting for more than 70 percent of global poverty reduction—a great achievement considering that its population makes up only one-fifth of the world's total. Nevertheless, China still faces huge challenges in eliminating absolute poverty. The global experience shows that pulling the last 10 percent of poverty-stricken population out of poverty is the most difficult part. Since the end of 2012, China has lifted more than 90 million rural people out of poverty, and the poverty rate has declined from 10.3 percent to 0.6 percent. By the end of this year, it will meet the goals on poverty reduction set in the Untied Nations 2030 Agenda for Sustainable Development 10 years ahead of schedule. To help such a large number of people shake off poverty in such a short period demonstrates the dramatic development and progress China has achieved in the new era.

"People-oriented development philosophy" is the defining characteristic of the Communist Party of China. Poverty reduction is the most wonderful Chinese story and also the most powerful narrative to dissolve the prejudice about China and change the perception of China. There is no leader in any other country who has set targets on poverty reduction with a specific timetable and make it a policy guideline. Robert Lawrence Kuhn, chairman of the Kuhn Foundation, wrote in his article: "Every poor family in China has its own file, each with its targeted plan to lift each above the line of absolute poverty."

"People" is the soul of China's poverty reduction story. Lifting hundreds of millions of people out of poverty is the most vivid demonstration of Chinese leaders' commitment to fulfilling "people's aspiration for a good life". As President Xi said, "The goal of poverty elimination can be achieved only through the efforts of the impoverished people themselves." People should be always the protagonists in China's poverty reduction story, and the writers of the history of the era.

China's anti-poverty achievements have created a China narrative in poverty reduction. Poverty elimination is a historic mission for humankind and a long-lasting problem plaguing the world. New developments in global poverty reduction efforts are shaping new anti-poverty theories; and China's practices in poverty relief create rich narrative resources. We should revolve around the new approach and the systematic theory of "targeted poverty alleviation" to create its own narrative system in poverty reduction with Chinese characteristics, and portray China's role in global poverty reduction.

Zhou Shuchun

Editor-in-Chief of China Daily

October 2020

中国观察智库

　　中国日报社中国观察智库，是中国日报依托遍布全球的高端资源和传播渠道，倾力打造的传播型智库。该智库汇聚全球中国问题研究的意见领袖、政治人物和商界精英，集纳海内外"最强大脑"的权威观点，建设中国研究的全球"朋友圈"，促进交流互鉴，提升研究水平，推动形成新理论、创造新智慧，影响并引领全球中国问题研究方向。致力于成为内容具有聚合性、权威性和工具性，传播效果具有穿透性的高端智库平台，并使其成为全球中国议题最权威的平台和风向标，服务于传播中国、影响世界、促进沟通和理解、推动建设人类命运共同体的使命。

　　《中国日报》是国家英文日报，创刊于改革开放之初。经过40年的发展，已经建成覆盖全球的集平面媒体、网站、移动新媒体、社交媒体、电邮简报以及系列品牌产品的全媒体传播网络，有效进入海外主流社会，形成传播优势，并积累了丰富的专业人才、分发渠道、运营经验和人脉资源优势，旗下的《中国观察报》与20余个国家的30余家权威媒体开展深度合作，期均发行500万份。《中国日报》是国内外高端人士首选的中国英文媒体，是讲述中国故事、传播中国理念、塑造中国改革开放形象的重要媒体平台。

About China Watch Institute

China Watch Institute is a communication channel facilitating research and analysis for China-focused institutions and thinkers around the world.

Powered by China Daily's core strength as a national flagship of international communication, China Watch Institute is a top-notch conduit for timely, detailed and thought-provoking research on China-related issues. It's in the best position to leverage its vast experience in communicating the China story to the world, especially to political influencers, opinion makers and business leaders by utilizing our incomparable network of China watchers and thinkers across the globe.

China Watch's global presence across a broad spectrum of media partners in more than 20 countries publishing in seven languages — such as The Washington Post, The Wall Street Journal, The Daily Telegraph, Le Figaro, Süddeutsche Zeitung, El Pais, Rossiyskaya Gazeta and The Mainichi Shimbun — gives it unrivalled reach around the world to increase cross-cultural communication.

The institute is committed to establishing itself as a high-end think tank platform which is inclusive, authoritative and a benchmark for global China issues.

China Daily, established in 1981 as the national English-language newspaper, has developed into a multi-media information platform combining newspapers, websites and Apps with a strong presence on Facebook, Twitter, Sina Weibo and WeChat. It serves more than 200 million readers all over the world and is a default choice for people who read about China in English. The group plays an important role as a channel for information exchanges between China and the rest of the world.

撰稿人
List of Contributors

[**Chapter I** **第一篇**] **伟大传奇**
The Great Legend

弗拉基米尔·诺罗夫 / Vladimir Norov

上海合作组织秘书长，乌兹别克斯坦前外长。

Secretary-General of the Shanghai Cooperation Organization, former minister of Foreign Affairs of Republic of Uzbekistan.

高大伟 / David Gosset

汉学家，中欧论坛创始人。

Sinologist, founder of the Europe-China Forum.

罗伯特·劳伦斯·库恩 / Robert Lawrence Kuhn

美国库恩基金会主席，中国改革友谊奖章获得者，《前线之声：中国脱贫攻坚》主持人、撰稿人。

Chairman of the Kuhn Foundation, China Reform Friendship Medal Recipient, the host and writer of the documentary *Voices from the Frontline: China's War on Poverty.*

胡鞍钢 / Hu Angang

清华大学国情研究院院长、清华大学公共管理学院教授。

Dean of the Institute for Contemporary China Studies, professor of the School of Public Policy and Management at Tsinghua University.

郝福满 / Bert Hofman

世界银行驻中国代表处经济部主任、首席经济学家。

Chief economist, World Bank's Country Director for China.

江诗伦 / Lauren A. Johnston

伦敦大学亚非学院副研究员。

Research associate at SOAS University of London, China Institute.

刘俊文 / Liu Junwen

中国国际扶贫中心主任。

Director general of the International Poverty Reduction Center in China.

阿拉文·耶勒里 / Aravind Yelery

北京大学汇丰商学院高级研究员。

Senior research fellow at HSBC Business School at Peking University.

伊凡娜·拉德杰维克 / Ivona Ladjevac

塞尔维亚贝尔格莱德国际政治经济研究所"一带一路"地区研究中心主任。

Head of Regional Center Belt and Road Initiative, Institute of International Politics and Economics, Belgrade.

尹树广 / Yin Shuguang

香港《文汇报》前副总编辑，中国国际战略研究基金会研究员。

Former deputy editor-in-chief of Hong Kong newspaper Wen Wei Po and researcher at China Foundation for International and Strategic Studies.

伍鹏 / Wu Peng

中国扶贫基金会国际发展部主任。

Director of the International Development Department of the China Foundation for Poverty Alleviation.

张弛 / Zhang Chi

中国社会科学院经济研究所助理研究员。

Assistant researcher at the Institute of Economics, Chinese Academy of Social Sciences.

穆罕默德·阿西夫·努尔 / Muhammad Asif Noor

巴基斯坦和平与外交研究所所长。

Director of Institute of Peace and Diplomatic Studies in Pakistan.

汉弗莱·莫希 / Humphrey P.B. Moshi

达累斯萨拉姆大学经济学教授，中国研究中心主任，坦桑尼亚公平竞争委员会主席。

Professor of economics of the University of Dar es Salaam, director of the Center for Chinese Studies, and chairman of Tanzania's Fair Competition Commission.

王刚 / Wang Gang

中国驻乌拉圭大使。

Chinese ambassador to Uruguay.

Chapter II

百年目标
The Journey

乔瓦尼·特里亚 / Giovanni Tria

意大利经济与财政部前部长。

Italian former minister of Economy and Finances.

万广华 / Wan Guanghua

复旦大学特聘二级教授、世界经济研究所所长。

Professor and director of the Institute of World Economy at Fudan University.

樊胜根 / Fan Shenggen

全球食物经济与政策研究院院长，国际食物政策研究所前所长。

Professor and director of Acadcmy of Global Food Economics and Policy at China Agricultural University, former director general of the International Food Policy Research Institute.

卡洛斯·阿基诺 / Carlos Aquino

秘鲁圣马科斯国立大学教授、亚洲研究中心协调员。

Professor and coordinator of the Center of Asian Studies at National University of San Marcos.

王华 / Hua Wang

法国里昂商学院副校长，创新管理和管理经济学教授。

Deputy president at Emlyon Business School, professor of Innovation Management and Managerial Economics.

蔡昉 / Cai Fang

中国社会科学院副院长、学部委员，中国社会科学院国家高端智库副理事长、首席专家。

Vice-president of the Chinese Academy of Social Sciences (CASS), chairman of the National Institute for Global Strategy of CASS.

高书国 / Gao Shuguo

中国教育学会副秘书长、研究员。

Deputy secretary-general and researcher of the Chinese Education Society.

林伯强 / Lin Boqiang

厦门大学中国能源政策研究院院长。

Head of the China Institute for Studies in Energy Policy at Xiamen University.

胡敏 / Hu Min

绿色创新发展中心主任。

Director of Green Development Program.

迭戈·蒙特罗 / Diego Mendero

绿色创新发展中心战略顾问。

Strategic advisor of Green Development Program.

蒋希蘅 / Jiang Xiheng

中国国际发展知识中心副主任。

Vice-President at the China Center for International Knowledge on Development.

洪勇 / Hong Yong

商务部研究院电子商务研究所副研究员。

Deputy researcher of E-Commerce Research Institute, Chinese Academy of International Trade and Economic Cooperation of the Ministry of Commerce.

章文光 / Zhang Wenguang

北京师范大学政府管理学院院长、农村治理研究中心主任。

President of School of Government, director of Research Center for Rural Areas at Beijing Normal University

利娅·林奇 / Leah Lynch

睿纳新国际咨询公司副总监。

Deputy director at Development Reimagined.

Chapter III

共同事业
Joint Effort

马凯硕 / Kishore Mahbubani

新加坡国立大学教授，新加坡前驻联合国大使。

Professor at the National University of Singapore, former Singaporean ambassador to the United Nations.

沈陈 / Shen Chen

中国社会科学院世界经济与政治研究所助理研究员。

Assistant research fellow of the Institute of World Economics and Politics at the Chinese Academy of Social Sciences.

保罗·鲁道夫·尤尼亚托 / Paulus Rudolf Yuniarto

印度尼西亚科学院地区资源研究中心高级研究员，复旦发展研究院访问学者。

Senior researcher at the Research Center for Area Studies of Indonesian Institute of Sciences, visiting scholar at Fudan University Research Institute.

凌迈 / Ehizuelen Michael Mitchell Omoruyi

浙江师范大学非洲研究所研究员。

Researcher of the Institute of African Studies at Zhejiang Nomal University, China.

Chapter IV
第四篇 未来可期
The Way Forward

伊恩·高登 / Ian Goldin

牛津大学全球化与发展学教授，曾任世界银行副行长。

Professor of Globalization and Development at the University of Oxford and former vice-president of the World Bank.

格雷厄姆·艾利森 / Graham Allison

哈佛大学肯尼迪政府学院首任院长、教授，哈佛大学贝尔弗科学与国际事务中心主任。

Professor and the first director of the Harvard Kennedy School, director of Harvard's Belfer Center.

李小云 / Li Xiaoyun

中国农业大学文科讲席教授、国务院扶贫开发领导小组专家咨询委员会委员。

Chair professor of Humanities at China Agricultural University, member of the Advisory Committee of the State Council Leading Group of Poverty Alleviation and Development.

俞子荣 / Yu Zirong

商务部国际贸易经济合作研究院副院长。

Vice-President of the Chinese Academy of International Trade and Economic Cooperation of the Ministry of Commerce.

朱海波 / Zhu Haibo

中国农业科学院农业信息研究所副研究员。

Associate professor of Agricultural Information Institute of the Chinese Academy of Agricultural Sciences.

孙靓莹 / Sun Jingying

中国社会科学院世界经济与政治研究所、国家全球战略智库特约研究员。

Researcher of the Institute of World Economics and Politics and National Institute for Global Strategy at the Chinese Academy of Social Sciences.

吉姆·奥尼尔 / Jim O'Neill

"金砖四国"概念首创者，英国财政部前商务大臣，英国皇家国际事务研究所主席。

Coiner of the term "BRIC", former commercial secretary to the UK Treasury and chair of Chatham House.

贝安之 / Andreas Pierotic

2014年至2019年任智利共和国驻华大使馆公使衔参赞兼经贸处处长，曾任智利外交部国际经济关系总局中国事务处处长。

Minister counselor and head of the Economic & Trade Department of the Embassy of Chile in China from 2014 to 2019, trade negotiator for the government of Chile, China desk in the General Directorate for International Economic Relations of the Ministry of Foreign Affairs of Chile.

杨小茸 / Yang Xiaorong

中国驻马达加斯加前大使。

Former Chinese ambassador to Madagascar.

尼亚兹·艾哈迈德·汗 / Niaz Ahmed Khan

达卡大学发展研究系教授和前主任，布拉克（BRAC）治理与发展研究所高级学术顾问，孟加拉国热带森林保护基金会主席，国际自然保护联盟（IUCN）孟加拉国前代表。

Professor and former Chairman of Department of Development Studies at University of Dhaka, senior academic adviser of BRAC Institute of Governance and Development, chairman of Bangladesh Tropical Forest Conservation (Arannayak) Foundation and former country representative-Bangladesh of IUCN-International Union for Conservation of Nature.

阿尔维·斯里约恩 / Alvy Al Srijohn

孟加拉国达卡市国家纺织工程与研究所发展研究系讲师。

Lecturer in Development Studies at the National Institute of Textile Engineering & Research (NITER), Dhaka, Bangladesh.

以文章出现先后排序，多于一篇的仅在首篇列出。
Order according to the arrangement of articles.

目 录
Contents

IV
Chapter IV
第 四 篇

The Way Forward

Challenges and Sustainable Development of
China's Poverty Alleviation

未来可期 · 中国脱贫的挑战与可持续发展

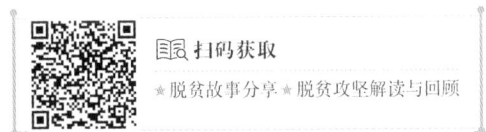

扫码获取
★ 脱贫故事分享 ★ 脱贫攻坚解读与回顾

第一篇

伟大传奇

Chapter Ⅰ

中国脱贫和全面建成小康社会的
世界意义

扫码获取

★ 脱贫故事分享
★ 脱贫攻坚解读
　　与回顾

/ 第一章 /
中国脱贫是对人类发展事业了不起的贡献

一、中国减贫成就给世界的启发[①]

中国是全球首个完成联合国千年发展目标中有关2030年前减贫任务的发展中国家。联合国秘书长安东尼奥·古特雷斯曾称赞中国为"减贫领域的世界纪录保持者"。

自1978年中国实行改革开放以来,中国累计已有近8亿贫困人口脱贫,占同期全球减贫人口总数的70%以上。放在世界范围内看,这一减贫数据甚至超过了今天拉丁美洲的人口总数。

英国海外发展研究院认为,中国减贫事业的成功得益于两大优势:一是经济长期保持较快增速,使减贫举措能够获得充足资金;二是政治体制稳定,有利于国家持续、稳定地制定和落实减贫政策。

比如,1952年至2019年,中国工业生产总值增长了近1000倍,年均增长率达11%,人均收入增长了70倍。除了中国,世界上还没有哪个国家实现过如此快速的经济发展。

在扶贫斗争中,中国通过吸引投资、推进工业化以及对国民经济各领域提供有针对性的发展援助,来扩大就业并实现对工业生产的合理分配。例如,2016年春,中国农业发展银行宣布计划于5年内投入4600亿美元用于农村减贫工作。

---

① 作者:弗拉基米尔·诺罗夫,上海合作组织秘书长,乌兹别克斯坦前外长。

在中国，正是农村居民率先感受到经济改革的积极影响。中国政府实行土地改革，同时提高谷物和农产品的收购价格，以激励农民增产。此举既可增加当地居民的实际收入，也可满足国内市场的消费需求。

中国政府根据各地资源禀赋协助改善当地基础设施。"要想富，先修路"口号成为中国式减贫的鲜明特色。时至今日，中国仍在实施一系列规模庞大的基建工程，目的就是要"村村通路、户户联网"，开车就能抵达这个国家的任何一个偏远角落。

在扶贫过程中，旅游业也成为富有吸引力的产业，有力促进了农村地区发展。旅游业能创造大量就业岗位和生产机会，特别是在开展其他类型经济活动十分困难的地区。中国统计数据表明，2011年至2014年，有超过1000万贫困人口（占中国最贫困人口的10%）借助旅游业成功脱贫。预计中国农村的300万旅游实体每年能够接待游客多达20亿人。

据中国文化和旅游部统计，2018年旅游业为中国国内生产总值贡献了9.94万亿元人民币（约合1.4万亿美元），约占当年中国国内生产总值的11.04%。同时，旅游业创造了近8000万个就业岗位，占中国就业总人口的10.29%。

2019年诺贝尔经济学奖得主、来自麻省理工学院的经济学家阿比吉特·巴纳吉和埃瑟·杜弗洛认为，受过良好教育、健康和饮食充足的人口会影响投资回报率，正是这些因素在推动快速发展和减贫过程中起到关键作用。

在改革开放初期，中国政府就意识到，只有更加重视国民教育和健康水平，才能从源头上消除贫困，防止贫困"代代相传"。

根据世界银行的数据，中国人口识字率从1982年的65.5%上升到2018年的96.8%，超过了86.3%这一世界平均水平。这是中国取得的又一个伟大成就！2019年中国对教育的投入达5.01万亿元人民币

（约合7066亿美元），比2018年增加8.74%。

2020年中国将有22842名教师被派往贫困地区支教，以帮助当地完成2020年至2021年教学计划。其中，21635名教师将在当地中小学从事九年制义务教育工作。上述举措是中国通过教育实施精准扶贫的关键一步。

在21世纪初，仅有不足三分之一的中国居民享有医疗保险。2006年中国开始实施医疗体制改革，使之能更多惠及农村贫困人口。

通过改革，已有近8亿中国农民获得了基本医疗保障。中国医保体系已基本实现城乡百分百全覆盖。这种国民获取医疗保健服务的平等性，是实现社会和谐的必要条件。

从本质上讲，中国已为其庞大人口提供了完善的社会保障机制，以保护国民免于承担巨额医疗费用。这为建设公正、繁荣的社会作出了巨大贡献。

同时，中国创新了脱贫模式。中国政府运用先进的信息通信技术，为偏远地区提供电子商务等现代科技应用的支持，为贫困地区的农产品找到了销路。

根据公开数据，2019年中国网民规模已达8.54亿人，其中超过2.25亿人是农村居民，全国互联网普及率则达61%。[①]2014年至2017年间，中国农村地区的网上零售额从1800亿元人民币增长到1.24万亿元人民币，年均增长91%，同期全国范围内的增长率则为35%。

今天，中国40%的人口生活在农村地区，土地退化加剧农村贫困。为此，中国政府实施了"三北防护林计划"，也被称为中国的"绿色长城"项目，旨在防止荒漠扩张。根据该计划，到2050年中国将实现35万平方千米国土的绿化目标。1978年至2017年，中国已种植了660多亿棵树，显著改善了当地生态环境，增强了居民健康。

---

① 数据来源：2019年10月第六届世界互联网大会。

改革开放40余年来，中国贫困人口减少了接近95%。对中国而言，扶贫不仅是重大的社会发展任务，也意味着巨大的国内发展资源。随着生活条件越来越好，中国人民对高质量产品的需求越来越大。为了不失去不断增长的国内消费市场，中国企业必须生产出技术含量更高、质量更优的产品。于是，减贫脱贫成为"中国制造"战略的重要组成部分。

世界其他国家也应以中国为例，学习和借鉴中国的扶贫经验。因为即使在大多数发达国家，贫困和衣食难保的情况也无法避免。中国的扶贫经验表明，政府专注于从根源上消除贫困并为居民创造条件以独立解决这一艰巨任务是多么的重要。

中国是世界第二大经济体，为世界贡献三分之一的经济增长。中国的部分工业水平位居世界前列，不仅能满足国内需求，也对推动世界经济恢复增长和在全球范围内消除贫困发挥关键作用。

根据联合国统计，中国之外的发展中国家减贫速度相当缓慢，贫困人口甚至还在增加。例如，撒哈拉以南非洲地区的极端贫困人口从1990年的2.78亿人增加到2015年的4.13亿人，占世界贫困人口的一半以上。

非洲国家普遍贫困的主要原因与债务缺口和公共债务急剧增加有关。过去的5—6年中，非洲国家的债务总额增长了一倍，2018年时占到当年国内生产总值的53%。撒哈拉以南非洲45个国家中，有33个是最不发达国家。

中国不仅同世界分享了扶贫经验，也向非洲等贫困人口较多的地区伸出了援手。2020年6月，中国国家主席习近平在中非团结抗疫特别峰会上发言表示，中方将在中非合作论坛框架下免除有关非洲国家截至2020年底到期对华无息贷款债务。

中国还呼吁二十国集团（G20）进一步延长对包括非洲国家在内的相关国家缓债期限，希望国际社会特别是发达国家和多边金融机构在非洲减缓债问题上采取更有力行动。

二、中国脱贫成就及其国际影响[①]

让贫困人口和贫困地区同全国一道进入全面小康社会是我们党的庄严承诺……中国共产党是为中国人民谋幸福的政党，也是为人类进步事业而奋斗的政党。中国共产党始终把为人类作出新的更大的贡献作为自己的使命。

——中国共产党第十九次全国代表大会报告

2017年10月18日

圣雄甘地曾说："贫穷才是最糟糕的暴力。""消除贫困"在联合国17个可持续发展目标中排在首位。

中华人民共和国成立以来最伟大的成就之一就是脱贫。2020年，中国将消除绝对贫困，实现全面建成小康社会的目标。中国人口占世界人口的18%，因其在世界人口结构中的重要比例，中国脱贫将为人类进步作出巨大贡献。

世界银行前行长罗伯特·佐利克在《2030年的中国》的序言中写道："中国在过去30年的经济表现是举世瞩目的。中国成功发展的故事，为其他国家效仿此成功模式提供了宝贵经验。"[②]

（一）中国治理模式、基础设施、教育、性别平等、医疗保健、可持续城市化：共同阐释中国发展

在发展经济学领域，有几个相互依存的因素共同阐释中国的发

---

① 作者：高大伟，汉学家，中欧论坛创始人。

② 世界银行与国务院发展研究中心联合课题组：《2030年的中国》研究报告，中国财政经济出版社，2013年。

展成就。

第一，中国的治理模式能高效地集中力量进行动员。具体来说就是，只要明确了目标，中国就能集中所有有用力量和资源以达成目标。

2012年，时任中共中央总书记胡锦涛在中国共产党第十八次全国代表大会报告中展示了同样的雄心："如期全面建成小康社会任务十分艰巨，全党同志一定要埋头苦干、顽强拼搏。"

2017年10月，中共中央总书记习近平在中国共产党第十九次全国代表大会报告中明确指出："让贫困人口和贫困地区同全国一道进入全面小康社会是我们党的庄严承诺。要动员全党全国全社会力量，坚持精准扶贫、精准脱贫。"

除了动员能力外，中国治理模式的另一优势是长期连续执政。在社会转型时期，连续执政对中国这样的大国起着至关重要的作用。

第二，中国坚持走自己的发展道路。在许多国家跟随西方思想和发展模式的情况下，中国不模仿任何国家，反而成为一位社会政治变革中的巨人。

1978年以来，邓小平将中国引上了改革开放的道路，实行社会主义市场经济，将政府宏观调控与市场经济相结合，显著加快了中国经济发展的进程。正如邓小平所说："不管黑猫白猫，捉到老鼠就是好猫。"

在脱贫攻坚战中，中国一直把注意力放在正确的地方。

第三，中国的发展进步得益于对基础设施的建设。中国走了一条正确的发展道路，用一句中国的俗话来表达就是"要想富，先修路"。中国的治理方式与其建设大型基础设施项目的能力之间有着明显的联系。从这个角度看，纵观历史，中国一直是基础设施建设强国（如都江堰灌溉系统、长城、大运河的建造）。

第四，与基础设施建设同样重要的是教育问题。中国的教育体制把整个国家的识字率提高到前所未有的高度。现如今，中国识字率达96%以上，而人口规模与中国相当的印度仅为71%。有研究表明，撒哈拉沙漠以南的非洲国家的识字率为65%，这会对经济社会的发展造成巨大障碍。

第五，教育促进了中国妇女的解放，促进性别平等的实现。"妇女能顶半边天"，人们经常引用毛泽东的这句名言，因为它蕴含着真理。第七任联合国秘书长科菲·安南把妇女地位和经济发展之间的联系阐释得非常清楚："实现性别平等的意义不仅仅是这个目标本身，更是应对减贫挑战的前提。"在联合国17个互相关联的可持续发展目标中，"性别平等"位居第五。

第六，随着改革开放的成功，中国已经有能力建立起基础医疗保健系统。随着2002年新型农村合作医疗制度的推出，基本医疗保险已覆盖8亿农村居民。

在2013年出版的《胜利大逃亡：健康、财富和不平等的起源》一书中，安格斯·迪顿写道："人类历史上最伟大的逃亡是摆脱贫困与早逝。"而正因其对贫困与社会福利的分析，安格斯·迪顿获得2015年诺贝尔经济学奖。

中国摆脱贫困的"逃亡"也是其摆脱早逝的"逃亡"。1949年，中国人的人均预期寿命是35岁。而今天，这个数字变成了77。2018年世界卫生组织数据有一大看点：这一年，中国人均健康预期寿命首次超过美国。美国婴儿出生时的人均预期寿命仍高于中国，但美国人最后10年的生命质量并不乐观。

第七，城市化相对和谐发展是脱贫的助力因素。"可持续城市和社区"是联合国可持续发展目标中的第11个。城市能带来就业机会，但世界上很多城市都和贫民区相伴相生。而中国能够避免世界上其他主要城市遇到的这一问题，这是一个了不起的成就。

（二）中国对世界的贡献

中国向世界传递的信号非常明确：贫困不是命定的，贫困是可以打败的。这对拉丁美洲、非洲和部分欧亚地区来说都是希望的信号。

虽然中国一派欣欣向荣的景象，但从全球来看，我们要做的还有很多。安格斯·迪顿在《胜利大逃亡：健康、财富和不平等的起源》一书中提醒我们："虽然世界其他地区的贫困率在下降，但贫困人口绝对数的下降很大程度是因为中国经济快速增长。所以，至少在过去十年间，除中国外其他地区的贫困人口绝对数是在不断增加的。"

数十年来，中国一直积极帮助其他国家。1982年5月6日，邓小平在会见利比里亚国家元首塞缪尔·卡尼翁·多伊期间谈到："中国对第三世界朋友尽的力量还不多，这是因为中国地方虽大，但很穷，还有许多困难。建国以来，我们做了一些事情，基本上解决了吃饭穿衣问题，粮食达到自给。这是很了不起的事情，旧中国长期没有解决这个问题……我们现在正在一心一意地搞建设，力争经济有较快的发展。到那个时候，我们可以对第三世界的朋友们多尽点力量。"①

在党的十九大报告中，习近平指出："中国共产党是为中国人民谋幸福的政党，也是为人类进步事业而奋斗的政党。中国共产党始终把为人类作出新的更大的贡献作为自己的使命。"这让人回想起邓小平在1982年对非洲领导人多伊说的那番话。

习近平还指出，中国"积极促进'一带一路'国际合作，努力实现政策沟通、设施联通、贸易畅通、资金融通、民心相通，打造国际合作新平台，增添共同发展新动力"。

邓小平提出的改革开放侧重于中国与世界之间的合作，提高中国内部的现代化水平。而习近平提出的"一带一路"倡议则开启了"中国改革开放的2.0时代"，推动中国在全球范围内的合作。

当代中国的最非凡成就之一，就是从思想、经验和投资的单纯接受者转变成全球安全与发展的贡献者。"一带一路"倡议正在影

---

① 《邓小平文选》第2卷，人民出版社，1994年，第405页。

响全球发展。

在很短的时间内，北京成功为建立新型国际金融机制积攒力量，以支持21世纪新丝绸之路的发展愿景。丝路基金、亚洲基础设施投资银行和金砖国家新开发银行都是年轻、有潜力的机构，能够将愿景变成现实。

"一带一路"倡议的本质是沟通，其内容是开放。它是一个可以把新的想法和现实结合在一起的项目，而不是一个死板的计划。除了一贯加强海、陆、空的联系，以科技发展为支撑的数字新丝绸之路将不断增强中国与世界之间的联系。

"一带一路"倡议的核心特征是包容。它不是东方牵制西方的计划，不是发展中国家削弱发达国家实力的机构，更不是对布雷顿森林体系和联合国机制的挑战。"一带一路"的目的只在于加强国际合作，为共同发展与和平贡献力量。

"一带一路"倡议能带领世界共同构建"人类命运共同体"，这是习近平对中国传统价值观的重新定义，是中国和平复兴的具体例证。

在党的十九大报告中，习近平还提到，中国"加大对发展中国家特别是最不发达国家援助力度，促进缩小南北发展差距"。

2018年，中国组建中华人民共和国国家国际发展合作署，这本身就是强有力的声明。随着自身的成功，中国向较不发达国家伸出了援手。中国国家国际发展合作署的官网上显示该机构的职能为"拟订对外援助战略方针、规划、政策，统筹协调援外重大问题并提出建议，推进援外方式改革，编制对外援助方案和计划，确定对外援助项目并监督评估实施情况等"。

中国为毛里塔尼亚、乌干达、利比亚、科摩罗和南苏丹提供医疗救助；为阿富汗、古巴、伊朗和索马里提供人道主义援助；支持突尼斯、加纳、马尔代夫和科特迪瓦的教育事业，并和巴基斯坦、尼日利亚、老挝展开科技合作。中国国家国际发展合作署成绩斐然。

在此背景下，中国与其他援助方应共同努力，不断开展经验交流。对于非洲和其他地区，欧盟和中国多多合作才是明智之举。

中国对世界所作的另一贡献则与世界银行有关。世界银行与中华人民共和国国务院发展研究中心联合编著了前文引用的《2030年的中国》研究报告。

中国自1980年起就和世界银行成为合作伙伴。1944年布雷顿森林会议宣布，世界银行的使命是"建立一个没有贫困的世界"。一开始，中国是国际开发协会的受助者。而27年后，中国变成了捐助者。2010年，中国成为世界银行第三大股东！

（三）中国面临的新挑战：不均衡和不断增长的期望

历史没有终点。消除绝对贫困的问题解决后，中国必然面临一系列新的挑战。

如今，中国和西方国家一样面临着发展不平衡的问题。2018年，人民日报网络版发表了一篇发人深省的文章《2017年中国基尼系数超过0.4》。从标题上看，收入不平等已经成为中国脱贫工作面临的重要问题。

在众多问题中，收入差距已经导致住房困难。在一些大省和一线城市，外来工因房价太高只能放弃工作机会。如果外来工在资源富足的地区无法永久居住，那么要将他们提升到中等收入水平将会十分困难。

我们经常提及的城乡差距和区域发展不平衡是联系在一起的。中国经济发展靠前的较多集中在沿海地区，内陆地区的发展比较参差。中国必须发展经济，让沿海的发达经济向内陆延伸。

西部大开发战略确实让沿海之外的地区得到发展（包括6个省、5个自治区和1个直辖市）。然而，区域发展不平衡仍是中国的一大问题。京津冀城市群和宏伟的粤港澳大湾区构想都势必为中国内陆地区发展带来机会。当然，这些规划都需要一定时间来实施。

中国面临的人口挑战也不可轻视。和许多邻国一样，中国的老龄人口规模庞大。这是个问题，持续强劲的经济增长需要年轻健康的劳动力来维持。

中国要找到促进平衡的办法，为此有必要进行财政改革，同时也要避免走进经济学家所说的中等收入陷阱。

中国人民期望提高后带来了一系列新的更复杂的问题。当最直接的物质需求得到满足之后，人们就想要提高方方面面的生活质量。生活在北京、上海、厦门、广州和深圳的高度连接的城市居民，对教育、医疗和空气质量的要求越来越高。这种从数量到质量的转变需要小心应对。

在党的十九大报告中，习近平肯定："必须认识到，我国社会主要矛盾的变化是关系全局的历史性变化，对党和国家工作提出了许多新要求。我们要在继续推动发展的基础上，着力解决好发展不平衡不充分问题，大力提升发展质量和效益，更好满足人民在经济、政治、文化、社会、生态等方面日益增长的需要，更好推动人的全面发展、社会全面进步。"

中国领导人充分认识到"发展不平衡不充分"这一中国转型新阶段的问题。这一认识使得中国能最大限度解决再平衡的问题，促进经济充分发展。

坚持走渐进式改革、分步骤开放的道路，中国必将战胜新的挑战，将世界的繁荣稳定推向新阶段。

三、前线之声：中国脱贫攻坚①

朱亚当是我的长期搭档，我们相识已有25年之久，经常一起探

---

① 作者：罗伯特·劳伦斯·库恩，美国库恩基金会主席，中国改革友谊奖章获得者，《前线之声：中国脱贫攻坚》主持人、撰稿人。

讨并讲述中国故事。几年前，我们接到邀请，拍一部中国扶贫纪录片，特别是全面记录在习近平主席领导下的中国扶贫攻坚壮举。习近平主席强调，到2020年中国将全面建成小康社会，使所有中国人脱离绝对贫困、极端贫困或赤贫，这是中国的"两个一百年"奋斗目标之一（2021年适值中国共产党成立100周年）。

无论中国国内生产总值和人均国内生产总值达到什么样的水平，除非每个公民都真正脱贫，否则中国就不能算是真正实现了这一目标。

如今，在西方世界，特别是在美国，人们对中国的各种举措感到担忧，并对中国的政策出发点抱有怀疑。我想，只要中国扶贫取得最终成功，这种陈词滥调自然不攻自破。

2020年初，新冠肺炎疫情来袭，中国正在励精图治，努力按照原计划实现其消除农村贫困和消除区域贫困的目标。当前形势下，中国还能实现这一目标吗？

新冠肺炎疫情暴发，中国经济逆风前行，到2020年底，中国的脱贫攻坚目标究竟会面临多大的挑战？采取了哪些减贫措施？实施如此大规模的国家项目，其组织结构如何？有什么制衡手段尽可能减少欺瞒行为（扶贫评估记录准确），并尽可能减少腐败（扶贫项目专款专用）？

一言以蔽之，中国体制中，是什么推动了扶贫工作的成功？

2019年7月31日，我们拍摄的纪录片《前线之声：中国脱贫攻坚》在美国公共电视网加州电视台（PBS SoCal）首播。在这部纪录片中，我们讲述了中国矢志打赢扶贫攻坚战、到2020年消除所有绝对贫困的内幕故事。这是第一部在国外播出的关于中国扶贫工作的深度纪录片，全面介绍了中国到2020年在全国范围内消除极端贫困的战略构想及相关努力。

这部纪录片的主创人员为：监制朱亚当、导演彼得·盖泽尔，以及笔者本人。能够作为影片主持人和撰稿人参与这个项目，笔者深感荣幸。

这部纪录片由中美摄制团队联合制作完成。在合作伙伴的大力支持下，片方国际电影摄制组得以深入探访中国各地，有机会接触到中国大规模的扶贫项目。我们见到了正走在脱贫道路上的农民、肩负脱贫重担的地方干部，还有专门负责考察脱贫成效的第三方评估人员。

纪录片的制作花费了两年时间，在此期间，摄制组走访了贵州、甘肃、山西、四川、海南和新疆等五省一自治区的贫困家庭，采访了中央、省、市、县、乡各级政府官员，记录了大量第一手扶贫资料。走访工作并不容易。摄制组不畏严冬酷暑，经常一连几个星期驻扎在最贫穷的地区。

这部纪录片通过六个案例，生动而贴切地描绘了中国的扶贫工作。这些案例突出了中国的扶贫战略以及实施该战略所需的体制和组织。纪录片对中国的精准扶贫计划进行了细致的记录，向观众讲述了实现精准扶贫的五种方法：一是发展产业，在当地创建可持续的小微企业；二是易地扶贫搬迁，迁移贫困地区人口；三是发展教育和培训；四是对生活在环境较差地区的居民进行生态补偿；五是加强社会保障和医疗补贴，向没有工作能力的人直接发放经济救助。

纪录片中的案例取材来自一线的真实故事：一位在偏远村庄工作的年轻党支部书记，一名通过教育改变命运的甘肃女孩，一个靠养骆驼脱贫的哈萨克族牧民，从贵州偏远山村迁出的老人，独立评价扶贫效果的第三方评估团队，还有协调扶贫工作、保证扶贫目标实现的地方各级党委书记。这些故事真实平凡，触动人心。

在其中一个案例中，镜头对准了海南省琼中黎族苗族自治县岭门村年轻的第一书记黄海军：他对贫困家庭进行精准识别，通过实地走访了解贫困家庭的情况，并针对每个家庭实施量身定做的救助措施。

片中还记录了基层扶贫工作人员真实的生活和工作情况，将各级扶贫官员的第一手资料原汁原味地呈现出来。

我曾经自以为是个"中国通"，随着摄制的深入，才知道自己对中国扶贫的了解不过皮毛而已。在节目制作过程中，我们惊讶地发现，中国为每个贫困户都完成了建档立卡工作，并制定了与之相对应的精准脱贫计划。

在美国人和中国人之间的跨文化合作中，我们对中国非凡脱贫攻坚计划实际运作方式有了更为深刻的了解。

2020年是中国计划在全国范围内消除极端贫困之年，又恰逢新冠肺炎疫情突然来袭。不难看出，中国政府在脱贫攻坚战中所表现出的强大动员能力，在"抗疫阻击战"中再次展现出来。

监制朱亚当强调："了解中国的扶贫方式可以帮助人们了解中国体制的运作方式。了解了脱贫攻坚，就了解了中国。"

导演彼得·盖泽尔在这部纪录片中采用了电影化的手法，以旁观者的视角冷静写实。进行影片剪辑时，他偏重于画面客观呈现而非讲述。盖泽尔说："在中国偏远地区领导一支跨文化团队，对这一非凡战略的运作方式有了更为深刻的认识。"故事娓娓道来，自然展开，贫困者坦露心迹。这种发自内心的声音，使观众能够亲身体验脱贫过程。

尽管世界各地都在与贫困作斗争，但没有什么能比得上中国大规模、全国性的村庄整体迁移。将贫困的农民从偏远地区转移到城市，提供住房和工作，使他们有机会过上更好的生活。

我们在贵州省惠水县看到，那里正在进行偏远山村的整体搬迁工作。村民们从偏远地区搬到了70千米外的新社区。

我们了解到，安置在这里的村民可以免费获得住房。一个四口之家拥有80平方米的居住空间，人均20平方米。所有的基本设施，包括沙发和床等家具、厨具以及电器，也统统由政府买单。

但是，这些文化程度不高、一直跟泥土打交道的人如何适应城镇生活，找到新的非农业工作呢？我参加了一个烹饪班，结识了一位农民，他正在学习烹饪，计划将来成为一名厨师。我见到了他一家三代人和他的几个朋友。几乎每个人都对新生活充满向往。

当然，并不是每个人都想搬到新社区。我见到了惠水县断杉镇戴井村党支部书记。书记介绍说，村委会不能强迫人们搬迁，政府政策也不允许这么做。他的工作是说服剩下的少数村民搬迁。

但是，中国幅员辽阔、官员仕途利益攸关、扶贫资金庞大，造假和贪污难以杜绝。中国绝不会任由伪造数据或挪用资金破坏其减贫目标。

为防止扶贫工作中出现不当行为而设立的一项制度让我印象特别深刻，即"第三方评估"。其设想是，由来自完全不同地区的团队担任第三方评估人员，他们不太可能认识评估对象，因此不会受到个人关系的影响。

他们的任务是评估扶贫工作的成绩与不足，以及相关领导干部的工作表现。

为了不给地方官员钻空子的机会，评估小组一般会临时决定他们去哪里进行检查，通常是在检查当天的上午。

国务院扶贫开发领导小组办公室负责指导第三方独立检查，对造假、瞒报的工作人员，依法追责、严肃处理，使扶贫成果经得起历史的考验和人民的检验。政府透明度越高，老百姓对政府的信心就越大。

中国精准扶贫固然取得了历史性的伟大成功，但无论过去还是现在，都面临各种挑战。

有些刚刚脱贫的人，在兴奋感消退之后，很可能在2020年之后再次返贫。如何预防这种情况？要使中国的减贫工作真正取得成功，就必须具有可持续性。

有些人勉强超过极端贫困线，生活水平远低于中国城市中等收入群体。只要这种情况存在，就很难实现中国的长远目标——全面建成小康社会。2020年绝不是这场扶贫攻坚战的终点。

想要真正消除一切形式的贫困，实现可持续发展，中国必须始终把扶贫项目当成头等大事，并坚持不懈，一步步实现最终目标。毋庸置疑，这又是一场"长征"。

那些认识到中国空前扶贫成就的人，还必须认识到这种成就与中国共产党的领导和强大的、有权威的政府之间的因果关系。尽管每种政治制度各有利弊，但没有如此强大的政府，中国不可能实现其减贫目标。

中国的宏大扶贫使命，在40多年的时间里帮助8亿人脱贫，在过去七年里帮助1亿贫困人口脱贫，这是史诗般的伟大成就。

未来的时代，人们记录文明史，中国精准扶贫时代无疑会是其中浓墨重彩的一章。

第二章
中国经济高速发展和摆脱贫困的成功经验

一、中国特色社会主义制度的优越性[①]

"中国奇迹"不仅体现在其经济快速发展从而带动全球经济增长上，也体现在中国社会发展的巨大进步上。

人类发展指数是联合国开发计划署根据国民预期寿命、受教育程度和人均国民收入等数据，用以衡量各成员国经济社会发展水平的指标。在中国共产党的坚强领导下，中国人民创造了人类历史上前所未有的发展奇迹：人类发展指数跃升至0.752。这意味着拥有14亿人口的中国已成功跻身人类发展水平较高的国家行列。而在70年前，仅有5亿多人口的中国只是一个人类发展水平极低的国家。在未来的5～7年，中国人类发展指数将至少达到0.8，跻身更高水平的国家行列。

1949年中华人民共和国成立以来，中国坚持以人民为中心，实现了跨越式发展，其为全人类发展作出的贡献超过了其他国家。中华人民共和国成立前，中国人类发展指数远低于世界平均水平，国家发展速度也低于世界平均水平。1950年以来，中国发生了翻天覆地的变化。中国坚持"三步走"战略，从消除绝对贫困到人民生活达到小康水平，最后基本实现现代化。中国人类发展水平从极低水

---

① 作者：胡鞍钢，清华大学国情研究院院长、清华大学公共管理学院教授。

平到高水平的快速发展，折射了其在经济、医疗和教育三大社会领域发生的历史性巨变。随着中国完成从低收入国家向中高收入国家的转变，中国不再是"东亚病夫"，而是"健康中国"。并且，中国已摆脱了高文盲率的困扰，成为拥有强大人力资源的国家。

中国特色社会主义制度是中国创造发展奇迹的决定性优势。"中国奇迹"绝非偶然，而是从量变到质变的过程。在此过程中，社会主义制度的优越性发挥了核心作用。坚持以人为本、致力于增进民生福祉等社会主义理念以及全心全意为人民服务的党的根本宗旨，是中国实现快速发展的主要驱动力。

将中国和印度这两个同样充满活力、具备发展前景、人口众多的发展中国家的人类发展指数进行比较，中国特色社会主义制度的优越性便充分显现出来。1950年中国人类发展指数仅为印度的87%，而2017年中国人类发展指数是印度的118%。在预期寿命和平均受教育年限这两项指标上，中国分别领先印度8年和4年。在医疗和教育领域，中国至少领先印度30年。按照目前的发展速度，印度要在2040年才能赶上中国目前的人类发展水平。

中国特色社会主义制度为什么能成为具有竞争力的制度优势？首先，它能够在长远目标下集中力量办大事，即在惠及全民的大事上，持续投入人力物力财力，尤其对医疗和教育两大领域的投入具有基本性、长期性、有效性的特点，而医疗和教育的进步也为自身的建设提供了发展红利。其次，在中国特色社会主义制度的指导下，中国高度重视市场的作用。充分处理好政府宏观调控与市场之间的关系，使政府与市场形成发展合力。

在取得举世瞩目的经济发展成就的同时，中国还保持着经济和社会稳定，并充分调动和发挥人民群众的积极性、主动性和创造性。在极度贫困、资源匮乏的年代，中国政府不断激发人民群众摆脱贫困的内生动力，兜底保障人民群众的基础教育和基本医疗。此外，中国的制度优势可以转化为政治优势、科学决策和民主决策优势。例如，在制定《"健康中国2030"规划纲要》和《中国教育现代化2035》的过程中，政府在网上广泛征求并充分参考人民群众的意见，这反映了人民群众在中国民主决策过程中的实质性参与。

中国是全球发展的最大贡献者。工业革命以来，在同等经济发展规模的大国中，只有中国成功实现了现代化。习近平总书记明确表示，中国将一以贯之为世界贡献中国智慧和中国方案。作为世界第一人口大国（美国和欧洲发达国家的人口合计不到中国的一半），中国发展水平的提高意味着世界上很大一部分人的生活将会得到改善。联合国开发计划署在2018年《人类发展报告》中的数据显示，2017年全球人类发展水平较高的人口总数达23.8亿，中国占比59.2%。如果以现阶段的走势持续发展，到2030年，当中国成功跻身高人类发展水平国家组时，该群体将增加14.5亿的人口，总人口数将达到28.9亿，占世界总人口的34.3%。

中国的现代化进程是一个坚持以人民为中心的发展过程，充分发挥了社会主义制度的优越性，充分调动了亿万人民群众的创造伟力。

二、中国减贫成功之道：回顾与反思[①]

（一）简介

1978年，中国开启了改革开放的历史征程，从而翻开了历史新的一页。40多年来，改革开放政策引领中国从一个封闭、贫穷的小经济体转变为中等偏上收入国家，并且，以购买力平价（PPP）计算，中国已成为世界第一大经济体。中国在减贫方面取得了巨大的

---

① 作者：郝福满、江诗伦。郝福满，世界银行驻中国代表处经济部主任、首席经济学家，主管世界银行在中国的经济分析与政策咨询工作。江诗伦，伦敦大学亚非学院副研究员。

成功，累计有8亿人脱贫。

　　经济的快速增长是中国减贫的主要驱动力。1978年后的40年里，中国经济年均增长9.4%，同期人均收入年均增长8.4%。经济快速增长在减少贫困方面也非常奏效：1981年至2012年间，中国人均国内生产总值（GDP）每增加一个百分点，贫困人口所占比例每年下降0.97个百分点（图1）[①]。

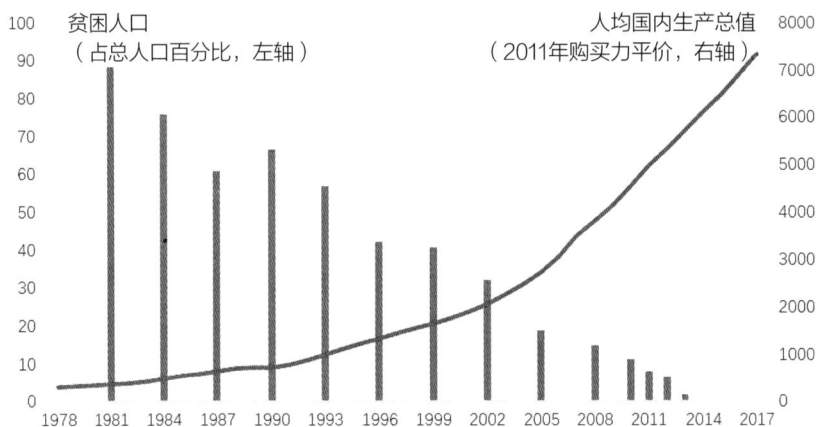

图1　1978—2017年中国人均实际收入及贫困状况

　　资料来源：基于《国家统计局家庭调查数据》和《世界发展指标》的世界银行估计数据。

　　无论采取何种贫困衡量标准，中国的扶贫工作均成效显著。改革开放之初，中国穷困人口占90%以上。到2019年，几乎已经消除了极端贫困。按照目前官方公布的全国贫困线，即农村地区每年2300元人民币（2010年不变价格），农村贫困人口的比例从1978年

[①] 按国内生产总值和人均国内生产总值（不变人民币价格）计算。2020年5月25日搜索的《世界发展指标》数据。

的97.5％下降到2017年的3.1％，即从7.704亿人减少到3050万人。国务院总理李克强在2020年5月向全国人民代表大会所作的政府工作报告中指出，2019年贫困人口进一步下降到占总人口的0.6％。

根据世界银行每人每日1.9美元（2011年购买力平价或国际可比价格）的国际贫困线标准，从1981年到2015年，总贫困人口指数从占总人口的88％降至0.7％。也就是说，贫困人口从约8.75亿下降到1000万。死亡率下降，同时预期寿命增加，这意味着，如今中国出生的儿童比20世纪中叶在中国出生的儿童平均寿命长30年。

中国的社会进步和经济发展令世人瞩目（表1）。自1981年以来，全球约有12亿人口脱贫，其中中国脱贫人口占了约74％。如果没有中国的减贫成功，联合国第一项千年发展目标（即1990年至2015年间极端贫困人口数减半）的实现将无从谈起。

表1 1981—2015年部分年份的极端贫困人口数

（单位：百万人）

国家和地区	1981年	1990年	1999年	2010年	2015年
中国	875.3	751.7	503.7	149.6	10
除中国以外的东亚和太平洋地区	237.4	233.1	189.2	69.8	37.1
欧洲和中亚地区	10.4	13.3	36.8	11.7	7.8
拉丁美洲和加勒比地区	50.2	66.4	69.6	36.3	25.3
中东和北非	18.3	14	10.5	6.9	14.1
南亚	515.3	537.1	535	403.6	215.2
撒哈拉以南的非洲	193.7	279.7	378.7	404.9	419.6
全球总人数	1906	1899.2	1728.5	1088.3	736.7
除中国以外的全球总人数	1030.7	1147.5	1224.8	938.7	726.7

资料来源：PovCalNET、《世界发展指标》和作者个人计算数据。

注：按照每人每日1.9美元（2011年购买力平价）这一世界银行国际贫困线标准衡量的贫困状况。

中国减贫的成功引发了人们对中国如何实现这一目标的极大兴趣。在这里讨论中国减贫的一些关键战略和政策。限于篇幅，无法面面俱到，只能介绍几个主要的方面。尽管如此，了解中国近几十年来的一些关键政策机制和优先事项，可能会对其他国家制定本国扶贫策略有所启迪。

（二）推动减贫的增长战略

很大程度上，中国在减贫方面的成功应该归功于改革开放带来的快速、持续经济增长。这种快速增长始于一个极低的基准线。20世纪70年代末，中国是世界上最贫穷的国家之一。

在某些方面，中国的经济改革采纳了主流经济学家提出的多种举措。中国坚持对外开放，逐步放开价格，实行多种所有制，加强产权制度，控制通货膨胀。（相对）持续的宏观经济稳定使高储蓄转化为高投资和快速的城市化进程，进而引发了快速的结构转型和生产率增长。以中国为例，在改革方面，支撑经济增长的是复杂的试验性、分散性和渐进性的改革开放进程。这一进程历尽曲折，应了中国人常说的一句老话："摸着石头过河。"

中国的改革开放始于农业领域。家庭联产承包责任制赋予了农户对土地的经营权，而政府提高了国家收购价格，鼓励农民种植经济性农作物。这些因素组合在一起，大大提高了农业生产力和农民收入，在1979年后的头十年中，这些因素在很大程度上推动了减贫。在工业领域，中国的策略并不是将国有企业私有化，而是放开政策，鼓励国内外民营企业参与竞争，共同发展壮大。到了20世纪90年代中期，非国有企业已成为经济、就业和收入增长的主要驱动力。

1980年，中国开始在沿海设立经济特区，拉开了对外开放的序幕。这些经济特区成为改革开放的"窗口"和"试验田"。外商投资是中国进口技术和专业知识的一种渠道，并日益与全球市场紧密联系在一起。2001年，中国加入世界贸易组织（WTO），成为全球供应链的首选基地，外商直接投资和对外贸易激增。21世纪初，改革深入到社会各领域，不断提高公民的教育、医疗保健和社会福利待遇。

同时，自1993年《中共中央关于建立社会主义市场经济体制若干问题的决定》以来，随着市场经济改革的全面推进，中国利用21世纪初的10年时间，采取各种措施，包括加大对高等教育和科学技术的投入，为不同的增长模式打下了坚实基础。政府的观点是，国家需要发挥主导作用，即市场在资源配置中的决定性作用。

人口红利进一步推动了人均收入增长。20世纪70年代初，尤其是20世纪80年代以来，人口增长率迅速下降，部分原因是中国的计划生育政策。但在之前，中国的人口增长非常迅速。这带来了很高的人口红利，这段时期，劳动年龄人口占总人口比重加大。在中国，这种情况从20世纪70年代开始，一直持续了大约40年。在人口红利期间，中国政策方向非常明确，极为重视吸引劳动密集型外商投资。这促进了对外贸易，同时采用了有针对性的激励措施，包括国内移民，使国民和国家受益于劳动力激增。

经济改革和人口增长放缓是中国大幅减贫的根本原因，但这远不是全部原因。下面将阐述中国减贫途径的其他一些特征。

（三）中国的减贫战略方针

1. 制度与激励措施

改革开放以来，扶贫工作得到了各级政府的政治支持。最初的体制改革刺激了经济增长。随后，1986年成立了一个专门的机构推动扶贫工作的进展，它便是国务院扶贫开发领导小组。同时，在各级政府内部，直至县级，均建立了扶贫开发领导小组办公室，即贫困地区开发办公室。

国务院扶贫开发领导小组监督贫困政策的制定，包括国家贫困线的界定和项目设计；贫困地区开发办公室监督地方一级的减贫项目落实情况。两者均得到了高层支持和资金扶持。减贫项目的主要目标是使人们获得可持续性生计，通过发展减贫，其中许多项目都向农村地区倾斜。邓小平认为："中国社会是不是安定，中国经济能不能发展，首先要看农村能不能发展，农民生活是不是好起来。"[①]这种政策倾斜和相关的项目落实，在很大程度上是由中国的扶贫机构推动的。这也使中国避免再次遭遇饥荒——由于大多数贫困人口来自农村，因此，农业生产力始终是重中之重。

中国减贫途径的另一个重要特征是激励政府官员。官员的晋升前景取决于其所在地区的经济成就，特别是在经济增长、就业、外商投资和人口控制方面实现特定目标。财政体制还将收入增长份额留给创收政府，由此激励增长。政府的官方激励措施与对投资者的激励措施大体一致，而政府各部门的扶贫机构则负责促进并确保一定程度的再分配。这套制度和激励措施并非一帆风顺，过度的增长动力和腐败一直是中央政府关注的问题，尽管如此，它们仍然在推动2020年取得既定减贫目标。

2. 战略上的差异化和包容性的增长

无论是时间上还是地域上，中国的减贫工作都并不是整齐划一的。20世纪80年代的减贫速度最快，并且随着贫困人口减少和经济增长变缓，减贫速度随之放缓。从地理上看，中国沿海地区的极端贫困人口迅速减少，而偏远的西南和西部地区的极端贫困人口减少则要缓慢得多。根据《中国农村贫困监测报告》，到2016年，浙江、江苏等沿海相对富裕省份的贫困率接近零，而甘肃、新疆等内陆偏远地区的贫困率超过12.5%。

可以从邓小平1986年作出的一项政治决策中认识到中国减贫的

---

① 《邓小平文选》第3卷，人民出版社，1993年，第77-78页。

地区发展差异现象："我们的政策是让一部分人、一部分地区先富起来，以带动和帮助落后的地区，先进地区帮助落后地区是一个义务。"①因此，出台沿海发展战略后，首先开放了沿海地区，并将投资和激励措施重点放在这些地区。目的是将中国有限的资源集中在可能带来最快经济增长的地区。直到21世纪初实施西部大开发战略以来，中国的经济政策才逐步向西部省份倾斜。

农业改革的初步成果逐渐落实之后，最贫穷人口的收入固然实现了大幅增长，但其从中国的经济增长中获得的收益却低于平均水平。沿海发展战略和权力下放的改革战略使这种情况更为凸显，与计划经济时代相比，市场放开后地方之间的贫富差异越拉越大。因此，收入不均衡迅速加剧，特别是在沿海和内陆省份之间以及城乡之间。在最近的20年中，贫困人口的人均收入增长率高于平均水平，收入不均衡状况有所缓解。

3. 逐步明确和有针对性的减贫议程

改革开放之初，仅仅依赖经济增长，特别是在农村地区，就取得了显著的扶贫成效。随后，中国贫困人口日益边缘化，例如，在偏远地区人口、残疾人或老年人等。中国的减贫议程和政策反映了这一转变。因此，在20世纪八九十年代，经济增长是扶贫议程中更为明确的要素。这些经济成果中，有一部分用于反哺较贫困地区的卫生、教育和扶贫议程。

中国制定了一项直接、更有针对性的减贫议程。总而言之，这是一个由经济增长推动的国家级项目，层层落实到省、县、村，又落实到户。其中，随着经济增长和收入增加，医疗保健和教育服务的质量和公平性逐步提高。早期经济改革的一个弊端是财政资源的急剧、不均衡下降，导致教育和卫生等政府服务的不均衡。现在，

---

① 此为1986年3月28日邓小平会见新西兰总理朗依时说的话。

针对这种不均衡现象出台了各种措施，包括重新分配财政资源、鼓励优秀教师到最贫困地区工作，以及借助教育配对，使教育资源丰富的地区和学校对较贫困的地区和学校提供教育帮扶。这反映出中国改革开放早期决策有意识地使一部分人和地区先富起来，最后通过"传帮带"不断融合，实现共同富裕。

中国推行扶贫到村到户方略，称为"精准扶贫"。想要真正实现精准扶贫，就必须了解贫困户和贫困户家庭成员信息。2014年前后，扶贫官员进行了一项大规模调查，针对最贫困人口创建了一个大型数据库，最初的贫困人口数据约为7000万人。随着中国扶贫工作进入啃硬骨头、攻坚拔寨的冲刺期，该数据库将不断更新，为旨在确保最后一批贫困人口顺利脱贫的基层官员和政策提供相关信息。

在这一进程中，中国动员了相关政府官员，将扶贫工作成效纳入其政绩指标。此外，大量公司、银行、非政府组织和慈善团体群策群力，为减贫事业添砖加瓦，作出一份贡献。这种"举国之力"的做法是中国独有的。

中国已逐步并专门利用技术为最贫穷的人口提供帮扶。中国电子商务蓬勃发展，已成为贫困和偏远社区销售商品和低价购买商品的工具。通过建设互联网访问基础设施，增强社区将产品推向市场的能力，政府在不断推动这方面的工作。大型电子商务公司同样热衷于扶持农村电子商务。人们还利用互联网和移动技术，使贫困人口能够享受更多的金融服务、医疗咨询和服务，以及接受教育的机会。

4. 国际发展伙伴关系

尽管中国在扶贫方面的成功是民族自豪感的源泉，但这种成功实际上也部分依赖于国际伙伴关系。首先，外国投资者是中国经济增长的基础。中国改革开放初期的多位领导人以及许多杰出的企业家和科学家曾在海外学府深造。此外，多边和双边的国际发展机构与中国建立了持续的伙伴关系，支持扶贫工作。

1980年，邓小平与时任世界银行行长麦克纳马拉会晤时为建立这种伙伴关系定下了基调。邓小平说："中国下定决心要实现现代化和发展经济。有了世界银行的帮助，中国能够更快更有效地实现这个目标。没有世界银行的帮助，中国也能做到，但可能要慢一点。"[1]为了建立这种伙伴关系，世界银行提供了直接和间接的扶贫援助。特别为农业、运输、能源、城市化、卫生、教育、社保以及扶贫等部门的改革提供了建议和财政资源。中国强调建设自身的改革能力，这意味着中国政府将可以从国际上获得的经验在国内进行推广，并推出最符合中国国情的具有中国特色的改革。

（四）展望

2020年初暴发的新冠肺炎疫情无疑加大了2020年减贫工作的难度，但中国政府仍然不畏艰难，正在努力实现这一目标。中国2020年又拿出1%的国内生产总值安排扶贫资金，确保达成减贫目标。无论如何，中国的减贫挑战绝不可能止步于此。首先，随着经济的日益繁荣，中国对贫困的定义可能会发生变化。大多数高收入国家的贫困线大大高于中国目前的国家贫困线。其次，新的挑战正在出现，特别是中国人口的迅速老龄化，这将减缓经济增长速度。而且，中国有数亿老人养老金不足，国家必须提供支持。最后，尽管中国的扶贫工作主要依赖经济增长和发展，但社会福利补助和定向扶持将是未来扶贫工作的支柱。成功建立和完善政府组织、项目和信息系统，对于中国不断达成减贫目标至关重要。

---

[1] 林重庚：《五十位经济学家回顾中国改革开放三十年》前言，2008年。应当指出的是，麦克纳马拉在与林重庚的对话中提及了这番言论，但并未列入当时邓小平与麦克纳马拉的会议正式记录。

三、中国精准扶贫——成果丰硕、意义深远①

2020年是中国决胜脱贫攻坚和全面建成小康社会的收官之年，中国即将在中华民族几千年发展史上首次整体消除农村绝对贫困现象。党的十八大以来，以习近平同志为核心的党中央把脱贫攻坚摆到治国理政的突出位置，实施精准扶贫精准脱贫方略，创造了中国减贫史上的最好成绩。精准扶贫成为推动全球减贫进程的重要经验，为实现联合国《2030年可持续发展议程》目标贡献了中国智慧和中国方案。

整体上消除绝对贫困目标即将完成。根据中国现行扶贫标准，中国农村贫困人口从2012年的9899万人减至2019年的551万人，年均减贫1000万人以上，农村贫困发生率由10.2%降至0.6%。按照世界银行每人每天1.9美元的国际贫困线标准，中国贫困发生率从1981年末的88.3%下降到2016年的0.5%，累计下降87.8个百分点。这意味着中国基本消除了整体绝对贫困。

贫困地区基础设施大幅改善。党的十八大以来，国家持续加大对水、电、路、网等基础设施投资力度。截至2019年底，贫困地区已基本解决通电和饮水安全问题；所在自然村通电话、通有线电视信号和通宽带的农户比重分别达到100%、99.1%和97.3%；所在自然村进村主干道路硬化的农户比重为99.5%；所在自然村能便利乘坐公共汽车的农户比重为76.5%；86.4%的农户所在自然村能集中处理垃圾。贫困地区生活环境和发展条件得到大幅改善。

公共服务和社会保障水平不断提高。贫困地区基本公共服务体系日益健全，社会保障水平稳步提升。截至2019年3月，全国92.7%的县实现义务教育均衡发展，更多的农村孩子享受到更好更公平的

---

① 作者：刘俊文，中国国际扶贫中心主任。

教育。医疗服务体系不断完善，文化设施建设持续推进。2018年，有文化活动室的行政村比重为90.7%，比2012年提高16.2个百分点，群众文化生活日益丰富。

选择适应国情的扶贫路径，做好顶层设计。20世纪80年代以来，中国区域性贫困人口大规模减少，但减贫的边际效果不断下降，贫困人口更加分散，贫困问题特殊性更加突出，原有扶贫路径难以适应新的减贫要求。2013年，习近平总书记适时提出"精准扶贫"，核心是从实际出发，找准扶贫对象，摸清致贫原因，因地制宜、分类施策，开展针对性帮扶，解决"扶持谁、谁来扶、怎么扶、如何退"四个核心问题，提出扶持对象精准、项目安排精准、资金使用精准、措施到户精准、因村派人精准、脱贫成效精准"六个精准"要求，实现了精准要求和扶贫脱贫的有机统一。

精准识别贫困对象，解决"扶持谁"的问题。2014年5月，国家对贫困户和贫困村建档立卡工作出台专门文件，为贫困精准识别提供制度保障。2014年，全国组织80万人深入农村开展贫困识别和建档立卡工作，共识别12.8万个贫困村8962万贫困人口，构建起全国统一的信息系统和大数据管理平台。为及时反映贫困最新特点，实行动态调整管理机制，2015年至2016年，全国动员近200万人开展建档立卡"回头看"，运用大数据比对等方法进一步精准识别贫困对象，剔除识别不准人口，补录符合标准人口。2017年至2019年，实施动态管理，增加脱贫措施和返贫情况等内容，扶贫信息进一步及时准确规范。建档立卡有效解决了"扶持谁"的问题，为实施精准扶贫精准脱贫政策措施和考核评估等工作打下坚实基础。

建立扶贫责任体系，解决"谁来扶"的问题。坚持"中央统筹、省负总责、市县抓落实"的管理体制，形成省、市、县、乡、村五级书记抓扶贫工作格局。建立起干部驻村帮扶制度，从全国县级以上机关、国有企事业单位累计选派300多万名干部驻村帮扶，解决扶贫"最后一公里"难题。形成专项扶贫、行业扶贫、社会扶贫等多方力量、多种举措有机结合的大扶贫格局，东西扶贫协作不断深化，东部267个经济较强县（市、区）结对帮扶西部406个贫困县，中央层面共有320个单位定点帮扶592个贫困县。同时，组织引导民营企业"万企帮万村"精准扶贫行动等。

推进实施扶贫工程，解决"怎么扶"的问题。建立需求导向的扶贫行动机制，通过深入分析致贫原因，逐村逐户制定帮扶计划和专项扶贫措施，与精准识别结果和贫困人口发展需求相对接。通过发展生产脱贫、易地搬迁脱贫、生态补偿脱贫、发展教育脱贫、社会保障兜底等"五个一批"工程，实施健康、教育、金融、交通等十大扶贫行动，开展职业教育、小额信贷、企业帮扶等十项扶贫工程，形成了大量有效的扶贫模式。引导和支持有劳动能力的贫困人口依靠勤劳双手创造美好生活，激励贫困人口立志强智阻断代际传递，织牢社会保障网确保应扶尽扶、应保尽保。

严格脱贫考核评估，解决"如何退"的问题。围绕脱贫人口"不愁吃、不愁穿，义务教育、基本医疗、住房安全有保障"的标准，开展严格的考核评估。考核结果作为省级党委、政府主要负责人和领导班子综合考核评价的重要依据。对扶贫不力的干部进行严肃问责。

中国在减贫方面所取得的巨大成就不仅对中国本身意义重大，对国际减贫事业也产生了深远影响，有力推动了全球减贫进程。中国是首个实现联合国千年发展目标的发展中国家，对全球减贫贡献率高达70%以上。2020年全面脱贫目标完成后，中国将提前10年实现联合国《2030年可持续发展议程》的减贫目标，直接推动世界减贫进程，并带动周边地区快速减贫。东亚和太平洋地区贫困人口占全球的比重由1981年的59%（11亿贫困人口）下降到2013年的9%，减少10.4亿贫困人口，中国的贡献率为82%。东亚和太平洋地区成为减贫速度最快的区域。

为世界减贫提供了中国经验。中国以政府为主导，有计划有组织地扶贫开发，特别是党的十八大以来实施的精准扶贫精准脱贫方略，为全球减贫提供了有效的中国智慧与中国方案。联合国秘书长安东尼奥·古特雷斯致"2017减贫与发展高层论坛"的贺信中称："精准减贫方略是帮助最贫困人口、实现《2030年可持续发展议程》宏伟目标的唯一途径。中国已实现数亿人脱贫，中国的经验可以为其他发展中国家提供有益借鉴。"

增强了国际社会减贫的信心。当前，全球仍然有7.66亿贫困人口，84%分布在撒哈拉以南非洲和南亚，贫困程度深、减贫难度大。中国精准扶贫实践的成功不仅印证了扶贫道路和方略的正确性和有效性，也通过经得起历史检验的减贫成就和模式，为世界各国更有效地进行贫困治理提供了中国方案，让许多深陷贫困的发展中国家看到了希望，进一步坚定了战胜贫困的信心。

力所能及开展对外减贫合作。中国在与贫困的斗争中不断发展，始终担当履行大国责任，力所能及地向其他发展中国家提供不附加任何政治条件的援助，支持和帮助广大发展中国家特别是最不发达国家消除贫困。中国将与国际社会加强合作，共同落实《2030年可持续发展议程》，努力实现合作共赢。

四、人口红利和改革发展塑造出理想的模式[①]

在20世纪，随着世界各个国家采用各自特有的方式实现繁荣、经济增长和现代化，可持续增长越来越多地被放在"发展"与"公平"两大全球框架下进行讨论。在二战后的全球建设中，工业革命

---

① 作者：阿拉文·耶勒里，北京大学汇丰商学院高级研究员。

或科学突破导致欠发达社会的收入增长受到限制。随着越来越多国家获得独立并开展国家建设，增加收入变得越发艰巨。

全球增长指数和发展衡量标准因地域和人口而异，发达国家、发展中国家、低收入国家的发展任务和发展策略各不相同，所以这些国家的经济发展周期并不一致。尽管各国经济增长模式千差万别，其核心问题都是一样的，那就是如何减少贫困。联合国开发计划署发布的2019年度《全球多维贫困指数》报告显示，在101个国家和地区中，有13亿人（占23.1%）处于"多维贫困状态"。贫穷成了一种生存状态，代表着生活困顿、心态脆弱和能力有限。贫穷不仅意味着经济收入低下，往往还会引发教育、健康、收入差距等一系列连锁反应。

中国的经济转型算得上是20世纪最伟大的成就之一。中国通过转变经济政策，成功提升了人民生活水平。与21世纪其他重大框架体系事件和现象相比，中国的成功是历史性的。中国经济发展面临的挑战与发达经济体大相径庭。中国通过改革与现代化建设，积累了大量革命性经验，为其他发展中国家树立了榜样。

有各种形容词来诠释中国经济崛起，通过这些描述可以从各个方面了解中国的巨大转变。西方国家、亚洲其他邻国以及遥远的非洲和拉丁美洲国家都见证了中国的崛起，并将其视为奇迹，许多国家将其奉为经济发展的典范。中国在实现重大转型的同时也向世界分享了它的发展成果，带动了一些亚洲国家的发展。亚洲国家是中国崛起过程中的最大受益者，以至于21世纪也被称为"亚洲世纪"（或亚洲全球化）。在改革过程中，市场成为塑造现代中国的主要力量和行为主体，中国人的创业精神也对国家崛起发挥了重要作用。省政府、机构和人民群众所扮演的角色决定了各级机关和受惠于改革的微观经济实体的形态和规模。所有这些变量共同作用，实现了史无前例的经济高速增长。中国通过保持意识形态与政府治理之间的平衡，使改革产生了前所未有的回报。值得深入研究的是，这些改革的核心领域是什么。

除了快速增长的指标外，中国在可衡量的扶贫脱贫方式方面也名列前茅。为什么说可衡量呢？这就是中国独一无二之处。一方面，中国调动了近乎所有的经济力量驱动全球增长；另一方面，它大幅降低了全球贫困率的中位数。

20世纪初，中国的贫困率急剧飙升。战争频繁，加之各种内乱，中国进入了历史上最艰难、最糟糕的时期。兵连祸结，封建王朝土崩瓦解，民生凋敝，贫困加剧，整个国家和社会都陷入了困厄苦难的泥潭。20世纪上半叶，社会不平等现象加剧，失业率和贫困率上升，出现了各种意识形态矛盾和抗争运动。

中华人民共和国成立后，贫穷仍然是困扰中国共产党的关键问题之一。中国共产党结束了旧中国四分五裂的混乱局面，上台执政，收拾残局。西方列强的剥削以及战争和军事冲突造成的破坏，与中国政府和人民面临的社会危机交织在一起。

20世纪中叶，中华人民共和国成立时，中国人口高达5.4亿，是1500年（明弘治十三年）人口的3倍。对于新政府来说，在有限的资源下集中精力减贫脱贫是一项几乎不可能完成的任务。本已十分紧张的资源必须满足人口急剧增长的需要。

因此，在中国进入经济改革实验的探索性时期，消除贫困实乃当务之急。扶贫一直是中国政府的首要任务之一，也是国家坚持以人为本、深化改革的基石。中国政府很早就意识到公共健康缺乏保障是贫困现象普遍的原因之一。

卫生状况现实严峻，领导层逐步转变观念，制定国家卫生政策作为立国方针大计。如果说扶贫是长远目标之一，那么，公共卫生就是增强经济结构改良的重要手段。

在任何经济体系中，人口都是一个重要杠杆，而中国是20世纪继承了过去人口红利的经济体之一。如果说中国的人口数量带来了巨大的人口红利，那么完善国内公共卫生体系无疑等于创造了"增加值"。中国在减贫方面的成功也加强了它应对其他挑战的能力，改变了中国城乡发展的轨迹。在过去的70年间，中国着力提高公共卫生水平，使其成为经济增长和国力增强的"引擎"。

中国为世界减贫事业作出了杰出贡献。数字不会说谎，显示了中国数十年来在扶贫脱贫方面的决心。

自从经济开放和放宽对生产和资本积累的其他管控以来，扶贫工作一直稳步进展，值得注意的是，中国扶贫项目是全球减贫工作的重头戏。例如，从1981年到1990年，中国使1.52亿人脱贫，而在同一时期，全球减贫人数仅为3100万人。

20世纪90年代，这一数字不断攀升，达到2.37亿人。这些数字反映了中国扶贫模式的成功。从1999年到2010年，中国的扶贫工作使2.89亿人脱贫摘帽，占世界减贫总人数的54.9％。

从1990年到2010年，中国脱贫人口达到5.26亿人，约占全世界的75.7％。中国在扶贫脱贫方面的成功与联合国千年发展目标提出的计划相吻合，其中包括自2000年联合国千年首脑会议以来的八项发展目标。

截至2017年底，中国贫困人口减少到3046万人，贫困率下降至3.1％。中国正在积极推进落实《2030年可持续发展议程》，实现该议程是中国改革里程碑之一，也带来了更全面的社会效益。

迄今为止，中国对全球减贫的贡献率超过70％，成为世界上减贫人口最多的国家。中国在全球减贫方面起到了"火车头"的作用。按照世界银行每人每日1.9美元的国际贫困线标准，从1981年到2013年，中国使8.5亿人摆脱了极端贫困。据世界银行统计，中国极端贫困人口比例从1981年末的88.3％下降至2013年末的1.85％。

中国曾经是世界上最贫穷的国家之一，但照此速度发展，中国必将在2020年底彻底消除绝对贫困、全面建成小康社会，千百年来困扰中华民族的绝对贫困问题即将画上历史性句号。中国减贫成果与近70年来的一系列改革密不可分。根据联合国的一份报告，全球减贫事业成就的76%左右来自中国。中国不仅自身积极发展扶贫项目，还帮助其他发展中国家和新兴经济体开展减贫工作，分享成功经验。中国国际扶贫中心为来自亚洲、非洲与大洋洲发展中国家的官员举办讲习班和培训班，使这些国外官员深入了解中国扶贫成就，并借鉴中国经验。

纵观历史，中国在经历了20世纪的一系列社会和政治巨变后，一跃成为世界第二大经济体，想来真是难以置信，堪称一场梦幻之旅。而中国在减贫方面的巨大变革和所取得的实实在在的成就更是令人瞩目、令人惊叹。中国的成功并非来源于任何书本或现成理论，而是国家不断调整政策、反复摸索尝试的结果。这些政策和实践反映了中国政府坚持以人为本、造福社会的决心，是中国共产党与中国特色社会主义先进性的具体体现。

五、决心和奉献是中国扶贫工作的关键因素[①]

如果有人在20世纪50年代初或60年代初陷入沉睡，2020年才醒过来，肯定会对世界的剧变大感震惊。在这个人眼里，想必凭空多出了无数世界奇迹，而中国无疑就是奇迹之一。

与其他国家一样，中国历经了多次战争浩劫。但是，与其他国家不同，中国实现了"大飞跃"。数十年来，中国人民披荆斩棘、呕心沥血、笃定前行。经历这次飞跃后，中国从一个积贫积弱的国家一跃

① 作者：伊凡娜·拉德杰维克，塞尔维亚贝尔格莱德国际政治经济研究所"一带一路"地区研究中心主任。

成为世界第二经济体和有影响力的践行者，国际地位大大提升。

在1949年中华人民共和国成立之前，中国是全球经济最不发达的国家之一。与所有不发达国家一样，中国面临种种问题：人均预期寿命、婴儿死亡率、文盲率、收入差距、城乡差距、区域差距、性别差距、工农业差距等。封建制度结束后，中国随即进入新的社会制度，没有任何可供借鉴的经验。襁褓中的新中国，百废待兴。人民教育程度较低，疆域辽阔，充斥着各种社会矛盾。

中华人民共和国宣告成立后，中国进入了新的发展时期。第一代领导人毛泽东提出"共同富裕"这一概念，同样具有重大历史意义。共同富裕思想是在对国情进行深入调查的基础上，通过计划经济体制、农业合作和工业现代化等途径，积极探索脱贫致富之路。

毛泽东认识到，要实现国家繁荣昌盛，除了脱贫别无选择。因此，他把脱贫致富视为国家大业。与此同时，毛泽东认为，这是新中国社会建设的先决条件。因此，他明确了几个前提和主要方面：其一，坚持社会主义，作为脱贫的保障；其二，把"共同富裕"作为脱贫的目标；其三，解放和发展生产力。

实践经验印证了他的思想。在随后的几年乃至几十年中，事实证明，借助意识形态和政治方法发展经济、动员最广泛的社会力量参与脱贫致富，极为重要。此外，毛泽东坚持"实现所有农民群众共同富裕"的目标。达到这一目标的唯一途径是"逐步实现国家的社会主义工业化，并逐步实现国家对农业、手工业和资本主义工商业的社会主义改造……使农民群众共同富裕起来"。同时，解放和发展社会生产力是解决社会基本矛盾的根本措施，也是推动社会进步的根本动力。

对于薄弱的经济发展基础，这些观点非常合理。新中国成立时，有40％~50％的人口处于赤贫状态。脱贫被认为是巩固和发展社会主义制度的前提。为此，政府建立了计划经济体制，实施了土地改革，着重发展工业化，改善了教育和医疗，保障了城市的充分就业，提供了大力推动国民经济增长和改善人民生活条件的社会福利和社会救助制度。

数据显示，在连续实施5个"五年计划"期间，从1952年到1978年，国民经济年均增长率达到7.3％，而工业总产值年均增长率为11.4％。从前，中国没有能力建造汽车、飞机或拖拉机，而后来情况发生了变化，中国工业突飞猛进，扩展到了500多个工业门类。考虑到当时中国在经济上被西方封锁，其资金、人才、资源和经验匮乏，这一成就尤为伟大。

虽然取得了明显的进展，但仍有许多工作要做，主要是需要政策向扶贫工作侧重，这对中国政府来说是沉重的负担。诚然，政府大力维护城乡发展之间的平衡，但改变赤贫的面貌需要采取更为复杂的措施，需要贫困人口自立自强。此外，农村地区的要求更高，自然条件严峻，自然灾害频发，疫病也时有发生。因此，尽管众志成城、热情高涨，但技术和生产力水平低下、贫穷因素复杂和经济扶持不足，这些因素削弱了贫困人口提升自我发展能力的前景。要突破瓶颈，必须寻找新的解决方案。

毫无疑问，中国发展的最初阶段始于新中国的成立，之后又进入了一个新阶段，即1978年开始的改革开放阶段。

1978年12月，中共十一届三中全会在北京召开。这是中国近代发展的历史性转折点，也开启了脱贫致富的新时代。

在这一阶段，衡量中国改革成功与否的标准从国家的政治意识形态转变为务实的立场。换句话说，在坚持共同富裕的前提下，中国共产党认识到了中国独特的政治和体制优势，并不断扩大和创新扶贫措施。这一次的措施不仅在农村严格推行，并在全国推广。这个设想的目的不仅是为了推动贫困地区的经济和社会发展，更是为了进一步推动整个国家的经济和社会发展。

　　当时的中国领导人邓小平是一位审慎且高瞻远瞩的务实型领袖，他提出了著名的黑猫白猫论："不管黑猫白猫，捉到老鼠就是好猫。"提出这种观点作为经济发展思想，需要巨大的魄力和勇气。邓小平主张，在经济领域，政府应该鼓励地方、企业、工人和农民通过辛勤劳动获得更多的收入，过上更好的生活。他的设想是，要让一部分人先富起来，树立典型和榜样，充分发挥模范带头作用，带领周围的人共同致富，其他地方的人就会纷纷向他们取经学习。邓小平认为，这种途径可推动整个国民经济的持续发展。邓小平指出："社会主义的本质，是解放生产力，发展生产力，消灭剥削，消除两极分化，最终达到共同富裕。"①

　　1983年，中共中央发表了《当前农村经济政策的若干问题》，指出了十一届三中全会的重要意义，中国农村由此发生了众多变化。影响最深远的是引入了农业生产责任制和家庭联产承包责任制。地方政府因地制宜推行制度变革，实行以家庭承包经营以及农村集体经济统分结合的双层经营体制。这一制度极大地调动了广大农民的积极性，解决了亿万贫困人口的温饱问题。

　　落后的农村地区，尤其是中西部广大农村地区，得到了国家扶贫攻坚计划的重点扶持。1982年启动的"三西"农业建设专项，就是有计划、有组织、大规模扶贫开发的鲜明例子。这一举措从根本上解决了甘肃河西、定西和宁夏西海固地区的贫困问题。

　　1986年，中国政府开始实施有计划、有组织、大规模的农村扶贫攻坚，制定了以发展为导向的政策。一方面，政府将重点转向改善贫困地区的生产生活基础设施以及增强地区整体经济社会发展能力。另一方面，政府大力改善贫困人口的健康并提高其文化素质，改变了以往的扶贫方式。政府还设立了专门机构，以确定贫困标准和重点扶持

---

① 《邓小平文选》第3卷，人民出版社，1993年，第373页。

领域，划拨专项资金，并制定专项配套政策。这些措施取得了立竿见影的成果。从1986年到1993年，贫困县农民人均纯收入从206元增加到483.7元。农村贫困人口由1.25亿人减少到8000万人，年均减少640万人。换句话说，贫困农民的比例从14.8％下降到8.7％。

　　尽管成果显著，但扶贫攻坚计划依然任重道远。为此，1994年，中共中央、国务院颁布了《国家八七扶贫攻坚计划（1994—2000年）》，不断深入推进扶贫和发展。在这一时期，以江泽民同志为核心的党中央将扶贫开发纳入国家发展战略，深入解决扶贫标准、扶贫内容和扶贫对象等具体问题，进一步完善了扶贫的思想内容和工作体系。当时的首要任务是解决剩余贫困人口的温饱问题，巩固扶贫成果，从温饱型向小康型转变，全面推进贫困地区经济社会发展。

　　实施这项"七年计划"后，到2000年，贫困人口减少到3000万人，而农村地区的贫困人口比例从30.7％下降到3％左右；国家重点扶贫县贫困人口从1994年的5858万人减少到1710万人。

　　到2000年底，贫困地区通电、通路、通邮和通电话的行政村分别达到95.5％、89％、69％和67.7％。贫困县的经济社会发展速度也大大加快。1994年至2000年间，国家重点扶持县的农业产值增长了54％，年均增长率为7.5％；工业产值增长了99.3％，年均增长率为12.2％。人均纯收入从648元增加到1337元，年均增长率为12.8％。

　　此后，以胡锦涛同志为总书记的党中央对扶贫开发提出了更高的要求，把扶贫开发的重要性和目标置于更深更广的范畴内考量。胡锦涛强调，扶贫开发是"以人为本"思想的重要体现，是科学发展观的根本要求。胡锦涛指出，必须"从人民群众的根本利益出发谋发展、促发展，不断满足人民群众日益增长的物质文化需要，切实保障人民群众的经济、政治和文化权益，让发展的成果惠及全体人民"[1]。

---

[1] 《十六大以来重要文献选编》（上），中央文献出版社，2005年，第850页。

　　在西部大开发的战略背景下，各地政府进一步协调城乡经济发展。政府贯彻工业反哺农业、城市反哺农村的战略措施，全面推进农村经济社会发展，惠及农村地区的大多数贫困人口。2006年1月1日起废止《中华人民共和国农业税条例》，取消了各种农民赋税。随后，政府出台了多项补贴措施，其中包括种子补贴、农机设备补贴、物资补贴等。与此同时，政府还出台了农业免税试点项目、农村义务教育等其他优惠政策。除了这些政策和措施外，中央政府还逐步建立健全农村社会保障体系，推进农村饮用水、电力、道路和沼气等基础设施的建设。中央政府还在"三农"以及扶贫开发等方面加大了财政拨款力度。从2003年到2010年，相关中央财政支出从2144.2亿元增加到8579.7亿元，年均增长21.9%。

　　21世纪的前十年，中国政府将扶贫对象设定为扶贫标准以下的人口。中央政府确认了592个国家扶贫开发工作重点县。为了解决这一突出问题，政府实施了推动全村扶贫开发的模式，并通过教育发展、工业化、安排就业而非直接补助、移民搬迁和财政扶持等途径，在一些特殊困难地区实施符合当地特点的扶贫项目，在一些特殊困难地区实施因地制宜的扶贫开发。

　　贯彻扶贫攻坚的同时，地方政府也高度重视人权。中央政府对22个人口不足10万的人口较少民族给予了特别扶持，颁发了《扶持人口较少民族发展规划（2005—2010年）》，并向人口较少的民族及其社区投入了37.51亿元的帮扶资金，以加快其发展步伐。此外，通过实施《中国妇女发展纲要（2001—2010年）》，政府制定了一项专门的妇女扶贫计划，该计划优先考虑缓解妇女贫困程度，减少贫困妇女数量。

　　中国共产党第十八次全国代表大会确定了下一个十年的发展方向。习近平主席把扶贫开发作为总体发展战略的核心。与此同时，政府努力实现极为重要的战略使命：全面建成小康社会。这一任务需要纳入"五位一体"总体布局和"四个全面"战略布局，据此进行决策。"五位一体"总体布局与社会主义现代化建设全面接轨，其中包括经济建设、政治建设、文化建设、社会建设和生态文明建设，而"四个全面"包括全面建成小康社会、全面深化改革、全面依法治国、全面从严治党。消除贫困、改善民生、实现共同富裕的思想，已成为习近平新时代中国特色社会主义思想当中的重要治国方略。

习近平新时代中国特色社会主义思想已成为党和人民的重要指导思想。这一思想深受儒家思想的精神启发，融入了毛泽东的革命思想和邓小平式的改革理论。正因为如此，这一思想蕴含着系统的内容体系，即"八个明确"和"十四个坚持"，包括坚持全面深化改革，坚持新发展理念，坚持党对人民军队的绝对领导，坚持人与自然和谐共生，坚持"一国两制"和推进祖国统一等。

在脱贫方面，引入长效机制，解决其实际问题。为此，《脱贫攻坚责任制实施办法》得到发布，"中央统筹、省负总责、市县抓落实"的脱贫攻坚工作机制得到完善。除此之外，脱贫攻坚政策、脱贫攻坚资金投入、脱贫攻坚监管和脱贫攻坚评估体系也得到了建立。

在中共中央和国务院的有力领导下，经国务院扶贫开发领导小组的全面协调以及地方政府的积极配合和社会的参与，所采取的措施已见成效。

据世界银行统计，按照国际贫困线标准（每人每日1.9美元）计算，40年来，中国成功减少了7亿多贫困人口。在这些方面，"中国在经济快速增长和减贫方面取得了前所未有的成就"。更重要的是，中国是世界上第一个实现联合国《2030年可持续发展议程》减贫目标的发展中国家。事实胜于雄辩，中国提前十年实现了这一目标，堪称全球减贫事业的领导者。

有数据表明，2019年中国农村人民生活水平仍在不断提高。例如，2019年前三季度，贫困地区农村居民人均可支配收入为8163元，比2018年同期增长10.8％。

中国在减贫方面的突出经验可为其他国家所借鉴，特别是中国愿意为建设人类命运共同体作出贡献。正如习近平主席睿智地指出，霸权主义抬头是对世界体系的严重破坏和威胁。因此，必须建立伙伴关系，以推动造福于全人类的开放、创新和包容性发展。普通民众的生活质量决定了我们的未来。

最后，用一句中国谚语结束本文——"不怕慢，就怕站"。

第三章
希望的信号：中国为发展中国家减贫带来了启迪与赋能

一、从"你吃了吗"到"你瘦了"①

中国曾经对贫穷有着切肤之痛，对美好生活充满渴望。人们见面打招呼时会说"你吃了吗"，这是亿万中国人在艰难年代的生活写照，彼时中国人的温饱问题还未得到解决。

改革开放40年后的今天，中国人的问候语已悄然发生变化，变得多元起来，许多人开始用"你胖了"或"你瘦了"打招呼。

问候语的变化折射出中国人已基本解决温饱问题，向着更注重生活质量的方向转变。

中国有句谚语"一锹挖不出一口井"，它与西谚"罗马城不是一天建成的"意思相近。1961年，我出生在中国东北城市哈尔滨，妈妈至今还常说："怀你时，根本吃不上鸡蛋牛奶，看着商店的上海'大白兔'奶糖，馋得直流口水。"20世纪70年代，做铁路工程师的父母每月从各自微薄的56元工资中，寄给农村爷爷奶奶和姥姥姥爷各15元，因为农村的生活更艰难。爷爷奶奶则把乡下的地瓜干和花生米寄给我们。

城乡亲人情同手足，互通有无，这既是中国传统农业社会紧密

---

① 作者：尹树广，香港《文汇报》前副总编辑，中国国际战略研究基金会研究员。

家庭关系的现实写照，又是孔夫子倡导的以"仁爱"为核心的儒家思想的延续。这一优良传统构成了中华民族生生不息的精神源泉，培养了中国人勤劳、忍耐和乐观的性格，亦成为克服生活磨难的益世良方。

1978年，中国终于迎来历史转折关头，邓小平开启了中国改革开放的里程碑进程。那是中国恢复高考的第二年，我幸运考上黑龙江省重点中学——哈尔滨市第一中学高中部。我只有一个想法：一定要考上大学。1978年，日本故事片《追捕》热映，镜头中闪现的东京摩天大楼、川流不息的车流，让所有中国人的心灵受到强烈震撼。对外开放成为所有中国人的共识。

当时，我不敢想象有朝一日能拥有一辆小汽车，能到东京旅游。由于中国当时实行计划经济体制，绝大多数日用品都要凭票供应，我家只有一台缝纫机和收音机，一家四口人挤在一间12平方米的屋子里。

邓小平被誉为中国改革开放总设计师。40年前，他提出"贫穷不是社会主义""发展是硬道理""让一部分人先富起来"等一系列大胆论断，回想起来，至今还让人激动不已。

1987年，中共十三大提出社会主义初级阶段理论，这一邓小平理论的精髓奠定了改革开放政策的理论基础，统一了中国共产党人的思想和行动。邓小平的"富民理论"不仅成功促成中国特色社会主义市场经济体制的确立，更为2020年全面实现脱贫攻坚、全面建成小康社会提供了坚实制度保证和物质条件。

2013年11月，习近平主席首次提出"精准扶贫"方略，中国扶贫之路开始从粗放化走向精细化的历史演变。习近平身体力行，不仅每年多次去农村指导减贫工作，还为这项工作制定了关键绩效指标（KPI），作为各级领导干部的政绩考核重点，强调要"久久为功"和"抓铁有痕"。所以，中国的减贫事业取得了世界瞩目的成就不是偶然的。

改革开放让近8亿中国人彻底摆脱了贫困，贫困率降低了94％。截至2019年，中国的极端贫困人口下降到551万人，仅占14亿中国人的0.4％。中国成为第一个实现联合国千年发展目标中减贫目标的发展中国家。

2019年，联合国秘书长安东尼奥·古特雷斯在参观中华人民共和国成立70周年阅兵仪式时由衷地感叹："中国让8亿人脱贫，谱写了人类减贫历史的辉煌篇章。"

2020年，新冠肺炎疫情使全球经济陷入深度衰退之中，中国经济也受到前所未有的冲击。但中国政府迎难而上，依然将消灭551万绝对贫困人口作为2020年全年优先任务之一不动摇。

中国在与贫穷作斗争的事业中取得了举世瞩目的成就。2017年2月，古特雷斯在慕尼黑安全会议的讲话中对此称赞道："中国成为全球减贫作出最大贡献的国家。"作为一名从事新闻报道几十年的中国媒体人，笔者认为中国"减贫奇迹"的成功原因可概括如下：

一是减贫成绩单是中国40年改革开放政策的必然结果，改革开放政策为全面减贫成效提供了保证。40年来，中国减贫的深化与改革开放的进程几乎同步：从沿海地区转向中西部欠发达地区、从大城市转向广大农村、从北上广深和省会转向三四线中小城市，才可能像打鱼收网那样，形成2020年的精准扶贫决战阶段，最终将使551万绝对贫困人口走出困境。

二是形成了一整套切实可行的减贫政策和实施机制。在国家历次"五年计划"中，均包括有减贫内容。中央政府设有专门的国务院扶贫办，一名副总理亲自抓落实。省、市、县、乡四级行政管理部门均设有扶贫职能机构。

三是中央预算每年都拿出大量财政资金用于支持扶贫。

四是中国宪法规定中国是单一制国家，有利于政府在全国范围内落实政策，这也有利于为高效落实减贫措施提供经验和动力。

五是确定了基建扶贫、易地扶贫、教育扶贫、卫生扶贫、金融扶贫、产业扶贫、旅游扶贫、互联网扶贫等八大重点扶贫领域。这八大领域不仅符合中国具体国情和特点，而且同当下方兴未艾的互联网经济、数字经济等新经济革命结合了起来，给中国减贫装上了科技的翅膀。

2013年下半年，习近平主席提出"一带一路"倡议，这为国际减贫合作提供了新契机。在全球范围内，"一带一路"合作正顺利推进，这可以使中国与沿线国家的合作成果惠及更多人，使沿线各国更多人就业、更多人喝上干净的饮用水、更多孩子获得受教育的权利等。

1995年夏，我曾去内战中的"中亚山国"塔吉克斯坦采访。从哈萨克斯坦开车去之前，我问一位当地同行朋友："需要点什么？"他不假思考地回答："带一袋子白面（25公斤）和白糖吧！"当我到达首都杜尚别，得知当时人均收入才5美元，连米面油糖都没有，我理解了"贫穷"的真正含义。至今，当时的情景历历在目。

所以，和平与发展应是国际社会永恒的主题，国际减贫合作任重而道远。

渴望公平，摆脱贫穷，是各国人民的梦想，是人类文明进步的标志之一。20世纪的两次世界大战、许多国家的内战悲剧都让人们认识到和平与发展弥足珍贵。

联合国千年发展目标和《2030年可持续发展议程》将"消灭贫困和饥饿"列为全球首要目标和议程，国际减贫路漫漫。只要各国政府和人民齐心协力，国际减贫事业一定会取得更大成就。

二、中国减贫经验对其他发展中国家的启示和意义①

中国是第一个实现联合国千年发展目标的发展中国家，为全球减贫事业作出了重大贡献。中国自1978年实施改革开放政策以来，使7亿多贫困人口摆脱了贫困，对过去40年世界减贫事业的贡献率超过70%。当前，中国正在实施精准扶贫精准脱贫方略，并向世界宣布，到2020年底实现现行标准下农村贫困人口全部脱贫，彻底消除绝对贫困的目标。无论是从宏观层面还是从微观层面来说，中国在减贫领域的经验对于很多发展中国家都极具价值。

从不同的视角和维度，可以归纳总结出很多中国减贫经验。从宏观层面来说，中国的减贫经验可以归纳为四个方面：一是坚持改革开放，保持经济快速增长，为大规模减贫提供环境和经济基础。二是制定一系列有利于贫困人口发展的制度政策，形成大规模持续减贫的政策基础。这些制度包括明确农民对土地的使用权和收益支配权的土地制度、积极的就业政策、保障所有学龄儿童接受教育的义务教育法、在城市实行基本医疗保险、在农村实行合作医疗的政策，以及建立了以社会保险、社会救助、社会福利、优抚安置和社会互助为基础的社会保障制度等。三是实施专项扶贫开发计划，增强贫困地区和贫困人口的自我发展能力。中国先后实施《国家八七扶贫攻坚计划（1994—2000年）》《中国农村扶贫开发纲要（2001—2010年）》《中国农村扶贫开发纲要（2011—2020年）》，同时，针对特定人群组织也实施了妇女儿童、残疾人、少数民族发展规划。四是坚持动员全社会参与，发挥中国制度优势，构建了政府、社会、市场协同推进的大扶贫格局，形成了跨地区、跨部门、跨单位、全社会共同参与的多元主体的社会扶贫体系。

---

① 作者：伍鹏，中国扶贫基金会国际发展部主任。

从微观层面来说，中国的减贫经验也可以归纳为四个方面：一是建立健全从中央到地方的扶贫组织体系，实行责任、任务、资金和权力"四个到省"的扶贫工作责任制。二是根据国情确定了贫困线，并且使用了多维化的贫困评定标准，将"两不愁、三保障"，即不愁吃、不愁穿，义务教育、基本医疗和住房安全有保障作为脱贫标准。三是实施了精准减贫方略，注重抓"六个精准"，即扶持对象精准、项目安排精准、资金使用精准、措施到户精准、因村派人精准、脱贫成效精准，确保各项政策好处落到扶贫对象身上。四是结合时代的发展，不断探索减贫新模式，如东西协作扶贫、定点扶贫、劳动力转移培训扶贫、易地搬迁扶贫、产业扶贫、教育扶贫、科技扶贫、生态扶贫、社会保障兜底扶贫、旅游扶贫、构树扶贫、光电扶贫、资产收益扶贫、金融扶贫、电商扶贫等。

中国的减贫成就和经验得到世界各国的高度认可，其他发展中国家在学习中国的减贫成就和经验方面存在极大需求。然而，因为不同国家的政治体制、发展阶段不同，对于中国的减贫经验肯定不能简单地照抄照搬，需要根据自身的实际情况有针对性地学习借鉴。在如此丰富的中国减贫经验中，以下几个方面尤其值得其他发展中国家学习借鉴：

一是中国政府在国家层面制定减贫中长期规划，确保实现减贫工作目标的经验。这些规划都是根据当时经济社会发展实际情况，在减贫目标、减贫对象与重点、基本方针、内容和途径、政策保障（含资金投入）和组织领导方面都有明确要求，确保扶贫目标的实现。发展中国家可以借鉴中国这方面的经验，在国家层面制定中长期减贫规划，统一共识、凝聚资源、降低各级沟通和决策成本、提升减贫工作效率，实现减贫目标。当然，只制定减贫规划是不够的，还需要持之以恒地贯彻执行。一些发展中国家往往也有制定很详细的减贫路线图，但是要么政府没有财政预算支持，成为被束之高阁的字面规划；要么就是因为频繁的领导人更替，导致规划被迫中途放弃，得不到持续的贯彻和执行。

二是中国建立自上而下的完整减贫机构，为减贫提供组织保障的经验。中国政府依托行政体系在国家层面设立国务院扶贫办，负责统筹全国扶贫开发工作，在省、市、县、乡各级都设立了相应的扶贫部门，形成了自上而下完整的减贫机构，以政府为主导高效开展减贫行动。但是，有些发展中国家行政机构越往下，能力会越弱，到了乡镇级别，行政机构的执行能力非常有限，一般靠部落酋长或其他社区领袖来管理，减贫规划往往不能有效地贯彻执行，从而使规划的减贫效果大打折扣。实践证明，中国自上而下完整的扶贫机构体系对保证完成中国减贫任务起到关键作用，发展中国家可以根据本国实际，建立类似的减贫组织体系，如果政府的行政体系不足以支撑，可以与社会组织建立合作伙伴关系，共同完成减贫组织体系的建设，确保国家层面的减贫规划能高效地贯彻执行。

三是通过建档立卡，把贫困人口精准识别出来的经验。中国通过群众评议、入户调查、公示公告、抽查检验、信息录入等程序，开展到村到户的贫困状况调查和建档立卡工作，识别贫困人口。贫困人口识别出来以后，针对扶贫对象的贫困情况确定责任人和减贫措施，确保减贫效果。发展中国家每年能接收到大量来自国际发展机构的减贫援助资金，但是有很大一部分减贫援助资金在中间环节消耗掉了。仔细研究后发现，国际发展机构为了保证项目公平公正，在筛选受益对象方面花费很多，他们往往需要雇佣一批兼职人员深入社区，通过问卷调查、社区商议等程序，把需要帮助的贫困户识别出来，而且其调研的样本量往往是实际资助人数的一倍以上，耗费了大量的人力和物力，才能识别出令各方满意的受益人。然而，这并不是一家发展机构在做这样的动作，所有开展减贫项目的国际发展机构都在做同样的事情，重复消耗大量本来就稀缺的减贫资源。如果发展中国家借鉴中国建档立卡经验，由政府把需要帮助的贫困户统一识别出来，其他减贫参与机构只要瞄准这些被识别出来的贫困户开展项目，就能节省大量的前期识别费用，从而把宝贵的减贫资源更多地用在受益人身上。

四是可以借鉴中国接地气的减贫模式。中国是世界上最大的发展中国家，在没有脱贫之前，经济社会发展基础与绝大部分发展中国家差不多。所以，在同样基础上发展出来的中国减贫方法和模式，对发展中国家有极大的参考借鉴价值。中国减贫技术在发展中国家取得成功的案例很多，比如中国扶贫基金会在埃塞俄比亚实施的非洲水窖项目就是其中之一。2011年非洲之角发生旱灾的时候，中国扶贫基金会项目人员在实地调研时发现，当地解决贫困农户饮水问题的方式要么用卡车运水，要么打深井泵水，这两种方式投入成本都非常高。由此，中国扶贫基金会项目人员想到了中国干旱地区使用的水窖技术，通过雨季收集雨水储存在水窖里，旱季提取使用的方式，低成本解决贫困家庭的饮水困难。中国水窖项目引入埃塞俄比亚之后，因为投入成本更低，深受当地贫困农户欢迎，目前已经实施三期，完成120口水窖的援建。

中国的成功经验使国际社会看到了希望：贫困是可以消除的。中国的减贫经验是一个富矿，值得其他发展中国家探究和借鉴。当然，无论是中国政府还是民间社会，都非常愿意把中国的减贫经验分享到有需求的发展中国家，为这些国家早日实现联合国《2030年可持续发展议程》目标作出贡献！

三、减贫与经济发展齐头并进[①]

中华人民共和国成立以来，中国取得了举世瞩目的经济社会发展成就，也在减少贫困方面取得了长足的进步。特别是改革开放以后，中国有7亿多人摆脱了贫困，超过了拉丁美洲的总人口，为世界贫困人口的减少作出了卓越贡献。

中国减贫70年积累的丰富经验，对于世界其他国家来说具有很好的借鉴意义。不过，一些西方国家从自身角度分析认为，中国之所以能够取得如此巨大的减贫成绩，主要是因为抓住了特殊的历史机遇，利用世界生产体系转移的过程，成为世界工厂，在国际贸易中充分利用廉价劳动力的优势，使得经济发展迅速，才取得了巨大的发展成就。这种发展机会不可复制，因此他们认为中国的减贫经验并不具有可复制性，仅是一种偶然现象。

这实际上是机械地看待经济发展的过程，属于刻舟求剑，也误解了经济发展和减贫的逻辑关系。每个时代都有每个时代的发展机遇，经济发展也并不必然带来大规模减贫，反而有可能导致两极分化，增加相对贫困人口。

中国减贫取得成功，经济发展在其中起到的作用仅仅是一个方面，减贫理念和政府的作用同样也至关重要。发达国家经济社会发展较为成熟，贫困人口比例相对固定，政府、民间、企业有着较为完善的互动救助体系，中国的减贫经验可能对发达国家来说意义有限。不过，对于广大发展中国家来说，中国的减贫经验有许多积极的意义。这些国家一方面要大力发展经济，另一方面也要解决贫困问题，如何同时处理好这两个问题，在经济发展的同时带动减贫的实现，是这些国家面临的重要命题。在我们来看，这些国家在减贫

[①] 作者：张弛，中国社会科学院经济研究所助理研究员。

中应注意以下几点：

第一，要将减贫的方法和目的统一起来。减贫的最终目的是保证人民基本生存条件，提高人民生活质量。中国改革开放前的减贫工作，就是主要通过提升人民总体的生活条件来实现的，虽然人均收入水平按世界标准来看比较低，但人民群众的生活质量已经达到比较高的水平。党的十八大以来开展的精准脱贫工作中强调建立长效脱贫机制，防止返贫发生。减贫不能仅仅提供资金、食物、药品等物质支持，还需要建设相应的基础设施，提高贫困人口的生活质量和生活能力，实现真正脱贫。

第二，要在发展中解决贫困问题。必须在发展中加大减贫工作的投入，让贫困人口享受发展的红利。同时，要防止发展过程中出现两极分化，产生新的贫困问题，应合理调节社会收入分配水平。

第三，既要发挥好政府的主导作用，也要尊重人民的首创精神。减贫工作具有正外部性，政府推动这项工作对整个社会具有积极的意义。从国家层面进行减贫，需要统筹规划，协调各方面的利益和关系，综合利用各种资源，政府在这些方面具有其他机构或者组织无法比拟的优势。减贫事业需要大量的资金支持，通过政府信用背书有利于资金的调度使用。因此，减贫工作的顺利推进，需要一个国家通过政府制定周密的计划，从上而下依次推动，并建立有效的监督反馈机制。与此同时，还应充分尊重人民的首创精神，正确对待人民在减贫事业中的创新和探索，将合理有效的经验通过政府制度化、法规化，促进上下良性互动，调动人民的积极性，共同推动减贫事业取得成功。

中国的减贫经验和启示对于全人类来说都十分珍贵，值得推广学习，让更多的国家受益。

通过援助项目帮助发展中国家减贫。中国一直以来通过多种援助项目帮助发展中国家发展，特别是在非洲各国，在中国的帮助下修建了许多铁路、公路、医院等基础设施，极大改善了当地居民的生存条件。中国对非洲的援助工作，与许多发达国家只提供物质支持不同，中国通过帮助非洲国家发展产业，提升当地的经济发展水平，帮助非洲从根本上解决贫困问题。通过援助项目，中国为发展中国家带去先进的技术和理念，也同这些国家建立起友谊的纽带，是一种推广中国减贫经验的直接方法。

通过"一带一路"倡议、亚洲基础设施投资银行等，传播中国的减贫经验。中国经历了国家由弱到强的发展历程，清楚发展中国家减贫的真正需求，但在西方国家主导的组织中缺少话语权，往往很难发出声音。随着中国国力的不断增强，中国主导建立的许多新的国际组织，如中非合作论坛、上海合作组织等，这些国际组织可以成为很好的传播平台。比如在这些国际组织中成立专门的减贫指导机构，由中国人负责领导；或是在举办的国际性会议中，设立关于减贫工作的分论坛，着重介绍中国经验，让更多的发展中国家有机会学习中国的减贫经验。

中国近年的发展成就吸引了许多发展中国家的官员来中国取经学习。他们通过一段时间的系统学习，掌握中国的发展经验，便能够指导自己国家的发展。

四、中国发展经验为巴基斯坦指明方向[①]

中国为扶贫事业付出了艰苦卓绝的努力，使将近8亿人成功脱贫，这是21世纪屈指可数的伟大奇迹之一。中国励精图治，迎难而上，最终成为繁荣昌盛的经济大国。凭借开拓进取和高瞻远瞩的领导层、一以贯之的政策、强而有力的方针和卓有成效的方法，应对

---

① 作者：穆罕默德·阿西夫·努尔，巴基斯坦和平与外交研究所所长。

各种挑战，革新传统生产操作模式，大力应用先进技术，推动农业扶持和改革进程，这是整个中国扶贫攻坚计划进程的重要纲领。

中国不仅增强了自身的整体经济实力，还引领绝大多数中国人民脱离贫困的泥淖，对全球减贫的贡献率超过70％。中国是巴基斯坦的战略盟友，中巴关系是巴基斯坦外交政策的重要组成部分。在危机之时，中国更是巴基斯坦的重要伙伴。中国的经济发展进程大大带动了巴基斯坦的发展。

中国已经成为区域和全球经济大国，启动了庞大的项目工程和"一带一路"倡议，中巴经济走廊成为其中的关键环节。中国正在借助中巴经济走廊为巴基斯坦提供广泛支持，旨在建立长远发展的互通互联项目。随着中巴经济走廊的全速推进，"共同富裕"这一中国梦有了强大的推动力。

核心问题是，中国取得了如此划时代的瞩目成就，对巴基斯坦有什么意义和启发。巴基斯坦拥有2.2亿人口，地理位置优越，是一个发展中国家。70多年来，以减贫为重点、实现全面发展一直是巴基斯坦整个社会经济的核心原则。

尽管巴基斯坦政府矢志不移、笃定前行，并进行了政策层面的改革，但由于存在冗繁复杂的社会结构和行政问题，实现减贫目标依然任重道远。巴基斯坦国内外最新的各种发展报告，无不揭示了巴基斯坦令人担忧的贫困状况。例如，根据最新的联合国开发计划署人类发展指数，巴基斯坦在189个国家中排名第150位。

巴基斯坦政府总理伊姆兰·汗上任后不久就宣誓要为人民谋福祉，借助中国对巴基斯坦人民的全力支持，消除贫困，改善民生。除政府主导的各种项目外，中巴经济走廊已进入第二阶段，在这一阶段，除了关注互联互通、能源、农业和工业发展外，其中一个重要使命是促进社会经济发展，大力减贫。

习近平主席不仅带领中国人民实现了伟大目标，他在国家治理方面的远见卓识大大激励了巴基斯坦领导人。习近平主席带领中国崛起，同时也推动了全球经济发展。作为"一带一路"倡议的重要组成部分，中巴经济走廊正在改变整个格局，加快巴基斯坦减贫步伐。

对巴基斯坦来说，另一个重要的好处是，中国通过中巴经济走廊向巴基斯坦提供援助，扶持其建设强大的铁路、公路和通信项目网络，增强了巴基斯坦建设支持其边缘化社区的能力。这使从农场到小企业以及国家和地区之间的联系越发紧密。巴基斯坦正在借助瓜达尔港为中国贸易打入全球市场提供最短、最安全和低成本的通路。还必须指出的是，这不仅对中国大有裨益，而且也为巴基斯坦的经济繁荣提供了契机。巴基斯坦可有效利用这些发达的网络，在区域和全球层面建立商业、贸易和经济事务方面的接触和联系。

巴基斯坦能够在各个领域及时了解研究、知识和技术等方面的所有最新发展成果。无论是农业、供水系统和资源管理、电子商务、工业发展与合作、战略资产建设，还是能源领域，巴基斯坦都在不断寻求并接受中国的援助。

例如，在中巴经济走廊规划初期，巴基斯坦面临着严重的能源危机，但现在巴基斯坦已能满足自身能源需求。互联互通正在助力工业成为巴基斯坦经济基础的生命线。此外，巴基斯坦各地发生严重蝗灾之后，中国提供了帮助以及创新的应急对策。巴基斯坦的电子商务和商业，与中国各大电子商务公司建立联系，借此东风，蓬勃发展。

巴基斯坦是中国的盟友，也是中国改革开放和社会经济发展可持续政策的受益者。巴基斯坦力图通过改变整个民族的精神面貌，大力灌输发展理念，这是一大关键因素。

任何发展进程，想要获得成功，都需要构建一个因地制宜的宏伟蓝图，从而实现长远目标。对巴基斯坦来说，同样重要的还有，中国的发展模式保持了中国特色，因势利导，可应对各种新的变化和挑战。在整个发展过程中，中国并没有因循守旧，而是冲破藩篱，与时俱进。巴基斯坦需要向中国借鉴这些重要经验，坚持一以贯之的方针政策，根据自身具体国情求真务实，打造符合自身需求的本土模式。发展必然是个长期坚定的过程，不管政府当权者是谁，都绝不能背离初衷。

最后，由于中国的改革开放，包括启动中巴经济走廊，巴基斯坦也在推行财政紧缩政策，力图消除社会各阶层的腐败现象，特别是在执行发展项目的过程中。巴基斯坦还极为重视公务员制度改革，并提供充分的支持，包括对高效、廉洁、守信的行为实行奖励。

纵观中国发展经验，可明白一个道理，一个国家的命运掌握在那些廉洁守信、勇于担当、急流勇进、在逆境中起领导带头作用的人手中。正是这样的一些人，披肝沥胆，不辜负脚下这片土地，引领中国不断走向繁荣富强。2020年，正是中国全面建成小康社会宏伟目标的实现之年，中国人民终于得以品尝社会经济发展结出的累累硕果。

五、非洲需要深谋远虑的减贫领导力[1]

近20年来，人们对非洲的看法发生了巨大变化：从"毫无希望"的大陆变成了"充满希望"的大陆。这种变化的基础是从20世纪70年代和80年代的经济负增长和停滞增长转变为随后几年的经济正增长和相对稳定的增长。然而，尽管民生和福利有所改善，非洲在人们心目中的形象，仍然是一个战乱频仍、处处饥荒和极度赤贫的大陆。数十年来，寻求政治、战略、计划和项目以解决贫困问题的政治家、学者、研究人员、政策制定者和发展伙伴，一直在关注"非洲崛起"

---

[1] 作者：汉弗莱·莫希，达累斯萨拉姆大学经济学教授，中国研究中心主任，坦桑尼亚公平竞争委员会主席。

的悖论（一方面是根深蒂固的困顿，一方面是急于求成的增长）。

虽然非洲已在全球、区域和国家各个层面制定了一系列政策，部分已予以实施，但与全球其他发展中地区相比，非洲大陆的减贫速度一直非常缓慢。这种令人沮丧的局面，再加上经济专家的预测表明，世界上的穷人将越来越集中在非洲，人们呼吁社会各界紧急行动起来，携手努力，解决非洲普遍存在的贫困问题。

事实上，造成非洲贫穷的原因有很多，包括冲突、环境退化和人口高速增长。

但是，根本原因在于，急于求成的增长既没有实现包容性，也没有带来经济结构的转型。一方面，农业是大多数人的生计来源，生产率低下，却占据了主导地位；另一方面，经济去工业化，这证明了转型的延迟。

这种状况无论在理论上还是在实践上都是矛盾的，这突出了两个部门之间的共生关系，某种意义上，从提高生产率的角度来看，农业部门的发展是减贫和推进工业化的最可靠方法。事实上，亚洲国家，特别是中国的发展经验，就是这一现象的明证。这些国家成功的工业化经验不仅提高了农业部门的生产率，而且还可以大大减少贫困和不平衡现象，这值得非洲国家借鉴和学习。中国是非洲的第二大贸易伙伴，并且中非之间有各种各样的合作安排，非洲国家迫切希望这种合作成为实现结构转型和减贫的强大推动力。在减贫工作中，非洲可以借鉴中国的社会经济模式，从中学到很多东西。这种模式能够在相当短的时间内大幅减贫。

在全面建成小康社会的进程中，中国积累了丰富的减贫经验：保持经济持续稳定增长，不断出台有利于贫困地区和贫困人口发展的社会政策，把扶贫开发纳入中国总体发展战略，并将经济发展作为减贫脱贫的根本之举。其他重要经验还包括充分落实扶贫目标，优先发展农业，全面推进农村经济社会发展，优先建设贫困地区的道路、供水、供电、供气和住房等基础设施，并鼓励社会参与，发挥政府、社会和市场的导向作用。

在中国40多年的改革进程中，中国采用了一种兼容并蓄的社会经济发展模式，过去如此，现在也是如此。这种模式已使7亿多人脱贫。

确实，尽管面临新冠肺炎疫情的挑战，但2020年3月的中央扶贫工作会议明确指出，本年度的扶贫攻坚目标保持不变，即到2020年底，确保中国的551万贫困人口、52个贫困县和1113个贫困村全部脱贫摘帽。

这一史无前例的成就为非洲大陆提供了又一个借鉴性经验。非洲大陆仍有4亿多人处于赤贫状态，非洲领导人要想有效地消除贫困，必须采纳中国发展模式的一些关键方面，并加强与中国在各个经济领域的合作。

《摆脱贫困》是习近平主席的个人著作，收录了他任中共宁德地委书记期间的重要讲话和调研文章，共29篇。全书紧紧围绕闽东宁德地区如何脱贫致富、加快发展这一主题，提出了一系列方法，如改变思想观念、经济发展和管理以及领导决策。读了这本书，我们深有感触，其中许多问题似乎与非洲的情况极为相关。但是，我们并不是主张全盘照搬，而是主张根据非洲大陆的实际情况加以借鉴。我们已经确定了三个关键领域，这些领域似乎与非洲的情形息息相关，但是在当代减贫工作中却明显被忽视了。应使这些已确定的领域进入各级决策者的视线，由此制定相关方针政策，逐步引领非洲摆脱贫穷。

首先且最重要的是需要转变观念。正如习主席书中所说，"扶贫先要扶志，要从思想上淡化'贫困意识'"。换句话说，这意味着贫穷不是悲观的宿命，完全可以面对并最终克服。事实上，所有发达国家都曾在过去的某个时期陷入贫困，这既是减贫工作的启示，也是减贫工作的动力。

其次是需要利用现有资源与贫困作斗争。在大多数情况下，在贫困地区，最丰富的资源就是农业，包括农作物、林业、牲畜和海产品。必须开发资源，对资源有效调配与利用，这是使一个国家摆脱贫困的主要途径。这就是习近平主席所说的"经济大合唱"。同样，这些地区的工业化应以资源为基础，生产加工农产品。这方面突显了农业与工业之间的紧密联系。建议在起草工业政策时，重点应放在"紧紧围绕工业发展农业，以发展工业来支援农业"。

动员人民群众和加强干部队伍建设，是解决贫困问题的关键因素。习近平主席强调："各级领导干部要深入实际，深入群众，坚持从群众中来到群众中去。"[1]习近平主席进一步描述了领导干部应具备的素质，包括忠心赤胆、克己奉公、勤勉踏实、清正廉洁、谦虚谨慎。习近平主席认为，领导干部要想获得人民的信任和支持，这些素质缺一不可。此外，习近平主席还认为，领导干部必须大公无私，理性务实，提倡办实事需要科学思考和科学论证。

六、"中国智慧"助力乌拉圭减贫[2]

2020年是中华民族伟大复兴进程中具有里程碑意义的一年，中国将彻底消除绝对贫困，全面建成小康社会，实现第一个百年目标。新中国成立70年来，尤其是改革开放以来，中国7亿多人成功摆脱贫困，占同期全球减贫人口的70%以上。

中国共产党人的初心和使命，就是为中国人民谋幸福，为中华民族谋复兴。以习近平同志为核心的党中央提出扶贫攻坚的执政理念，就是要让全中国人民共奔小康、实现共同富裕。习近平总书记

---

[1] 《摆脱贫困》，福建人民出版社，1992年。
[2] 作者：王刚，中国驻乌拉圭大使。

强调："小康路上一个都不能掉队！"①这是中国扶贫事业的庄严承诺，也是不断深入开展扶贫工作的行动指南。

近年来，随着脱贫工作进入攻坚期，中国把精准扶贫作为基本方略，强调对扶贫对象实施精细化管理、对扶贫资源实施精确化配置、对扶贫对象实施精准化扶持，在扶持对象精准、项目安排精准、资金使用精准、措施到户精准、因村派人精准、脱贫成效精准上想办法、出实招、见真效，因地制宜，对症下药，实现贫困人口精准脱贫。

今天的世界，发展不平衡不充分问题仍然普遍存在，南北发展差距依然巨大，贫困和饥饿依然严重。贫困及其衍生出来的饥饿、疾病、社会冲突等一系列难题依然困扰着许多发展中国家。习近平主席提出构建人类命运共同体的理念，要着力解决发展失衡、治理困境、数字鸿沟、分配差距等问题。

中国秉持共建共治共享的减贫理念和开发式扶贫理念，将产业扶贫与稳定脱贫相结合，将"输血式"扶贫与"造血式"扶贫相结合，将精准扶贫与绿色发展相结合，将自身扶贫与国际扶贫相结合。

中国在推进国内扶贫事业发展的同时，也一直是全球减贫事业的积极倡导者和有力推动者。过去70年，中国累计向近170个国家和国际组织提供援助资金4000多亿元，实施各类援外项目5000多个，派遣60多万名援助人员，为发展中国家培训各类人员1200多万人次，为120多个发展中国家落实千年发展目标提供了帮助。

2018年11月1日，中国政府在乌拉圭首都蒙得维的亚市援建了一所小学，即将竣工。新校舍距离老校舍两个街区，配备9间教室，并将专门设立一间"孔子课堂"。校长苏姆女士说，得益于中国的帮助，学校的硬件有了很大的提高，课程设置也更加丰富，孔子学院

① 2017年10月25日，习近平在十九届中共中央政治局常委同中外记者见面时的讲话。

的老师现在定期来授课。学校已连续两年组织师生访华，在华游学经历激发了孩子们的学习热情和动力，他们归来后纷纷表示，这是一次励志之旅，决心将来一定要考上大学，有此鸿鹄之志在乌贫寒子弟中十分难得。乌拉圭驻华大使卢格里斯说，中国的援助给孩子们带来了希望，"在卡萨瓦耶区，当孩子们看到新的校舍，他们会相信将有更好的未来在等着自己"。

中国愿在"一带一路"框架下，秉持正确义利观，同包括乌拉圭在内的世界各国携手合作，集思广益，共同应对贫困问题的挑战，为推动人类命运共同体建设，共同创造人类的美好未来而不懈努力。

第二篇

百年目标

Chapter II

中国精准扶贫的经验与创新

扫码获取

★ 脱贫故事分享
★ 脱贫攻坚解读
　与回顾

/ 第一章 /
高质量就业和收入增长

一、经济增长是关键驱动力①

自20世纪70年代末经济体制改革以来，中国已有8亿人摆脱了绝对贫困，创造了人类减贫史的奇迹。到2020年底，中国有望提前10年完成联合国《2030年可持续发展议程》制定的减贫目标。这一历史性的成就对全球减贫的贡献率高达70％以上。

这主要是由于总体经济增长改变了世界经济，部分是由于在过去几十年中为消除贫困而试行和实施的专门性政策，特别是旨在消除农村极端贫困的精准扶贫战略启动之后。

1978年中国开始经济体制改革，以及随后实行中国国际贸易和对外投资开放，逐步开放国际市场，经济迅速增长，由此达成了这项史无前例的成就。中国脱贫攻坚的故事是整个中国经济的成功故事。当然，在这个过程中也遇到了无数艰难曲折。

中国的经济发展需要管理大量人口从农村到城市的迁移，涉及农业生产、制造业乃至服务业等各行各业。

这些重大变化也造成了经济发展不平衡现象，在经济快速增长期，这是不可避免的。随着越来越多的人摆脱了极端贫困，其中许多人成为中产阶级，中国不得不应对快速发展的沿海省份与相对落

① 作者：乔瓦尼·特里亚，意大利经济与财政部前部长。

后的内陆省份之间的发展不平衡，以及增长率较高的省市内部的社会和经济不平衡。因此，减贫成功也是兼顾这些不平衡并使其得到控制方面的成功。

减贫的成功还在于中国有能力在"私有经济日益增长下的市场经济发展"和"中央政府宏观调控下分散管理的计划经济"之间取得平衡。在以国内人口大量流动为特征的过渡时期，要确保劳动力的增长和教育卫生水平的提升，就更加印证这一能力的重要性。在这一时期，经济增长和摆脱贫困这两个基本因素越来越多地依赖于私人储蓄。

对于一个需要在经济快速增长和包容性增长之间寻求持续平衡的国家来说，中国的脱贫攻坚一直是一项发展战略。如今，中国需要针对部分人口和落后地区的发展采取专门的包容性政策。

但是，要了解中国为全球减贫作出了多大的贡献，我们还应该考虑中国经济增长对于其他新兴经济体和发展中国家增长动力的直接影响，以及中国的成功如何为我们提供了借鉴性经验，其中甚至改变了我们如今看待发展中国家国际发展合作机构发展政策的方式。

关于中国经济增长对全球经济，特别是对亚洲和非洲其他发展中经济体和新兴经济体经济增长的直接影响，我们应该考虑，随着中国工资水平的提高和中国经济的转型，中国如何成为复杂的全球供应链网络的中心，为一些低收入发展中经济体逐步提供了低附加值的生产。

实际上，中国已经从依赖出口和投资支撑的增长转变为依赖国内消费支撑的增长，从制造业转变为通过广泛利用制造业外包而日益以服务为导向的体系，并且，最终从通过外国直接投资引入创新转变为内生创新。就这样，中国沿着国际供应链跃上了附加值梯级，在密集的生产链和国际贸易网络中推动和转移技术，这在包容国际贸易、外国投资流和向许多低收入发展中国家提供技术转移的过程中发挥了重要作用。

中国使得众多发展中国家借鉴开放国际市场和外商投资的中国发展模式发挥比较优势。从这个角度来看，中国还对传统的扶贫开发合作和援助政策产生了整体性影响。

同时，在传统的南北援助效果不佳的时候，中国在南南发展合作中也发挥了日益重要的作用。基本上，西方捐赠机构和多边发展机构的官方援助方案未能帮助低收入国家突破阻碍工业化和经济发展的基础设施瓶颈。

出现这一障碍的原因是发达国家划拨给援助发展的资源减少。大多数发达国家的公共预算困难，特别是在金融危机之后，加剧了这一现象。而且许多开发项目的效果收效甚微，这些项目大多只是为了缓解极端贫困状况，而不是改革经济，使之走上平衡发展和包容性增长的道路，从而大范围地减贫。从这个意义上来说，中国的发展道路是个启示，南南合作已发展成为贸易、援助以及公共和私人投资等工具的结合。

中国的发展道路被指控为向已负债国家发放开发贷款的"债务陷阱外交"。然而，这个问题值得商榷，因为中国对贫困国家的援助部分弥补了发达国家和开发银行干预力度的下降，而且不仅要考虑债务与国内生产总值比率，还应考虑这些贷款是否被用于旨在为基础设施投资提供资金，从而有效地减少贫困，在中长期内推动经济增长。

分析人士和决策者都对中国在非洲和亚洲的发展政策的有效性进行了辩论，可以肯定的是，近20年来，中国的国内经验及其与发展中国家和新兴国家合作的方式改变了发展经济学，也改变了多边开发银行制定政策和计划的方式。

在此背景下，意大利与中国在减贫方面的携手合作已有40年的历史。

自中国政府于1978年出台对外开放政策以来，意大利在华发展合作一直非常活跃。意大利是中国发展初期最早向中国提供援助的国家之一，在很长一段时间内，意大利是通过赠款和援助信贷额度计划向中国提供援助的主要国家之一。随着中国经济的发展，援助的类型也发生了变化，从粮食援助、支持教育和培训的计划和项目，到后来的农村地区扶贫专项。

意大利保护和加强中国文化遗产的援助计划也变得重要，原因有两个。首先，这些计划将意中这两个拥有与世界上最悠久的文化遗产的国家联系起来。其次，这些计划通过发展旅游业增加了收入，帮助贫困地区的发展。并且还因为，一个国家的遗产和历史文化意识是集体动员的重要因素。

但是，在我看来，意大利为中国减贫作出的最重要贡献是借助双边贸易、技术和科学合作以及意大利各个先进工业部门的私人投资流。换句话说，中国在脱贫攻坚方面的成功得益于前所未有的经济增长，意大利在基于近几十年来逐步加强的两国经济互补性的商业关系和经济合作中也做出了贡献。

如今，在中国的积极经验和意中两国分别与低收入国家进行经济合作的经验的基础上，两国可以合作制定联合计划和项目，消除世界其他地区的贫困。意中两国可以通过多边开发银行合作设计可持续投资计划，在这些多边开发银行中，两国已经分担了战略任务，并且可以根据第三方开发协定以及在"一带一路"倡议的框架内进行合作。

人们越来越普遍地认为，全球扶贫将以经济合作为条件，推动一个将近80亿人口居住的高度互联互通的世界的经济增长，这是至关重要的。在这个世界上，所有国家，特别是最贫穷的国家，其命运取决于能否通过融入全球经济，利用各个经济体的经济比较优势。同时，已经摆脱贫困桎梏的国家采取的这种合作行动符合全球利益。实际上，扶贫攻坚是一项全球性公益事业，抗击气候变化和健康保护同样如此，只有在一个彼此合作的全球化世界中才能取得成功。

二、金砖国家的减贫历程：增长与收入分配的作用[①]

贫困、增长、不平衡之间存在错综复杂的"三角"关系。聚焦金砖国家的减贫历程，可以比较增长和贫富差距的变化在其中所发挥的作用。

我们的研究显示，在金砖国家中，2004年之前，中国的贫困率最高；2004年之后，印度的贫困率最高，俄罗斯最低，南非和巴西则在中间。

考虑到中国巨大的人口基数和显著的贫困率下降幅度，中国无疑是减贫最为成功的国家。根据亚洲开发银行的研究，如果不考虑中国，由192个国家元首签署、联合国发布的千年发展目标的贫困目标就不可能如期实现。事实上，长期以来，中国对全球减贫的贡献巨大，在1990年至2015年千年发展目标推行期间，中国对全球减贫的贡献率达到63.9%。同时期，中国对全球经济增长的贡献率在30%左右。中国的经济增长成就十分显著，而中国在消除绝对贫困方面的成就更为举世瞩目。

在金砖国家减贫成就的背后是各国持续出台的推进经济发展、减少贫困的政策。2018年世界银行发布的《中国系统性国别诊断报告》中指出，中国在过去的25年取得了世界上绝无仅有的减贫成绩，与中国实行的大规模开发式扶贫紧密相关。印度推出了农村就业保障计划和包容性增长财政政策等反贫困措施。巴西实施了主要依靠经济发展来减轻贫困的"无贫困计划"。俄罗斯政府将改革战略聚焦于经济的复苏，进而减少了贫困。南非的黑人经济振兴法案和《2030国家发展计划》都把社会经济发展作为重要目标。

金砖国家之间比较而言，从减贫途径上看，金砖国家均是扶贫救

[①] 作者：万广华，复旦大学特聘二级教授、世界经济研究所所长。

助和扶贫开发两手抓，既重视"输血"工作，也重视增强贫困地区和贫困人群的"自主造血"功能。中国更是提出包含产业帮扶、劳务协作、人才支援、支撑保障在内的多角度全方位扶贫开发模式。

从减贫主体上，中国广泛动员全社会力量参与扶贫开发，鼓励民营企业、社会组织、个人参与扶贫，形成多元主体共同扶贫的中国特色扶贫开发道路。

从减贫精准度来看，从2013年起，中国将精准扶贫作为扶贫工作的基本方针，建档立卡、明确扶持对象；分工清晰、明确扶持责任人；因地制宜、明确扶持方法。其他金砖国家虽然强调精准（如俄罗斯的公共社会援助法，也强调精确瞄准），但实际政策体现并不充分。

那么，在金砖国家（尤其是中国）取得减贫成就的过程中，经济增长和收入分配分别起了什么作用呢？

我们的研究发现，所有金砖国家的减贫成就主要归功于经济增长，收入分配只充当了辅助的角色。更为遗憾的是，与"劫富济贫"相反，金砖国家在不少年份里的贫富差距发生恶化，致使贫困率上升。由此可见，严格控制收入分配不均、千方百计促进包容性增长是金砖国家乃至全球共同面临的巨大挑战。而联合国《2030年可持续发展议程》里已经添加了关于收入分配不均的指标。

经济增长对贫困率下降至关重要，但这并不意味着可以忽视收入分配的作用，因为收入分配与贫困直接相关，并会间接影响经济增长。从根本上说，巴西、俄罗斯、南非相对较慢的减贫速度是由于其日益严重的收入不平等。金砖五国中，南非的基尼系数一直处于最高位置，巴西次之，其基尼系数一直处在45%～55%之间。

从趋势上看，除了巴西，其他四国的基尼系数均有所上升，南非从1975年的58.4%上升到2015年的60.2%；印度从1973年的38.1%上升到2012年的47.2%；中国自改革开放以来，收入分配不均程度也在逐渐攀升，从1978年的28.4%上升至2008年的43.3%，尽管近年出现些许下降，但在2015年仍然处于高位的41.1%；由于苏联解体，俄罗斯在1990年至1995年期间基尼系数急速上升，接着缓缓下降，从1996年的37.4%下降至2016年的33.3%。就巴西而言，尽管其基尼系数从1970年的50.3%下降至2017年的46.5%，但下降程度十分有限。

这些国家的收入分配问题阻碍了其减贫进程。

金砖五国是新兴与转型经济体的代表和典范，人们大多关注这些国家的经济增长，而往往忽视其收入分配和贫困问题。人们需要改变这种观念，不仅因为减贫和收入差距是联合国《2030年可持续发展议程》里最为重要的指标，而且因为经济增长受到贫困和收入分配不均的高度影响。比如，包括巴西在内的拉丁美洲国家面临经济停滞、掉入中等收入陷阱的主要根源就在于收入差距大。又如，收入分化及其分化所导致的犯罪，是南非难以获得国外直接投资的根本原因之一。

改革开放后的中国是世界上发展最快、扶贫攻坚最为成功的经济体，但同时也经历了贫富差距的不断攀升，并引起了一系列社会经济问题，其中最为紧迫的是国内消费疲软。不难理解，当富人不再增加消费（富人有钱不消费），而穷人想消费却没有钱时，国内消费需求显然无法拉升。换言之，中国储蓄率过高的诟病与贫富差距紧密相关，并且与其对应的内需不振在逆全球化浪潮中无疑会拖累中国的经济增长。

当然，经济增长会带来贫困的下降，这就是所谓的水涨船高；即便没有增长，当收入分配得到改善时（比如通过财政转移的"劫富济贫"），贫困率也会下降。事实上，很多地区或国家的贫困完全可以通过改善收入分配而得到解决。即便是诸如印度这样的国家，如果没有收入差距或收入差距很小，按照世界银行每人每天1.9美元或3.2美元甚至5.5美元贫困线计算，贫困就会消失，因为印度的人均国内生产总值（GDP）已经超过了2000美元。需要说明的是，尽管人均GDP不等于人均收入或人均消费，但世界银行的贫困标准仍需要用各国的购买力平价进行平减。对发展中国家而言，其物价往往较低，购买力较高，以购买力平价表示的贫困线往往大大低于以官方汇率表示的贫困线。

展望未来，中国除了应该设法减少储蓄，增加居民消费，以便在经济缓行的情况下仍然能够保持一定的减贫速度，还应该重视贫富差距加大较快的问题，这抵消了经济增长的减贫效应，影响了经济增长的持续性。而其他金砖国家在防止收入分配不均的同时，更需要控制消费，增加储蓄，以通过扩大投资拉动经济增长。最后，中国在治贫过程中高效发挥了政府、社会各界和国际合作的作用，这些都是其他国家可以借鉴与学习的。

第二章
乡村振兴、城乡发展一体化与人口结构变化

一、振兴农村经济是减贫的关键因素①

2020年5月28日，国务院总理李克强在十三届全国人大三次会议闭幕后的记者会上披露，中国仍有6亿人每个月的收入不足1000元（约合140美元）。新冠肺炎疫情暴发之前，根据官方的国家贫困线估计，中国约有500万贫困人口。该贫困线相当于世界银行对极端贫困的定义（按购买力平价计算每人每天1.9美元）。由于疫情暴发，之前超过贫困线的人，其中一部分可能再次返贫。但是中国政府重申了在2020年消除极端贫困的决心，并将通过多种政策和财政扶持计划，扩大最低生活保障和失业保障的覆盖面。中国毫无疑问能够达成这一目标。但问题是如何守住消除极端贫困的战果，并在振兴农村经济方面取得进一步进展，从而在2035年之前实现除基于收入的极端贫困以外的各种目标，如教育、保健、住房、农村生活条件和环境。借鉴其他国家的经验非常重要。

从1971年到1979年，韩国实施了一个以社区为基础的综合性项目——新村运动，将农村发展列为国家政治议程的优先事项。该项目旨在缩小农村地区和快速发展的城市地区之间日益扩大的收入和生活质量差距。该项目首先把重点放在村级自助项目，随后农民尝

---

① 作者：樊胜根，全球食物经济与政策研究院院长，国际食物政策研究所前所长。

到了甜头，新村运动由此逐步演变为自发的运动，迅速扩展为在灌溉、农业投入（特别是现代种业）、电气化和交通运输方面的一系列投资。女性俱乐部帮助妇女发起创收项目并参与决策。从1970年到1979年，农村家庭收入增长了5倍，与城镇家庭收入持平。那些亟待将国家项目与地方参与联系起来的国家，可从这种模式中获得一些启示。

20世纪50年代至80年代，随着工业化和城市化进程的加快，日本面临人口锐减、农田荒芜和农村自然资源退化的问题。20世纪90年代以来，日本已启动了多个项目，振兴农村产业，搞活农村经济。这些项目除了投资农村基础设施以及改善当地居民和移民的生活条件外，还有一个特点，就是促进包容性的城乡联系，通过农贸市场和合作社将当地农民与城市消费者联系起来。与中国一样，随着年轻人向城镇迁移，日本的农村人口正在逐步老龄化。2000年，日本实施了一项强制性的社会长期护理保险计划，为农村地区的老年人提供价格低廉的家庭和社区服务，例如家务帮工、成人日托和家护。

在泰国，开发利基产品和增强农村地区自立能力一直是减贫的关键因素。政府制定了"一乡一品"（OTOP）计划，推动泰国7255个乡镇或分区的产品生产和销售，从而激发了当地的创业精神，并为贫困农民带来了替代性收入。泰国还出台了多项以农村为基础的举措，包括有机水稻种植、手工艺品生产和乡村旅游，增加当地就业和可持续生计。泰国在社区发展方面的经验凸显增强社区自身能力的重要性，必须使其能够抵御1997年亚洲金融危机和2009年全球经济衰退等外部经济冲击，为提高社区成员的生活质量提供稳定的基础。这种策略的一个关键要素是人民知情、主动参与，使经济发展基于其自身的需求和愿望。

传统上，欧盟采用农业补贴政策为农民提供保障。不过，2000

年以来，欧盟开始对其农业补贴政策进行改革，为农民提供直接收入补贴和环境服务补贴。欧盟设立了一个专项资金，用于发展农村地区，包括投资农村基础设施。欧盟的新农业政策引入了目标更明确、更公平的保障措施，激励农民采取对气候友好、可持续发展的做法。

20世纪初，美国的农业和农村逐步繁荣。但在20世纪六七十年代，很大一部分农村人口迁往城市。最近有一种新兴趋势，人们正在离开城市，住在离市中心两三个小时车程的地方。如此一来，居住空间变宽敞了，还可以呼吸到郊区或农村的新鲜空气，与此同时，并不妨碍其享受城市的优质医疗、娱乐和其他便利设施。最近美国公布了一项1.5万亿美元的基础设施投资计划，其中很大一部分资金将用于改善农村基础设施，包括交通、水电和网络宽带接入。电子商务和远程办公等新技术和工作模式也展现出了振兴农村、创造商业和发展机会以及保持城乡联系的潜力。

中国已经成功控制了新冠肺炎疫情，目前，经济正在全面复苏。消除贫困不仅是2020年的短期目标，而且还应成为长期消除收入以外贫困（包括医疗卫生、教育、生活条件以及农村生态环境）的关键出发点。这些也是农村振兴的主要目标。无论从短期还是长期来看，中国政府均应在借鉴国外成功经验的基础上结合自身特点，借助农村振兴，考虑采取以下多维度的扶贫战略：

第一，必须振兴包括农业和粮食在内的生产部门以及农村地区的生产后价值链，同时运用部分财政刺激政策为返乡农民提供保障。在2020年全国人大会议上，国务院总理李克强宣布了一项3.6万亿元的财政刺激计划，以应对新冠肺炎疫情带来的经济减速，引领中国经济逐步复苏。由于制造业、建筑业和服务业的经济停滞或增长势头放缓，许多农民无法返回城市工作。因此，失业补助应当用于帮助修建农村地区的公路、电信、灌溉等基础设施以及其他生产性资产。还可利用一揽子计划帮助返乡农民创业，重振农村经济和就业。韩国、日本和泰国的"一乡一品"战略以及农村文化和农业旅游激励政策，可在这方面为中国提供宝贵经验。1997年亚洲金融危机和2008年全球金融危机期间，韩国、日本和泰国为振兴农村所采取的社会保障政策，可为中国制定振兴政策提供有益的经验。

第二，必须重新重视或优先考虑农村居民（特别是儿童和妇女）的教育、医疗卫生和营养。从长远来看，包括教育和医疗卫生在内的未来人力资本是达成减贫目标、改善农村居民福祉和实现农村现代化的基础。这些投资首先包括改善中小学教育。教育制度的完善会对人类发展的诸多指标（包括收入、工资和劳动生产率）产生强烈的正面影响。同时，还应重新设计政策，重点改善农村居民的营养状况，而不是粮食自给。为妇女儿童提供营养健康的饮食，是全面改善人力资本发展的重要组成部分。在这方面，泰国的经验尤其重要。社区领导和专家确定了营养、医疗卫生和教育基本的最低指标，这些最低指标转化为反映地方优先事项的目标，可监测进度。此外，在泰国，社区志愿者在实现这些指标方面也起到了至关重要的作用。

第三，改善环境是农村振兴的关键因素。过去，由于过度使用化肥和农药以及过度开采地表水和地下水，农村自然资源和环境严重退化。农村可通过保护性农业、雨水集蓄、生态补偿等改善城乡环境质量，这为社区成员管理生态系统资源和保护生物多样性提供了动力。采用以社区为基础的水和森林管理系统，也为共享繁荣、环境可持续性和社会凝聚力提供了机遇。获得清洁饮用水和卫生设施，包括建造更多的厕所和垃圾处理设施，也应纳入振兴计划。借助这些举措，可改善农村生活条件，吸引人们留在农村发展甚至从城市中心返乡。中国可效仿欧盟共同农业政策的成功改革，将农业补贴转化为对农村基础设施和改善环境的投资。应加大支持力度，促进蔬菜、水果、豆类和渔业等营养食品的研发、生产和价值链发展。

第四，韩国、日本和泰国的改革实践证明，增强农村村庄和社区的能力并对其进行激励是振兴农村最成功的战略之一。应根据人民的意愿发展经济，在这方面，治理权下放至关重要。保证参与性、透明性、问责制并在财政权力与所赋职能之间取得平衡的分权治理系统，可对当地情况、需求和期望做出及时响应。

第五，加强城乡联系，包括物质、经济、社会和政治联系，对于振兴农村和可持续消除城乡贫困至关重要。城镇经济增长增加了粮食需求，并刺激了城镇人口饮食结构变化。新的需求可为农村生产者改善其生计提供机会。价值链断裂和协调不力削弱了城乡联系，阻碍了粮食安全和营养方面的发展。对农村基础设施和中间城镇的投入（优质的乡村公路和支线公路、电力、仓储设施、通信和信息）可建立城乡联系并打造经济活动的枢纽，使小农户和城镇人口受益。在美国，新兴的卫星城镇通勤距离最多一两个小时，并且使用IT技术在家办公。这是中国经济复苏可借鉴的良好实例。在荷兰，利用现代化温室和ITC平台等技术，实现城乡一体化粮食系统，使城乡消费者从中受益。这是中国可借鉴的另一个实例。

二、政策向农村倾斜是扶贫工作的重心①

中国正在推行一系列政策，旨在实现到2020年消除绝对贫困的目标。这是人类的一项巨大成就，并为世界其他国家和地区树立了榜样。

1949年中华人民共和国成立之初，政府实行土地改革，从而开

---

① 作者：卡洛斯·阿基诺，秘鲁圣马科斯国立大学教授、亚洲研究中心协调员。

始改善了90％以上农村人口的生存条件。

但是，最令人瞩目的成就是1978年中国实行改革开放以来的经济腾飞。据报道，1978年起，中国经济的奇迹使近8亿人摆脱了贫困，这在世界历史上是前所未有的。

1979年初，中国出台措施，力争全面实现四个现代化：工业现代化、农业现代化、国防现代化、科学技术现代化。农业现代化非常重要，大多数穷人生活在农村地区并从事农业工作。农业现代化基于几个要素：

农民可以耕种自己的土地并转让剩余的土地。分田到户提高了农民的生产积极性，从而增加了产量，增加了农民的收入。

政府开始努力改善道路等基础设施，扶持农村地区实现现代化，并使农产品以更快捷的途径、更低廉的价格进入市场。另外，一些金融机构向农业部门提供贷款，并帮助农民购买必要的工具，以提高生产力。中国有多家面向农村地区的金融机构，其中最大的农业金融机构是中国农业银行。

为了减轻农村地区的贫困，中国政府从2006年起彻底取消了农业税。从历史上看，农业部门的税收是政府的主要收入来源。这项延续2000多年的税收政策正式退出中国的历史舞台。

农村市场发展迅猛，农民不仅可以依托土地出售农产品，还可以饲养牲畜获利或进行农产品加工。

另外，2005年，政府决定取消农业税，免除农村义务教育阶段学生学杂费，农民的生活开始大大改善。

随着农业现代化和农民收入的增加，另一项齐头并进、推动中国扶贫脱贫进程的措施是工业现代化。工业现代化必然性的两个因素：首先，农业现代化提高了农民生产率，农村出现了大量富余劳动力，他们背井离乡从农村走向城市，谋求个人和家庭生活的改善和发展；其次，工业部门的收入较高。

因此，大量农民离开农村去往城市就业，从事制造业工作。在这方面，中国政府实施的政策是成功的。这些政策让大量农民工从事对外出口的制造业，从而使中国成为世界工厂。

自1978年以来，中国实行招商引资的政策，外企与中国企业合资，开始为国外市场生产廉价商品。中国也在教育和科技方面加大了投资，开始生产具有更高附加值的先进商品，工人收入迅速增长。

政府采取的另一项政策是针对特殊群体的一系列具体措施。中国是一个幅员辽阔、地域广袤的大国，地势高低起伏，地形复杂多变，有些人的贫困是由来已久、根深蒂固的。

很多人生活在人迹罕至的地区，崇山峻岭，甚至未通公路。中国有55个少数民族，在新中国成立之前有些少数民族生活非常贫穷。中国政府给予少数民族特殊待遇，改善他们的处境。

例如，约占人口8.5％的少数民族历来享有特殊待遇，计划生育政策比汉族更为宽松，政府还会给予各种财政补助，帮助他们发展并摆脱贫困。这些政策包括在这些地区发展农业和畜牧业、建设高速公路和乡镇企业等。

中国政府制定了很多政策帮助其实现消除绝对贫困的目标，其中一些对许多国家，特别是发展中国家有很大的借鉴意义，综上所述，可归纳为以下几点：

第一，需要制定政策，帮助提高农业产出以及农民收入。为此，重要的是提供扶贫资金，帮助贫困农民获得必要的生产工具。在许多国家，农民无法获得政府贷款，税赋繁重，只能持续在贫困中挣扎。

第二，提供灌溉工程和道路等有形基础设施，不仅能提高生产力，而且可缩短农产品到市场的产销链。不仅农民受益，消费者也可购买到更便宜的食物。

第三，富余的贫困农民进入城市，一旦找不到工作，就会成为城市贫困人员，生活并无实质性改变。因此，只有大力发展工业和制造业，才能吸纳富余的农民工。

第四，教育是政府出台的最重要政策之一，人们可以掌握更先进的技能，谋求高薪工作。只有这样，人们才能彻底摆脱贫困。

第五，在许多国家，有些人需要政府予以特别关注，例如生活在偏远地区的人、有特殊需要的人，如老弱病残群体、弱势群体或受歧视群体。对于这些人群，政府必须出台财政补贴等特殊措施，帮助这些人克服不利条件。

新冠病毒大流行对所有国家来说都堪称重创，在许多国家，大量人口将陷入贫困。中国是第一个受新冠肺炎疫情影响的国家，但应对得当，快速高效地控制了疫情导致的死亡人数和经济损失。例如，根据国际货币基金组织（IMF）于2020年6月发布的经济预测，2020年世界经济将出现负增长，全球平均增长率为–4.9％，发达经济体为–8％，新兴市场和发展中经济体为–3％～0％，但中国将实现1％的经济正增长。

我相信，中国政府将尽一切努力，引导经济回到正轨，并实现更高速的增长。消除中国的绝对贫困迫在眉睫，但切勿忘记，从21世纪初开始，中国一直是世界经济的引擎。因此，世界期冀中国实现自身的目标，而其成功经验可供其他国家借鉴和参考。中国的发展离不开世界，世界的繁荣也需要中国。

三、借助农村工业化推动扶贫工作[①]

2010年是全球制造业的转折点。中国超越美国成为全球制造业第一大国[②]。中国占全球汽车制造业产值的19.8％，略高于美国的

---

① 作者：王华，法国里昂商学院副校长，创新管理和管理经济学教授。

② 彼得·马什：《中国超美成世界头号制造业大国》，2011年3月14日，引自：https://www.cnbc.com/id/42065544。

19.4％。自2010年以来，中国逐步提高生产力并加强密集的技术创新，保持了这一新的领导地位。

21世纪，在汽车生产领域，中国汽车产业处于全球领先地位。21世纪头十年，中国汽车销量不到200万辆。2020年之前的几年，中国汽车销量增长达两位数，2010年达到1800多万辆（乘用车和商用车），2018年达到近2800万辆。如今，中国的汽车产量是美国的2倍多、日本的约2.9倍，远远超过任何欧洲国家的汽车行业。

表1　2000年、2010年和2018年前十大汽车生产国汽车产量[①]

（单位：辆）

	国家	2018年	2010年	2000年
1	中国	27809196	18264761	2069069
2	美国	11314705	7743093	12799857
3	日本	9728528	9628920	10140796
4	印度	5174645	3557073	801360
5	德国	5120409	5905985	5526615
6	墨西哥	4100525	2342282	1935527
7	韩国	4028834	4271741	3114998
8	巴西	2879809	3381728	1681517
9	西班牙	2819565	2387900	3032874
10	法国	2270000	2229421	3348361
全球总产量		95634593	77629127	58374162

对外开放和外商直接投资带动的工业化中国汽车产业崛起主要推动力量有两个，一是20世纪70年代末和80年代对外开放政策，二是紧随

---

① 资料来源：https://en.wikipedia.org/wiki/List_of_countries_by_motor_vehicle_production.

其后的20世纪90年代外商直接投资的逐步增长。跨国公司组建了中外合资企业，将其全球供应商带到了中国。从20世纪80年代到21世纪头十年的约30年内，中国逐步在国内建立了完整的汽车产业价值链。

在中国汽车产业取得举世瞩目增长的同时，还有另一个以农村为基础的汽车产业共存。20世纪90年代后的几年中，中国农村汽车产业出产了数百万辆汽车。农村汽车产业的发展是中国工业化进程中的一个独有现象。农村汽车产业的发展既不依赖于直接技术转移，也不依赖于外国公司投资。该产业立足于农村客户需求，为农民工创造了大量就业机会，这是工业化和减贫的重要方面。

从20世纪80年代至21世纪头十年，除了新兴的农用车小众市场，中国农村市场几乎被忽略。农用车是一种新车型，有三轮农用车，也有四轮农用车。大多数三轮农用车都是用单缸柴油机制造的，最初是为固定式农业机械专门设计的。然后，对其进行调整改良。如此一来，这些农用车满足了农民的多种目的，可用于农业活动，也可用作载人载货，而且价格较为低廉，平均不到传统轻型卡车或货车价格的一半。1999年，农用车产量飙升至峰值，达到300万辆，是同年传统乘用车的3倍。2010年农用车总产量约为2200万辆。

中国传统汽车产业得到了中央政府的大力支持，与此形成鲜明对比的是，农用车扎根基层谋求发展，并未得到中央政府的大力扶持（Sperling，Lin，and Hamilton，2005[①]）。20世纪80年代中期之前，农用车被归类为一种农业机械。农用车生产由农业部管理，与传统汽车相比，农用车税赋较轻。

农用车发展初期，数以百计的农村小企业蜂拥而入，其中一些得到了地方政府的扶持。严格的行业监管和技术标准加速了产业整合。

[①] Daniel Sperling, Zhenhong Lin, Peter Hamilton, 2005, Rural vehicles in China: appropriate policy for appropriate technology, Transport Policy, 12(2), March 2005, pp.105–119.

符合农用车新规范的企业数量从2001年的204家降至2002年的120家。市场集中度加快。前十大三轮车生产企业市场占有率从59.5%增至65%，前十大四轮车生产企业市场占有率从93%增至96%。

（单位：辆）

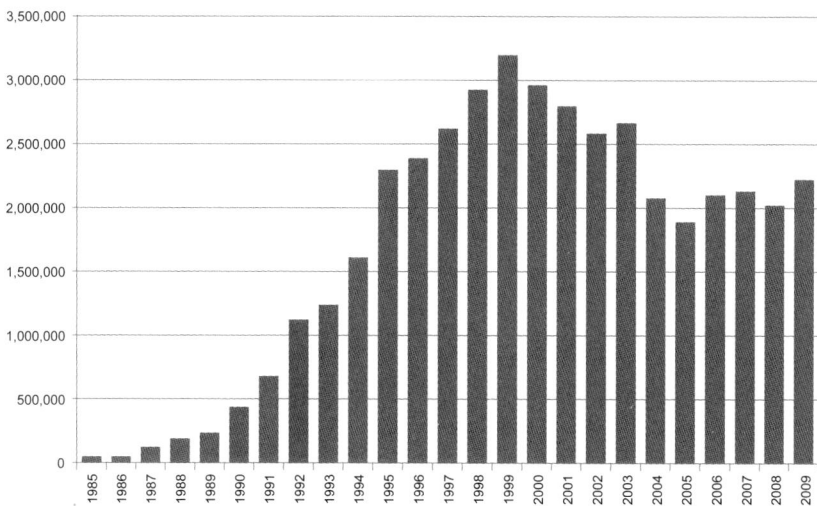

图1　1985—2009年中国农用车产量[1]

21世纪头十年末，居住农村附近的城镇居民收入增加，催生了新的出行需求。2007年，多个行业的公司开始生产一种乘用低速电动汽车（Wang and Kimble，2010a）[2]。常见的低速电动汽车结构简单，最高时速40～70公里，续航距离为80公里、100公里或150公里，成本为2万元～4万元（约合3100～6200美元）。低速电

---

[1] Wang, H., Kimble, C., 2012a. The Low Speed Electric Vehicle – China's Unique Sustainable Automotive Technology?, in: Sustainable Automotive Technologies 2012. Springer, pp. 207 – 214.

[2] Wang, H., Kimble, C., 2012b. Business Model Innovation and the Development of the Electric Vehicle Industry in China, in: The Greening of the Automotive Industry. Palgrave Macmillan.

动汽车是中国节俭创新的一个生动案例，挖掘了金字塔底层的营销潜力。与农用车消费人群不同，低速电动汽车消费人群主要分布在三、四线城市以及小城镇和乡村。

低速电动汽车非常透彻地彰显了农村地区低收入消费者的价值主张。低速电动汽车平均价格为2.5万元（约合3900美元），比传统的紧凑型汽车便宜得多，后者的价格至少为4万元（约合6200美元）。低速电动汽车的能源成本也低于小型汽油动力汽车。行驶100公里，电费约为6元（约合0.9美元），而汽油则为49元（约合7.5美元），约高7倍。此外，低速电动汽车的充电解决方案比加油简便得多。农村家庭拥有私人停车位，可通过普通的220伏电源插座为铅酸电池充电，省去了开几公里车到加油站加油的麻烦。简而言之，与农用车类似，低速电动汽车这款产品由消费者驱动，而非国家驱动。

农用车和低速电动汽车的年市场规模均超过100万辆，说明二元经济结构成效显著，未来可期。这种二元经济由专设的农业和工业部门组成（Lewis，1954）[1]。尽管中国在20世纪70年代后期改革开放后取得了令人瞩目的经济增长，但2018年农村家庭人均年收入仅为14617元（约合2107.3美元），不到城镇家庭人均年收入的三分之一（39250元，约合5658美元）。根据2019年《中国统计年鉴》的数据，中国仍有农村人口5.52亿人，占中国总人口的39.4%。农村人口购买力低，生产和消费方面的交通需求较为单一，为低成本汽车奠定了坚实的基础，而低成本汽车是传统汽车制造商尚未开发的巨大市场。

另外，与工业化汽车集群相比，中国农村低成本、低价位汽车的工业化和大量生产为新的增长理论提供了丰富的研究素材。这是一股创建本土汽车细分市场的浪潮。没有外商直接投资的直接参

---

[1] Lewis, A., 1954. Economic development with unlimited supplies of labor. The Manchester School, 22(2), pp.139 - 191.

与，也没有中央政府的官方扶持。这是一种基于低收入人群的需求以及国内成熟的汽车或机械行业跨行业技术溢出而形成的一种产业化形式。农村和小城市的民众既是这些产品的生产者，又是这些产品的消费者，从而形成了一个工业化、城市化的新经济圈，并为二元经济结构的动态演变作出了积极贡献。从长远来看，通过提高农村地区的收入水平、人力资本、技术密集度以及增加农村地区的熟练工人，完全有可能实现经济融合（Banerjee and Newman，1993；Mesnard，2001；Rapoport，2002；Yuki，2007）。[1]

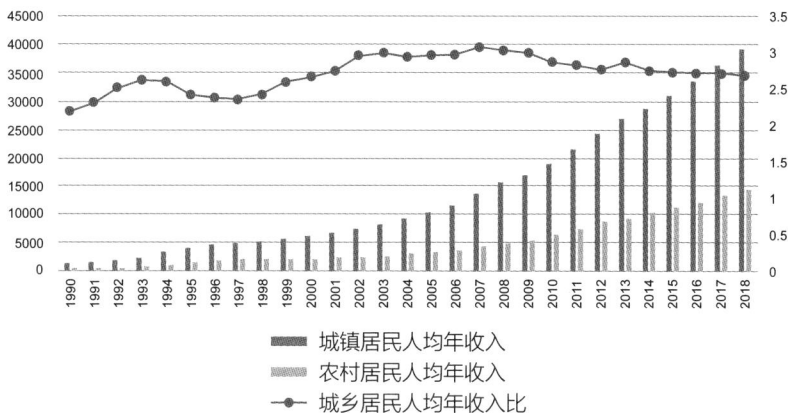

图2　1990—2018年中国城乡人均收入[2]

在以二元经济结构为特征的转型期经济体，特别是在人口众多的国家，存在两种汽车产业。一种是针对主要生活在大城市的中产阶

---

① Banerjee, A. V. and Newman, A. F. (1993). Occupational choice and the process of development. The Journal of Political Economy, 101 (2), 274–298.

　Mesnard, A. (2001). Migration temporaire et mobilite intergenerationnelle. Louvain Economic Review, 67 (1), 59–88.

　Rapoport, H. (2002). Migration, credit constraints and self-employment: a simple model of occupational choice, inequality and growth. Economics Bulletin, 15 (7), 1–5.

　Yuki, K. (2007). Urbanization, informal sector, and development. Journal of Development Economics, 84, 76–103.

② 资料来源：http://www.stats.gov.cn/tjsj/ndsj/.

级人口，另一种是针对农村乡镇人口。农用车和低速电动汽车的价格低廉、行驶成本低、使用方便，为低收入消费者提供了明确的价值选择。

中国的市场极为庞大，足以试验许多不同类型的技术，并将这些技术整合到各种不同的产品类型。农用车和低速电动汽车是技术成熟的产品。在巨大市场需求的驱动下，数百家汽车制造商争相投入生产。激烈的竞争促使该产业走向整合，产生规模经济和大规模生产，这是工业化的典型标志。

与中国传统汽车产业不同，这种工业化主要是由农村市场需求驱动的，并且由当地民营企业组织，没有跨国公司的技术支持和资金投入。它是本土工业发展的例证。

农用车和低速电动汽车创造了数以百万计的就业机会，并为减贫作出了贡献。该产业涵盖零部件供应商、生产商、经销商和售后服务提供商的子行业。该产业还存在地理邻近现象。这些农用车和低速电动汽车的产业集群位于农村人口众多的省份。这些产业正在借助地缘优势吸纳劳动力。

有趣的是，中国低速电动汽车产业还处于开拓海外市场的初期阶段。外国机构买家（例如政府、警察部门、医院、邮局和机场）购买低速电动汽车作为"绿色解决方案"，同时还降低了成本。甚至，美国私人消费者也购买低速电动汽车作为第二或第三辆备用汽车。低速电动汽车在美销量从2008年的5000辆增加到2010年的约2万辆（Wang and Kimble，2010c）。[1]

农用车和低速电动汽车的发展是中国农村工业化减贫的生动案例。政府应进一步平衡高科技驱动型工业化和覆盖40%农村人口

---

[1] Wang, H., Kimble, C.: Leapfrogging to Electric Vehicles: Patterns and Scenarios for China's Automobile Industry. International Journal of Automotive Technology and Management11(4), 312－325 (2011).

的"低科技"（节约型技术）工业化之间的关系。针对二元经济的二元产业政策可能在减贫方面更加有效，这将进一步扎实推动工业化。对于发展中国家，特别是人口众多的发展中国家，中国的这种产业发展和体制环境具有重要的启示作用。

/ 第三章 /
办好人民满意的教育

一、挖掘教育红利[1]

人们普遍认为，中国经济在改革开放时的迅猛增长得益于该国的人口红利。 1980年至2010年期间，中国在15～59岁范围内的劳动年龄人口以年均1.8％的比率增长。 这使中国形成了古代儒家学派推崇的理想人口格局，即生产者多而消费者少。 这个格局保障了充足的劳动力，更优秀的人力资本，处在高位的资本投资回报率且资源能够再分配（生产能力），也因此带来了前所未有的高速发展。在同样的时期里，国内生产总值的年增长率是10.1％。

自2010年以来，劳动年龄人口逐渐减少，人口抚养比拔高，这使得经济增速放缓。一些学者建议中国能够利用并应当利用其第二次人口红利所带来的优势。 然而在接受这个建议之前，我们应该首先弄清楚第二次人口红利是什么以及我们在哪里可以找到它。

传统观点认为，第二次人口红利是因人口抚养比下降而使得储蓄水平到达高位的这样一种利好情形。根据这种观点，在老龄化社会中，如果人们把应急储蓄的必要性认作一种动力，并且假如有一个资金充沛的养老保险金制度，那么处在高位的储蓄存款利率还是可以形成的。 以

---

[1] 作者：蔡昉，中国社会科学院副院长、学部委员，中国社会科学院国家高端智库副理事长、首席专家。

上就解释了第二次人口红利是如何形成的。

但是在劳动适龄人口的机会之窗关闭之后，仅仅依靠一个低的人口抚养比来刺激中国经济增长是不够的。通过让资本投资与劳动投入互相配合，中国使自己在高增长时期免受资本回报率衰退的困扰。这就是人口红利的精髓。因此，在劳动力供给无法做到无限制的时代，寻找阻止资本回报率衰退的方法是中国获得再一次人口红利时面临的真正挑战。

第一次人口红利可以说算是一次短暂的有利条件，它并没有成为一个驱动经济增长的持久的力量。在经济发展的靠后阶段，经济增长不能再依赖人口的总规模及其年龄结构。取而代之的是，未来的经济增长必须依靠可以被培养并因此而得以稳定持续存在的资源。经济理论和发展经验表明，全要素生产率（TFP）和人力资本是最重要的可持续的增长驱动力，这两个驱动力互为先决条件并互相支撑。

从本质上讲，全要素生产率是一种分配效率，或是在恒量的情况下有效分配生产要素带来的收益。由于生产要素分配的优劣程度取决于工人的技能熟练度和企业家精神，那么提高全要素生产率就需要改善人力资本，这更像是一个人口优势。大量的实证研究表明，以工人平均受教育年限衡量的人力资本不仅对经济增长作出了直接而重大的贡献，而且还同步通过提高全要素生产率来对经济增长作出了间接贡献。

除了通过在实践中学习来提高人力资本外，教育是人力资本在总体上能够积累的主要原因。此外，各种层次和类型的教育所奠定的基础决定了在实践中学习的有效性。教育的发展首先体现在教育在数量上的增加，通常以学年数来作为衡量标准。教育的发展也有其在质量方面的维度，但质量的提高是需要建立在数量的增长这一基础上的。假如教育的质量是一个确定值，那么受教育年限的增加就意味着人力资本的全面提高，反之则不一定成立。 教育具有外在性这一特征，这也是为什么我们应该通过增加数量来提高教育质量。

质量是效率的一种形式。在经济活动中，效率的提高需要通过充分的竞争和有创造性的破坏来达到，也就是说，要让高效率的企业进入市场，让低效率的企业退出市场。但是，与物质生产不同的是，教育不仅仅是提供生产要素的一种方式，还是实现人类全面发展目标的一种方式。因此，在教育发展的过程中只能有创造，而不应该有破坏。那么毫无疑问，学校不能破产，这样学生的学习过程也不能被中断。

培养技能和人才需要教育规模的扩展。也就是说，努力增加进入劳动力市场的新人所接受的教育年限相当于同时提高教育的数量和质量。 中国和其他国家的经验表明，一旦九年制义务教育完成全覆盖式的普及，那么增加在义务教育阶段之前和之后的时期受教育年限的机会之窗就能进一步打开，在中国，就是指学前教育和高中。

将义务教育阶段延长至包括学前教育和高中教育，将在经济和社会上带来益处。

首先，在科技迅猛发展的时代，满足经济增长和社会发展需求的教育能够产生高额的社会收益率。研究表明，学前教育的社会收益率是所有教育阶段中最高的。

其次，义务教育阶段对于阻止贫困的代际传递起到了至关重要的作用。调查表明，学前教育的差距会使得城市和农村儿童站在不平等的起跑点上，而在高中和大学两个阶段，农村青年相较于城市青年入学比例低是导致社会阶层固化的根本原因。

最后，政府为这些阶段的教育买单可以减轻家庭的经济负担并减少机会成本，以此帮助提高年轻家长的生育意愿，这在低生育率时期是至关重要的。

二、教育减贫的中国实践[①]

贫困是人类发展的最大挑战，智力贫困是贫困产生的深刻根源。习近平总书记在中央扶贫开发工作会议的讲话中指出："治贫先治愚，扶贫先扶智。教育是阻断贫困代际传递的治本之策。"2020年是全面建成小康社会和扶贫攻坚的收官之年，也是基本实现教育现代化的收官之年。

其实，中国的教育减贫从1949年新中国成立时就已经开始。当时，中国人均国内生产总值只有49美元，全国人口80%以上是文盲，农村地区文盲率接近95%。毛泽东曾经这样描述道："中国是一穷二白，穷就东西少，白就是文化程度不高。"他向世界宣告："我们将以一个具有高度文化的民族出现于世界。"[②]改变一穷二白面貌是中国共产党和全体人民的历史使命。

1949年12月23日，在部分地区依然燃烧战火的背景下，第一次全国教育工作会议召开，一场人类历史上最为宏大、长达70多年的教育减贫"大战"从此拉开序幕。其重视程度之高、政策密度之强、动员范围之广前所未有。中华全国总工会1949年发出《关于工会文化教育经费用途的暂行规定》，明确规定工会文化教育支出中教育费应占60%。1950年，周恩来以政务院总理名义发布的《关于开展职工业余教育的指示》明确指出，职工业余教育的内容以识字为主。1950年，政务院批准《关于开展农民业余教育的指示》，首次提出扫除文盲的对象和标准——为全球教育扶贫创立了先例。

从1951年起，一场由政府领导、群众组织参与的识字运动在举国上下全面展开。到1953年底，全国共扫除文盲近408万人，首战

---

① 作者：高书国，中国教育学会副秘书长、研究员。
② 《毛泽东文集》第5卷，人民出版社，1996年，第345页。

初捷。到1981年，全国共扫除文盲1.4亿人。其中，扫除职工文盲约1000万人，职工中文盲减少到5％左右；扫除农民文盲1.3亿人，农村青壮年中的文盲减少到25％左右。

1978年至2000年，中国人均受教育年限从5年上升为7.79年，文盲人口从2.4亿人下降为9960万人。2000年至2010年，15岁以上文盲人口再次下降3977万人，文盲发生率首次突破5％，降至4.88％。教育减贫取得关键性胜利，中国也是6个人口大国中唯一一个全面实现联合国全民教育目标的发展中国家。

党的十八大以来，中国持续深入推进精准扶贫、精准脱贫工作。2012年12月29日，习近平总书记在河北省阜平县考察扶贫开发工作时指出："到2020年稳定实现扶贫对象不愁吃、不愁穿，保障其义务教育、基本医疗、住房，是中央确定的目标。"教育成为扶贫目标的重要指标，一场针对贫困地区、贫困人口的教育扶贫攻坚战正式开始。

贫困地区教育发展水平落后的原因是多方面的，有经济因素、政治因素、文化因素、传统因素、个体因素。由于教育发展水平与机会差距，在贫困地区出现恶性循环，即政府教育投入不足—教育水平落后—教育机会短缺—劳动力素质不高—经济发展缓慢—教育投入不足。为此，从中央到各地政府全面加大对贫困地区和贫困人群的教育投入，全社会共同支持贫困地区发展，将教育公平作为社会公平的重要手段，从单纯的"输血"转向"造血"功能的培育和发展。

2018年，教育扶贫工程正式启动，这是重点对集中连片特殊困难地区的680个贫困县实施的一项重大民生工程。2018年2月，《深度贫困地区教育脱贫攻坚实施方案（2018—2020年）》进一步确定：到2020年，深度贫困地区教育总体发展水平显著提升，实现建档立卡贫困人口教育基本公共服务全覆盖。保障各教育阶段建档立卡学生从入学到毕业的全程全部资助，保障贫困家庭孩子都可以上学，不让一个学生因家庭经济困难而失学。

为解决贫困大学生上学难的问题，教育部、中国人民银行等有关部门经过多年努力，已经建立起以奖学金、学生贷款、勤工助学和学费减免为主体的、多元的资助高等学校经济困难学生的政策体系，学生资助工作做到各个教育阶段全覆盖、公办民办学校全覆盖、家庭经济困难学生全覆盖，"应助尽助"，基本实现了"不让一个学生因家庭经济困难而失学"。全国共资助学生达到5.2亿人次，资助经费总投入达到8864亿元。

1978年至2019年，全国农村贫困人口减少至551万人，农村人口的贫困发生率从30.7%下降到0.6%。2010年至2020年间，全国农村人口人均受教育年限增长幅度快于城镇地区，城乡差距呈现明显快速缩小趋势。中国人均受教育年限从1982年的5.2年提升到2018年的9.35年。据预测，到2035年时，中国受高等教育人数的比例将超过25%，人均受教育年限也将上升至11.5年左右。

要进一步解决好部分农村和贫困地区辍学率较高的问题，对辍学高发区进行重点监测，确保2020年全国九年义务教育巩固率达到95%以上。教育部明确指出，到2020年各省（区、市）高中阶段教育毛入学率均要达到90%以上。

教育是反贫困的重要手段，更是阻遏智力贫困代际传递不可替代的重要工具。教育减贫是一条将过重的人口负担转变为人力资源的发展道路。70多年来，中国在扫除文盲的成功探索和伟大实践中，形成了一套扫除文盲工作行之有效的思路、模式和方法：

第一，领导体制。中国共产党和中央人民政府将教育扶贫工作确定为基本国策，由党和政府最高领导层亲自设计、组织、参与和发动，形成了科学的扫盲工作领导体制。

第二，制度优势。社会主义制度是中国教育扶贫工作取得成功的巨大制度优势。党和政府充分发挥理论、政治、组织、制度和密切联系群众的优势，一切从人民的利益出发，人民生活全面改善。

第三，社会动员。社会动员能力是中国政府的重要战略能力。70多年来，在党中央、国务院领导下，动员一切可以动员的力量，举全国之力，打赢了一场全民参与教育扶贫的人民战争。

第四，合作机制。中国政府真诚地与国际组织合作，虚心学习世界各国扫除文盲的成功经验，接受联合国教科文组织等国际组织的指导、帮助和援助，积极支持和参与国际组织的扫除文盲工作，真诚地履行一个负责任大国的国际扫盲责任。

中国人民在摆脱了经济贫困的同时，基本消除了智力贫困。中国创新了教育扶贫的思想、理论和模式，为人类消除贫困作出巨大贡献、提供先进经验。

第四章
绿色减贫的成效与前景

一、能源扶贫的双重红利①

党的十八大以来，党和国家坚决打赢脱贫攻坚战的决心和信心，加快了中国脱贫的步伐，到2020年，中国将实现现行标准下农村贫困人口的全面脱贫。

为确保这一目标的实现，国家各部门纷纷立下战书，通力合作，从教育、医疗、交通、就业、培训等领域全方位进行改善。中国的扶贫模式也从先前传统的基于农业和资源的开发式扶贫向生计替代式扶贫转变，由救济式扶贫转为开发保障式扶贫，呈现出多元化的扶贫方向。

在所有的扶贫措施中，能源项目由于具有支持贫困地区经济发展、提高能源普遍服务水平和减少农村环境污染等重要作用，成为目前实现贫困地区低碳减排和减贫双目标的重要途径。不难发现，目前中国尚未实现脱贫的人口主要聚集于西部或其他贫困山区，这些地区由于地处偏远，加之交通不便、通信闭塞，很难实现脱贫的目标，但这些地区同时拥有得天独厚的光照条件和水资源，对于这种情况，能源扶贫就显得尤为重要。

能源扶贫是指在政府引导下，以能源企业为主的各方合力帮助贫困地区实现脱贫。目前能源扶贫的主要形式包括分布式光伏、水电

---

① 作者：林伯强，厦门大学中国能源政策研究院院长。

以及生物质能源等。

一方面，中国光伏产业发展迅速，产业竞争力不断提高；另一方面，电力缺乏、光照充足、分布式能源成本较低的农村地区也是光伏发电的一个重要市场。在贫困地区进行光伏扶贫，可以践行"绿色经济"理念，改善生态环境，尽最大可能利用新能源。利用当地廉价的小水电和生物质能源，可以促进农村相关产业发展，增加农民收入。

中国的能源扶贫还体现在改造贫困地区农网，以配合光伏项目和水利扶贫。2018年，中国向贫困地区下达405亿元的农网改造升级投资，用于推进农村电网改造升级，提高农村供电能力和供电质量。事实上，中国除西藏外的地区已实现供电区域内自然村动力电全覆盖，有效推动贫困地区电动农业机械的应用，促进贫困村经济发展。

能源扶贫不仅可满足贫困家庭自用需求，而且有利于保护生态环境，改变了贫困居民以木柴为燃料的状况，不仅可以减少农民砍柴劳动量，提高农民收入，而且改善了居民厨房卫生面貌，实现退耕还林，也获得了良好的环境和经济效益。

虽然扶贫取得了瞩目的成绩，总结一下近年来的相关能源扶贫信息，实施能源扶贫的过程中主要还存在以下几个问题：

一是新能源补贴相对滞后影响了扶贫效果。能源扶贫项目通常由政府出资20%～30%作为启动资金，其余来源于企业垫资、融资或银行贷款。由于项目投资回收期较长，即使采用较低利率的扶贫信贷，投资回收期还是比较长。如果投入运行的扶贫项目如村级光伏项目扶贫电站不能及时纳入补贴目录，就不能及时得到收益。当然，部分项目纳入国家补助目录，但因为申报材料信息不真实等问题，影响了补贴资金的及时拨付。

二是一些能源扶贫项目前期建设质量不高，且缺乏后期维护。有些偏僻贫困地区的村级电站是由村集体组织建设和运行维护的，由于缺乏专业知识和相关经验导致后期维护不足而影响项目运行，已经出现有些项目在选址、设计、安装及施工方面因缺乏统一标准、能源设施管理方式落后、管护技术不足、运行方式不合理等，导致部分设备运行性能不达标、运行效率低甚至停止使用等问题，不仅项目无法取得预期效果，甚至可能成为负担。

三是贫困户本身动力不足也会制约能源扶贫效率。如果能源扶贫方式是给予资金和物质，可能使得扶贫对象对资金和物质产生依赖，难以形成正确的致富观，也难以学习和掌握操作技能。如果能源扶贫的对象以老年人和残疾人为主，教育程度以及劳动投入水平等也客观上影响了扶贫效果。而且，现实中可再生能源资源禀赋特征与贫困户的实际情况可能存在矛盾。可再生能源如风能、太阳能、小水电等的项目具有初始投入大、后期投入小、成本高且回收期长的特点，与贫困户资金缺乏且要求快速见效之间存在矛盾。短时间内难以改变贫困户的生活理念和环保认知，以及一些地方的文化封闭和青壮年劳动力外流，导致了清洁能源应用的人力资源难以保障，这些都限制了清洁能源的广泛应用。

四是如果能源扶贫项目由政府包办而缺乏相关利益方的参与，就会使清洁能源应用缺乏灵活机制和取得应有的效益。比如说，少数民族地区现有投入使用的清洁能源系统大多来自政府规划的扶贫项目，的确存在教育培训及维修指导不到位、设备维护不足等问题，使得有些清洁能源系统无专人维护而处于闲置状态，清洁能源的效益也难以持续体现。

五是地方政府监管缺位可能造成消极扶贫。政府只采用资金资助和优惠政策的措施来激励能源扶贫，而忽略了政府监管这一可以保障能源扶贫实效的重要环节，造成部分产业采取消极扶贫策略。另外，地方政府还可能因为重视指标改善，急功近利，支持本不应该受到支持的项目。

为实现2020年全面脱贫的目标，加快中国全面建成小康社会的步伐，2019年中国在能源扶贫方面推出了以下新政策：

第一，在前期开展试点、光照条件较好的5万个建档立卡贫困村实施光伏扶贫，保障280万无劳动能力建档立卡贫困户户均年增收3000元以上。就在前不久，财政部提前下放了2020年1136亿元的扶贫资金和56.75亿元的可再生能源补贴，切实缓解由于新能源补贴相对滞后对扶贫效果的不良影响，这对于光伏扶贫、农村分布式户用光伏无疑是重大的利好消息。

第二，在总结试点经验的基础上，建设农村小水电扶贫装机200万千瓦，让贫困地区1万个建档立卡贫困村的100万贫困农户每年稳定获得小水电开发收益，助力贫困户脱贫。

经过不懈的努力，贫困地区能源扶贫已经取得了显著成绩。但受制于客观因素，中国农村能源基础设施仍相对薄弱，能源普遍服务水平较低，清洁能源资源开发程度不高。目前，精准扶贫已经到了"重塑鱼塘生态"的关键环节，应做好精准扶贫能源方案，从产业扶贫着手，加速转变能源扶贫模式，把资源向深度贫困地区倾斜，完善能源开发收益分配机制，提高贫困户收入，增强贫困地区的"自我造血"能力。全心全意做好定点扶贫工作，大力开展贫困地区电网的升级改造，因地制宜发展新能源项目，结合产业力量，发挥"光伏+"的优势，以能源扶贫为契机，寻找更多的经济发展机会。

二、发挥中国绿色软实力[①]

2019年，在北京举行的第二届"一带一路"国际合作高峰论

---

① 作者：胡敏、迭戈·蒙特罗。胡敏，绿色创新发展中心主任。迭戈·蒙特罗，绿色创新发展中心战略顾问。

坛上，中方强调将切实落实建设绿色"一带一路"的承诺，出台了《关于推进绿色"一带一路"建设的指导意见》《"一带一路"生态环境保护合作规划》等系列实施政策，确保"一带一路"建设的清洁、绿色。

如何兼顾谋求发展和保护生态对于我们来说并不陌生。与20年前的中国一样，改善电力供应是"一带一路"沿线国家促进就业、开展扶贫和发展公共卫生事业的重要前提，是政策的重中之重。但这种发展的需要，可能会对缓解长期的全球气候变化风险带来不利影响。

中国在"一带一路"倡议中大力推广清洁能源，亚洲基础设施投资银行参与了多个清洁能源项目，其中包括世界最大的清洁能源项目之一的埃及本班太阳能公园。而在阿根廷，中国国家开发银行和中国进出口银行为建设阿根廷考查里电厂——拉丁美洲最大的太阳能发电厂，提供了85%的资金。

然而，从发展投资的角度来看，国外对环境管理的标准比中国国内更复杂、更严格。世界银行的一份报告指出，中国对外投资的政策指导越来越多，但仍缺乏有关实施、监督和执行等方面的重要细节。而这只是问题的一方面，"一带一路"伙伴国的环境、能源和气候政策也同样重要。

世界资源研究所的一份报告建议，中国的投资要符合《巴黎协定》下的国家自主贡献方案。但上述建议只能解决部分问题。以印度尼西亚为例，即使履行了协定中关于能源发展的承诺，到2050年印度尼西亚煤电比例仍将增长5倍。总的来说，伙伴国制定的关于使用何种电器、驾驶何种汽车、建造何种建筑、使用何种能源等方面的法律法规和相关政策，是影响当地能源消耗和温室气体排放的关键因素。

那么，中国能够提供什么帮助呢？在硬实力方面，中国可以制定更严格的对外投资环境标准；而更重要的是，中国可以为"一带一路"伙伴国提供资金和技术支持，分享中国在清洁能源、环境和气候政策方面的经验，这一方面，我们可以称为"绿色软实力"。

打赢污染防治攻坚战，中国仍在路上。在过去几十年里，中国已经建立了较为完备的法律法规体系，并陆续出台了一些符合世界标准的环境保护和清洁能源使用的战略规划。例如，中国设立了比美国和欧盟更严格的发电厂污染排放标准。国际清洁交通委员会的数据显示，中国制定的轻型车"国六标准"为全球最严格的排放标准之一。

"一带一路"沿线发展中国家面临的很多问题都是中国经历过的，可以借鉴中国的经验。相较于发达国家，中国在环境保护和二氧化碳排放量控制上的经验，或许更适合他们。比如，中国煤电产能过剩的问题也可能出现在"一带一路"沿线的中亚国家。中国可以与伙伴国分享相关的经验教训。

各国政府应根据行业标准区分中国与其他"一带一路"沿线国家的政策，并确定温室气体减排潜力最大的国家。政府之间的对话应将重心放在最有效的政策上，与矿业相关的生态保护标准、能源密集型产业能源效率、与基础设施建设相关的绿色标准等具有普适性，可适用于"一带一路"沿线国家。

中国善于制定和执行清洁能源、节能减排等综合规划。约旦是"一带一路"框架下中国三大投资对象国之一，中国的大部分投资都流向油页岩开发项目，这些项目均符合当地能源供给多样化的要求。约旦拥有丰富的太阳能和风能资源，以及廉价的沙漠土地。绿色和平组织的一份报告显示，到2050年，从技术可行性出发，上述资源能够满足当前电力总需求的6倍。通过切实可行的长期规划，约旦能够在可再生能源发电方面取得更大突破。

为实现合作共赢，我们应首要倡导政策共商与技术合作。在相关战略框架已成功搭建的前提下，我们需要落实具体的行动，例如，"一带一路"沿线国家环境政策、标准沟通与衔接是中国"一带一路"生态环境合作规划25个重点项目之一。2019年4月25日，在北京举行的第二届"一带一路"国际合作高峰论坛上，中国国家发展和改革委员会、中国能源基金会、联合国亚洲及太平洋经济社会委员会、联合国工业发展组织共同发起了"一带一路"绿色高效制冷行动倡议，其中一项动议就是呼吁加强环境标准方面的对话与合作。这是朝着正确方向迈出的坚实的一步。

第五章
数字技术与电商助力扶贫

一、中国减贫新模式：数字技术如何助力减贫[①]

数字技术日益广泛地应用于经济社会活动各领域，正在深刻改变现代社会的生产方式和人们的生活方式。对于发展中国家来说，在用数字技术提高效率的同时，也要防止数字鸿沟和贫富差距扩大风险，形成更具包容性的数字经济。在中国，以数字技术为依托的电子商务、数字普惠金融和大数据精准扶贫管理等对于减少贫困发挥了积极作用。

其一，电子商务促进贫困人口增收和增能。中国拥有世界上增长最快的电子商务市场，约占全球电子商务交易额的40%以上。众多贫困人口在电子商务的蓬勃发展中受益。例如，在政府政策支持下，全国电子商务进农村综合示范项目帮助近300万建档立卡贫困户实现增收。2019年，全国832个贫困县网络零售额达1076亿元人民币（约合157亿美元）。

电子商务平台大幅降低了小微商家连接大市场的门槛。许多在地理位置、信息获取、发展能力等方面处于边缘地位的农村人口通过电子商务在线展示他们的农产品和手工艺品，并找到买家，提高了产品销量，增加了收入。其次，电子商务带动产业链上下游发

---

① 作者：蒋希蘅，中国国际发展知识中心副主任。

展，创造了就业机会，为农村劳动力提供多样化的选择。农村网店零售业带动中国农村就业人数逾2800万人。此外，农村电商还惠及有养育责任的女性、老年人，为这些劳动能力较弱的贫困人口提供就业机会。阿里巴巴电商平台上的创业者男女比例接近1∶1，而整个商业领域这一比例约为3∶1。

更重要的是，电子商务能够促进思维模式转变，提供摸索和学习契机，激发贫困人口的创业潜能。2015年4月至2017年3月，在淘宝大学网络课堂上，来自765个国家级贫困县的112万名贫困县学员学习了559门课程。

其二，数字技术让金融服务更普惠。融资难、融资贵一直是小微企业和贫困群体生存和发展的瓶颈。世界各国在提供普惠金融方面有很多探索，但始终面临成本和信用两个难题。但是，高成本和信贷缺口仍然存在，因为这是贫困人口获得贷款的两个主要障碍。2016年，二十国集团（G20）峰会发布的《二十国集团数字普惠金融高级原则》标志着普惠金融的全球实践正式进入数字化阶段，为解决这两项难题提供了新的解决思路。

在中国，传统金融机构更多运用数字化手段，提高边缘群体金融服务的可获得性和便利性。各地金融部门有效支持粮食等大宗农副产品收购实现全程非现金结算，以非现金支付方式发放养老保险、医疗保险以及财政涉农补贴资金等，为农村人口提供极大便利。

中国首家基于云计算的商业银行——网商银行，自2015年成立四年来，为全国146个贫困县、超过400万客户提供无接触贷款。2017年，京东推出了数字农贷。数字农贷项目上线两年后，就与山东、河北、河南等地100多家农民专业合作社合作，累计放款约10亿元，逾期率和坏账率均为零。

其三，大数据成为辅助政府精准扶贫的技术手段。大数据使贫困识别的精准度得到提高，并使公平性得以保障。2014年，民政部开始推动各地大数据信息核对平台建设。

截至2019年10月，中国省级和地市级大数据信息平台覆盖率已经分别达到了96.8％和91.9％。实际上，利用各部门大数据组网对贫困家庭进行前置性甄别正逐渐成为主流。同时，探索、利用大数据对贫困地区进行综合分析，帮助制定有针对性的帮扶措施。大数据分析结合气候、地貌等自然信息以及家庭人口、个人能力、经济财务等社会信息，系统深层次地分析县、村、户各级的致贫原因，为扶贫到村到户提供强有力支撑。

但是，大数据的应用水平还需要大幅提升。目前中国只有5.9％的地市利用数据库进行过专门的数据开发，1.8％的地市曾经向上级机关提交过基于大数据分析的决策报告。

综合扶贫、教育、工商、民政、卫计等领域的大数据实时共享及动态比对，可以提高扶贫财政资金等公共资源利用效果。大数据还可以跟踪和监测不同地区、机构的扶贫进度和效率。

多维度的贫困大数据信息甚至可以帮助政府选择更加合适的扶贫项目、制定合理的贫困标准。以上海为例，大数据广泛用于上海市年度贫困标准的认定。基于大数据的调查研究，例如《基于核对数据的最低生活保障研究》，为民政部等部门出台国家政策实施标准提供了有益帮助。

其四，大数据有助于提高扶贫资源利用效率，推动循证决策。综合扶贫、教育、工商、民政、卫计等领域的大数据实时共享及动态比对，可提高扶贫财政资金等公共资源利用效果。

数字技术正在中国的减贫中发挥积极作用。但是，应注意，这得益于三方面条件：

第一，中国农村地区（包括大多数贫困地区）传统和数字基础设施的广泛覆盖。截至2020年3月，中国的互联网覆盖率达到64.5％。行政村通光纤和通4G的比例均超过98％，贫困村通宽带比例达到99％，广大群众的电脑或手机上网需求得到保障。电网、道路等传统基础设施建设覆盖中国绝大多数居民点，提供了稳定的电力供应和交通运输。

第二，政府与数字平台企业的有效合作关系，促进发展。各级政府对数字经济发展持开放鼓励态度，积极与数字平台企业开展合作，更好地甄别和扶助贫困人口，实现精准扶贫。

第三，数字平台企业采取了具有包容性的商业模式。通过电子商务、金融服务和与之配合的助贫扶弱公益项目，数字平台企业可以赋能贫困地区的女性、年轻人、残疾人和小微商家。借助数字平台，这些群体能够对接大市场，获得低成本发展空间，通过创业和就业摆脱贫困。

二、电商扶贫——现代农村经济发展的助推器[①]

自2014年起，商务部会同财政部、国务院扶贫办已累计在1231个县级市开展电子商务进农村综合示范工作，覆盖国家级贫困县832个。2018年，这832个国家级贫困县的网络零售额达1804亿元（约合259亿美元），同比增长49.3%，农村电子商务创造了3000多万个就业岗位，惠及1000多万人，其中300万人实现了增收。以甘肃省环县为例，电子商务助力居民家庭平均收入从2015年的750元、2016年的1100元、2017年的1560元提高到2018年的2450元。

农村电子商务的成功离不开大型电商公司的支持。超过800个淘宝村如雨后春笋般涌现于省级贫困县。以山东省曹县为例，12个贫困村通过创建淘宝村成功脱贫，全县2万余人（即全县五分之一人口）获利于电子商务从而实现脱贫致富。拼多多是一家团购电商平

[①] 作者：洪勇，商务部研究院电子商务研究所副研究员。

台，在其平台注册的国家级贫困县商户数量有14万家，年订单总额达162亿元，创造就业岗位30多万个。此外，商务部在指导电商扶贫方面也发挥了重要作用。2017年，商务部开通电商扶贫频道汇总信息平台，集中反映电商扶贫的最新情况。

近年来，尽管中国农村电子商务发展迅速，但仍处于起步阶段，未来还有较大的发展空间。

加快农村电子商务发展，首先要提高电商扶贫的精准和实效。在一些农村电商试点项目中，存在低收入家庭目标定位不准确、资金配置不合理、应对措施缺乏针对性等问题。例如，不同地区的自然条件、经济发展水平和物流成本不同，会导致农村电子商务区域发展不平衡。然而在财政专项资金的使用过程中，却未能充分考虑不同区域的差异性，采取平均分配资金的方式。一些县级电子商务监管部门对项目缺乏整体规划，不敢使用资金或缺乏必要的专业技能，从而使得专项资金执行进度缓慢。

其次，要坚决清除形式主义和官僚主义。部分县级电子商务公共服务中心长期闲置，只有在上级检查时才开放使用；物流配送中心的部分仓库距离太远，无法充分利用网络效应，从而被闲置；某些地区盲目提高村级服务中心的高覆盖率，导致资源配置过剩，供过于求。

再次，要解决农村电子商务人才短缺的问题。农村缺乏电子商务营销、运营和设计等领域的专业人才，农村常住人口主要为老人和留守儿童，该群体对于学习使用互联网不感兴趣。并且，由于电商培训占用了村民的农务时间，他们不愿意参加。培训内容和方式往往"一刀切"，无法满足村民多样化的学习需求。培训课程重理论轻实践，某些电商培训中心局限于教授如何开设网店、发布通知、接受订单等基础技能，缺乏对产品设计、推广、运营、平面设计、客户关系管理、仓库管理等专业技能的全面培训。由于课程不够接地气，学员很难将所学知识应用到网络创业中去。

加快推动乡村振兴和脱贫致富，关键要培育具有竞争优势的产业，创新县级电子商务发展模式，拓宽农村电子商务发展渠道。一是整合线上零售和批发平台，包括一亩田、中农网、农融网等B2B商品交易平台，阿里巴巴、美菜网等农产品批发平台，本来生活网、易果网等垂直生鲜电商平台，以及其他农产品电商平台。二是将农村电子商务融入跨境产业链，把优质农产品销往国外，参与全球市场竞争，为世界各地提供淡季产品，并推动产品差异化和转型升级。三是利用微信、微博、今日头条、抖音、快手等社交媒体，助力农村电子商务发展。借助网络乡村引流，讲好故事，打好网红牌。为电商平台和贫困县创造合作机会，比如，电商平台帮助有发展潜力的农村企业家开发产品、推广品牌和开展培训，使双方达成长期合作。

三、电商扶贫大有可为[①]

电商扶贫把先进互联网技术与最贫困的地区和人群结合起来，创造性地采取了一系列行之有效的帮扶措施，助力脱贫攻坚，衔接乡村振兴。数据显示，2019年底全国贫困县实现网络零售额2392亿元人民币，同比增长33%，带动贫困地区约500万农民就业增收。

第一，完善交通、互联网、电力、物流、仓储电商基础设施。截至2020年6月，全国具备条件的乡镇和建制村100%通硬化路，贫困村通光纤比例从2017年的不足70%提升到98%，有96.6%的乡镇设立了快递服务网点，832个国家级贫困县全部建立电子商务服务中心，实现贫困地区县、乡、村三级农村电商管理与物流配送网络全

---

① 作者：章文光，北京师范大学政府管理学院院长、农村治理研究中心主任。

覆盖。

第二，发展特色扶贫产品。贫困地区因地制宜发展特色产品，如陕西柞水木耳、甘肃礼县苹果、云南西盟山林百花蜜等；加强农产品质量安全检验检测，制定产地认证、质量追溯、冷藏保鲜、分等分级、产品包装、冷链物流等环节标准；开展"名特优新""三品一标""一村一品"等农产品认证，实施电商扶贫产品的标准化、规模化、品牌化。

第三，健全服务支持体系。一是基层扶贫队伍带动，通过组织贫困人口参与电商扶贫，让贫困户了解并分享技术进步带来的红利；二是银行和支付平台在小额信贷、支付方式等方面加大支持力度，为电商扶贫发展提供动力；三是电商扶贫协会等社会组织发展，为贫困户提供电商产品集货、分级包装、品牌营销、物流配送、售后保障等规范化服务，支持电商扶贫行稳致远。

第四，搭建企业合作平台。国务院扶贫办通过签订扶贫战略合作协议、政策鼓励支持等方式，把京东、苏宁、阿里巴巴、拼多多、供销E家、邮乐购、乐村淘等一大批电商销售平台与贫困地区生产者联结起来。2020年"618"促销活动，京东开场一小时内农产品成交额同比增长超17倍，淘宝和天猫有超过120万贫困县卖家入驻。云南省祥云县依托云南邮政打通洋芋销售"最后一公里"，解决了因新冠肺炎疫情造成的农产品滞销难题。

第五，赋能农村创业主体。预计2020年底，全国电商知识技能培训将超过1000万人次，培养农村青年电商高端人才100万名以上，基本实现每个贫困村至少有一名电商扶贫人才。积极鼓励贫困地区高校毕业生返乡创业，大力支持贫困村青年、妇女、残疾人依托电子商务就业创业。开展"巾帼脱贫行动"，扶持贫困妇女参加电商培训，有122万妇女学习了相关技能，在全国创建了636个"全国巾帼脱贫示范基地"。

第六，构筑扶贫"大格局"。中国精准扶贫是政府、社会、市场协同推进的扶贫"大格局"。通过"东西协作"，实现东部地区市场、技术优势与贫困地区劳动力、资源、土地优势互补。通过"希望工程""光彩事业"等项目，推动社会多方力量参与扶贫，撬动社会资源支持脱贫攻坚事业。通过"定点帮扶"，加大对贫困地区资源支持力度，2020年上半年中央企业开展消费扶贫专项行动，集中购买受新冠肺炎疫情影响严重的178个县1800多种滞销农产品9.27亿元，减少疫情对贫困地区的不利影响。

电商扶贫不仅推动贫困地区发展、提高贫困群众收入，更为脱贫攻坚、产业兴旺和乡村发展打开了新局面。

为脱贫攻坚按下"加速键"。电商扶贫摆脱了地理位置偏远、交通条件不便等对农产品销售的束缚，让优质农产品"山里人卖得出，城里人买得到"，在促进贫困地区产业发展、实现贫困户就业增收方面的减贫带贫效果显著。面对新冠肺炎疫情的挑战，电商扶贫解了贫困户燃眉之急，缓解了农产品滞销风险，2020年"6·18"促销活动期间销售数据再创新高。以电商扶贫为代表的农村数字经济已经成为"三农"发展新动能，为贫困县如期实现脱贫摘帽提供有力保障。

为产业兴旺搭起"致富桥"。电商扶贫通过整合产、供、销、购等资源要素，动员社会力量参与脱贫攻坚，是打赢脱贫攻坚战的"有力武器"。一方面，打通农产品上行通道，使贫困地区农产品直接融入市场经济产业链和国际国内供应链；另一方面，改变传统农产品生产销售方式，赋能龙头企业、合作社、个体户等市场主体，形成更加稳定的利益联结机制，为全面建成小康社会后实现农村产业兴旺打下坚实基础。

为农村发展注入"新活力"。精准扶贫注重扶贫与扶志扶智相结合，从单纯地给钱给物转变为物质扶贫与技术扶贫、教育扶贫相结合。电商扶贫充分调动贫困户积极性，激发内生动力，培养了数以百万的新型农民，吸引大批人才返乡创业，"数字成为新农资，手机成为新农具，直播成为新农活"。

当今世界面临百年未有之大变局，中国人民顺应时代潮流，在危机中育新机、于变局中开新局，创造性地采取电商扶贫举措，为世界减贫事业提供了中国智慧、中国方案。

首先，中国拥有坚强领导核心。中国共产党的领导是中国脱贫攻坚取得成功的根本保证。只有中国共产党才能带领一个14亿人口的大国，在40年间实现8亿人脱离贫困，开人类历史之先河，为世界减贫作出巨大贡献。脱贫攻坚目标之高远、任务之艰巨、时间之紧迫前所未有，全国各族人民在党的集中统一领导下，采取有效措施统筹人力物力，调动各方资源，创新探索，攻坚克难，彰显了巨大政治优势。

其次，坚持精准扶贫基本方略。电商扶贫严格落实"六个精准"要求，是精准扶贫基本方略在实践中的具体体现。第一，电商扶贫措施精准，各级电商主管部门结合电商扶贫新业态的特点，因地制宜发展电商扶贫产业链，将精准带动贫困户就业增收作为电商扶贫出发点，不片面追求规模，注重帮扶质量。第二，电商扶贫责任精准，各级电商主管部门注重考核，发挥绩效评价指挥棒作用，压实主体责任，严格落实资金和项目管理制度，提高资金分配和使用效果。第三，电商扶贫成效精准，各级电商主管部门依托商务部乡村站点监测管理系统，指导电子商务示范县加强部门数据和信息共享，统一统计电商扶贫在带动扶贫增收、产品销售、就业创业、品牌培育等各个方面的成效数据，开展试点、推广、普及的渐进发展之路，精准发挥扶贫效果。

同时，发挥中国特色社会主义制度优势。充分发挥社会主义制度集中力量办大事的优势，在中国深度贫困地区持续开展基础设施和公共服务"补短板、强弱项",为电商扶贫发展夯实基础。调动全社会力量共同参与脱贫攻坚,形成扶贫"大格局",东西部产业优势互补,上下同心同行,把扶贫与扶志扶智相结合,开发式扶贫与保障性扶贫相统筹,为电商扶贫发展提供历史性机遇。运用整体思维完善脱贫攻坚顶层设计,把脱贫攻坚工作纳入全面的战略布局,开辟出一条中国特色的脱贫攻坚道路。

四、"淘宝村"可为非洲借鉴[①]

走进肯尼亚的城镇或村庄,随处可看到小棚房和装潢精美的商店上写着"Mpesa"。Mpesa是由肯尼亚及坦桑尼亚电信运营商Safaricom推出的移动银行服务,相当于中国的微信支付和支付宝、缅甸的Wave Money和美国的Apple Pay。Mpesa创立于2007年,几年后移动支付才在中国开始普及。Mpesa主要通过短信和在线服务开展业务,并已使约18.6万户家庭(占肯尼亚家庭总数的2%)摆脱贫困。Mpesa还大大提升了肯尼亚女性的地位。如果某个家庭有一定流动资金,妇女就有机会脱离农业生产,从事商业活动。

在减贫方面,中国已经有了相当于Mpesa的在线版本——淘宝村。2019年,世界银行和阿里研究院联合发布的一项报告称,自2015年以来,这些村庄帮助了成千上万的中国农民脱困致富。其中,女性受益最大。根据阿里研究院提供的数据,在电子商务领域,企业家(网店店主)的男女比例大致相等,而传统企业中男女企业家的比例为3∶1。但是这些村庄的运营模式是什么?肯尼亚乃至整个非洲大陆是否可借鉴这种模式?

淘宝村是指"活跃网店数量达到当地家庭户数10%以上、电子

---

① 作者:利娅·林奇,睿纳新国际咨询公司副总监。

商务年交易额达到1000万元以上的村庄",堪称电子商务巨头阿里巴巴的创新之举,旨在使农民借助网店业务摆脱贫困。2016年,即淘宝村启动两年后,由国务院扶贫开发领导小组办公室等部门联合出台了《关于促进电商精准扶贫的指导意见》。该意见要求,到2020年在贫困村建设"电商扶贫站点"6万个以上,贫困县农村电商年销售额比2016年翻两番以上。

阿里巴巴的农村淘宝计划实际上起到了抛砖引玉的示范作用,其他电商公司纷纷效仿并按政府规定扩大规模。作为中国精准扶贫战略的一部分,地方政府扶持开设电子商务和服装生产培训班,提供了低息贷款,并鼓励成功的企业家优先考虑雇用贫困农民。青年企业家在中国农村电子商务发展进程中也发挥了举足轻重的作用。政府最新政策,鼓励超过13万名应届毕业生返回家乡,并针对各种项目开设网店、提供相应服务,带领亲朋好友共同创业。

在中国,电子商务或数字贸易已经成为促进贸易、创造就业、增加收入和减少贫困的强有力工具。在非洲,也是如此。然而,尽管一些非洲国家在移动支付领域处于领先地位,非洲在电子商务方面仍然非常落后。在中国,电商市场是由两家大型科技巨头主导的。而在非洲,电商企业众多,还有大量初创企业,电商企业遍布非洲23个国家,数量约为264家。非洲最大、资金最雄厚的电子商务平台Jumia仍未实现盈利,销售分布仍然非常不平衡。2017年,在肯尼亚、南非和尼日利亚三个国家的消费者数量超过非洲消费者总数一半。

但是,电子商务仍然潜力巨大,前景可期。

非洲青年人口增长率全球最高,就业岗位稀缺,而且需求极为迫切。根据非洲开发银行的数据,非洲大陆近4.2亿15~35岁的青年人中,失业率高达三分之一。这些青年人对手机的使用非常娴熟,而手机正是最流行的网上购物工具。据世界银行报告,非洲有6.5亿移动用户，超过了美国或欧洲的移动用户数量。在一些非洲国家，手机使用普及率甚至超过了清洁水源、银行账户或电力。非洲的中产阶级也不断壮大，高达3.3亿人，集中在埃及、尼日利亚、南非、阿尔及利亚和摩洛哥，他们有强烈的消费欲望。越来越多的非洲制造品牌和产品在非洲大陆（包括较大的老牌市场以及卢旺达、塞内加尔和埃塞俄比亚等新兴市场）生产。从时尚产品到护肤产品，非洲产品备受推崇和期待。

这一切都预示着非洲数字贸易领域的巨大增长机会，而新冠肺炎疫情大流行为包容性电子商务及相关数字解决方案、工具和服务蓬勃发展提供了千载难逢的机遇。

以我在中国和非洲的工作和生活经历，我很清楚，想要在非洲沿袭中国的模式绝非易事。

首先，非洲由50多个国家组成，各国政策、市场规模、消费者特点、语言和其他差异使得协调和物流障碍重重，难以实现规模经济。

事实上，非洲的重心大多放在引入技术和搭建平台。这两者相对容易，而关键是建设基础设施，如公路、铁路、机场、互联网门户等。因此，在非洲，各电商公司常常陷入困境，很难与基础设施相当完善的海外廉价商品竞争。

非洲面临的第一个挑战是物流。可以设想一下，如果物流更为通畅便捷，整个非洲的卖家生态系统势必会充满生机、丰富多元。如果借助资金和贷款，对城镇中的众多中小企业进行电子商务和产品营销方面的培训，很可能达到与淘宝村极为相似的积极效果。非洲村庄完全可以建立自己的电子商务中心。非洲拥有庞大的、受教育程度越来越高的青年人口，政府扶持、鼓励青年企业家在农村地区建立电子商务中心的计划可以充分利用这些人才。

第二个挑战是基本的"工作方式"，其阻碍了电子商务在整个非洲大陆的蓬勃发展。

例如，在中国有54％的人使用移动支付进行网上购物。然而，由于对产品和快递缺乏信任，90％的非洲人口采用的购买方式是货到付款而非移动支付。在农村地区，如果快递人员只负责送货不负责收款，这对于电商公司来说尤其麻烦，而且成本高昂。由于地址和邮政系统不够完善，这方面的挑战长期存在。快递员要花大量时间才能找到网购客户，成本太大，尤其是在农村地区。

尽管客户熟悉像Mpesa这样的移动支付服务，但这些系统的开发是为了提供包容性商务，而不是像在中国那样建立信任，提供便利。只有10％~15％的非洲人口使用银行账户。因此，大多数非洲在线零售商店和服务要求客户有银行账户或与之关联的付款服务，这无疑限制了客户群体。

面对物流和"工作方式"这两个挑战，非洲的电子商务能否像中国一样，在非洲减贫中发挥作用？

我认为，答案是肯定的，尤其是着眼于解决这两个重大挑战。我们还认为，中国（和其他国家）可以通过两种具体方式在这方面提供帮助。

首先，扶持非洲本地电子商务公司，而不是与之竞争。一直以来阿里巴巴都对非洲市场非常感兴趣。对本地企业家提供扶持，并在淘宝和天猫上出售一些非洲特产，如卢旺达咖啡豆。在新冠肺炎疫情期间，阿里巴巴与埃塞俄比亚航空公司建立了新的合作伙伴关系，为捐赠的医疗设备提供跨境物流。这些关系可以使阿里巴巴在非洲大陆快速发展，但这也会使非洲本土的电商企业不断退出市场。因此，阿里巴巴、亚马逊等合作伙伴应对现有的非洲电子商务平台进行投资，并提升其扩大市场范围的能力，而不是自己占领市场。

其次，了解非洲各国政府和私营部门的需求。中国的成功得益于对电商企业进行投资，使企业得以发展壮大。尽管非洲初创科技企业的股权融资迅速增长（2018年达到11.6亿美元），但流入非洲的外国直接投资总额有限，仅占全球总额的3.5％。非洲中产阶级消费市场不断增长，非洲的数字贸易也随之增长，新冠肺炎疫情暴发后，提供了独特的投资机会。非洲各国政府为遏制新冠病毒在整个非洲的传播而采取的措施表明，他们愿意采取迅速行动，保障人民群众的安全健康。鉴于上述理由，目前投资非洲恰逢其时。电子商务是一个绝佳的机会，电子商务同样可以创造就业机会并减少贫困。"淘宝村"在这方面堪称典范。

希望在不久的将来，肯尼亚的城市和村庄不止Mpesa一家，而是百花齐放，共创繁荣。

第三篇

共同事业

Chapter III

中国脱贫与全球发展的

相互关系

扫码获取

★ 脱贫故事分享
★ 脱贫攻坚解读
　 与回顾

第一章
中国为世界脱贫注入"授人以渔"的
可持续动力

一、人权与务实①

大部分宣扬人权的人都出身于富裕的社会，他们根本不了解穷人有着更基本、更重要的需求。他们总是强调投票权如何重要，但是，如果人们连饭都吃不饱，拥有投票权又有什么意义呢？

因此，倡导人权首先应实现五项基本权利：一是生命安全权；二是温饱权；三是基本医疗保障权；四是受教育权；五是能够获得收入并养家糊口的工作权。如果这五项权利不能得到保障，那么其他的人权也注定沦为空谈。

这五项权利是最基本的。理解这一点，对于世界其他国家正确认识中国近年来的故事非常重要。过去40年，中国比世界上任何国家、比人类历史上任何时期都更快速、更全面地保障了其公民的这五项基本权利。

这一成就之所以更为卓越，是因为从1840年鸦片战争到1949年中华人民共和国成立前，在长达一个世纪的时间里，中国人民遭受了巨大的痛苦。那段时期的中国人饱受外敌侵略、内战和饥荒，医疗物资匮乏，教育资源奇缺，面临大量失业。要想了解中国人民取

---

① 作者：马凯硕，新加坡国立大学教授，新加坡前驻联合国大使。

得的成就有多大，首先要看看他们之前的生存条件有多么艰苦。

在此前相当长的一段时间里，中国农民的生活条件一直没有得到改善，绝大多数中国农民过着非常艰苦的生活。人们没有足够的口粮，也匮乏教育和医疗资源。人均寿命极低。透过一些统计数据，中国发展速度之快一目了然。在1980年，中国农村贫困人口比例接近100％。而到了36年后的2016年，农村贫困发生率降低了95.5％，仅为4.5％。

把目光从农村扩大到整个中国，减贫成就同样令人瞩目。1980年，中国90％以上的人口（9.81亿人）每天的生活费不足3.2美元。到2016年，这一比例已下降到5.4％，下降幅度颇为明显。

中国的减贫成就在整个人类发展史上绝无仅有，对全世界来说颇为重要，其中一个重要原因是，即使是当今的2020年，广大亚非拉地区仍有许多人生活在贫困线以下。其中，南亚贫困人口占比为53.9％，东亚为12.5％，撒哈拉以南非洲为68.1％，拉丁美洲为10.4％。

全球赤贫人口总数高达20亿人，占世界人口的26.4％。对于这些地区，中国减贫经验具有借鉴意义。我们需要为这20亿人做的最重要的事情就是帮助他们摆脱贫困。

直到最近，仍有许多经济学家认为消除贫困是一项不可能完成的任务。但中国用事实告诉我们，情况并非如此，彻底消除贫困是完全可以做到的。

这就是我们要把中国的故事传播到世界每一个角落的原因。那么，问题来了，中国是如何成功完成这一看似"不可能完成"的任务的呢？答案其实很简单：中国在国内和国际层面采取了一些正确的政策，实现减贫目标。

在国内方面，当我还是新加坡国立大学李光耀公共政策学院院长时，我就教导我的学生们，国家要想成功，就必须遵循神奇的MPH公式。

在这里，MPH并非指每小时英里数。MPH是指三个治国准则：任人唯贤（meritocracy）、求真务实（pragmatism）和诚实正派（honesty）。

M代表"任人唯贤"。中国一直实行"任人唯贤"的人才任用原则。任人唯贤，意味着中国政府能够选拔最优秀的人在其众多机构中工作，提高治理能力。治理能力提高了，才能制定出改善人民生活的正确政策。

P代表"求真务实"。关于求真务实，最好的定义就是已故中国领导人邓小平的那句名言："不管黑猫白猫，抓到老鼠就是好猫。"

中国善于从世界各地的最佳政策和实践中汲取营养，并结合自身实际贯彻执行。这种务实作风值得各国学习，用来解决世界上的诸多问题。

H代表"诚实正派"。归根结底，历史告诉我们，要想成为繁荣昌盛的国家，必须有效打击腐败，确保国家资源用于民生福祉，杜绝中饱私囊等官场丑恶现象。

在国际方面，中国坚持正确的政策导向，积极融入以自由规则为基础的国际秩序。如果能够在全世界推广中国减贫经验，我们就有望实现有史以来人类境况的最大改善。

二、精准扶贫：中国扶贫之路及其全球性影响[①]

消除贫困是联合国《2030年可持续发展议程》的首要目标，也是最艰巨的发展挑战。2019年，诺贝尔经济学奖授予三位发展经济学家，以表彰他们通过实验性方法在缓解全球贫困研究领域作出的突出理论贡献。中国创造了人类历史上规模最大的减贫奇迹。1981

---

① 作者：胡鞍钢，清华大学国情研究院院长、清华大学公共管理学院教授。

年至2015年，中国绝对贫困人口减少了8.74亿人（根据世界银行贫困线标准每人每天1.9美元），占同期全球减贫人数（11.73亿人）的74.5％。中国为全球减贫事业作出了巨大贡献。中国的扶贫战略，特别是精准扶贫的实践和理论，对世界具有重要意义。

2020年，中国将结束已延续数千年的绝对贫困，将全面建成小康社会，消除绝对贫困，提前10年率先实现联合国可持续发展目标。

中国的扶贫之路为全球贫困治理提供了中国智慧。2013年，习近平主席首次提出"精准扶贫"理论，成为解决贫困问题的根本战略。精准扶贫理论主要包括"六个精准"，即扶贫对象精准、项目安排精准、资金使用精准、措施到户精准、因村派人（第一书记）精准、脱贫成效精准。同时，精准扶贫要求落实"五个一批"，即发展生产脱贫一批、易地搬迁脱贫一批、生态补偿脱贫一批、发展教育脱贫一批、社会保障兜底一批。精准扶贫是中国现有贫困人口全部脱贫的有效战略，也是扶贫理论和实践的重大创新。

中国精准扶贫仍面临重大挑战。首先，贫困成因复杂，积重难返，脱贫困难。其次，扶贫过程中存在"坐等帮扶""望穷却步"等问题。主观因素可能会阻碍减贫进度。最后，即使彻底消除了绝对贫困，仍然会存在相对贫困和返贫现象，需要培养穷困人口的"自我造血"能力。消除绝对贫困是脱贫攻坚战的"最后堡垒"，直接关系到扶贫的质量和效果。面对造成贫困的各种主观和客观原因，中国必须深入推进精准扶贫战略。

中国应继续实行精准扶贫，并在未来不断完善扶贫措施。成功的扶贫需要"天时地利人和"，其中最重要的方面是"人和"，依托人民群众的力量。推进精准扶贫，应注意以下几点：

第一，授人以鱼，不如授人以渔。扶贫不能一味依赖"送钱"。必须改变旧的、过时的生产方式和经营方式，推广新技术、新项目、新想法。

第二，扶贫应为贫困人口提供基本保障。应该建立更完善的保障机制，以提高穷人的容错率，减少其风险规避心态，使他们敢于尝试。

第三，扶贫路上"手拉手"。扶贫开发过程中存在各种不可预见的问题。必须提供充分的指导和及时的解决办法，确保成功减贫。

第四，"扶贫先扶志"。扶贫工作需要帮助贫困群众树立起摆脱困境的斗志和勇气。应该从贫困群众自身的角度，对其困难和心境有更深入的认识。

第五，必须引入科学的扶贫措施，如承诺机制、监督机制、提醒制度等。事实证明，这些措施在帮助他们追求长远利益、抵御眼前诱惑、提高参与率、减少扶贫项目退出率等方面是行之有效的。

作为一个拥有14亿人口的泱泱大国，中国是全球减贫事业最重要的"试验田"。中国从一个贫困国家起步，现在已成为世界上最大的经济体（按购买力平价计算），并将全面建成小康社会。中国扶贫的成功向世界提供了全球贫困治理的中国榜样、中国经验和中国战略。

/ **第二章** /
国际减贫合作与交流

一、"一带一路"助推非洲摆脱贫困[①]

消除贫困是联合国《2030年可持续发展议程》的首要目标。目前，全球大约有7亿极端贫困人口，其中一半以上生活在撒哈拉以南非洲。在世界最贫困的20个国家中，有16个来自非洲。西方国家曾长期向非洲国家提供援助和减免债务，但撒哈拉以南非洲的极端贫困人口却从1990年的2.9亿人上升到2010年的4.14亿人。正如《无用的援助》一书中所说，西方国家援助和减债更多是为了体现它们的"宽宏大量"，却没有提升非洲国家自身解决贫困问题的能力。

与非洲类似，中国也曾有数量庞大的贫困人口，其中大部分聚集在农村。通过修建水坝、灌溉、公路等基础设施，中国农村得到了巨大改善。1994年至2000年间，中国平均每年修建约4.2万公里的农村公路，推动当地农产品和剩余劳动力的自由流动。经济开发区吸引了很多劳动密集型产业，创造了大量就业机会，最大限度地发挥中国的人口红利。

中国的脱贫经验受到了包括非洲国家在内的国际社会的广泛关注。2016年，"非洲晴雨表"一份关于非洲人如何看待中国影响力的调查显示，中国发展模式的受欢迎程度为24%，大约三分之二的非洲

---

① 作者：沈陈，中国社会科学院世界经济与政治研究所助理研究员。

人认为中国的影响力是"或多或少积极的"或"非常积极的"。习近平主席提出的"一带一路"倡议得到了非洲国家的支持和响应，截至2020年6月，已有43个非洲国家签署了"一带一路"相关合作协议。

受新冠肺炎疫情影响，非洲国家的防疫成本和卫生开支大大增加，非洲各国正努力恢复经济、保障就业，避免部分人口返贫或加剧贫困。习近平主席在中非团结抗疫特别峰会上提出，中非应加强共建"一带一路"合作，加快落实中非合作论坛北京峰会成果，并将合作重点向健康卫生、复工复产、改善民生领域倾斜。"一带一路"倡议有利于中非在经贸融资、产业转移、技术交流等方面的合作，推动中非合作的转型升级。

基础设施不足是制约非洲发展的最大瓶颈。例如，电荒是非洲普遍存在的问题，过去曾出现过某跨国企业向非洲捐赠上千台笔记本电脑，却发现当地没法给笔记本电池充电的情况。对于依赖电力的工业企业来说，电荒会严重阻碍非洲的工业化进程。在运输方面，非洲国家极度依赖公路交通，铁路运力则较为有限，因此城际铁路运输费用非常昂贵。城际铁路运力的严重不足限制了当地企业的生产力，难以达到生产的预期目标。在通信方面，非洲电子通信的计费方式也相对落后。

改善非洲基础设施一直是中非合作的重点。20世纪六七十年代，中国耗资4.5亿美元修建全长1860公里的坦赞铁路。"一带一路"倡议提出以后，中国更加重视非洲铁路、公路、航空、港口、电力和电信的建设，推动非洲地区的互联互通。据美国布鲁金斯学会数据，中国对非基础设施投资年均约100亿美元，占非洲所有基础设施项目外来资金的三分之一。2016年10月，埃塞俄比亚首都亚的斯亚贝巴至吉布提的铁路正式通车。次年5月，连接肯尼亚首都内罗毕和东非最大港口蒙巴萨的蒙内铁路也全线开通。亚吉铁路、蒙内铁路是"一带一路"在非洲的"旗舰项目"，这些项目使当地的基础设施建设实现公路、港口、铁路的全面配套，创造了大量的就业机会，并带动沿线工业园区、旅游业和房地产的投资。

在过去很长一段时间，西方媒体将中非经济合作看作是政策性银行、基础设施和自然资源的组合。具体来说，中国政策性银行与非洲国家签署了一笔担保协议，以非洲国家的自然资源为担保获得一笔优惠贷款，再用优惠贷款在非洲国家兴建基础设施。该模式曾被西方媒体认为是为了满足中国国内的资源能源需求。但如今，中非经济合作的融资选择大大增加，政策性银行的作用减弱。同时，中国国有企业和民营企业共同构成投资的主体，尤其是民营企业已经成为中非经济合作的重要增长点。

2017年，麦肯锡一份名为《下一个世界工厂：中国投资如何重塑非洲》的研究报告中，详细描述了中国企业在非洲的投资浪潮。2017年有超过1万家中国企业在非洲运营，主要集中在尼日利亚、赞比亚、坦桑尼亚和埃塞俄比亚等国。这些企业有约三分之一属于制造业，绝大多数是小微企业。根据美国传统基金会的研究，中国对非投资组合已经呈现出多元化趋势，除了矿产资源、基础设施等传统优势项目，还包括房地产、银行、金融、保险、物流和零售等不同行业的投资。"一带一路"倡议实施以来，中国对非洲国内生产总值增长的贡献率每年都在5％以上。此外，还出现了一批了解非洲、扎根非洲的中国商人和技术人员，这些人才已成为中非经贸可持续发展的宝贵资源，有利于向非洲进行各领域的技术转移。

普惠是一种以人为本的发展理念，包括人与人、人与自然、人与社会的全面发展，涉及人类发展指数、绿色发展指数、社会福利指数、幸福指数等多个评价标准。习近平主席指出："要积极引导经济全球化发展方向，着力解决公平公正问题，让经济全球化进程更有活力、更加包容、更可持续，增强广大民众参与感、获得感、幸福感。"在2017年5月举行的"一带一路"国际合作论坛上，习近平宣布中国将向沿线发展中国家提供20亿元人民币（约合2.92亿美元）紧急粮食援助，向南南合作援助基金增资10亿美元，在沿线国家实施100个"幸福家园"、100个"爱心助困"、100个"康复助医"等项目。在发达国家纷纷陷入"援助疲劳"的情况下，中国与其他发展中国家团结互助，这有利于解非洲等发展中地区的燃眉之急。

普惠发展致力于减少贫困人口和促进社会公平，但并不完全等于向弱势群体提供慈善救助。除了维持基本生存需求的人道主义援助，普惠发展绝大部分通过贸易、金融和技术培训等方式展开。2015年以来，中国已为非洲提供了3万个政府奖学金的名额，并培训了20万名各类职业技术人员，帮助非洲国家提升劳动力素质。2019年世界银行发布《"一带一路"经济学：交通走廊发展机遇与风险》报告，该报告提出"一带一路"倡议的全面实施可帮助3200万人摆脱中度贫困，全球和"一带一路"沿线的贸易额增幅将分别达到6.2%和9.7%，沿线发展中国家的外国直接投资增幅将达到7.6%。推动普惠贸易、普惠金融、普惠教育，提升发展中国家的自主生产能力，促进非洲的工业化和出口贸易，避免因援助依赖带来永久贫困。

2004年，时任英国首相的布莱尔组建非洲委员会时曾说："提到非洲，总是给人一种荒凉的感觉。我曾在许多场合说过，我认为非洲是整个世界良知上的一块伤疤。"事实上，非洲大陆本身并不贫瘠，这里拥有世界40%的自然资源储备、60%未开垦的土地和10亿日益增加的劳动力。非洲没有理由继续贫困下去，非洲人民可以用自己的双手来创造财富。换言之，非洲需要的不是同情和援助，而是全球的团结与合作。这正是"一带一路"倡议和中非团结抗疫特别峰会的价值追求。

二、印尼：乘着"一带一路"的东风破浪前行[①]

中国和印尼是"一带一路"倡议的优势互补战略合作伙伴。中国愿意将"一带一路"倡议与"全球海上支点"战略结合，这将促进中国和印度尼西亚区域综合经济走廊的发展。

在2019年4月的"一带一路"论坛上，印尼和中国签署了价值640亿美元的23项投资和贸易合作谅解备忘录。对于印尼来说，这笔资金将重点用于四个经济走廊的开发项目：北苏门答腊是马六甲海峡地区的物流枢纽，北加里曼丹以其世界级的水力资源而闻名，北苏拉威西岛和巴厘岛则是中国人的热门旅游地。

据报道，印尼和中国已经在北苏门答腊瓜拉丹戎草拟了一份合作框架协议，这是印尼和中国的首个合作项目。2019年11月14日，印尼国有企业与荷兰鹿特丹港务局和浙江省海港投资运营集团的代表签署了瓜拉丹戎港开发协议书（HoA）。

除上述四个项目外，还有其他合作项目，例如雅万高铁、爪哇多地中型发电厂、加里曼丹中部的坑口燃煤电站、西爪哇省绒果尔经济特区、吉打拜综合工业区、苏门答腊油棕补种，以及西爪哇省勿加西的美佳达（Meikarta）综合工业区。

中国推动了大规模的基础设施建设、能源和交通项目以及制造业转移。印尼希望通过这一合作平台获得技术转移和培训等，并利用劳动力和旅游业等优势推动经济增长。

然而，除了所谓的债务陷阱问题外，人们对"一带一路"倡议下中国和印尼合作的长远利益，以及这种合作如何在减贫方面改善人民福祉，尚心存疑虑。

[①] 作者：保罗·鲁道夫·尤尼亚托，印度尼西亚科学院地区资源研究中心高级研究员，复旦发展研究院访问学者。

印尼中央统计局2019年的调查显示，印尼贫困人口约2600万人，占总人口的9.82％。实际数字还要更高，因为印尼政府设定的贫困线门槛很低，而且贫困统计数据与现实有出入。此外，新冠肺炎疫情对印尼经济造成了严重冲击，出口减少，外国直接投资和旅游收入下降，将有更多人陷入贫困。据基准预测，印尼2020年国内生产总值增长率将下降至2.1％，而悲观预测将下降至−3.5％。基准预测，是指经济增长下滑且复苏迅速。相反，所谓悲观预测，是指经济进一步萎缩，然后缓慢复苏。

（单位：％）

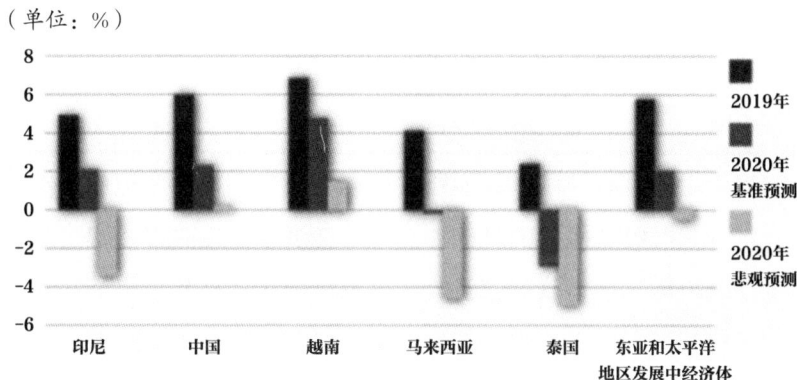

图1　经济增长预测①

印尼政府在《2020年国家中期发展计划》中将消除贫困列为重中之重。政府一直在发放大量现金和非现金福利，例如用于当地发展的乡村基金，并发行医疗福利卡和食品折扣，以消除偏远乡镇和城市地区的贫困。但是贫困仍然是一个不容忽视的大考验。脱贫攻坚的领域极为广泛，例如贫困趋势、社会援助、社会保障、社区项目和创造更多更好的就业机会。除此之外，这项工作还需要与国际

① 来源：世界银行，2020年。

社会齐头并进，推动减贫项目。在这方面，"一带一路"倡议无疑可推进印尼的减贫项目，印尼可从中受益。

对于不发达国家，基础设施投资和减贫是两个最紧迫的公共政策问题，两者之间有千丝万缕的联系。"一带一路"倡议的概念将基础设施投资与可持续创造就业维系在一起。这项提案已扩展到涵盖非基础设施投资，包括数字经济、文化纽带和人文交流。"一带一路"倡议还旨在满足在整个地区创造贸易、就业、旅游、移民和教育的迫切需求。因此，这项倡议将着力在全球范围内实现人员、思想、资本或网络的交流，以及社会文化交流。实际上，这项倡议在经济利益方面具有巨大潜力，包括参与建立基础设施连接，这些连接可影响中国与"一带一路"伙伴国家之间的货物和人力资源流动。

中国正在建设复杂的交通系统、水坝、港口、通信系统、相应的卫生设施和清洁用水、道路、桥梁，机场和水力发电厂现在是"一带一路"投资模式的基础。其中，亚洲基础设施投资银行是主要的金融机构，也有其他银行共同参与。许多项目将对当地社区产生重大影响，从而在当地、区域甚至全球范围内创造新的机会。在所有这些方面，决策者和利益相关者应充分利用"一带一路"的独特性，推动地方和国家经济发展。

对于印尼而言，必须进行基础设施方面的投资，与此同时，中国恰好可以满足印尼的需求。在三个方面，基础设施建设对印尼经济至关重要。首先，运输和物流基础设施、能源基础设施、水资源管理基础设施（灌溉和公共饮用水）以及信息和通信技术基础设施的发展将推动其竞争力的提升。其次，需要发展基础设施，解决印尼当前的供应危机。最后，众多部门的基础设施问题成了吸引外国直接投资和推动工业增长的障碍。

此外，"一带一路"给印尼带来的好处还包括中国的技术转移（技能和培训）以及基础设施投资。印尼群岛还可以利用人口优势。印尼海洋统筹部部长卢胡特·潘查丹表示，在实施"一带一路"项目的三个省（巴厘岛除外），贫困率有望降低至9%以下。同时，还必须避免债务陷阱等潜在问题。在"一带一路"合作中，印尼不应采用政府间的G2G模式，而应采用企业间的B2B模式，缓解国家预算中的债务风险。

世界银行的一项研究报告显示，截至2017年，中国使8亿人摆脱了贫困。中国是全球最早实现千年发展目标中减贫目标的发展中国家。尽管贫困标准不断提高（从1978年的100元/人提高到2005年的693元/人），但中国扶贫脱贫工作依然成果斐然。1986至2006年间，中国农村贫困人口从2.5亿人减少到2150万人，贫困人口的比例从30.7%下降到1.6%。这也证明中国实现了联合国千年发展目标中的减贫目标。中国向120多个国家提供帮助，推动其实现千年发展目标，对全球减贫贡献超过70%。这是人类历史上的"中国奇迹"。

（单位：万）

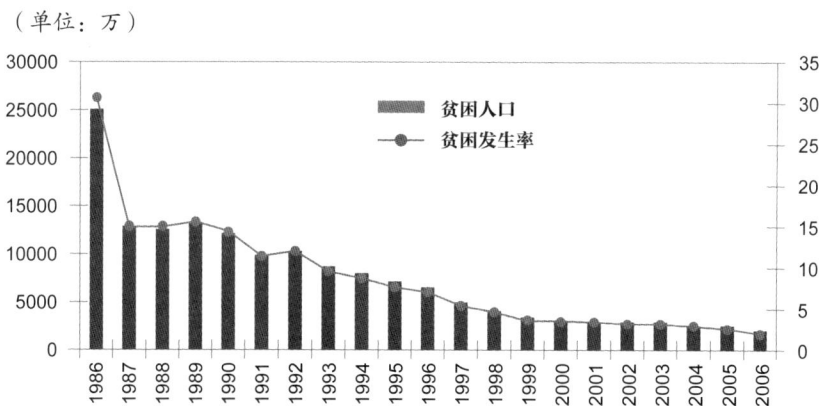

图2　1986年至2006年中国农村贫困人口及贫困发生率[1]

基于这个成功案例，包括印尼在内的"一带一路"伙伴国家完

---

[1] 资料来源：国务院发展研究中心，2006年。

全可以向中国学习。中国的扶贫经验值得其他国家借鉴。除基础设施外，还可以学习中国政府如何制定扶贫战略。据国务院扶贫开发领导小组办公室称，中国扶贫成功有四个驱动因素：改革开放（体制创新）；经济增长和基础设施建设；城乡一体化发展；扶贫开发和自力更生。这些方案为正在考虑减贫战略的国家提供了重要的经验和启示。

中国政府制定了适合国情的战略。扶贫不仅提供资金、食品或药品等扶助，而且还建立了相应的基础设施，改善人民群众的生活质量和谋生能力。除国务院扶贫开发领导小组办公室外，相关省、自治区、直辖市和地（市）、县级政府也成立了相应的组织机构。

这些战略和政策的实施产生了重大影响：加快了欠发达地区的发展，改变经济重心的轨迹，并大大减少了中国的贫困人口。

"一带一路"为不发达国家带来了新一轮的机遇，特别是在基础设施建设方面，推动了这些国家的公路、铁路、桥梁和港口建设。这项倡议不仅打开了国有和私有基础设施投资的"泄洪闸"，而且还促进了劳动力和旅游业的流动，以及在教育和减轻贫困方面的合作。因此，"一带一路"倡议应在各国人民、人才流动和社会文化领域之间建立更多的合作关系，不仅是经济往来，还应形成中国与其他国家之间的深层次互联互通和共同繁荣的人文交流。

三、中非扶贫合作与经验交流[①]

非洲是一个由50多个国家组成的大陆，与中国国情不尽相同，近几十年来在减贫方面的经验极度匮乏，收效甚微。尽管中国与诸多非洲国家有不少相似之处，但事实上，中国也曾一度处于糟糕的

---

① 作者：凌迈，浙江师范大学非洲研究所研究员。

境况，甚至有些方面还不如一些非洲国家。当年中国面临的脱贫艰巨程度丝毫不亚于如今的马拉维。

但是，自改革开放以来，截至2014年，中国国内生产总值（GDP）年均增长率约为10％，人均GDP增长近49倍。中国占全球经济的份额从1978年的2.7％上升至2019年的16％；人均GDP从1978年的155美元上升至2019年的1万美元以上。1981年，按每人每天1.9美元（2011年购买力平价）的标准计算，中国的贫困率为88.3％；2010年，这一数据降至11.2％（Liu，2020）[1]。据世界银行预计，全球极端贫困人口（每人每天生活费不足1.9美元）的数量已从1990年的18.5亿人下降至2015年的约7.36亿人。同期，中国已帮助6.027亿人脱贫，占全球总脱贫人口的54％。即每天脱贫人口高达25万人，或每分钟脱贫200人（World Bank，2017）[2]。

中国为全球减贫作出的贡献超过了任何其他国家。40年来，中国脱贫人口高达7亿多人，甚至超过了整个欧洲2016年的总人口数（7.41亿人）。此外，2018年，农村贫困人口平均年收入上升至10371元（约合1530美元），经通胀调整后同比增长8.3％。中国只用了20多年便取得了全世界用200年所取得的成就：从贫困线（每天1.25美元）以上人口占五分之一变成贫困线以下人口占五分之一。（Chandy，2015）[3]这一瞩目成就很大程度上归功于这段时期内的经济快速增长。中国的发展经验表明，确保经济增长跨部门、跨地区并使贫困人口广泛参与具有重要意义。

---

[1] Liu, X.(2020). A Critique of Precision Precision Poverty Alleviation: Does China Approach Adequate Policy Tools? Journal of Business and Adminstration Studies Vol. 14, No.1.

[2] World Bank. (2017). "From Local to Global: China's Role in Global Poverty Reduction and the Future of Development." The world Bank, Washington, DC.

[3] Chandy, L., Kato, H., and Kharas, H. (Eds) (2015). The Last Mile in Ending Extreme Poverty. Brookings Institution Press.

在对其他发展中经济体（特别是其中几个仍依赖发展援助的非洲国家）来说，可借鉴中国减贫成就的关键方面包括：中国如何与国际援助机构合作，如何发展农业和农村，如何扩建基础设施，以及如何营造良好环境推动企业蓬勃发展和创造就业机会。此外，中国在减贫方面的成就可能还要部分归功于1986年首次推出的区域精准扶贫计划，当时331个县被确定为国家重点扶持贫困县。（Zhang et al，2003）[1]2001年，随着农村贫困人口的减少，调研发现，将县列为扶贫单位已不再适合中国国情；此后，乡镇取代了县，成为扶贫基本单位，使扶贫更为精准。

自2013年习近平首次提出精准扶贫之后，中国的脱贫工作取得了辉煌成就。但中国领导集体清醒地认识到，脱贫攻坚计划仍然任重道远。截至2015年底，仍有6000余万农村人口生活在贫困线以下，全国有14个连片特困地区、832个贫困县、12.9万个贫困村。习近平主席是一位有雄心壮志的领导人，他决定进一步采取措施，全面落实扶贫对象帮扶到户，拟于2020年之前全面消除中国的绝对贫困。

中国政府设定了一个新的宏伟目标，从2016年起每年都要完成1000万以上贫困人口的脱贫任务，并计划到2020年使剩余的4335万农村人口全部脱贫。鉴于巨大的城乡差距和地区差距，中央政府和地方政府深刻认识到，2020年农村贫困人口全部脱贫这一目标的完成并不意味着中国反贫困事业的终结。2020年后，随着长期困扰中国农村的原发性绝对贫困的消失，中国农村贫困将进入一个以转型性的次生贫困和相对贫困为特点的新阶段。

中国的领导集体在减贫方面的重大成就，植根于坚实、有针对

---

[1] Zhang, L., Huang, J., and Rozelle, S. (2003). China's War on Poverty: Assessing Trageting and the Growth Impacts of Poverty Programs. Journal of Chinese Economic and Business Studies,1(3), 301–317.

性的全面协调的扶贫战略，此外，还依赖于国家领导能力、目标坚定、自力更生、万众一心。中国政府有一种特殊能力，能不断认识到在其他国家已尝试的众多理论和思想对本国的建设性意义。中国政府能够在其政策方针中践行这些理论和思想体系。因而，这些理论和思想体系在国家层面内得以持续下去，层层落实到经济、生态和社会经济状况各不相同的各级政府。中国在扶贫方面取得了瞩目成就，这主要归功于中国人民的无私贡献、通过国家产业政策实行的强有力领导和体现的奉献精神、经济高速发展、扶贫宏观经济政策、政府扶贫政策以及精准扶贫项目。所有这些均可归纳为三个方面——亲贫经济增长政策；农村社会保障网；以发展为导向的扶贫战略和计划（Lin Jian et al.，2009）[1]，从而表明中国政府在扶贫领域的政策是卓有成效的。

中国政府制定了一项政策，让发达的东部省份与较为落后的西部省份进行结对帮扶。这一政策体系通常称为"对口支援"。左常升（2018：34）认为，发达省份可向与之结对的经济欠发达省份提供各方面的资源投入和扶助[2]。

为缩小东西部地区经济发展差距，建立了东西部对口扶贫体系。对口扶贫双方本着优势互补、互利双赢、长期合作、共同发展的原则，在政府援助、企业合作、社会援助、产业发展、干部交流、人才培养和劳动力转移等领域，采用多种形式开展多层次的扶贫合作。中国前领导人邓小平指出，在改革开放进程中，先富裕起来的地区应该对贫困地区进行帮扶。这项扶贫战略旨在确保所有中国人实现共同富裕。

---

[1] Liu J., X. Li and F. Liu. (2009). A Study on Povety Reduction in Rural China. Beijing: China Finance and Economics Press.

[2] Changsheng, Z. (2018) (ed) "The Evolution of China's Poverty Alleviation and Development Policy (2001–2015). Springer, pp. 34.

习近平主席于2013年强调了精准扶贫计划落实到"个人"的重要性。习近平主席提出，扶贫工作应该更加精准，从而使有限的扶贫资金发挥最大的作用。自从习近平主席发表讲话以来，中国的扶贫政策注重"授人以渔"，而非"授人以鱼"。向贫困人口提供资产和机会，帮其立业，助其奋发，规避纯粹的"施舍"。扶贫项目旨在提高贫困农村家庭的创收能力。中国政府创新了农村扶贫机制，使政府能够为基本公共服务、人力资本开发以及对农业、企业和基础设施的大量投资不断扩大扶持力度，形成滚雪球效应。

2015年，中国政府进一步强调，必须坚决打赢脱贫攻坚战，确保到2020年所有贫困地区和贫困人口一道迈入全面小康社会。也就是说，应制定缩小经济发展差距的战略规划和政策措施，解决衣食住行问题，消除贫困，通过解决气候变化带来的一系列问题改善环境，提高自主能力。如果中国能够通过消除贫困和缩小发展差距实现2020年的如期脱贫目标，这将是中国改革开放的又一个里程碑。中国将提前10年实现联合国《2030年可持续发展议程》的第一目标：消除一切形式的贫穷。因此，"十三五"规划中对扶贫脱贫提出了具体的要求和措施。这是中国领导集体首次将减贫作为中国五年规划的重要组成部分，并把脱贫攻坚任务作为一项强制性指标。

2016年，世界银行报告申明，中国政府扶持项目包括提高贫困人口的收入、实施早期儿童发展、提供优质的教育和卫生医疗、面向贫困家庭的现金转移支付、农村基础设施建设和住房改造补贴等。这些措施都是减贫的有效途径。此外，据伊泽伦（2019）称，中国政府已将其2019年扶贫资金的一部分提前划拨给了地方政府。[1]已划拨给28个省、自治区和直辖市的扶贫资金总额高达130亿美元，

---

[1] Ehizuelen, M.M.O. (2019). China's Last Lap in Eradicating Poverty by 2020.ChinaDaily, 14th March, 2019. Retrieved 17 April 2020 from global.chinadaily.com.cn/a/2019/14/WS5C89b8da3106c65c34ee93a.html.

占2018年总额的86％。这130亿美元专项拨款中，一部分用于扶持新疆、西藏、云南部分地区，甘肃、四川等特困地区。扶贫专项资金涵盖多个领域，包括改善民生、农村基础设施资金、农业补贴、贴现贷款。[①]此外，预计每年将创造1300万个城市就业机会，使近年来的失业率保持在4％的低水平（Hu，2018）[②]。

此类扶助的目标是激发贫困户自主脱贫的内生动力，提高贫困户自主脱贫的积极性。中国人民对美好生活的向往极为强烈。多部门协同、有针对性的战略、卓越领导才能、不懈创新（例如农村淘宝等农村电子商务），已成为中国扶贫的核心推动力。中国在减贫方面取得的种种成就得益于中国政府强有力的领导、大规模的资源调配能力与创新实践能力。为了使亿万中国人民摆脱贫困，中国领导人毅然走出舒适区，以经济现代化为中心，开辟改革开放新道路，"摸着石头过河"，逐渐走出困境。

所有这些举世瞩目的成就表明，尽管2020年新冠肺炎疫情形势严峻，但中国一定会在临近胜利的节骨眼上"百尺竿头，更进一步"，取得扶贫攻坚战的最终胜利。只要全国人民众志成城，中国就能实现"两个一百年"奋斗目标和中华民族伟大复兴的中国梦。这种发展模式应成为非洲一体化的驱动因素。难怪发展经济学专家断言，中国的经济快速转型及其非凡发展轨迹可为非洲提供借鉴。中国过去的社会经济状况与非洲国家十分相近，但在一段时期后却取得了举世瞩目的经济增长。

在国内开展脱贫攻坚战的同时，中国还积极扶助其他发展中国家，例如非洲各国。这些国家希望借鉴中国的减贫经验，帮助非洲4

---

① 同上页。

② Hu, B. (2018). China's Economic Transformation. DOC Research Institute. Retrieved 6th July, 2019 from https://doc-research.org/2018/01/chinas-economic-transformation/.

亿多贫困人口脱贫。2018年9月召开的中非合作论坛北京峰会上，习近平主席重申了他在三年计划中支持非洲扶贫的庄重承诺，为非洲大陆提供600亿美元资金支持，推动实现联合国减贫目标（2030年之前在全球范围内消除极端贫困）以及2063年非洲议程。研究表明，贫穷和失业是非洲的主要问题。众多非洲国家无法实现以减贫为核心的千年发展目标。（Asante，2017）[1]从这个意义上来说，中国的600亿美元资金支持对非洲的可持续发展至关重要。

非洲和中国商定，中方将在加强自身减贫努力的同时，增加对非援助，在非洲实施200个"幸福生活工程"和以妇女儿童为主要受益者的减贫项目。这些项目包括南南合作援助基金。该基金将推动非洲实现联合国《2030年可持续发展议程》的目标、制定2015年《约翰内斯堡行动计划》，其中包括进一步加强减贫经验分享。除此之外，中国重申将继续举办中非减贫与发展会议，并将其列为在中非合作论坛框架下的正式分论坛。这一举措使中非双方可共同探索扶贫政策和战略，同时逐步建立一个多层次的政府间和社会间扶贫对话平台。我们正是在这一背景下着眼于非洲国家汲取中国扶贫经验的潜力。

从农业带动经济增长和农村家庭收入多样化的角度看，中国农业快速发展对非洲国家的减贫工作有一定借鉴意义。首先，政府的扶贫工作广泛集中于农村地区，因此中国的扶贫项目特别注重农村和农业的发展。但是，考虑到两种不同的国情，在广泛借鉴中国经济增长和减贫战略经验时，非洲国家应倍加谨慎。

尽管中国文化多元，幅员辽阔，但中国一直是个统一国家，而非洲则是由50多个国家组成的大洲，其社会、经济和环境条件各不相同。中国的社会政治和人口状况比非洲更占优势。但是，中国成

---

[1] Asante, R. (2017). "China's Security and Economic Engagement in West Africa: Constructive or Destructive?" China Quarterly of International Strategic Studies, Vol. 3, No. 4, pp. 575–596.

功改善了农村人口的生活水平，非洲完全可以借鉴。另外，非洲国家需要了解中国小农经济是如何发展起来的，同时也要从中国农业发展面临的一系列困难中汲取经验，例如如何解决社会发展不平衡（城乡差距加大）、农村土地所有权不清、农业高度集约化所导致的环境污染和自然资源退化等问题。

经济的持续高增长是减贫的必要条件，这对非洲国家来说仍是所要面临的巨大挑战。中国工业和服务业的增长是基于40多年前开始的农业改革。非洲可从中国政府的这些政策中吸取经验，学习中国吸引和规范外国投资以推动工业化和技术发展的策略与方法。

快速的经济增长和积极的宏观经济、工业和社会政策，推动中国跻身于中高收入国家和全球经济强国的行列，非洲国家同样渴望在不久的将来成为中等偏上收入国家。在这一时期，通过双边贸易和资金流动，或者间接地通过增长溢出效应和贸易条件的影响，中国的转型对非洲国家的发展道路产生了越来越大的影响。

尽管中国的减贫经验看起来都不错，但是非洲国家在学习借鉴的过程中应注意以下四个方面：

第一，直到20世纪70年代后期，中国大部分经济资源都处于国家控制之下，并且借助体制改革，这些资源在农村地区得到了公平的分配。中国赋予了贫困人口自主权。非洲的权力和政治结构完全不同，充斥民事和军事官僚主义、政治和宗教力量、拥有大量土地的农村精英阶层以及根深蒂固的氏族制度。中国的整个改革进程中，中国领导集体一直将目标锚定贫困地区。然而，非洲的贫困地区中，拥有土地的家庭极少，很难分配土地等经济资源。

第二，与中国相比，非洲的国家机构往往比较薄弱，这对减贫项目的开展以及向非洲人提供关键的社会服务和基础设施都产生了不利影响。

第三，非洲人口增长迅猛。高生育率造成的高抚养比率似乎是经济增长和减贫的一个制约因素。

第四，充斥极端主义和恐怖主义，社会治安状况糟糕，这可能是制定和贯彻扶贫政策的严重制约因素。

中国的经验教训对非洲国家具有重要意义。中国通过基础设施的建设、政府主导的扶贫开发改善了贫困地区的生产条件，为中国扶贫作出了巨大贡献。政府扶贫项目还向贫困人口提供小额贷款和培训，增加贫困人口收入并提升其自主脱贫能力。

有鉴于此，中非双方互相学习、共同进步是至关重要的，也是明智可取的。非洲各国需要根据自身的历史、文化和经济特点，选择性地借鉴中国扶贫经验。也就是说，在借鉴国外扶贫经验的本土化过程中，非洲国家应形成具有非洲自身特色的减贫模式。对中国而言，减贫合作过程中，指导思想应为建设人类命运共同体，原则应为基于合作的平等、包容性和多样性，尊重非洲扶贫战略的自主性，调动各方面的力量开展综合扶贫措施。

另外，中非双方应根据自身的能力分享发展经验，努力深化合作，从逻辑上讲，其核心应为"我做了什么"，而不是"你需要做什么"（互相追赶，互相学习）。应努力加强合作，使中国学者更为深入地了解非洲的贫困与发展情况，并在中国传播这些信息。应加大中非扶贫资金投入，开展联合研究和交流，深化减贫经验分享、强化培训和能力建设活动。

第四篇

未来可期

Chapter IV

中国脱贫的挑战与可持续发展

扫码获取

★ 脱贫故事分享
★ 脱贫攻坚解读
　与回顾

第一章
下一个百年的挑战

一、中国的减贫奇迹与经验[①]

几十年来，全球贫困人口在不断减少：20世纪60年代，全球约有50%的人生活在极端贫困中（见图1）。过去40年间，中国为此作出的贡献一直名列前茅，消灭了全球70%以上的贫困。

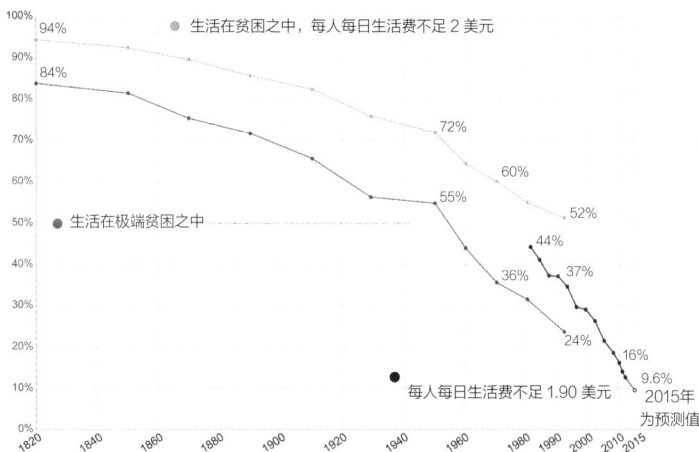

图1　1820—2015年贫困人口占世界总人口比例[②]

---

① 作者：伊恩·高登，牛津大学全球化与发展学教授，曾任世界银行副行长。

② 数据来源：1820—1992 Bourguignon and Morrison（2002），《世界公民贫富差距》，《美国经济评论》；1981—2015世界银行（PovcalNet）。
可视化交互数据来自OurWorldinData.org。作者马克思·露丝通过CC-BY-SA协议授权。

中国贫困人口的减少是一段具有历史意义的成功故事。40年来，中国政府有条不紊地开展了脱贫运动，用一代人的时间把中国变成了一个中等收入国家。

据世界银行统计，自改革开放以来，中国超过7亿人脱离了贫困，中国贫困人口比例由20世纪90年代初的60%左右降低到2014年的不到2%（见图2、图3）。而这一切都是通过齐心协力的经济现代化实现的。

（单位：%）

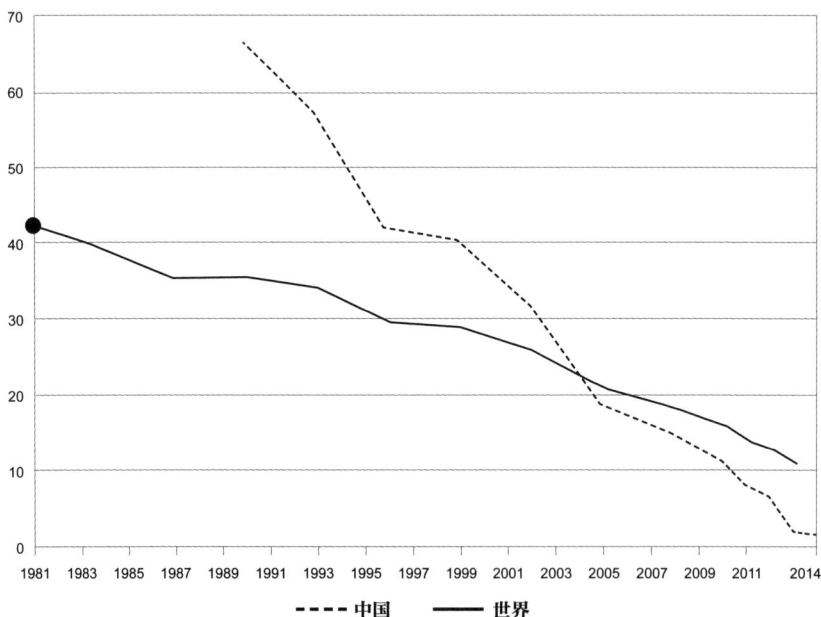

图2　1981—2014年中国和世界贫困人口（国际标准）[①]

---

① 数据来源：世界银行。

（单位：%）

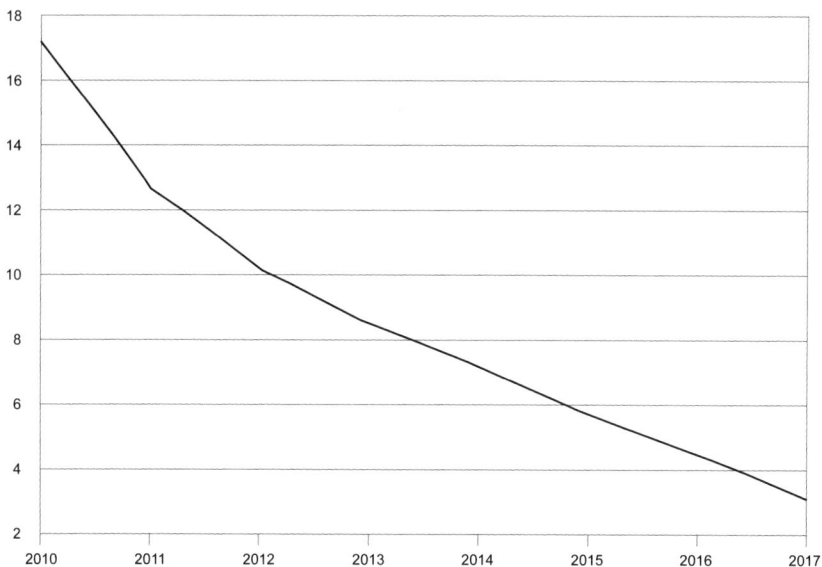

图3　2010—2017年中国贫困人口（国家标准）①

　　40年前的中国，农业从业人口占75%以上。而如今，这一比例降到了25%以下，制造业和随后出现的服务业取代农业成为最大的就业领域。这和城市化的推进、全民教育和健康卫生服务的承诺，以及净水和电力的供给有关。40年前，中国只有20%人口生活在城镇，至2016年近14亿中国人中有超过60%的城镇居民（见图4）。自2000年以来，城市财富增长了4倍多（见图5）。40年来，在城市化不断推进的同时，中国人的预期寿命增加了12年，达到了77岁。平均收入增长超过40倍，如果按购买力计算，人们的平均收入增长更是超过了60倍。

---

① 数据来源：世界银行。

（单位：百万）

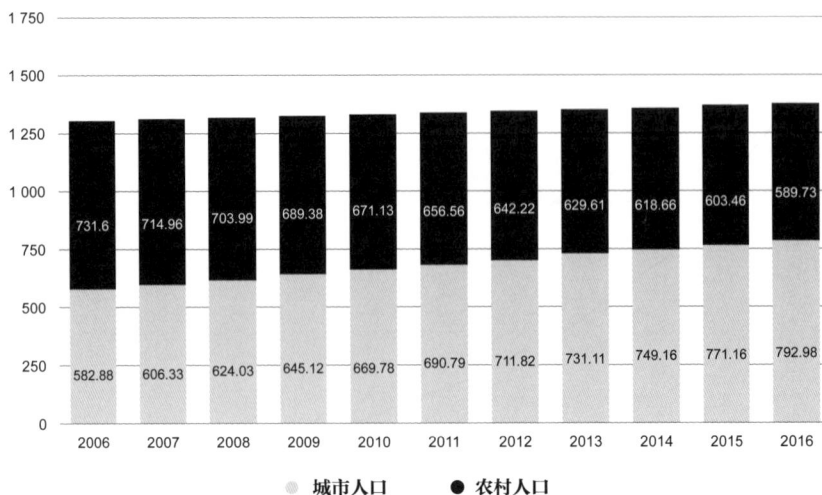

图4　2006—2016年中国城市和农村人口[①]

（单位：元）

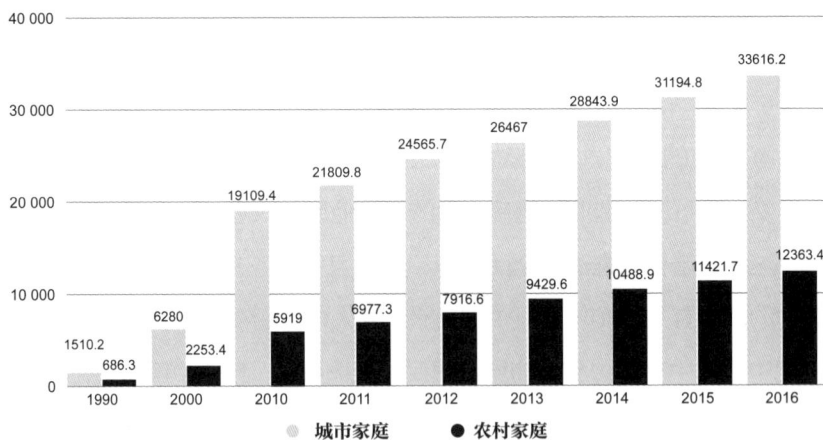

图5　1990年、2000年和2010—2016年中国农村和城市地区人均收入[②]

---

① 数据来源：中国国家统计局。

② 同上。

习近平主席在2015年减贫与发展高层论坛上宣布，中国政府的目标是在2020年实现中国贫困人口全部脱贫。考虑到中国所取得的非凡经济成就，这一目标似乎并非不切实际。

那么，中国是怎样取得如此辉煌的成就的？发展中国家可以从中国减贫的举措中学到什么？

中国成功的关键在于，改革开放后，中国在经济强劲增长的同时，还专门针对减少贫困制定了发展政策。经济合作与发展组织认为，以发展为导向的领导方式、建立国家共识，这两者都是中国能消灭贫困的主要原因。为此，国家需要严格执行发展和社会政策，设立一套衡量政策绩效的统一系统，私营和公共部门需要在国家统一的共同目标激励下一起努力。设立准确的发展目标、鼓励包括公有和私营部门在内的全国人民一同为取得成果而努力，这两点在中国减贫战略中起到了重要作用，为其他正在和贫困作斗争的发展中国家树立了榜样。

如果没有连贯有效的政策执行机制，这些雄心勃勃的目标是不可能实现的。中国的一大独特之处在于其在动态学习中试验发展政策的方式：如果某项政策经测试有效就在全国范围内进行推广，反之就撤销。事实证明，这样的方法非常有效。自从中国开始扶贫脱贫工作以来，试行各种政策一直很普遍：某项政策出台后会先在一些地方施行，政府会据此评估该项政策的有效性，然后在全国范围内推行有效政策。而这都要归功于这个幅员辽阔的国家对来自全国各地的公务员的监督和轮换。

比如说，在20世纪70年代末出台的促进农业生产力提高的土地所有权制度，正是农村家庭联产承包责任制试验成功的结果。市场政策、资本自由流动的逐步放开、贸易改革和金融交易所一开始都先在经济特区进行了试点，自由贸易区和经济技术开发区代表了中国渐进性和实验性政策制定的成功。

位于华中地区的长沙等城市的发展，正是这一独特发展战略的一大例证。长沙起点低，是一个相对落后的地区。但近几十年来，这座城市发展惊人：2000年至2012年间，长沙人均国内生产总值增长了3倍，产业结构由重工业和制造业转变为高附加值的资本密集型产业，比如汽车和传媒通信行业。这是通过国家干预（尤其是中部崛起计划）和有效的权力下放实现的。国家投资研发和劳动培训计划，同时推行政策促进不同城市与省份之间的内部竞争。这些措施确保了高新产业的发展和经济的快速增长，促进了越来越多快速发展的城市和地区改善教育和基础设施。地方上则由"领导小组"体系帮助协调国家、地方和企业的活动，以便实现有效增长。与此同时，地方政府还会推进有利于当地人力资本发展的项目，吸引人才，从中国其他地区、国际组织、其他国家以及国际专家汲取经验。

就像在其他发展领域密切监测结果、谨慎规划试验一样，政府会通过试验和纠错改善结果，然后将经验推广到越来越多的地区和人民之中，一直以来这都是中国减贫战略的核心。致力于广泛、深入地完成任务，通过实践并根据地方情况来理解最佳国内外案例——这两者双管齐下是中国最重要的经验。

实施政策所需的资金一方面来自政府对基础设施和技术创新方面的投资，另一方面则来自对国际资源和投资的负责使用。而负责使用国际资源和投资，同时也有利于中国学习、消化国际上一些最佳实践案例，并根据自身情况调整应用。这种乐于检验国际经验、乐于与地方社区协商并调整实施改革的开放心态，是我们可以从中国的案例中学到的另一项重要经验。

早期，最初的减贫政策创造了大量的就业机会，私营、公共投资，交通运输和通信基础设施的建设带来了新的岗位，工人被转移到了服务业和制造业生产部门。如今，超过80%的就业与大约60%的投资来自私营部门（见图6）。

（单位：%）

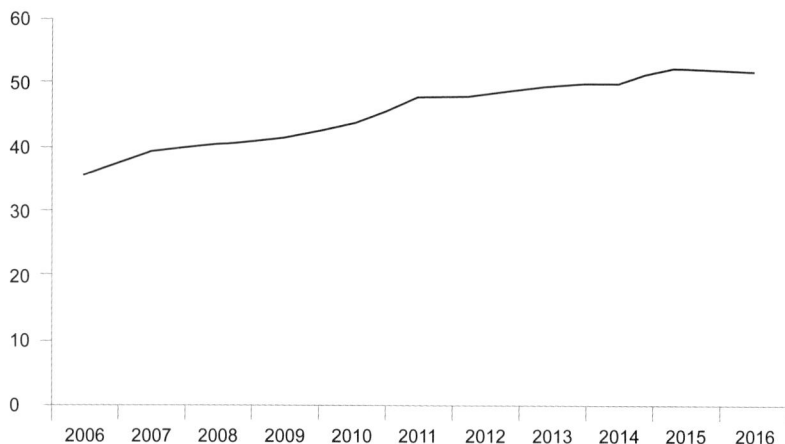

图6　2006—2016年私营部门投资占总投资比例①

　　如果没有搭建起令人惊叹的教育、社会和科研机构网络，如果没有形成广泛的交通和通信线路，这一切都不可能实现。随着社会基础越来越坚实、社会影响越来越深远，中国政府为贫困人口打造了一块摆脱贫困的跳板，激发他们的责任感，让他们有机会获得教育和科技资源。在这一过程中，自力更生是一个关键，无论是在个人、社区、城市还是在机构层面都是如此。要想进入顶级教育机构或成为公务员都得经过激烈的竞争，而且这些竞争的参照依据都是优异的成绩表现，因此全中国上下准备之完善、能力水平之高在发展中国家堪称前所未有。

　　中国发展的状况虽然令人惊叹，但同样也存在风险，尤其是，

---

① 数据来源：中国国家统计局。

中国的这种快速发展在环境上是否具备可持续性。因此，中国需要减少水和能源的大量使用，克服污染问题，解决对化石燃料的依赖。中国政府意识到了这些挑战，并将它们纳入了2020年消灭极端贫困的目标之内。中国政府渴望维护社会稳定，获得可持续发展所带来的好处，因此他们已经开始研究和制定广泛的环保政策。习近平主席曾表示，要把中国建设成为生态文明的国家。面对气候变化问题，中国一马当先，在再生能源方面的发展脚步明显加快，短时间内成为最大的太阳能和风能生产国和使用国。通过这些努力，中国在2005年至2017年成功实现了碳强度下降46%，提前超额完成了2020年以前减少45%碳强度的目标。

重新造林也一直是中国政府的重点工作。1978年起，中国共种植了超过660亿棵树，比如干旱的西北地区，如今已经拥有了先进的种植技术，可以种出一道"绿色长城"，阻止荒漠化蔓延。另一项值得关注的大规模植树造林计划则在河北省，政府希望在这个中国受污染最严重的地区之一种植超过100万英亩树木。环境问题是促成这一计划的重要动力，但除此之外，公共健康问题和经济方面的考虑也是相当重要的因素。呼吸道和心血管疾病被认为是中国最主要的两项疾病，而河北省人民正遭受污染的严重影响。

中国经济快速发展带来了一些副作用，日益突显的环境问题是其中之一，而另一个副作用则是日益加剧的贫富差距。过去，中国社会非常贫穷，但同时也是世界上收入差距较小的社会之一。改革开放后，收入的快速增长带来的必然结果就是，一些人比其他人更快实现了脱贫致富。中国的基尼系数近年来一直徘徊在0.4以上（见图7），高于世界标准。基尼系数越高，就意味着社会贫富差距越大。尽管根据这个标准，美国、巴西和墨西哥都比中国高，但大多数亚洲和欧洲国家的基尼系数都低于中国。一定程度上来说，贫富差距加大的原因在于收入的增加，体现在中国工业的发展为农村贫困人口创造了大量的就业机会，同时由于城市福利政策的出台、城市公共服务的提高，农村人口在城市工作能获得更高的收益，因此使得农村人口大量向城市转移。2015年城市占据了80%的财富，而1975年这一比例仅为30%。中国的贫富差距加剧问题呈现出了很强的地域性，反映了城市和农村地区之间的差距——城市地区收入增加比农村地区更快。

数值

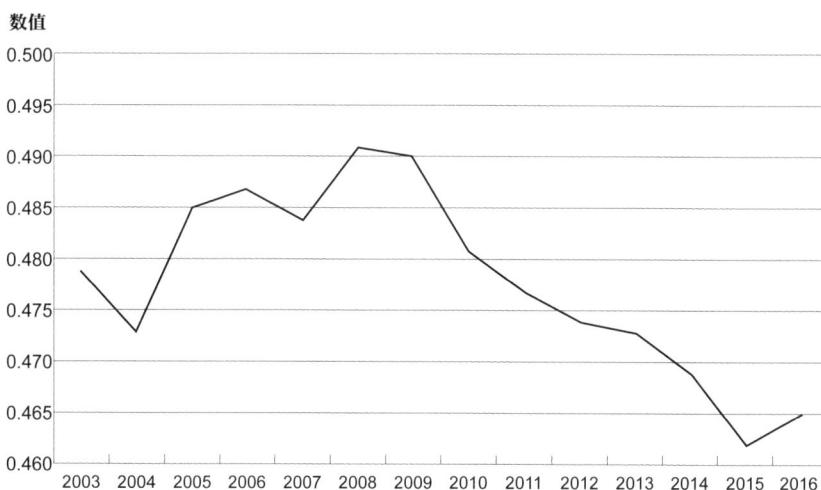

图7　2003—2016年中国基尼系数[①]

　　然而，有证据显示，通过在偏远的农村地区采取有针对性的干预措施、引入最低工资制度、努力解决腐败问题，这一趋势近些年出现了逆转。中国政府在推动经济从投资驱动型转变为消费驱动型之余，还把提高低收入人群购买力放在了首要位置。针对如何减少不平等问题发布官方指导文件，这是政府朝着这一目标迈出的重要步伐。这进一步巩固了中国作为社会政策新兴全球领导者的地位。

——————————————

① 数据来源：经合组织。

中国不仅是世界经济强国，而且还参与了国际管理。除了努力实现国际环保标准、带头应对气候变化问题外，中国在解决全球贫困问题上也发挥了越来越重要的作用。中方投资往往对准亚洲和非洲大陆，一来提供援助，二来为它们更好的交通、通信和市场发展及基础设施建设作出贡献。中国在亚洲基础设施投资银行、新开发银行和"一带一路"倡议的项目中发挥的领导作用同样也反映了中国对全球共同发展更广泛的国际承诺。

当然，中国的经验并不是应对贫困的唯一办法。每个国家开始治理贫困问题时的条件情况、时间节点都是独一无二的，面对的障碍和机会也各不相同。中国的模式并非通用的样板，但却可以启发其他国家在制定政策、作出决策时进行参考，并根据自身情况调整使用。一个值得注意的例子是，中国对农村生产力早期且持续至今的关注，实现了减少饥饿、提高农村贫困人口收入的双重目标。中国的增长策略依托的是对人力资本增长和基础设施在刺激经济繁荣发展上所起作用的深入理解，这为其他发展中国家提供了宝贵的经验：提供人们负担得起的教育和医疗服务，并为最贫困的家庭提供慷慨的援助补贴，有助于改善社会流动性。

过去40年间，中国展示了贫困是可以被打败的。中国提供了重要的经验教训：只要有决心，可持续发展的全球目标是可以实现的。在持续努力消灭国内贫困，进一步改善人民生活的同时，中国还将重视环境可持续性，关注低收入群体，进一步巩固扶贫成果。在过去40年取得的独特成就的基础上，中国正越来越多地投身于消除全球贫困的事业，鼓舞所有致力于实现可持续发展目标的国家。

二、合作共赢才是上策[①]

40年前，中国向世界打开大门，启动国家经济发展规划。在人类历史上，难道有任何其他比中国的改革开放更成功、帮助更多民众脱贫的扶贫计划吗？

想象一下所谓的"贫困金字塔"。1978年，中国有10亿人口，平均每10个人中就有9个生活在世界银行划定的"极端贫困线"（即每人每天1.9美元）以下，天天为吃饱肚子而发愁。

如今，贫困金字塔已经倒转过来。13亿多中国人的平均热量摄入增加了一倍，绝大部分人已经摆脱了饥饿之苦。前几代中国人，为了让自己和子女吃饱穿暖没日没夜地忙碌。如今，人们能够同餐共饮，享受家庭之乐。

自1978年起，中国经济持续数十年快速增长。根据"72法则"（以1％的复利计息，72年后，本金翻倍），中国经济几乎每七年翻一番。一部分中国民众的生活水平甚至提高了50倍。可以说，改革开放40年奇迹般的经济增长，比中国过去4000多年历史所创造的福祉还要更大、惠及的人数还要更多。

2004年，世界银行行长罗伯特·佐利克说，中国凭"一己之力"就让全球步入实现减贫目标的正轨。用他的话说："1981年至2004年，中国成功帮助超过5亿人口摆脱极端贫困。这无疑是减贫史上最伟大的飞跃。"

2017年，世界银行行长金墉指出，中国的成就堪称"人类历史上最伟大的故事之一"。他表示，中国已使8亿人口摆脱了极端贫困之苦，并且国民的人均寿命延长了10多年。

[①] 作者：格雷厄姆·艾利森，哈佛大学肯尼迪政府学院首任院长、教授，哈佛大学贝尔弗科学与国际事务中心主任。

依靠具有中国特色的市场经济，中国成功实现了经济飞跃，超越美国成为世界第一大经济体（按购买力平价计算）。

中国人民应该为自身努力和政府领导带来的伟大成就感到自豪。但也要认识到，当时，稳定的国际经济和安全秩序为亚洲奇迹（尤其是中国发展奇迹）提供了大前提。

在我们这个互通互联的世界中，有许多"小型核危机"（面对毁灭性挑战时，没有一个国家可以独善其身）。新冠病毒就是一个典型的例子。病毒没有护照，不分国界。当疫情蔓延成为全球性流行病时，没有一个国家可以完全封锁其疆界，因此每个国家都处于病毒威胁之下。无可否认的是，如今全世界77亿人都生活在这个小小的星球。正如肯尼迪总统在解释与苏联共存、共同面对核危机的必要性时所指出的那样："我们都呼吸着相同的空气。我们都珍惜着孩子的未来。我们也都是血肉之躯。"

新冠病毒大流行是一种"小型核危机"。对于保护生物圈使公民可以呼吸新鲜空气，管控金融危机以避免经济大萧条（及其政治后果），阻止大型恐怖主义的扩散等问题，紧密合作与良好伙伴关系为彼此带来的不仅仅是互惠互利。其实在这些领域中，如果没有对方的精诚合作，任何一个国家都无法确保其最重要的生存利益。

第二章
中国脱贫事业可持续发展

一、中国如何实现减贫目标①

深入研究中国改革开放的整个过程，可以得出这样的结论，过去40年来，中国不仅创造了经济增长奇迹，而且创造了社会稳定奇迹。创造双重奇迹的主要原因是，改革开放通过做大蛋糕，惠及千千万万普通中国人，随着国家经济发展，这增加了人们的幸福感和满足感。

减贫的实践和结果是这种共同发展的最好体现。回望1981年，当时中国人口占世界人口的22.4％，生活水平低于世界银行绝对贫困线标准（按2011年购买力平价计算每人每天低于1.9美元）的人口占世界贫困人口的46.4％。2018年，尽管中国人口占世界总人口的18.4％，但几乎所有中国人的生活水平都超过了绝对贫困线。五分之一的人类摆脱了贫困的泥沼，这个故事无疑向世界展示了中国在减贫方面的智慧和能力。

"把蛋糕做大"是公平分配的前提。1978年至2018年，中国国内生产总值（GDP）的实际年增长率为9.4％，不仅是这一时期的世界最高水平，而且在世界经济史上的其他任何时期同样没有先例。这样的增长速度使中国的生活水平有机会追赶发达国家。

根据世界银行按人均GDP的收入分类，1978年中国改革开放前

---

① 作者：蔡昉，中国社会科学院副院长、学部委员，中国社会科学院国家高端智库副理事长、首席专家。

夕，中国是低收入国家中最贫穷的国家之一。受益于人口红利和那段时期的全球化优势，中国在1993年和2009年分别跨过了中等偏低收入门槛和中等偏高收入门槛。2018年，中国人均GDP达到9771美元，已接近高收入门槛。

中国并没有止步于此。中国政府认为，经济增长、技术进步和全球化成果应由所有人共同分享。以下是中国经验分享的本质。首先，中国在这一时期的经济增长模式可以表现为一个资源再分配的过程，在这一过程中，同时实现了就业增长、收入增加和生产率提高。其次，随着劳动力市场的发展，对社会保障的需求越来越高，由此建立并完善了社会保障体系。此外，中国政府很早就启动了国家农村扶贫计划，并在计划落实的各个阶段都制定了具体目标。

经济发展模式的所有这些特点使中国成为世界减贫的杰出榜样和最大贡献者。根据世界银行的数据，1981至年2015年间，世界贫困人口的数量从18.927亿人减少到7.53亿人，而中国贫困人口的数量从8.778亿人减少到960万人。

也就是说，在这一期间，中国不仅丰富了人类脱贫攻坚经验，而且，中国为全球减贫事业作出了实际的重大贡献，贡献率高达76.18％。2015年，中国贫困线标准已高于世界银行最新贫困线标准。此后，中国继续以这一标准开展农村扶贫工作。2018年，中国农村贫困人口为1660万人，贫困率低至1.7％。

中国减贫事业的成功，是传统教科书所没有的，为以人为本的发展观树立了一个活生生的全新榜样。在实行扶贫战略的国家中，存在减贫成效递减的现象。一些学者和实务人士甚至认为这是减贫规律。随着减贫工作的成功，贫困人口减少到相对较少的人口比例，政策效果趋于减弱。这是因为，在减贫工作后期，剩余贫困人口往往带有特殊的不利特征。也就是说，无论是残疾、疾病、高龄、受教育程度低等弱势群体特征，还是居住、生产、生态等不利地理条件，都使他们积重难返，无法完全摆脱绝对贫困。

结果，在许多国家，减贫工作在最后关头陷入了困境。在实物投资领域，如果任何投资者遇到资本回报率下降的现象，都有理由停止向该项目继续注资。投资项目和扶贫开发的根本区别在于，后者是与作为发展最终目标的人打交道。中央政府秉承以人为本的发展理念，决心打破减贫成效递减的所谓"规律"，郑重承诺，到2020年，现行标准下的贫困人口全部脱贫，在中国历史上消除绝对贫困现象。

尽管这一目标肯定会按计划和预期完成，但中国已经开始部署下一步任务，继续推进减贫工作，包括规范扶贫政策和机制，巩固已取得的成果，关注和应对新的贫困成因，应对可能引发冲击型贫困的风险，以更高的标准推行新的扶贫战略，解决相对贫困问题。

二、建立长效机制，巩固脱贫攻坚成果[①]

在以人民为中心的发展模式下，中国农村绝对贫困人口大幅减少。按照中国政府在1986年确定的贫困线，到20世纪末中国已基本解决了温饱问题，到21世纪初，中国农村绝对贫困已经消失。

中国1986年确定的贫困线是一个非常低的赤贫线标准。因此，2012年中国政府按照中国经济社会发展的客观实际调整了贫困线标准，并决定到2020年全面消除农村绝对贫困现象。需要指出的是，2012年至今我国农村扶贫开发的基本条件已与改革开放以来任何时期农村扶贫开发的客观条件大不相同。

首先，改革开放以来的很长一段时间，贫困群体与经济发展之间的关系一直都比较密切，如农业发展、乡镇企业发展等的参与主

---

① 作者：李小云，中国农业大学文科讲席教授、国务院扶贫开发领导小组专家咨询委员会委员。

体实际上都是贫困农民。但是进入21世纪以后，贫困群体已经很难在经济发展的主流行业中增加收益。其次，城乡差距、贫富差距持续扩大，这也加大了按照原有的扶贫方式推进扶贫开发工作的难度。再次，城乡基本公共服务的差距越来越明显。

在这样的条件下，要想解决剩余贫困群体的现实问题，通过一般性经济开发的活动和一般性扶贫开发的支持可能很难奏效。因此，要超越现有的制度和路径的局限来减少结构性因素的不利影响，从而实现到2020年消除农村绝对贫困的奋斗目标。

正是基于上述背景，2012年以来的农村扶贫开发工作主要以精准扶贫和脱贫攻坚的形式展开。脱贫攻坚的目标是到2020年完全消除农村绝对贫困现象，其主要内容包括消除以2011年农民年均可支配收入2300元为标准的农村收入型贫困，以及"两不愁三保障"（不愁吃、不愁穿，义务教育、基本医疗、住房安全有保障）等不同方面。截至2019年底，农村绝对贫困人口已经减少到551万人，97%的贫困建档立卡户实现了"两不愁三保障"的目标。从目前来看，我们完全有把握到2020年底实现脱贫攻坚的最终目标。即便我们受到了新冠肺炎疫情的影响，但是这也不会从总体上改变决胜脱贫攻坚的基本面。

就脱贫攻坚工作而言，目前我们面临的重要挑战是如何巩固脱贫攻坚的成果。目前所取得的脱贫成果在很大程度上源于两个方面：一是在政策法规推动下所实现的脱贫，二是在资源供给保障下所带来的脱贫。虽然我们在脱贫攻坚战中已经探索了一系列制度性的脱贫机制的创新，如教育扶贫、健康扶贫等，并在很多地方性的脱贫实践中触及政策问题，如河北省邯郸市的扶贫保险机制创新等，但从总体上说，脱贫攻坚是一种暂时性的消除贫困的扶贫方式，并未太多涉及系统性的机制问题。

对于很大一部分具有劳动能力、具备一定条件的已经脱贫的群体而言，他们是在脱贫攻坚政策的支持下，通过提高收入摆脱贫困的。从总体上估算，目前这一群体仍然有3000万人左右，该群体的大部分人收入刚刚跨越贫困线。这个群体无论遇到任何风险，都极易返贫。实际上，新冠肺炎疫情发生以来，这种类型的贫困群体规模有所扩大，返贫趋势更加明显。因此，决胜脱贫攻坚的重点在于巩固脱贫攻坚的成果，而巩固脱贫攻坚成果的重点在于防止返贫。

与脱贫攻坚战中的扶贫工作不同的是，防止返贫工作以及决胜脱贫攻坚的关键在于逐步建立应对贫困的长效机制。除了在特殊情况下对贫困群体施以紧急援助，扶贫工作还应当成为经济社会发展中的日常行动。

其一，需要及早研究城乡一体化的就业制度。随着越来越多的贫困群体进入非农产业，如果没有促进贫困群体就业的制度，已经摆脱贫困的群体还有可能返贫，新的贫困问题就会发生。

其二，应从贫困群体自身能力提升的角度，改革现有的产业扶贫政策。在脱贫攻坚战中，产业扶贫大部分是在政府推动下开展的，具有很强的行政推动性的特点。从长效机制来考虑，则需要建立一个可持续的基于贫困群体能力和市场需求的开发机制。

其三，由于贫困地区的人才匮乏，在脱贫攻坚战中通过政府部门、国企和帮扶单位，以及第一书记驻村，极大地改善了贫困乡村在领导和管理方面的人才匮乏问题。但是从长效机制的角度考虑，如何确保贫困乡村拥有稳定的人力资源供给，也是巩固脱贫攻坚成果的一个重要方面。

其四，巩固脱贫攻坚成果不仅需要应对因各种风险出现的返贫，更需要着眼于构建防止新的贫困发生的长效机制。从目前来看，教育和健康是最容易在短期内导致返贫和在中长期发生新的贫困的重要领域。

三、数字技术：新工具带来新价值，新合作助力新增长[①]

数字技术助力劳动生产率提高，培育新市场和新增长点，为中国的减贫立下汗马功劳，也可成为国际经济发展的新动力。探索数字发展合作，因地制宜转化中国数字化经验，对促进后疫情时代国际经济复苏和社会发展至关重要。

中国脱贫攻坚的成就举世瞩目，其中数字技术发挥的创新和驱动作用功不可没。探索数字发展合作，因地制宜转化中国数字化经验，对促进后疫情时代国际经济复苏和社会发展至关重要。

改革开放以来，中国约8亿人口摆脱了贫困，对全球减贫的贡献率超过70%。数字技术的发展和应用，对中国民众改变生产生活方式、促进民生发展发挥了重要作用。

以农业为例。过去，中国亿万小农经历了农产品难以对接大市场的困境，农产品滞销一度成为常态。随着"互联网+"理念的引入，数字技术逐渐融入农产品种植、加工、流通、销售等各环节，实现了农业提质增效。

比如，在阿里巴巴农村电商的"亩产一千美金"计划推动下，手机成了"新农具"。农民可以在手机APP上观测农作物生长情况，通过电商平台销售产品，跟踪物流，获取顾客对农产品的消费评价。在数字技术的带动下，原本分散的农产品价值链条各环节得以整合，实现了农业附加值的提升。

农村电商在中国取得的成就表明，数字技术带来的红利并非局限于高收入国家和大城市。只要条件合适，在发展中国家和农村，其带来的经济和社会效益也大为可期。

当然，应当看到，农村电商在中国获得的成功实践得益于一系

[①] 作者：俞子荣，商务部国际贸易经济合作研究院副院长。

列因素和条件，包括中国巨大的市场需求、日益完善的交通和数字基础设施、良好的营商环境、对民生发展的重视、电商政策利好，以及各方的积极行动。这也说明，技术发展有效性的影响因素错综复杂，打造全方位的数字社会不能一蹴而就，必须分阶段、分步骤推进数字化经验本土化。

全球数字合作的条件已基本成熟。

从硬件条件看，电信基础设施的有效部署推动互联网以更便宜、更方便、更快捷的方式从发达国家向发展中国家普及。2019年，全球手机普及率超过80%，发达国家互联网使用率为86.8%，发展中国家互联网使用率也达到47%，这为全球数字合作奠定了基础。

从发展中国家的意愿看，尽管发展中国家数字技术发展起步较晚，但多数国家已着手开展相关规划和布局。越南、泰国、菲律宾、马来西亚等东南亚国家将数字化明确列为国家优先发展的方向，积极推进数字基础设施建设，健全监管法律框架，推进无现金支付，完善物流配送。卢旺达、埃塞俄比亚、肯尼亚、尼日利亚等非洲国家在完善通信设施、电子商务、数字能力建设等方面的合作需求空间巨大。发展中国家将愈加青睐通过数字发展合作的方式促进其经济社会发展。

从数字发展合作的形式看，国际社会相继出台数字发展合作方案。世界银行在科特迪瓦推出电子农业项目，旨在解决百万农村家庭"上网贵"的问题。作物生产和价格信息实时可查，提高了小农生产力。更多年轻女性接受数字技术培训，促进了贫困地区女性就业。

近年来，中国已通过多种方式在广大发展中国家推进数字领域的国际发展合作，包括援建数字基础设施、搭建数字贸易平台、开展数字科研合作、推广远程教育等，这为提升发展中国家数字化综合水平奠定了基础。

在改善数字基础设施方面，中国过去为亚非国家援建了大量基础设施，为受援助国经济社会发展提供了动能。中国援助坦桑尼亚国家宽带骨干网项目使该国电话资费降低58%，互联网资费降低75%，偏远农村地区也能享受到现代通信的便利性。

在创新数字贸易环境方面，中国通过搭建跨境电商平台，以及在清关、仓储、物流、技术运用等方面提供便利和培训等途径，帮助中小企业和弱势群体享受贸易数字化带来的红利。

以阿里巴巴搭建的世界电子贸易平台（eWTP）为例，它旨在利用互联网建立一个成本低、效率快、货通全球的贸易枢纽。目前已有马来西亚、泰国、卢旺达、埃塞俄比亚、比利时等国加入eWTP。

2020年新冠肺炎疫情期间，马来西亚eWTP承担了医疗物资仓储、运输、分发等重任，成为世界卫生组织指定的亚太地区重要救援枢纽。eWTP对贫困国家特色农产品"走出去"也发挥了独特作用。2020年天猫"6·18"活动期间，"马来西亚榴莲交易额同比增长超200%""3000斤卢旺达咖啡豆秒光，农民每包多赚4美元"等现象成为电商数字合作促进经济发展的国际典范。

当前，中国参与数字国际合作已经有了一定的基础，未来可以从以下四个方面着手：

第一，因国施策，科学甄别示范性项目。精准识别受援国发展需求，选取经济增长示范性强、发展潜力足的民生领域开展数字合作。特别是对医疗、教育、农业等援助项目开展运营管理数字化改造。

第二，推进公私合作，积极引导领军企业出海。充分发挥私人部门技术和管理优势，特别是支持数字化领军企业顺势出海，发挥数字技术在应对疫情冲击、复工复产和恢复社会生活等方面的保障作用。

第三，开展能力建设，加快培育技术人才。依托中国援建的职业技术学校、人力资源开发合作项目、奖学金项目、数字企业培训平台等，积极为发展中国家传授数字化管理运营新理念、新方法。

第四，深化数字开放合作，合力促进国际经济复苏。积极利用联合国、二十国集团（G20）、金砖国家等多边平台，同相关数字科研机构加强对接，推广中国数字技术、标准和服务，凝聚发展共识，携手为促进疫情后经济复苏提供动能。

四、可持续产业扶贫应发挥政府与市场的协同作用[①]

精准扶贫战略实施以来，中国的脱贫攻坚工作取得了显著成效，贫困人口从2012年底的9899万人减至2019年底的551万人，贫困发生率由10.2%降至0.6%。到2020年底，作为最难啃的硬骨头深度贫困地区也整体消除绝对贫困。

因地制宜发展当地特色产业是推动脱贫攻坚的根本出路，是实现稳定脱贫的根本之策。

通过产业扶贫，贫困户不仅能够增加收入，而且能够提高家庭的人力资本，并最终脱离贫困陷阱。

国务院扶贫办统计指出，2018年实现脱贫的475.4万贫困户中，享受产业帮扶措施的有352.8万户，占74.2%。农业农村部统计，截至2019年9月，全国92%的贫困户已经参与带动作用明显的特色优势产业发展，已脱贫人口中主要通过产业帮扶实现脱贫的占到67%。尽管产业扶贫产生了良好的成效，但是不可否认，现阶段的产业发展依然处于依靠政府补贴的初级发展阶段，产业的市场竞争能力依然很弱，比如产业发展的组织化程度低、技术水平差、小农户的能力不足、产销对接不畅、品牌缺乏等问题，实现可持续产业扶贫依然面临诸多挑战。

可持续产业扶贫的形成受到多重因素的影响，包括基于资源禀

---

① 作者：朱海波，中国农业科学院农业信息研究所副研究员。

赋的产业选择、良好的企业发展环境、企业家精神的彰显、政府对产业发展的支持引导、公平而有激励的利益联结机制等。同时，对于深度贫困地区而言，由于地处偏远，远离市场，其市场机制不健全，其市场主体本身能力弱小，缺乏资本，因此政府在产业扶贫中发挥着至关重要的作用。但是政府的作用也必须以培养市场主体本身的竞争能力为主要目标，也即需要发挥好市场力量与政府力量的协同作用。

第一，政府在推动贫困地区可持续产业扶贫方面，既要积极有为，也要厘清边界。一方面，政府应积极有为。深度贫困地区的产业发展缺乏外源性支持，比如资金、技术、龙头企业引进等，政府应充分发挥资源动员能力，充当"水龙头"作用，积极引入资源；同时充分利用中央下拨的产业扶贫资金，发掘有潜力的产业，培育有能力的市场主体，积极谋划推进产业发展。

以2018年12月和2019年7月两次实地调研为例，云南省维西傈僳族自治县处于"三区三州"深度贫困地区，是国内为数不多的原生道地中药材之乡。2017年起，伟宏公司在县政府的引导支持下，围绕中药材种植加工，以"公司+专业合作社+基地+农户"的订单模式，推进深度贫困村村集体经济发展及建档立卡贫困户增收脱贫，与康普乡普乐村、札子村、阿倮村、阿尼比村、康普村签订了股份合作协议，5个村共投入资金230万元进入公司，每年每个村能够获得2万～4万元不等的分红，同时带动552户农户通过订单种植中药材模式增收，其中建档立卡贫困户209户，户均增收突破5000元。

另一方面，政府的作用应有边界。在产业发展上，政府并非万能，政府作用的发挥应在尊重市场规律基础上，发挥有限责任，做好物流基础设施建设、技术推广、技术培训、质量监督、公共品牌创建和具有外部性特征的维护等公共服务工作，降低交易成本。在微观层面上，应该让企业、社会服务组织、合作社和农户成为面对市场、参与竞争、自我决策、自担风险的独立经营主体，这样才能有效发挥政府在产业发展中的良性作用。

第二，打造优势特色产业，依靠龙头企业做深做强，依托品牌化实现价值增值。贫困地区产业发展首先要甄别具有市场潜力与本地比较优势的产业形态，只有基于贫困县自身自然生态环境、特色农林产品与劳动力等禀赋结构优势的产业发展，才能够形成有竞争力的产品，进而在资源整合、精深加工、配套产业服务等产业链上做深做强。例如，威宁彝族回族苗族自治县是隶属贵州省毕节市的深度贫困县，得益于土壤条件、高山冷凉气候环境，出产糖心苹果、高山洋芋、黄党参等农特产品。

在2018年12月和2019年7月两次实地访谈中发现，威宁彝族回族苗族自治县借助"数字贵州"发展战略，以"互联网+"为契机，确定"电商+现代山地高校农业园区+农户专业合作+种植养殖农户"的发展模式，大力推进威宁农特产品电商发展。以访谈的益民电子商务公司为例，该公司创立于2016年，得益于县政府对电商发展的重视，加上公司运营成本很低且专注于市场，公司得以迅速发展。2019年仅威宁的苹果、洋芋销售额就达到500万元。

对于产业链的拓展延伸，要重视上游产品的规模化、标准化，以及品质化生产，通过内置村社的合作组织推动小农的组织化。要重视生鲜农产品错季销售的冷链仓储及冷链物流体系建设，最大化避免季节性供过于求导致的"丰产不丰收"现象。要重视基于优质农产品产业链的品牌化建设，以品牌溢价创造更高的价值。

第三，贫困地区扶贫产业的发展，直接依靠贫困户显然行不通，深度贫困地区政府应加大产业发展市场化主体的支持培育力度，围绕有潜力的特色产业，依靠龙头企业、合作社等更具有能力的主体，从提升产业链竞争力和带贫能力着眼，加大对这些主体包含信贷、用地、发展奖补等支持政策，推动它们的发展。

另外，在促进产业的合作化、分工化和规模化过程中，一定要积极对接贫困户，开展技能培训、提供就业岗位，让贫困户真正嵌入到产业发展中，在产业发展中受益，并提高自身发展动力与能力，实现稳定且可持续的脱贫。

例如，在2019年12月的调研中发现，新疆喀什市莎车县晨光生物科技集团积极带动贫困户种植万寿菊，实现产业脱贫。起初当地农户对这个新生事物持怀疑态度，参与积极性不高。莎车县政府经过调研，认识到这一产业的良好前景，于是推动各乡干部与企业科技人员一起积极开展宣传工作，为农户提供种植万寿菊的培训，推动企业、合作社、农户形成产业发展联合体。现在，万寿菊已被莎车县农民称为"致富花"。

第三章
中国减贫实践助力全球贫困治理

一、中国扶贫经验对其他亚洲国家的启示①

亚洲各国资源禀赋各异，经济发展政策不同，因此，减贫效果和贫富差异也不同。

面对新冠肺炎疫情对全球经济的重大冲击、局部武装冲突不断、贸易保护主义盛行，亚洲国家只有通过深化多边合作、互学互鉴，才能实现整个亚洲的整体脱贫，维护亚洲地区的永久繁荣与稳定。

从总体上看，亚洲地区贫困现状总体向好。《2019年可持续发展报告》的最新数据显示，就亚洲国家而言，按照每人每天1.9美元的国际贫困线标准，亚洲国家目前的极端贫困发生率为1.85%，低于2%，总体消除了绝对贫困，趋势向好。

同时也要注意到，亚洲总体情况向好的前提下，有些国家还有相当数量的绝对贫困人口，这也是未来亚洲减贫的主要挑战之一。在亚洲，极端贫困人口超过千万人的国家有三个，分别是印度（3890万人）、印度尼西亚（1183万人）和孟加拉国（1181万人）。

博鳌亚洲论坛《亚洲减贫报告》分析显示，与非洲跨国家间贫困人口几乎均匀分布形成鲜明对比的是，亚洲贫困人口集中。而

---

① 作者：孙靓莹，中国社会科学院世界经济与政治研究所、国家全球战略智库特约研究员。

且，亚洲国家之间的收入差异与非洲国家性质不同，亚洲国家的贫困是发展中的不平衡，而非洲则是不发达所导致的不平衡，这也是亚洲贫困区别于世界其他地区的一个鲜明特征。此外，亚洲国家的贫困是基本消除极端贫困后收入不平等所产生的贫困。在亚洲减贫中，较为突出的问题主要包括青年失业、营养不足以及基础设施与公共服务落后，特别是医疗服务短缺，这也将成为未来亚洲各国减贫合作领域的重点。

中国的减贫经验对亚洲有特别的启示。中国式减贫可以被概括为两阶段减贫法。第一阶段是改革开放后，伴随经济起飞阶段的普遍式减贫，在这一阶段主要依靠经济增长消除贫困。第二阶段是在单纯经济增长无法解决由收入不平等带来的贫困时，通过政府主导，从国家政策层面实施精准扶贫，最终实现全民脱贫，摆脱极端贫困。

在第一阶段，改革开放政策奠定了中国经济内外循环的基础。出口、投资及内需"三驾马车"共同拉动经济增长，为减贫提供了良好的客观环境。工业化创造新的经济增长点，带动其他劳动密集型产业发展，为贫困人口提供了大量低门槛的就业机会，最终实现普遍式减贫。在此过程中，中国实事求是地根据发展阶段制定适宜的经济政策，例如适时引进外资企业以及允许民营经济发展，随之而来的大量劳动密集型产业扩大了工业化就业规模，有助于农村贫困人口通过进城打工的方式获得高于务农所得的工资性收入，整体降低了农村的贫困水平。中国还不断推进产业转型升级，持续提高工业经济效率，为促进经济增长和提高居民收入提供了持久动力。1979年至2018年，中国制造业劳动生产率从每人2734.2元提升至每人157514.4元，增长了56.6倍，劳动生产率的不断提升为就业人员工资增长奠定了基础。

由政府主导的精准扶贫是减贫第二阶段的核心。2013年中国政府启动了精准脱贫。精准脱贫是在中国经济社会的结构趋向于不利于减贫的条件下实施的立足社会公平的政治行动。精准脱贫将保护式和开发式扶贫有机对接，将中国的经济社会发展与减贫在制度层面进行了整合，构成了中国扶贫的新实践体系。

以上分析可以看出，中国式减贫对于亚洲减贫的重要启示是，在贫困人口较多的情况下通过经济迅速腾飞以解决大多数人口的贫困问题；另外，当贫困人口减少到20%以下，精准扶贫就会发挥关键作用。需要强调的是，精准扶贫是发展减贫过程中的政策累加而不是替代，原有的发展扶贫措施仍然也必须继续发挥作用。经济增长阶段是一国总体减贫效果最好的时期。抓住这一时期，通过发展经济实现大规模减贫，让广大劳动者参与到经济体系之中并获取相应的回报，是最实用、政府负担最小的办法。

秉承这一思路，亚洲国家应珍惜眼下的和平机遇期，在维护经济共同繁荣的多边框架基础上，进一步推动亚洲地区的产业链、供应链以及价值链深度融合，加速实现亚洲地区经济一体化。亚洲各国在要素禀赋互补、产业发展阶段互补以及技术合作代际传递等方面，有着广阔的合作空间和合作机会。

团结与稳定是21世纪亚洲发展的基础。对此，全球性、区域性大国均负有不可推卸的责任。主要国家之间保持稳定、可预期的双边关系，是亚洲地区开展政治、经济、社会等领域多边合作、实现共同发展的保障。政治和社会稳定、一以贯之的发展战略以及政府维护公平正义经济社会制度的坚定意志，是实现减贫的重要条件。中国的减贫经验也被来自柬埔寨、印度尼西亚、马来西亚和越南的经验反复印证。稳定压倒一切，亚洲各国应共同携手，尽一切力量维护各国内部以及区域间的安定局面，最终实现亚洲整体性脱贫。

二、中国经验对其他金砖国家的启示和借鉴[①]

2020年是人类历史上不平凡的一年。突如其来的新冠肺炎疫情及其造成的经济衰退，给国家和人民带来了严重的生命财产损失。联合国预测，此次疫情或将使之前所取得的减贫成果付之东流。但愿疫情的影响只是暂时的，毕竟全球减贫的成果也是我近40年职业生涯中最重要的成果之一。在当今复杂多变的时代，全世界都应该认识到，减贫是世界经济发展的伟大成就。

世界上许多地区的贫困人口都在大幅减少。比如，拉丁美洲的许多地区、苏联和东欧的部分地区、非洲的小部分地区以及北亚和东南亚的其他广大地区。但中国一直是全球减贫事业的中心。中国已经使大多数人民摆脱了贫困，并且取得了巨大的进步。中国不仅使数亿人摆脱了贫困，而且使大约一半人口的生活水平达到了七国集团主要经济体的标准。

在2001年参与起草金砖四国报告时，我写了一篇题为《全球需要更好的经济之"砖"》的论文，在文中我首次提出，巴西、俄罗斯、印度和中国代表了未来增长机遇，可能会在全球经济中扮演越来越重要的角色。在随后的几年中，我和当时的高盛同事进行了探讨，一致认为，到21世纪30年代后期，金砖四国的经济规模可与七国集团相比（以名义美元计算）。我们还认为，在金砖四国的经济规模达到七国集团的规模之前，中国的经济规模有望赶超美国。

目前，新冠肺炎疫情的阴影仍然笼罩着全球大多数国家和地区。展望未来，有个问题摆在面前：中国在减贫方面取得了如此令人瞩目的成就，那么其他金砖国家可从中国的减贫成功经验中汲取

[①] 作者：吉姆·奥尼尔，"金砖四国"概念首创者，英国财政部前商务大臣，英国皇家国际事务研究所主席。

些什么呢？中国的减贫经验对于大多数非洲国家，尤其是在撒哈拉以南的非洲国家（这个地区集中了目前全球大多数贫困人口），也许更为适用。

归根结底，经济增长有两个驱动因素：国家劳动力规模及其生产力。一个国家的劳动力最大的决定因素是人口趋势，那些出生率高和预期寿命长的国家往往劳动力动态良好，而唯一能真正显著影响劳动力规模的因素便是移民。人口众多的国家，尤其是人口结构比较年轻的国家，经济增长速度通常比其他国家更快。在这方面，与其他金砖国家相比，中国和印度拥有巨大的优势，毕竟全世界只有这两个国家的人口规模超过10亿人。

由此引出了经济增长的第二个决定因素，即生产力。尽管与其他金砖国家相比，中国并没有多少天然优势，但近几十年来中国的生产力增长更为强劲。这是各国可以向其他国家借鉴的方面。当然，事实上，每个国家都应该向其他国家学习和借鉴，扬长避短，择善而从。这点至关重要。

然而，提高生产力并非易事，也没有通用的方法。我和一些经济学家认为，有的政策或许能提高生产率，但我们也只是猜测，不敢确定。但是从非官方渠道提供的数据来看，以生产力水平和经济繁荣程度来衡量，大多数减贫成功的国家，它们的教育、人均预期寿命、医疗卫生、人力资源和硬件基础设施、现代科技等方面的提高和改善发挥了关键作用。此外，政府管理部门的连续性、稳定性和管理能力，以及宏观经济的稳定（包括国际贸易和投资、国债），也同样重要。中国在以上这些方面都比其他金砖国家做得更好。

我在高盛任首席经济学家期间不仅提出了"金砖四国"这一说法，还负责制定了"经济环境分数"（GES）。我们挑选了18个对经济可持续增长和提高生产力有显著作用的衡量因素，从0到10分对每个变量进行评分，分数越高代表经济可持续增长能力越强或生产效率越高，其中大多数变量已在前文中提及。高盛每年都会公布约180个国家的经济环境分数，但这项数据在2014年停止公布。

从2014年的数据来看，在国家和地区中，新加坡得分最高，为8.1分，而厄立特里亚最低，为2.5分。新加坡的经济成功本身就很重要，中国借鉴了大量新加坡的成功经验，从中受益良多。

在我看来，需要关注的是，韩国得分为7.83分，排在第3位。这一度让我感到惊讶，但可以看到，韩国在提高生活水平方面取得了显著成就，其经济走向不容忽视。从组成部分来看，韩国在教育和技术应用方面得分很高。有许多国家的领导人或政策顾问渴望提高本国生产力，我经常对他们强调说，韩国是一个值得学习的国家。该国拥有5000多万人口，而且并没有什么得天独厚的自然资源。

金砖国家中，中国得分最高，为6.03分。因此，我相信中国仍然可向新加坡和韩国等其他国家学习。西方大国的得分通常介于新加坡和中国之间，不过有趣的是，2014年中国的得分首次超过了意大利。

其他金砖国家GES得分依次为：俄罗斯5.51分、巴西5.43分、南非5.29分，印度4.22分。印度得分最低，比中国低100多位，分别位列第151位和第49位。

纵观指数构成，可以看出其他金砖国家可从中国学到很多东西，特别是其教育成就、技术应用以及宏观经济稳定性方面的众多指标。其中，最重要的是中国在国际贸易和投资方面的参与度。想要真正实现全民共同富裕的长远目标，中国必须在各个方面继续完善；而在其他方面，比如治理和法治方面，则需要取得长足进步。但是，如果其他金砖国家想在减贫方面取得像中国一样的巨大成功，就必须向中国学习。尤其是印度，必须借鉴中国经验，找到一个行之有效的经济发展模式，才能满足其迅速增长的人口的需求。

三、拉丁美洲可借鉴中国的扶贫经验[①]

拉丁美洲18个国家的国情各不相同，但即便是情况较好的几个国家，贫困和极端贫困也没有消除，更令人担忧的是，过去几年，贫困人口逐渐增多。联合国拉丁美洲和加勒比经济委员会最新数据显示，2018年拉丁美洲的贫困线以下人口比重为30.1％（1.85亿人），极端贫困线以下人口比重为10.7％（6600万人）。

一直以来，智利和乌拉圭是拉丁美洲的减贫大国。2018年，这两个国家的贫困人口比重均不到11％，乌拉圭的极端贫困人口比重则不到2％。拉美其他国家的情况则截然不同，这些国家中有40％以上的人口生活在贫困中，19％的人口生活在极端贫困中。

整个拉美地区，过去20年在持续、迅速减少贫困和极端贫困发生率方面收效甚微，预计在未来几年减贫人口也不会出现大幅减少。拉丁美洲很难实现联合国《2030年可持续发展议程》提出的目标：在2030年之前消除极端贫困和贫困人口减半。[②]

---

① 作者：贝安之，2014年至2019年任智利共和国驻华大使馆公使衔参赞兼经贸处处长，曾任智利外交部国际经济关系总局中国事务处处长。

② 据拉加经委会解释，对于拉丁美洲而言，到2030年的减贫总目标是贫困人口占比14.5％（2019年该指标为29.1％）。还有一个目标，到2030年拉丁美洲极端贫困人口占比3％。"由于家庭调查的收入计量方法存在某些局限性，因此不考虑极端贫困人口占比为零的情况，也就是说，即使消除了极端贫困，极端贫困率计量值也大于零。"见拉丁美洲和加勒比经济委员会：《2019年拉丁美洲社会全景》，圣地亚哥，2019年，第115、116页。

表1[①] 拉丁美洲（15个国家）：根据拉加经委会提供的2015—2018年公共数据估计的贫困率和极端贫困率[a]

	极端贫困人口				总贫困人口				2017-2018年变化	
	2015年	2016年	2017年	2018年	2015年	2016年	2017年	2018年	EP	P
阿根廷[b]	…	2.9	2.8	3.6	…	21.5	18.7	24.4	0.8	5.6
玻利维亚	14.6	…	16.4	14.7	34.7	…	35.2	33.2	−1.7	−1.9
巴西[c]	4.0	5.0	5.5	5.4	18.8	19.8	20.3	19.4	−0.1	−0.9
智利	1.8	…	1.4	…	13.7	…	10.7	…	…	…
哥伦比亚	11.3	12.0	10.9	10.8	30.6	30.9	29.8	29.9	−0.2	0.1
哥斯达黎加	4.6	4.2	3.3	4.0	17.4	16.5	15.4	16.2	0.7	0.8
多米尼加[d]	9.2	7.2	6.4	5.0	29.7	27.3	25.0	22.0	−1.5	−3.0
厄瓜多尔	7.0	7.5	7.0	6.5	23.9	24.3	23.6	24.2	0.5	0.5
萨尔瓦多	10.4	10.7	8.3	7.6	42.6	40.5	37.8	34.5	0.8	−3.3
洪都拉斯	19.0	18.8	…	19.4	55.2	53.2	…	55.8	…	…
墨西哥[e]	…	11.7	…	10.6	…	43.7	…	41.5	−1.0	−2.3
巴拿马	8.0	8.5	7.6	6.2	17.9	17.0	16.7	14.5	−1.4	−2.2
巴拉圭	7.3	7.9	6.0	6.5	23.4	24.0	21.6	19.5	0.5	−2.1
秘鲁	5.4	5.2	5.0	3.7	19.0	19.1	18.9	16.8	−1.3	−2.1
乌拉圭	0.2	0.2	0.1	0.1	4.2	3.5	2.7	2.9	0.3	0.3

资料来源：拉加经委会，根据家庭调查数据库（BADEHOG）和贫困/极端贫困人口官方数据。

a 从2015年开始提供拉加经委会贫困人口估计数据的国家。

b 拉加经委会估计数据是指每年第四季度数据。官方估计是指每年下半年数据。

c 从2016年起，拉加经委会的估计数据基于持续性全国家庭调查（PNAD-Continua）结果，与前几年的估计数据无可比性。所报告的官方数据参考了巴西地理统计局（IBGE）（2019）根据世界银行低收入/中高收入国家标准的估算结果。

d 拉加经委会数据基于全国劳动力调查结果，指的是截至2015年每年9月统计数据。从2016年开始，该数据基于一年一度的持续国家劳动力调查结果。

e 官方贫困人口衡量标准是多维的。因此，采用墨西哥国家社会发展政策

---

① 拉加经委会使用统一的通用数学方法对每个拉丁美洲国家进行评估。该方法旨在对贫困人口和极端贫困人口进行分类，分类评估标准是一个人的收入或其家庭收入是否低于贫困线或极端贫困线。考虑到各个国家的粮食价格和非粮食类需求，这些线代表的是使各个家庭能够满足其所有成员基本需求的收入水平。见拉丁美洲和加勒比经济委员会：《2019年拉丁美洲社会全景》，圣地亚哥，2019年，第91页。

评估委员会（CONEVAL）发布的估算数据作为非官方国家参考数据，即"极端贫困人口"是指"低于最低福利门槛的人口"，"总贫困人口"是指"低于福利门槛的人口"。

相反，与2014年相比，2018年拉丁美洲总贫困人口增加了2.3％，约2100万人；极端贫困人口增加率则更高，为2.9％，大约2000万人。因此，自2015年以来，拉丁美洲贫困人口总体上增加了，特别是极端贫困人口。[①]这为拉丁美洲各国按时完成可持续发展目标蒙上了一重阴影，形势不容乐观。

拉丁美洲和加勒比经济委员会对于拉美地区实现减贫目标最乐观的预测方案是，要求在2019年到2030年间拉丁美洲人均国内生产总值增长2％，收入分配不均每年减少1.5％，基尼系数每年减少1.5％[②]，所有这些目标的实现都可谓任重道远。

拉丁美洲消除贫困和极端贫困的当前形势是贫困率下降的不规律性和脆弱性。预计2020年拉丁美洲经济增长将大幅下滑（降幅可能高达4％以上）[③]，并且由于新冠肺炎疫情的影响，预计要到2022年至2023年之后才会出现缓慢复苏[④]。因此，拉美地区的当务之急是加强扶贫政策，各国政府要向中国学习，更加审慎地学习借鉴减贫的成功案例。

---

① 拉丁美洲和加勒比经济委员会：《2019年拉丁美洲社会全景》，圣地亚哥，2019年，第93页。

② 同②，第115、116页。

③ 拉丁美洲和加勒比经济委员会：《拉丁美洲和加勒比经济委员会和新冠疫情：经济和社会影响》，2020年4月3日，引自：https://repositorio.cepal.org/bitstream/handle/11362/45351/1/S2000263_en.pdf。

④ 高盛集团，路透社报道，2020年5月20日，引自：https://www.reuters.com/article/us-latam-economy-goldman-sachs/latin-americas-economy-to-shrink-record-7-6-this-year-goldman-sachs-idUSKBN22V2QB。

（单位：%）

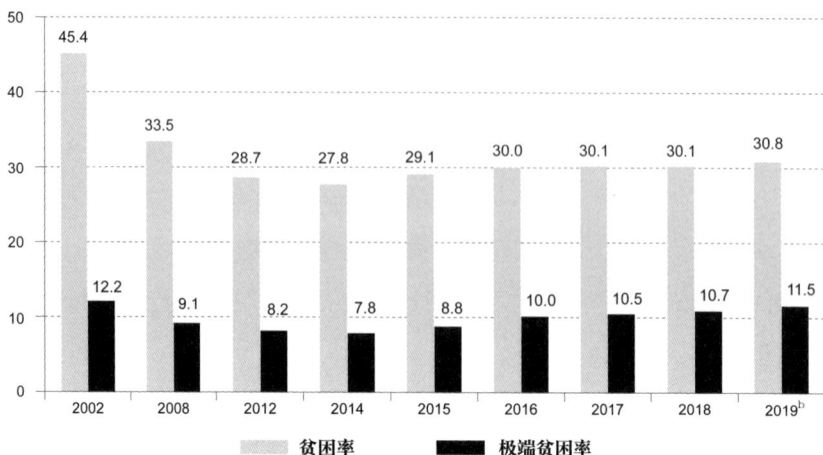

图1　拉丁美洲的贫困率与极端贫困率[a]

资料来源：拉加经委会，基于家庭调查数据库（BADEHOG）。

a　下列国家的加权平均值：阿根廷、委内瑞拉、巴西、智利、哥伦比亚、哥斯达黎加、多米尼加、厄瓜多尔、萨尔瓦多、危地马拉、洪都拉斯、墨西哥、尼加拉瓜、巴拿马、巴拉圭、秘鲁、玻利维亚和乌拉圭。

b　这些数据均为当时的预测结果。

表2　拉丁美洲（15个国家）：2018年按贫困率和极端贫困率对国家进行分类[a]

		贫困人口					
		15%以下	15%~20%	20%~25%	25%~30%	30%~35%	35%以上
极端贫困人口	5%以下	乌拉圭、智利	哥斯达黎加、秘鲁	阿根廷			
	5%~10%	巴拿马	巴西、巴拉圭	厄瓜多尔、多米尼加		萨尔瓦多	
	10%~15%				哥伦比亚	玻利维亚	墨西哥
	15%以上						洪都拉斯

资料来源：拉加经委会，基于家庭调查数据库（BADEHOG）。

a　仅包括提供2017年或2018年数据信息的国家/地区。除智利（2017年）外，均为2018年数据。

中国和拉丁美洲有共同的减贫目标，但在历史文化、地理位置和种族上却各不相同。因此，拉美国家不能直接照搬中国的减贫经验。

但是，在观察了中国近20年的政府制度建设后，我认为制度建设是一个未经探索的连接点，拉美国家可从中汲取宝贵经验，可以根据自身的实际情况进行调整。

针对扶贫体制建设，我从中国的经验中总结了四条可供拉美国家学习借鉴的要点，旨在在2030年实现消除贫困的目标。

第一，稳定的专门扶贫机构。

拉美各国政府都不重视在国家体制框架内建立和培养专门的扶贫专业人才。因此出现了减贫职责不明确（通常分散到几个独立的部门，如卫生、住房和教育部门）、地方民选官员不负责任或专门机构的高层官员不会从4~5年的总统任期中"脱钩"。因此，拉丁美洲的减贫机构不像中国那样有国家政策的特点，所有国家政策只与当前总统任期挂钩，没有延续性。

中国的减贫成功有赖于一个稳固的贫困治理体系，由成立于1986年的国务院扶贫开发领导小组办公室领导。领导小组为贫困地区制定有针对性的帮扶举措，设置自上而下的省、市、县、乡四级扶贫管理部门，与全国各级党委书记共同开展扶贫工作。①

无论中国领导层如何换届，扶贫机构均已牢牢制度化，担负着为中国人民谋求最高最长远利益的责任。这是拉美国家可从中国身上汲取的最大、最基本的经验借鉴之一：不仅要集中力量，还要把扶贫机构从其他机构的普遍做法中分离出来，使其官员和专业人员尽可能地与不断变化的政治环境隔离。而鉴于拉美国家的政治体系性质，其每隔4~5年就会经历一次更迭。

第二，适应性强的长期扶贫政策。

---

① 胡富国：《读懂中国脱贫攻坚》，外文出版社，2019年，第87、100页。

拉丁美洲国家缺乏强有力和稳定的专门扶贫机构，其直接后果是无法就减贫这一议题制定长期政策。从中国的经验来看，重要的工作领域与国家及时支持和维持政策的能力息息相关。基础设施、住宅和医疗卫生设施的建设或工农业的发展，是中国长期延续性扶贫政策的明显例子。这些政策在中国取得了成效，不仅需要扩大视野、加大执行力，而且还需要有分配持久预算的权力。

这种方略并不复杂，却有着无比深远的影响和冲击，拉丁美洲国家必须加以研究。拉丁美洲所有国家都有一个共同的特点，那就是这些国家未能分配长期预算，为持久的减贫政策提供资金。

此外，适应性是扶贫政策的关键要素。据我在中国的所见所闻，中国政府相关部门会不断根据新的环境条件对减贫领域的长期政策进行调整。中国的政策制定者会不断根据新发现、新知识、国外经验教训等对其长期政策的必要性进行审查。当今时代，信息和知识可以迅速共享和融合。中国政府机构已清楚认识到当今时代的这一特点，并将这作为其政策审查程序的组成部分。因此，拉丁美洲的政策制定者切记，制定长期的减贫政策并不意味着使其固化僵化。

第三，设计精准扶贫政策。

拉丁美洲国家扶贫政策的失败根深蒂固、来由已久，这些政策盲目投入各种无用的项目，不仅浪费了资金，还浪费了宝贵的时间。拉丁美洲朝着实现可持续发展目标走了很长一段路，虽然资金充裕，但扶贫方案却往往执行不力。与中国相比，很容易得出这样的结论：当前拉美减贫政策收效甚微的重要原因之一是，未对减贫政策进行精确设计，而且尚未对拉丁美洲的贫困人口进行深入普查和识别。

这可能是决策者面临的最大难题。实际上，在这方面中国同样也遇到了挑战性的问题，习近平主席亲力亲为、为扶贫工作出谋划策。2015年6月在贵州考察时，习近平主席提出了扶贫开发工作"六个精准"的基本要求，即扶持对象精准、项目安排精准、资金使用精准、措施到户精准、因村派人精准、脱贫成效精准。并要求扶贫政策决策者作出承诺,落实"五个一批"的脱贫措施:发展生产脱贫一批、易地搬迁脱贫一批、生态补偿脱贫一批、发展教育脱贫一批、社会保障兜底一批。[①]

诚然,中国扶贫机构制定的政策可能并不完全适用于拉丁美洲的具体情况,但同时也揭示了解决政策精准相关化问题的困难性和关键性。具体来说,如前所述,对于拉丁美洲,我认为拉美各国可从中国经验中受益匪浅,即建立相关机制,精准选择扶贫政策的受益者,并针对遴选的受益者制定相应措施。

一般而言,拉丁美洲在核定贫困人口方面通常缺乏精准性,特别是由于非正规经济在拉美普遍存在。在中国也存在这一现象,其主要区别在于中国拥有先进的技术以及本地公民身份核定和登记系统。这是拉丁美洲减贫决策者应采取的第一个重要步骤,确保不遗漏任何扶贫对象。精准登记人口信息是掌握有关家庭实际收入第一手信息的基本要求。尽管如此,拉丁美洲各国政府也应该认识到,人口登记也应该是动态的,因为贫困本身也是动态的:非贫困人口可能由于事故、健康问题、自然灾害等而陷入贫困。此外,贫困人口的核定和衡量不能只考虑收入,因为贫困是多维的,涉及教育、医疗、住宅等各个方面[②]。因此,完善贫困人口核定系统是大多数拉丁美洲国家应该做出改变的第一步。

另外,中国之前的扶贫政策是一种"漫灌"系统[③]。也就是说,当时的中国扶贫政策没有很强的针对性,更谈不上精准到户、落实到人。目前,拉丁美洲的情况正是如此。大多数拉美国家无法像中

---

① 胡富国:《读懂中国脱贫攻坚》,外文出版社,2019年,第89页。

② 同上书,第109页。

③ 同上书,第130页。

国那样实行"精准滴灌"系统，这不仅是因为没有落实前文提到的贫困户精准信息系统，更是因为没有目标长远、责任心强烈的专业化扶贫机构。

第四，扶贫目标的问责制。

拉丁美洲尚未推行针对高级减贫官员的强制性问责制。如前所述，拉美各国的减贫机构尚未脱离政府机构体系，而是受制于选举结果，缺乏延续性和独立性。因此，负责政策设计和执行的高级官员往往没什么减贫经验，也不对行政机构负责。这些官员不是专职官员，而是一些政客，其职业道路并非终身致力于公共部门，行政制裁对其职业前途没有重大影响。

此外，由于各部委部门与其他地方政府之间责任分散，削弱了减贫官员的责任感。因此，拉丁美洲公共行政机构的设置模式只会助长责任淡化、官员问责制的缺失，由此导致减贫工作效果平平。

不同的是，中国认识到，增强官员的扶贫责任心是达成宏伟既定目标的关键。因此，中国实行了一种制度，在这种制度中，往往有针对性地设计和实行相应政策，相关扶贫官员（均为公职人员）必须随时调整。这些官员对扶贫政策的落实情况和成效，对他们的职业晋升途径至关重要。因此，国务院扶贫开发领导小组办公室有权每年对省、市、县、乡从上至下各级扶贫领导班子进行检查和考察[1]，奖励扶贫成果，惩治违规行为。中国扶贫制度依赖先进的技术（各省之间的标准化统计交叉评估系统、应用程序级数据收集系统和大数据评估平台）和第三方组织（例如研究机构和社会组织）对扶贫成果进行考核，这些成果包括：受监管官员落实政策的成效、贫困人口的精准识别和精准退出、精准预算、扶贫对象的满意度以及总体目标的完成度（例如温饱问题、义务教育、基本医疗和住房）。

---

[1] 胡富国：《读懂中国脱贫攻坚》，外文出版社，2019，第141页。

各级扶贫官员的强烈责任感是中国扶贫工作取得成功的重要原因。拉丁美洲的扶贫政府组织必须审慎考量职业专业人员、责任、问责制、检查和结果评价等，并使其适应其自身的体制。

四、中国减贫经验对非洲的借鉴①

我在马达加斯加工作4年来，经常有非洲朋友问我，中国是如何在短短几十年时间内使8亿人口摆脱贫困？中国创造反贫困奇迹的秘诀是什么？在中国驻马使馆历次举办的宣介中国的活动中，图书展台上习近平主席的《摆脱贫困》一书总是最受欢迎。在全球减贫事业中，中国方案、中国智慧正在受到越来越多国家的重视和称赞。

中华人民共和国成立以来，中国实现了从站起来、富起来到强起来的历史性转变，用几十年时间走完了发达国家几百年走过的工业化历程。国家经济的发展也给中国人民带来越来越大的获得感和幸福感，中华人民共和国成立之初到2018年，中国人均国民收入从约70美元升至9470美元，国民受教育程度从80%以上人口是文盲到九年义务教育巩固率达94.2%，居民预期寿命从35岁提高到77岁，中国完成了世界上最大规模人口整体脱贫，形成4亿多人的世界最大规模中等收入群体。中国坚持以人民为中心的发展思想，实现了快速发展与大规模减贫同步，贫困人口共享改革发展成果。

中国70年减贫历程告诉我们，道路决定命运。鞋子合不合适，只有脚知道。中国减贫事业所取得的辉煌成就，靠的是中国共产党的坚强领导和制度优势，靠的是全体中国人民艰苦奋斗，靠的是走出一条符合自身国情的中国特色社会主义道路和中国特色扶贫开发道路。

----

① 作者：杨小茸，中国驻马达加斯加前大使。

中国与马达加斯加等非洲国家有着相近的历史遭遇，有着尽快摆脱贫困的共同目标。谈到中国特色扶贫开发道路对正在与贫困"开战"的马达加斯加等非洲国家的启示，我想主要有以下几点：

一是树立坚定信心。中国作为世界上最大的发展中国家，在一穷二白的基础上自力更生、艰苦奋斗，成为世界上减贫人口最多的国家，也是率先完成联合国千年发展目标的发展中国家。

非洲大陆是发展中国家最为集中的大陆，有着良好的自然禀赋，有着勤劳智慧的人民，正处在经济腾飞的前夜，是一片充满希望的热土。中国能做到的，非洲也一定能做到。有一位马达加斯加朋友对我说，从数字上看，许多非洲国家人均国内生产总值数额不低于中国1978年改革开放之前的人均数字，中国通过改革开放实现了经济腾飞，非洲国家也应坚定信心，加强与中国交流借鉴，实现经济振兴。

二是开展经验交流。"授人以鱼，不如授人以渔"。马达加斯加正在积极实施国家振兴倡议，中国的经济发展和扶贫经验对马达加斯加具有一定借鉴意义。例如，马达加斯加当前把发展作为重中之重，重视推进工业化和农业现代化，而中国始终坚持把发展作为解决贫困的根本途径，积极推进产业化扶贫，双方思路不谋而合。马达加斯加是世界上生物多样性最为丰富的国家之一，中国高度重视绿色扶贫，注重把贫困地区的生态优势转化为经济优势，积累了丰富经验。马达加斯加发展需要更多专业人才，中国坚持把扶贫与扶智相结合，向马达加斯加提供职教培训设备，迄今已邀请数千名马达加斯加专家赴华参加各类经济技术合作培训，帮助马达加斯加培养有用人才。

三是加强援助对接。中国高度重视把对非援助与非洲发展需要相对接。"要想富，先修路"。针对马达加斯加基础设施落后状况，20世纪80年代中国政府为马达加斯加援建了2号国道，成为连接首都塔那那利佛和最大经济城市塔马塔夫港的经济命脉，中国援外人员克服困难无私奉献，5位援外人员为此付出了宝贵的生命。近年来，中国援建的机场路、"鸡蛋路"等顺利推进，特别是"鸡蛋路"可以解决马达加斯加最主要鸡蛋产区运输难、破损率高的问题，有利于促进当地产业发展和民生改善。

需要强调的是，中国作为最大发展中国家，对非援助属于南南合作范畴，体现的是穷帮穷的真诚兄弟情谊。中国坚持真实亲诚理念和正确义利观，援助不附加任何政治条件，答应非洲兄弟的事会尽心尽力办好。

2020年是中国历史上具有里程碑意义的一年。因为在这一年，中国彻底消除绝对贫困，全面建成小康社会，实现第一个百年奋斗目标。中国在奋力消除自身贫困的同时，也将积极推动全球减贫合作，促进互利共赢，实现共同发展。

五、中国减贫经验对于孟加拉国及其他国家的借鉴①

中国减贫成功主要源于三个阶段的体制改革。体制改革的第一阶段体现在土地制度。家庭联产承包责任制取代了集体经济组织（人民公社）。这项措施极大鼓舞了农民的生产积极性，打破了农业生产经营和分配上的"大锅饭"。体制改革的第二阶段体现在农产品市场。逐步的市场自由化对农产品市场进行了重组。由此，农产品价格飙升。到1984年，农民的工资与工人的工资相差无几。体制改革的第三阶段体现在乡镇企业增多，吸收了大量农村剩余劳动

---

① 作者：尼亚兹·艾哈迈德·汗、阿尔维·斯里约恩。尼亚兹·艾哈迈德，达卡大学发展研究系教授和前主任，布拉克（BRAC）治理与发展研究所高级学术顾问，孟加拉国热带森林保护基金会主席，国际自然保护联盟（IUCN）孟加拉国前代表。阿尔维·斯里约恩，孟加拉国达卡市国家纺织工程与研究所发展研究系讲师。

力，农村经济结构得到了优化[1]。

但是，中国幅员辽阔，情况复杂，每个地区的改革都有不同的问题。因此在1986年5月16日，成立了"国务院贫困地区经济开发领导小组"，1993年更名为"国务院扶贫开发领导小组"。领导小组的核心职责包括考察中国欠发达地区的贫困状况、制定解决贫困地区问题的方案等。国务院扶贫办是该领导小组的常规办公室。在各省、自治区、直辖市、地级市和县均设有类似但规模较小的下属办事处（Xiaoyun和Remenyi，2008）[2]。

面对不平衡和发展差距的问题，中国政府制定了《中国农村扶贫开发纲要（2001—2010年）》，确定14.8万个贫困村，制定一系列农村减贫计划。中国政府采取的另一项创新举措是解决"三农"（即农业、农村、农民）问题，包括降低农业税、免除义务教育阶段农村学生学杂费、推行农村合作医疗等。

中国从"问题"的角度看待贫困这一概念。中国政府高度重视贫困状况，制定了详细的扶贫政策、计划和方案。此外，应该指出的是，在努力缩小收入差距的同时，中国政府成功保持了经济发展的正常运转。由此看来，中国的决策者从一开始就意识到，除非国民收入分配平等和公平，否则实现高经济增长就没有任何意义（Yan，2016）[3]。

孟加拉国和其他南亚国家可从中国的扶贫经验中吸取经验。需要指出的是，这些借鉴经验和实践技巧并非普遍适用，也并非绝对正确，但具有一定指导意义。旨在借鉴中国经验，探索和提供思

---

① Khan, A. R., & Riskin, C. (2001). Inequality and Poverty in China in the Age of Globalization. Oxford University Press.

② Xiaoyun, L., & Remenyi, J. (2008). Making poverty mapping and monitoring participatory. Development in Practice, 18(4–5), 599–610.

③ Yan, K. (2016). POVERTY ALLEVIATION IN CHINA. SPRINGER-VERLAG BERLIN AN.

路，供其他国家在谨慎考虑各自（特定）的背景、条件和实际情况后加以采纳和实施。

中国政府从一开始就意识到不平衡问题，提前计划并制定了应对不平衡和其他相关问题的对策。中国的案例充分说明，任何发展举措和议程，都必须从一开始就着眼于认真思考和规划社会经济不平等问题。这点至关重要。

为缩小收入分配差距，中国采取了许多有针对性的政策措施，保护和保障弱势群体（如农民、工人）的利益。例如，在农民和工人的收入水平之间取得平衡，并使这些弱势群体免受自然灾害和市场失灵等突发状况冲击。后来，这些措施帮助中国缓解了城乡发展的不平衡。

不平衡和不公正日益加剧，给孟加拉国带来了巨大的挑战，也给该国在减贫方面的其他令人瞩目的进展蒙上了阴影（参见Matin，2017）[①]。一位分析人士提出了一个孟加拉国经济发展相关问题：经济趋势表明，按购买力平价计算，孟加拉国现在是世界第三十一大经济体，到2030年将成为第二十八大经济体。预计到2050年，孟加拉国将成为第二十三大经济体，跻身发达国家之列。无疑，这表明该国经济增长速度是惊人的。但是，如果我们最终成为一个"不公平经济增长"的国家，那么这种增长进程就会变得毫无意义。

探索上述问题答案的过程中，中国的做法可能会提供有益的启示。中国动用其庞大的人力资源，生产低成本创新产品，从而在出口导向型产业中获得竞争优势。中国在研发方面投入大量资金。科学技术及许多学术领域的研究得到国家的支持和鼓励。这些研究可作为政策制定的参考和判断的依据。南亚国家可考虑采纳这种模式。

[①] Matin, K.A. (2017) "Economic Growth and Inequality in Bangladesh", Paper presented at the 20th Biennial Conference on Economic an Ethics of the Bangladesh Economic Association. held during 21–23 December, 2017 at Dhaka.

尽管中国的基础设施和资源非常贫乏，但中国最终取得了高速经济增长和巨大科学成就。这在国际上极为罕见。在国家层面，中国是令人鼓舞的经济发展例证。孟加拉国和其他南亚国家可借鉴中国发展之路，"使不可能成为可能"。在南亚地区许多国家（包括孟加拉国）"向东看"的背景下，以及中国在全球秩序中的影响力和地位日益提高，中国的经济发展案例有趣且令人鼓舞，可供其他国家研究和探讨，相互学习、互惠互利。

The Great Legend

China's Poverty Alleviation and Building an
All-Round Moderately Prosperous Society
to the World

扫码获取

★脱贫故事分享
★脱贫攻坚解读
　与回顾

Chapter I **The Great Legend**
China's Poverty Alleviation and Building an All–Round Moderately
Prosperous Society to the World

01

China's Poverty Alleviation Is a Great Contribution to Humanity

I. China's Poverty Alleviation Achievements Are an Inspiration to the World[①]

China is the world's first developing country to reach the UN Millennium Development Goals of eradicating extreme poverty and hunger. According to UN Secretary-General Antonio Gutterres, China is a country that has made "the greatest anti-poverty achievement in history".

After launching the reform and opening-up in 1978, China has pulled nearly 800 million people, or 70 percent of the world's total, out of poverty. In global terms, this figure exceeds the total population of Latin America.

The Overseas Development Institute of the UK believes that China's success in reducing poverty is based on two main factors. First, the economy sustained relatively high growth rates over a long period and so poverty reduction measures had sufficient resources. Second, political stability facilitated continued and steady efforts to develop and implement poverty reduction policies.

For example, Chinese industrial production grew by almost 1,000 times between 1952 and 2019 at an average rate of 11 percent per year. Per capita incomes increased 70 times. Not a single country in the world has seen such dynamic development.

---

① By Vladimir Norov, Secretary-General of the Shanghai Cooperation Organization, former minister of Foreign Affairs of Republic of Uzbekistan.

In fighting poverty, China's reforms were based on investment and industrialization, as well as targeted economic development assistance to individual economic sectors, employment incentives and rational location of industrial facilities. For example, the Agricultural Development Bank of China planned, in the spring of 2016, to invest about $460 billion in the reduction of rural poverty.

It was the rural population that was the first to see the effects of economic reforms in China. China managed to motivate inhabitants to increase production with land reforms. In parallel, they increased procurement prices for grain and agricultural products, something that made it possible to boost real incomes and saturate the domestic market.

The Chinese government helped to modernize infrastructure in poor regions based on local resources. The slogan, "If you want to get rich, first build roads", became an important stratagem in the context of the Chinese-style war on poverty. Even now, a major infrastructure project is being implemented to extend transport links to every village and doorstep of each house, and its aim being to enable motorists to reach every remote locality in the country.

Tourism has also emerged as a lucrative industry assisting the development of rural areas: this sector creates a broad spectrum of jobs and productive capacities, particularly in areas where other types of economic activity often prove difficult. Chinese statistics show that tourism helped to lift 10 million residents, or 10 percent of the poorest population, out of poverty between 2011 and 2014. It is expected that 3 million rural tourist agencies will be able to receive 2 billion tourists per year.

According to the Ministry of Culture and Tourism of the PRC, tourism contributed 9.94 trillion yuan ($1.4 trillion) to China's GDP in 2018, which amounts to 11.04 percent of its total GDP. The tourist sector has also created nearly 80 million jobs, which accounts for 10.29 percent of the total employed population.

An educated, healthy and well-fed population influences the rate of return on

Chapter I **The Great Legend**
China's Poverty Alleviation and Building an All-Round Moderately
Prosperous Society to the World

investment; therefore, this factor clearly plays a key role in kick-starting rapid development and eliminating poverty, according to Abhijit Banerjee and Esther Duflo, the recipients of the 2019 Nobel Prize in Economic Sciences who are from the Massachusetts Institute of Technology.

Since the beginning of the reform and opening-up, China has recognized that an increased focus on education and improving public health can eradicate poverty and prevent poverty from being passed on from one generation to another.

According to the World Bank, the literacy rate in China increased from 65.5 percent in 1982 to 96.8 percent in 2018, with the global average rate being 86.3 percent. This is one more extraordinary achievement. In 2019, China spent 5.01 trillion yuan ($706.6 billion) on education, which is 8.74 percent higher than the year before.

In 2020, 22,842 teachers will be assigned to teach the 2020−2021 academic year in poor regions. This team includes 21,635 teachers who will be involved in compulsory education and work with local schools. This measure is an essential step toward targeted elimination of poverty through education.

At the start of the 21st century, fewer than one-third of the Chinese had access to health insurance. Since 2006, China has been carrying out major reforms in the healthcare system to make it more accessible for poor rural people.

As a result, some 800 million rural residents have been provided with basic multi-level medical insurance that is now available to almost 100 percent of the population. Equal access to healthcare services is an inherent factor in social harmony.

Substantially, China has provided its enormous population with social security that protects people from incurring heavy expenses on healthcare; this is an immense contribution to building a just and prosperous society.

Concurrently, China is implementing an innovative model to counter poverty.

For example, advanced information and communication technologies are used to ensure that remote areas are supported by e-commerce and other modern technological applications. They are also used to market and sell agricultural products in poor regions.

Publicly available statistics show that in 2019 internet users in China accounted for 61 percent of the population (854 million), including 225 million rural residents. Between 2014 and 2017, online retail trade in rural regions grew from 180 billion to 1.24 trillion yuan, amounting to total annual growth of 91 percent, with the overall national growth being 35 percent. [1]

Forty percent of the Chinese today live in rural areas; therefore, land degradation disproportionately affects poor villages. Under the Great Green Wall project aimed at stopping desertification, there is a plan to plant trees and shrubs on 350,000 sq km of the country's territory by 2050. As many as 66 billion trees were planted toward this goal as of 2017, which contributed greatly to improving the environment and public health in China.

Over the 40 years of reforms, the poverty rate in China plummeted by almost 95 percent. This is not only an important social goal for China but also a tremendous domestic resource. As their wealth increases, the Chinese are becoming more demanding when it comes to product quality, which stimulates Chinese companies to produce high-quality and technology-intensive products in pursuit of the expanding domestic market. Consequently, countering poverty is an important aspect of the Made in China strategy.

Other countries should follow China's example because poverty and life below the subsistence level are not uncommon even in the most advanced economies. China's experience in fighting poverty demonstrates how important it is to focus on identifying the root causes of poverty and creating conditions in which the population can independently progress toward resolving this complicated issue.

---

[1] Data source:The 6th World International Conference in October 2019.

Chapter I **The Great Legend**
China's Poverty Alleviation and Building an All–Round Moderately
Prosperous Society to the World

China is the second-largest economy in the world, and it contributes a third of annual global economic growth. Some of the Chinese industrial corporations are world leaders in their industries. These assets not only meet domestic demand but also play a key role in facilitating the recovery of the world economy and eradicating poverty globally.

According to UN statistics, poverty alleviation rates in other developing countries are slow while the population living in poverty is even increasing. For example, the number of people living in extreme poverty in sub-Saharan Africa increased from 278 million in 1990 to 413 million in 2015, which accounts for more than half of the poor population in the world.

Endemic poverty in Africa is mainly caused by its massive debt load and the exponential growth of national debt. The cumulative debt of African countries has doubled in the past five to six years and reached 53 percent of their GDP in 2018. Thirty-three of the 45 sub-Saharan African states are considered least developed countries.

China has shared its poverty reduction experience with the entire world, including providing aid to Africa and other regions with high numbers of people in poverty. In June 2020, President Xi Jinping addressed the China-Africa Summit on Solidarity against COVID-19 emergency, where he announced that within the Forum on China-Africa Cooperation (FOCAC) framework, China is ready to waive African countries' interest-free government loans that are due to mature by the end of 2020.

China is urging all G20 countries to further extend the period for relieving the debt burden, including African countries, and hopes that the international community— in particular, developed countries and international financial institutions—will take more assertive action to alleviate Africa's debt burden.

II. China's Achievement in Poverty Alleviation and Its Global Signicance[①]

Seeing that poor people and poor areas will enter the moderately prosperous society together with the rest of the country is a solemn promise made by our Party (...) The Communist Party of China strives for both the wellbeing of the Chinese people and human progress. To make new and greater contributions for mankind is our Party's abiding mission.

——*Report at the 19th National Congress of the the Communist Party of China (CPC), October 18, 2017*

On the list of the 17 United Nations' Sustainable Development Goals (SDGs), the eradication of poverty, what Mahatma Gandhi called "the worst form of violence", rightly comes the first.

One of the most significant achievements of China in the past 70 years since the founding of the People's Republic of China is related to poverty alleviation. 2020 will mark the year in which China will eliminate extreme poverty and achieve the objective of building a "moderately prosperous society". Given the demographic importance of China—18% of the world's population—this positive development is a major contribution to the progress of mankind.

In his foreword to *China 2030,* former president of the World Bank, Robert B. Zoellick affirmed: "China's economic performance over the past 30 years has been remarkable. It is a unique development success story, providing valuable lessons for other countries seeking to emulate this success." [②]

---

① By David Gosset, sinologist, founder of the Europe-China Forum.

② From *China 2030* by the World Bank and the Development Research Center of the State Council of the People's Republic of China, 2013.

(1) Chinese governance, infrastructure, education, gender equality, healthcare, controlled urbanization: the interdependent factors explaining China's development performance.

There are several interdependent factors which explain China's performance in the field of developmental economics.

First, Chinese governance allows for highly effective collective mobilization. More specifically, once China has clearly identified an objective, the Chinese government is able to tap into all available resources to reach its goals.

In 2012, in his report at the 18th National Congress of the CPC, Hu Jintao, former generd-secretary of the CPC, had expressed a similar ambition: "Completing the building of a moderately prosperous society in all respects by 2020 is an arduous task, and all the comrades in the Party must work single-mindedly and with fortitude to reach this goal."

In the report at the 19th National Congress of CPC in October 2017, Xi Jinping, the general-secretary of the CPC, clearly noted: "Seeing that poor people and poor areas will enter the moderately prosperous society together with the rest of the country is a solemn promise made by our Party. We should mobilize the energies of our whole Party, our whole country, and our whole society, and continue to implement targeted poverty reduction and alleviation measures."

Besides the capacity to mobilize, one of the advantages of Chinese political governance is its continuity over a long period of time. This continuity is essential in transforming a society as large as China's.

Second, China has also been able to follow its own development path. While many countries opted to follow the Western paths of development, China refused to imitate, and on the contrary, it proved to be a gigantic socio-political innovator.

In 1978, Deng Xiaoping put his country on the path of the reform and opening-up. China carried out socialist market economy, combining a planned economy with a market economy, which has obviously accelerated China's economic progress.

As Deng Xiaoping famously said: " It does not matter whether the cat is black or white, as long as it catches mice."

In its battle against poverty, the Chinese authorities have been able to remain focused on the right priorities.

Third, the capacity to put in place solid infrastructure has allowed China to progress. China rightly followed a sequence which is expressed by its very common saying: "Want to be rich? Build roads first!" There are obvious connections between Chinese governance and the capacity to deliver on huge infrastructure projects. From this perspective and taking history into consideration, it can be said that China has always been an infrastructure superpower (e.g. the Dujiangyan irrigation system developed in 300 BC, the building of the Great Wall and the Grand Canal).

Fourth, in parallel with this attention to infrastructure, China's education system took the country's literacy rate to an unprecedented level. While over 96% of the Chinese population is considered literate, it is only 71% for India, which is comparable in terms of demographic size. Some studies show that the literacy rate for sub-Saharan Africa is around 65%, which is obviously a serious obstacle to social and economic progress.

Fifth, it has to be noted that education contributed to the emancipation of Chinese women, which contributes to gender equality. One often quotes Mao Zedong's words, "Women hold up half of the sky", because this expression contains the truth. The seventh UN Secretary-General Kofi Annan articulated very well the connection between the status of women and economic development: "Gender equality is more than a goal in itself. It is a precondition for meeting the challenge of reducing poverty." In the United Nations'17 interdependent Sustainable Development Goals, "gender equality" is presented as the fifth goal.

Sixth, following the success of the reform and opening-up, China has been able to set up a basic healthcare system. With the New Rural Co-operative Medical Care System (NRCMCS) created in 2002, 800 million rural residents has gained access to basic healthcare coverage.

Chapter I **The Great Legend**
China's Poverty Alleviation and Building an All-Round Moderately
Prosperous Society to the World

In *The Great Escape: Health, Wealth, and the Origins of Inequality* (2013), Angus Deaton wrote: "The greatest escape in human history is the escape from poverty and death." It is for his analysis on poverty and welfare that Angus Deaton received the Nobel Memorial Prize in Economic Sciences in 2015.

China's great "escape" from poverty has also been a great "escape" from death. In 1949, life expectancy in China was 35. It is now 77. In 2018, the data of the World Health Organization showed an interesting phenomenon. In that year, China had overtaken the United States of America in healthy life expectancy at birth for the first time. American newborns can still expect to live longer overall but the last 10 years of American lives are unfortunately not expected to be healthy.

Seventh, a relatively harmonious urbanization can also be seen as an element contributing to poverty alleviation. "Sustainable Cities and Communities" is the eleventh goal of the SDGs. Cities provide jobs, but there are many cities around the world that are associated with slums. That China managed to avoid this phenomenon affecting so many urban centers across the world is a remarkable achievement.

(2) China for the world

The signal that China is sending to the world can't be clearer: poverty is not a destiny. It can be defeated. It is for Latin America, Africa or some Eurasian regions a message of hope.

While things are looking rosier within China's borders, more efforts are certainly needed at the global level. In *The Great Escape: Health, Wealth, and the Origins of Inequality*, Angus Deaton reminds us: "although the poverty rate has fallen in other regions of the world, the fall in absolute numbers of poor has been driven in large part by the rapid growth of China, so that, at least until the past ten years, the absolute number of non-Chinese poor has continued to increase."

China has been for decades willing to help other countries. On the sixth of May 1982, while he was exchanging views with Samuel Kanyon Doe, Liberia's Head of

State, Deng Xiaoping told his interlocutor: "China has not given much help to its third-world friends. That is because our country, although vast in territory, is very poor and still faces many difficulties. Since the founding of our People's Republic, we have essentially solved the problems of food and clothing and have become self-sufficient in grain. That in itself is quite remarkable, because these problems remained unsolved for so long in old China (…) We are now devoting all our efforts to construction and the rather rapid development of our economy. When we have succeeded, we shall be able to do more for our friends in the third world." [1]

At the 19th National Congress of the CPC, Xi Jinping explained: "The Communist Party of China strives for both the wellbeing of the Chinese people and human progress. To make new and greater contributions for mankind is our Party's abiding mission." How is it possible not to draw parallels to Deng Xiaoping's remark to his African counterpart in 1982?

In the same speech at the 19th National Congress of the CPC, Xi Jinping mentioned more details: "China will actively promote international cooperation through the Belt and Road Initiative. In doing so, we hope to achieve policy, infrastructure, trade, financial, and people-to-people connectivity; and thus build a new platform for international cooperation to create new drivers of shared development."

While the opening-up orchestrated by Deng Xiaoping was mainly about synergies between Beijing and the world serving China's internal modernization, Xi Jinping structured the Belt and Road Initiative (BRI) and launched an "opening-up version 2.0", taking this cooperation beyond China's borders.

One of the most singular aspects of the Chinese contemporary story is the transformation from a mere receiver of ideas, practices and investments into a contributor of global security and development. The Belt and Road Initiative is already shaping the international agenda.

---

[1] In *Selected Works of Deng Xiaoping*, Vol.2, 1975-1982.

Chapter I **The Great Legend**
China's Poverty Alleviation and Building an All-Round Moderately
Prosperous Society to the World

In a very short period of time, Beijing was able to gather momentum for the creation of new international financial mechanisms to support its vision of a 21st century New Silk Road. The Silk Road Fund, the Asian Infrastructure Investment Bank (AIIB) and the New Development Bank (NDB) are young, promising institutions positioned to transform a vision into reality.

Being essentially about connectivity, the content of the Belt and Road remains open. It is a project that can integrate new ideas and realities more than being a rigid program. Besides the traditional land, maritime or air connections which will be reinforced, digital New Silk Roads backed by evolving technologies will increasingly enrich the relations between China and the world.

Inclusiveness defines the Belt and Road vision. It is not a plan of the East to contain the West, an enterprise of the South to weaken the North, a challenge to the Bretton Woods or the UN mechanisms, but merely aims at more global synergies for co-development and peace.

One of the paths leading to what China's President Xi Jinping calls, in a reinterpretation of Chinese classical universalism, a "community of shared future for mankind", the Belt and Road Initiative is a concrete illustration of China's peaceful renaissance.

At the 19th National Congress of the CPC, Xi Jinping also added: "China will increase assistance to other developing countries, especially the least developed countries, and to do its part to reduce the North-South development gap."

In 2018, when Beijing established the China International Development Cooperation Agency (CIDCA), it was also a powerful statement. Following its own success, the People's Republic is organizing its aid to less advanced countries. As explained on the China International Development Cooperation Agency website, the agency "aims to formulate strategic guidelines, plans and policies for foreign aid, coordinate and offer advice on major foreign aid issues, advance the country's reforms in matters involving foreign aid, and identify major programs and supervise and evaluate their implementation."

Medical help in Mauritania, Uganda, Libya, Comoros and South Sudan; humanitarian support in Afghanistan, Cuba, Iran and Somalia; education programs in Tunisia, Ghana, the Maldives and Ivory Coast; and technical collaboration in Pakistan, Nigeria and Laos, the China International Development Cooperation Agency has made great contributions.

In this context, China and other donors have to coordinate their efforts and constantly practice sharing experiences. In relations with Africa, but also other regions, it would be wise for the European Union and China to develop more synergy.

Another example of "China for the world" can be taken in relation with the World Bank, which worked with the Development Research Center of the State Council of the People Republic of China on the *China 2030* report previously quoted.

China began its partnership with the World Bank in 1980. The motto of the institution created at the 1944 Bretton Woods Conference is "Working for a World Free of Poverty". China started as a recipient of support from the International Development Association. 27 years later, China became a donor. In 2010, China became the World Bank's third largest shareholder!

(3) China and its new challenges: inequalities and evolving expectations

There is no such a thing as the end of history. After solving the issue of eradicating extreme poverty, China is certainly facing a new set of challenges.

Inequalities are now a problem for China as it is in the West. In 2018, People's Daily Online published a revealing article "China's Gini coefficient exceeded 0.4 in 2017". Based on the title, income inequality had become a relatively serious problem in China.

Uneven incomes have led, among other problems, to difficulties in relation with housing. Migrant labor is being priced out in some of the higher end provinces and cities. This is an issue because it limits the opportunities that those migrant laborers can enjoy. If migrant laborers cannot establish themselves in resource rich

Chapter I **The Great Legend**
China's Poverty Alleviation and Building an All–Round Moderately
Prosperous Society to the World

areas through permanent residence, then bringing them up to the same level of China's growing middle-income group will be that much harder.

What is often referred to as the urban-rural gap is to be combined with geographic imbalance. Most of the economic development is still clustered along the coasts, while the interior is mixed in its development. China has to proliferate the economic development that has been trapped along the coast and start to move inland.

The grand strategy of development of the West did contribute in bringing development beyond the coastal areas (6 provinces, 5 autonomous regions and Chongqing). However, territorial inequalities within China remain an issue. Plans for the Jingjinji Metropolitan Region (Beijing-Tianjin-Hebei), or even the ambitious Greater Bay Area vision, will certainly create opportunities for China's inland areas. Of course, these initiatives will require time to be fully implemented.

China's demographic challenge is another issue that should not be underestimated. Like many of China's neighbors, China boasts a sizable elderly population. This is an issue, as continuing robust economic growth requires a population that is young, healthy, and able enough to maintain it.

While China will have to find the ways to reduce inequalities—here fiscal reforms, among others, will be necessary—it will also have to avoid what economists call the middle-income trap.

More generally, it can be argued that it is the changing expectations of the Chinese people that poses a new set of more complex problems. After the most immediate material needs are satisfied, more qualitative aspects of life have to be addressed. The urban and hyper-connected Chinese population living in Beijing, Shanghai, Xiamen, Guangzhou and Shenzhen is increasingly demanding better education, better healthcare and better air quality. This transition from quantity to quality will have to be carefully managed.

At the 19th National Congress of the CPC, Xi Jinping affirmed: "We must recognize that the evolution of the principal contradiction facing Chinese society represents a historic shift that affects the whole landscape and that creates many new demands for the work of the Party and of the country. Building on continued efforts to sustain development, we must devote great energy to addressing development's imbalances and inadequacies, and push hard to improve the quality and effect of development. With this, we will be better placed to meet the ever-growing economic, political, cultural, social and ecological needs of our people, and to promote well-rounded human development and all-round social progress."

China's leadership has perfectly identified the "imbalances and inadequacies" which characterize the new phase of China's transformation. It therefore maximizes the chance for rebalancing and for fixing its inadequacies.

By continuing its progress on her own path of gradual reform and managed opening-up, China will certainly overcome her new challenges and, by doing so, will take the world to another level of stability and prosperity.

III. Voices from the Frontline: China's War on Poverty[1]

Several years ago, continuing our 25-plus years in communicating the China story, I and Adam Zhu, my long-time partner, were asked to focus on China's poverty alleviation campaign, especially as championed by President Xi Jinping, who stressed for China to become a "moderately prosperous society" by 2020—the first of the country's "centenary goals" (the 100th anniversary of the Communist Party of China being in 2021)—not a single Chinese citizen could be living in absolute, extreme or abject poverty.

No matter how large China's GDP, no matter how large China's GDP per capita, China could not claim to have achieved this goal unless and until every citizen was living above the line of absolute poverty.

---

[1] By Robert Lawrence Kuhn, chairman of the Kuhn Foundation, China Reform Friendship Medal Recipient, the host and writer of the documentary *Voices from the Frontline: China's War on Poverty*.

Chapter I **The Great Legend**
China's Poverty Alleviation and Building an All-Round Moderately
Prosperous Society to the World

Today, in the Western world, especially in the US, there is concern about China's actions and suspicion of China's motives. Poverty alleviation, to me, is the best disruptor of such stereotypes.

China was on course to meeting its target of eradicating poverty in rural areas and eliminating regional poverty by 2020 when the COVID-19 epidemic struck. Can China still achieve its goal?

What was the extent of this monumental challenge of poverty alleviation by 2020, notwithstanding the hurricane-force headwinds of COVID-19? What were the measures instituted to alleviate poverty? What was the organizational structure to implement such a massive national project? And what were the checks and balances to make sure there was minimal fraud—ensuring the assessments and recordings of poverty alleviation were accurate? And could it be sure there was minimal corruption—that the funds allocated to poverty alleviation were in fact going to poverty alleviation?

In short, what is it about China's system that enables such success?

On July 31, 2019, PBS SoCal, the PBS flagship public television station, premiered our documentary, *Voices from the Frontline: China's War on Poverty* —our inside story of China's race to eradicate all absolute poverty by 2020. It is the first in-depth documentary about China's poverty alleviation campaign to be broadcast abroad, portraying the country's strategies and structures in eradicating extreme poverty.

Executive Producer Adam Zhu, Director Peter Getzels, and I, as host and writer, were privileged and proud to participate.

Working with our partners, our international film crew had unprecedented access to travel across China and be embedded in the country's massive poverty alleviation programs. We met poor villagers, local officials and special monitors, as well as those being lifted out of poverty—those assigned to do the lifting and those recruited to do the checking.

The production of the documentary took two years, during which the film crew visited poor households in six regions—Guizhou, Gansu, Shanxi, Sichuan, Hainan and Xinjiang—and interviewed government officials at the central, provincial, city, county, township levels, recording a large amount of first-hand information. It wasn't easy: the poorest areas, for weeks at a time; summer, winter, the heat, the cold.

The documentary provides a textured and intimate portrayal of China's poverty alleviation by following six cases that highlight China's strategy and the systems and organization needed to implement it. Focusing on the six cases, the documentary presents the Chinese concept of "targeted poverty alleviation" and explains the "five methods" for achieving targeted poverty alleviation: industry, creating sustainable micro-businesses; relocation, moving people from remote areas; education and training; ecological compensation for those living in environmentally vulnerable areas; and social security, medical subsidies and direct payments to those who cannot work.

It captures in verité style grassroots stories: the young Party secretary working in a remote village; the Gansu girl who changed her fate through education; the Kazakh herder who lifted himself out of poverty by raising camels; the elderly of Guizhou who were relocated out of the mountains; the third-party evaluating teams whose independent checks enabled greater accuracy and honesty; and the Party secretaries at five levels of local government who coordinate their tasks and pledged to achieve their poverty alleviation goals.

Our cameras followed Huang Haijun, the young first secretary of Lingmen village, Qiongzhong county, Hainan province: providing "precision" identification of poor families, visiting impoverished households to understand their circumstances and implementing assistance measures customized to each household. The documentary also recorded the living and working conditions of grassroots poverty alleviation workers and presented first-hand accounts of poverty alleviation officials at all levels.

As much as I thought I knew China, I was startled to discover that every poor family in China has its own file, each with a targeted plan to lift each above the line of absolute poverty.

Our cross-cultural collaboration between Americans and Chinese led to insights about how China's extraordinary poverty alleviation program actually works.

While 2020 is the year that China intends to eliminate all absolute poverty nationwide, it is also the year of the novel coronavirus, and when one looks at how the Chinese government mobilized to fight the contagion, similarities between China's war on the epidemic and China's war on poverty are striking.

"Understanding China's approach to poverty alleviation can help people understand how China's system works," said Executive Producer Adam Zhu, stressing "when you understand poverty alleviation, you understand China".

"Directing a cross-cultural team in remote parts of China led to insights on how this extraordinary program works," said director Peter Getzels, who took a cinematic approach to the documentary, using a verité or observational style and editing in a way that shows more than tells. Stories unfold naturally, poor people give accounts candidly—making a visceral impact and enabling viewers to experience the poverty-alleviating process for themselves.

Although poverty is being fought the world over, there is nothing anywhere like China's relocation of whole villages on a massive, national scale—moving people from remote rural areas to cities, providing homes and jobs, giving them a real chance at a better life.

I travelled to Huishui county, Guizhou province, where the relocation of whole villages was underway. From remote mountain hamlets, villagers were being moved to new community, 70 kilometers away.
I learned that housing is free for villagers who relocate there. A family of four receives up to 80 square meters of living space, 20 per person. The government also covers all basic amenities, including sofas, beds, kitchenware and TVs.

But how can these rural men, who were farmers, learn new, non-farming jobs?

I joined a cooking class and got to know one of the former farmers, who was learning to be a chef. I spent time with three generations of his family and several of his friends. Almost everyone was appreciative of their new lives.

Yet, not everyone from the villages agrees to move to the new communities. I travelled to Daijing village to meet the Party secretary. His job was to convince the few remaining villagers to relocate. It is policy that neither he nor the government can force people to relocate.

But in such a massive country, with career stakes high and funding vast, cheating and stealing are no surprise. China will not allow falsifying data, or misappropriating funds, to undermine its poverty alleviation goals.

One of the aspects of poverty alleviation that impressed me the most was the system put in place to mitigate fraud, called "third-party evaluation". The governing idea is that since the third-party evaluators would be coming from completely different regions, they would not likely know any of the officials whom they would be evaluating and thus not be swayed by personal relationships.

The task is to evaluate both the successes and the challenges of the poverty alleviation process—and to assess how officials are doing their jobs.

To ensure that local officials do not prepare for inspection visits, the evaluation team decides where they will go only at the last minute, often the same morning of the inspection.

I commend the State Council Leading Group Office of Poverty Alleviation and Development for its independent checking and inspecting, avowing that if there is any false report or fraud, officials will be held accountable and dealt with seriously, so that the results of poverty alleviation can stand the test of history and the people. The greater the transparency of the government, the greater the trust of people in the government.

China's targeted poverty alleviation campaign, for all its historic success, still

Chapter I **The Great Legend**
China's Poverty Alleviation and Building an All-Round Moderately
Prosperous Society to the World

faced or faces some challenges.

What's to prevent those who are pushed just over the line of extreme poverty, after the excitement dies down, after 2020, from falling back down below it? For China's poverty reduction to be counted a true success, it must be sustainable.

Living barely over the line of extreme poverty, far below standards of living enjoyed by China's urban middle class, hardly makes for a society of common prosperity, China's long-term goal. The fight against poverty cannot end in 2020.

To truly eliminate all poverty in China, and to do it sustainably, poverty alleviation programs must continue to be an ongoing process and an ongoing priority in China. It is, indeed, a "Long March".

Those who recognize China's unprecedented poverty-alleviation success must also recognize its causal relationship to China's system of one-party-leadership rule and a strong, command-down government. While all political systems have trade-offs, without such strong authority, it would not be possible for China to reach its poverty alleviation goals.

China's grand poverty alleviation mission, lifting now over 800 million people out of poverty over 40-plus years, and 100 million of the intractably poor over the past seven years, is an epic achievement.

In the ages to come, when the histories of civilizations are written, China's targeted poverty alleviation epoch will be featured.

02

China's Success in Rapid Economic Progress and Poverty Alleviation

I. The Advantages of Socialist System with Chinese Characteristics[1]

China's "miracle" is embodied not merely in its rapid economic development, which has contributed and is contributing greatly to global economic expansion, but also in the huge progress of its social development.

The Human Development Index (HDI) is a composite measure of life expectancy, education and and per capita income used by the United Nations Development Programme to rank countries into four tiers of human development. Under the leadership of the Communist Party of China, the Chinese people have striven to raise China's HDI to 0.752, which means that with a population of 1.40 billion, China is now a high human development country, while only 70 years ago, when its population was just over 500 million, it was an extremely low human development country. In the next five to seven years, China will join the very high human development group (with an HDI of 0.80 or higher).

Since the founding of the People's Republic of China in 1949, China's people-centered human development has made huge leaps. Moreover, China has made a bigger contribution to the world's human development than any other country.

---

[1] By Hu Angang, dean of the Institute for Contemporary China Studies, professor of the School of Public Policy and Management at Tsinghua University.

Chapter I **The Great Legend**
China's Poverty Alleviation and Building an All–Round Moderately
Prosperous Society to the World

Before the founding of the PRC, China's HDI was extremely low, well below the world's average, and the country's development rate was also lower than the world average. Since 1950, China has been undergoing great changes. The country is adhering to a three-step process in which it has gone from overall absolute poverty to the enrichment of part of the population, to eventually common moderate prosperity. The rapid speed of development from extremely low to high human development reflects the historic changes taking place in contemporary China. It is a miracle that encompasses three aspects of society, namely the economy, health and education. As China has made the transition from a low-income country to a medium-to-high income one, so too it has ceased to be the "sick man in East Asia", instead it has become Healthy China, while also overcoming a high illiteracy rate to become a great power in human resources.

The fundamental advantage in bringing about the human development miracle is the socialist system with Chinese characteristics. It is not by accident that China has created such a miracle; rather, it is a process of quantitative to qualitative change. The socialist institutional advantage is the core factor at play. The primary driving forces are the socialist principle of investing in people, the socialist goal of expanding people's substantive freedom, and the fundamental purpose of the CPC of wholeheartedly serving the people.

A comparison of HDI between China and India, the two most dynamic and promising developing countries with large populations, fully reflects the role played by China's socialist institutional factor. In 1950, China's HDI was only 87 percent that of India, while in 2017, China's was 118 percent that of India. In the indicators of life expectancy and mean years of schooling, China leads India by 8 and 4 years respectively. China is at least 30 years ahead of India in terms of health and education development. This means that at the current rate of development, India will reach China's human development level in 2040.

Why is it that socialism with Chinese characteristics represents such a competitive institutional advantage? First of all, it enables the State to focus on the big picture over the long term; that is, to input continuous human capital investment in all the people. In particular, investment in people's health and education is a basic, long-term and effective asset, the dividends of which are long-standing and far-reaching. Second, the socialist system with Chinese characteristics places high significance on the role of the market. As a result, government macro-control and full market vitality can combine and cooperate with each other in a concerted manner.

While achieving spectacular economic development, China can also maintain significant economic and social stability. Furthermore, China can organize and mobilize the people. In the era of extreme poverty, when the resources at hand were meager, China extensively mobilized people to break through the poverty trap and achieved basic guarantees for education and health. In addition, China's institutional advantages can translate to political advantages, and to scientific and democratic decision-making. For example, in the process of designing the "Healthy China 2030 Plan" and the "Education Modernization 2035 Plan", the government solicited public opinions online, and these were fully taken into account before the finalization and publication of the plans. These examples reflect the substantial public participation in China's democratic decision-making process.

China is the largest contributor to global human development. Since the Industrial Revolution, no country as large population as China has realized modernization. As President Xi Jinping has made clear, China will always be a contributor to global development. As China has the world's largest population, improvements in China's human development mean that a significant proportion of the world's people will be better off. According to data provided by the United Nations Development Program in the Human Development Report (2018), in 2017 the total population of the world's high human development group was 2.38 billion, of which China accounted for 59.2 percent. If China's development trend continues, by 2030, when China successfully enters the very high human development group, it will increase the total population of that group by 1.45 billion; at that stage the very high human development group will include 2.89 billion people, more than a third (34.3 percent) of the world's total population.

In short, the process of China's modernization is a process of continuous investment in people. It makes full use of the advantages of the socialist system to input the human capital of more than a billion people.

Chapter I **The Great Legend**
China's Poverty Alleviation and Building an All–Round Moderately
Prosperous Society to the World

II. China's Poverty Alleviation Success: Review and Lessons[1]

1. Introduction

Against a backdrop of autarky, turbulence and widespread poverty in the late 1970s, in 1978 China turned a page in its history with the launch a policy agenda known as "reform and opening-up". Over four decades, this agenda guided China's shift from a small, closed and poor economy to a higher middle income country and the world's largest economy in purchasing power parity (PPP) terms. It produced a dramatic success story with respect to poverty alleviation, with around 800 million people getting out of poverty.

Rapid economic growth was the main driver behind China's poverty reduction. China's economy grew by an average of 9.4 percent per year for the 40 years after 1978, and income per capita grew by 8.4 percent annually over the same period. Rapid growth was also highly effective in reducing poverty: between 1981 and 2012 the share of the population in poverty fell annually by 0.97 percentage points for each percentage point increase in GDP per capita (Figure 1).[2]

---

[1] By Bert Hofman and Lauren A. Johnston. Bert Hofman, chief economist, World Bank's country director for China. Lauren A. Johnston, research associate at SOAS University of London, China Institute.

[2] Calculated with GDP and GDP per capita in constant RMB. Data from the World Development Indicators, accessed on May 25, 2020.

Figure 1   China's Real Income per Capita and Poverty 1978—2017

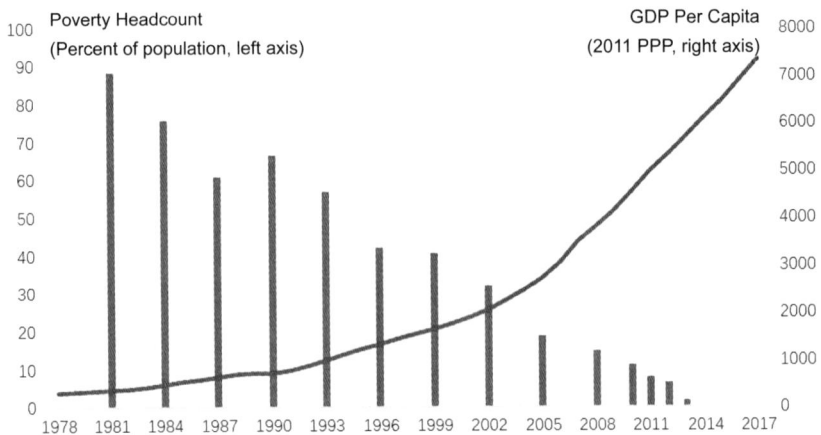

Source: World Bank estimates based on NBS Household Survey Data and World Development Indicators.

Across alternative poverty measures poverty alleviation in China has been dramatic. At the onset of reforms, nine out of 10 people in China were poor; by 2019, extreme poverty was practically eliminated. Based on the current official national poverty line, of 2,300 yuan per year for rural areas (at 2010 constant prices), rural poverty declined from 97.5 percent of the rural population in 1978 to 3.1 percent in 2017, that is from 770.39 million to 30.5 million people. Premier Li Keqiang's report to the National People's Congress on May 2020 noted that in 2019 the poverty headcount had further declined to 0.6 percent of the population.

Using the World Bank's international poverty line of $1.90 per day (at 2011 PPP or internationally comparable prices) the headcount poverty index fell from 88 percent of the total population to 0.7 percent between 1981 and 2015. This translates to a fall from some 875 million living in poverty to 10 million. Parallel declines in mortality and rising life expectancy mean that a child born in China today will, on average, live three decades longer than a child born in China in the mid-20th century.

China's progress is impressive on a global scale (Table 1). Worldwide, some 1.2 billion people have escaped poverty since 1981, some 74 percent of whom

Chapter I **The Great Legend**
China's Poverty Alleviation and Building an All-Round Moderately
Prosperous Society to the World

did so in China. Without China's success, the first goal of the United Nation's Millennium Development Goal—halving the number of people living in extreme poverty between 1990 and 2015—would not have been achieved.

Table 1 Number of People in Extreme Poverty, 1981—2015

(Unit: million)

	1981	1990	1999	2010	2015
China	875.3	751.7	503.7	149.6	10
East Asia and Pacific ex China	237.4	233.1	189.2	69.8	37.1
Europe and Central Asia	10.4	13.3	36.8	11.7	7.8
Latin America and the Caribbean	50.2	66.4	69.6	36.3	25.3
Middle East and North Africa	18.3	14	10.5	6.9	14.1
South Asia	515.3	537.1	535	403.6	215.2
Sub-Saharan Africa	193.7	279.7	378.7	404.9	419.6
World Total	1906	1899.2	1728.5	1088.3	736.7
World Total ex. China	1030.7	1147.5	1224.8	938.7	726.7

Source: PovCalNET, World Development Indicators and authors' calculations.
Note: Poverty is measured at the World Bank's International Poverty line of $1.90 per day in 2011 PPP.

China's success has sparked considerable interest in how the country achieved this. Here, we summarizes some of the key strategies and policies that led to China's poverty alleviation. Given the limitations of the chapter, this is far from an exhaustive account. Nonetheless, understanding some of the key policy mechanisms and priority choices of China over recent decades may help officials in other countries shape their own poverty alleviation agenda.

2. A growth strategy to drive poverty alleviation

To a large extent, China's success in reducing poverty can be attributed to the rapid and sustained economic growth unleashed by reform and opening-up. This rapid growth sprung from a very low baseline—China was among the poorest countries in the world in the late 1970.

In some ways, China's reforms followed many of the prescriptions mainstream economists would recommend. China opened up for trade and foreign investment, gradually liberalized prices, diversified ownership, strengthened property rights, and kept inflation under control. Continued (relative) macroeconomic stability allowed high savings to be turned into high investment and rapid urbanization, which in turn triggered rapid structural transformation and productivity growth. In China's case, on the reform side, growth was supported by a complex experimental, decentralized and gradual process of the reform and opening-up often summarized by the analogy of "crossing the river by feeling the stones".

Reforms took off in agriculture. The household responsibility system gave families control over plots of land, while the government raised state procurement prices and allowed the planting of more profitable crops. Combined, these dramatically increased agricultural productivity and rural incomes, which accounted for much of the poverty reduction in the first decade after 1979. As for industry, rather that privatizing State-owned enterprises, China allowed competition of domestic and foreign owned private enterprises to grow alongside. By the mid-1990s, non-State-owned enterprises were the main drivers of growth, employment and income.

Opening-up was initiated with the establishment of the special economic zones in 1980, which became laboratories for market reforms. Foreign investment was a vehicle by which China imported technology and knowhow, and increasingly linked China to global markets. China's entry in the World Trade Organization in 2001 made it the preferred base for global supply chains, and foreign direct investment and foreign trade surged. In the 2000s, the reforms shifted to the social sectors, and access to education, healthcare and social welfare dramatically improved.

Meanwhile, with market reforms well-advanced since the 1993 decisions to establish a socialist market economy, China used the first decade of the 2000s to prepare for a different growth model, including deeper investment in higher education and science and technology. The government's view is that China needs to have a leading role, the "decisive role" of the market in resource allocation.

Chapter I **The Great Legend**
China's Poverty Alleviation and Building an All–Round Moderately
Prosperous Society to the World

Growth in per capita income was further boosted by a demographic dividend. Whereas China's population grew very rapidly until the early 1970s, afterwards, especially since the 1980s, the population growth rate fell rapidly in part as a result of China's population policies. This produced a high demographic dividend, a period of rising working-age population share. In China's case, this lasted for four decades from the 1970s. During its demographic dividend, China explicitly invested in attracting labor-intensive foreign investment; it promoted foreign trade; it used targeted incentives including for internal migration so that households and the nation would benefit from the surging labor force.

Economic reforms and slower demographic growth were fundamental to China's dramatic poverty reduction, but it was far from the whole story. Selective additional features of China's approach are elaborated in the next section.

3. China's strategic approaches to poverty reduction

(1) Institutions and incentives

Since the launch of the reform and opening-up, poverty alleviation has received political support from all levels of government. After initial reforms had spurred economic growth, a dedicated structure to drive poverty alleviation was established in 1986: the Leading Group on Poverty Alleviation and Development (LGPR). Concurrently, a LGRP office, known as a Poor Area Development Office (PADOs), was established within each rung of government, down to the county level.

The LGPR oversaw poverty alleviation policy formulation, including definition of a national poverty line and program design; the PADO oversaw program implementation at the local level. Both were backed up by top-level support and funding. Poverty alleviation programs were predominantly targeted at getting people sustainable livelihoods, i.e. poverty alleviation through development, and much of the programs were aimed at rural areas. Deng Xiaoping held the view that, "Whether Chinese society is stable or not, whether China's economy can develop or not, depends on whether rural areas can develop and whether the peasant life improves".[①] This focus and related implementation drive, to a large extent, was driven by China's poverty-related institutions. It also helped to avoid China experiencing another famine—agricultural productivity remained in constant focus as agricultural regions were home to most of the poor.

Another important feature of China's approach was to incentivize government officials. Their promotion prospects depended on the economic success of their region, in particular on meeting selected targets in growth, employment, foreign investment, and population control. The fiscal system also incentivized growth by leaving an incremental share of revenues raised with the revenue-generating government. Government official incentives were broadly aligned with investor incentives, while poverty alleviation institutions within each rung of government worked to promote and ensure some level of redistribution. The set of institutions and incentives have not been flawless, and excessive growth drives and corruption have been issues of concern to the central government, but nonetheless they have supported the success being marked in 2020.

(2) Strategically unequal—but ultimately inclusive—growth

China's poverty reduction was not uniform over time or across the country. The rate of poverty reduction was most rapid in the 1980s, and it slowed over time, as poverty itself declined and growth slowed. Geographically, extreme poverty rapidly declined in coastal China, while it was much slower to decline in the remote south western and western regions. According to the China Rural Poverty Monitoring Reports, by 2016 relatively prosperous coastal provinces such as Zhejiang and Jiangsu had poverty rates of near zero, whereas regions such as Gansu and Xinjiang had poverty rates above 12.5 percent.

Geographic inequality of poverty reduction followed from a political decision by Deng Xiaoping in 1986: "Our policy is to let some people and some areas get rich first to drive and help the backward areas. First advanced areas later have the

---

① Page 77—78, Volume 3, *Selected Works of Deng Xiaoping*.

Chapter I **The Great Legend**
China's Poverty Alleviation and Building an All-Round Moderately
Prosperous Society to the World

duty to help the backward areas." In line with this, coastal areas were opened up first through the Coastal Development Strategy, which focused investment and incentives on these regions. The aim was to cluster China's limited resources in the regions that could generate the fastest growth. Only from the 2000s did China's western regions become the policy focus through the Western Development Strategy.

After the initial results from the reforms in agriculture subsided, the poorest segments of the population benefitted less than the average from China's growth, even though they too saw their incomes rise substantially. This was reinforced by the Coastal Development Strategy, and the strategy of decentralized implementation of reforms, which led to a wider variation of outcomes than under central control. Income inequality hence rapidly increased, especially between coastal and inland regions and between urban and rural areas. In recent two decades, the poor have had per capita growth higher than average, and income inequality has started to fall again.

(3) A progressively explicit and targeted poverty alleviation agenda

At the start of the reform and opening-up, growth alone, especially in rural areas, delivered dramatic poverty alleviation. Over time, China's poor have become marked by greater marginality—for example, in terms of living in remote regions, being disabled or elderly. China's poverty alleviation agenda and policies have reflected this shift. Hence, in the 1980s and 1990s, growth was a more explicit element of the poverty alleviation agenda. A share of those fruits was incrementally re-invested in local health, education and poverty alleviation agendas in poorer regions.

More recently, a direct and more targeted poverty alleviation agenda has evolved. In sum, a national agenda fostered by growth became a provincial-level poverty agenda, a county-level agenda, a village-level agenda, and most recently a house hold-level agenda. Within that, as growth and rising incomes allowed, the quality and equity of access to health and education services was gradually increased. A downside of early reforms was a sharp and uneven decline in fiscal resources, casing inequality in government services such as education and health. Recent efforts are targeting that inequality, including via redistribution of fiscal resources, incentives for top teachers to work in the poorest regions, and by a matching process whereby richer educational regions and schools support a poorer region and school. This reflects a step in China's early decision to encourage some areas and people to get rich before others in the early period on the condition of a later process of convergence.

China's recent household level poverty alleviation agenda is known as "Targeted Poverty Alleviation". It was understood that reaching the final pockets of extreme poverty in China would require information at the household and individual family member level. Poverty alleviation officials led a massive survey around 2014 that has created a large database on the poorest, originally including some 70 million people. As the last stretch of China's absolute poverty alleviation agenda is run, this database is continuously updated and also serves to inform the "last mile" officials and policies seeking to ensure these people also rise above the poverty line.

In the process, China has mobilized not only government officials—for whom poverty reduction features in their performance evaluation,—but companies, banks, non-governmental organizations and charities are all contributing in their own specific manner to poverty reduction. This "whole of society" approach is unique to China.

China has progressively and deliberately adopted technology to support the poorest. China's thriving e-commerce has become a vehicle for poor and remote communities to market their goods and buy at lower prices. The government has supported this by building the infrastructure for internet access, as well as by supporting the capacity of communities for bringing goods to market. Large e-commerce companies have equally been keen to support rural communities in the use of e-commerce. Internet and mobile technology have also been used to expand access to financial services, medical advice and services, and education, among others.

Chapter I **The Great Legend**
China's Poverty Alleviation and Building an All-Round Moderately
Prosperous Society to the World

(4) International development partnerships

Although China's poverty alleviation success is a source of national pride, that success was in fact also built upon international partnership. First, foreign investors were fundamental to China's growth. Foreign universities were also central to training many of the earlier leaders of China's reform and opening-up, and many of its leading entrepreneurs and scientists. Moreover, international development agencies, multilateral and bilateral, have had a continuous partnership with Chinese officials to support the poverty alleviation.

Indeed, Deng Xiaoping himself set the tone for this partnership in a meeting with then World Bank President McNamara in 1980, when Deng remarked: "China is determined to modernize and develop its economy. With the World Bank's assistance, China will be able to achieve its goals faster and more efficiently. Without the World Bank's assistance, China will still do it, but it might take longer." [1] Into that partnership, the World Bank provided direct and indirect poverty assistance. It specifically offered advice and financial resources for sectoral reforms including in agriculture, transportation, energy, urbanization, health, education, social protection, and also poverty alleviation. China's emphasis on building its own capacity for reforms meant that its government could localize the lessons learned from international experience, and introduce reforms "with Chinese characteristics" that fit China's own circumstances best.

4. Outlook

The emergence of the COVID-19 pandemic in early 2020 made conditions for eradicating extreme poverty this year more challenging, but the government remains committed to the goal. It has allocated an additional 1 percent of GDP this year for targeted measures to ensure meeting the goal. Irrespective, China's challenge will not stop here. First, with increasing prosperity, China's notion of

---

[1] Edwin Lim, 2008, Preface to the book: Fifty *Economists Look at Thirty Years of Reform and Opening-up*. It should be noted that this remark was reported by McNamara in a conversation with Edwin Lim; the official notes of the Deng-McNamara meeting did not mention this.

who is poor is likely to change. Most high income countries have a poverty line that is substantially above China's current national poverty line. Second, new challenges are emerging, in particular the country's rapidly ageing population, which will slow the growth, but also require national support for some of the hundreds of million pensioners that have insufficient income in old age. Finally, although China has predominantly relied on growth and development for poverty reduction, welfare payments and targeted support will be the mainstay of poverty alleviation of the future. Building and refining the government organization, programs and information systems to deliver these will be important for China's continued success.

III. Fruitful Achievements and Far-Reaching Significance[1]

The year 2020 will mark China's victory in the fight against poverty and the completion of the building of a well-off society in an all-round way. China is about to eliminate absolute rural poverty for the first time in a country with a history of thousands of years. Since the 18th National Congress of the Communist Party of China, the Party Central Committee, with Xi Jinping at the core, has made poverty elimination a priority in national governance and has implemented the strategy of targeted poverty alleviation. Targeted poverty alleviation has become an important example for the global poverty reduction process and has contributed Chinese wisdom and solutions to the achievement of the United Nations 2030 Agenda for Sustainable Development.

Overall, the goal of eradicating absolute poverty is going to be completed soon. According to China's current poverty alleviation standards, the rural poor population dropped from 98.99 million in 2012 to 5.51 million in 2019, with an average annual reduction of over 10 million, and the incidence of rural poverty

---

[1] By Liu Junwen, director general of the International Poverty Reduction Center in China.

Chapter I **The Great Legend**
China's Poverty Alleviation and Building an All–Round Moderately
Prosperous Society to the World

dropped from 10.2 percent to 0.6 percent. According to the World Bank's international poverty standard of $1.90 per person per day, the incidence of poverty in China fell from 88.3 percent at the end of 1981 to 0.5 percent in 2016, a cumulative decrease of 87.8 percentage points. This means that China has basically eliminated absolute poverty.

Infrastructure in poor areas has improved significantly. Since the 18th National Congress of the CPC, China has continued to increase investment in infrastructure such as water, electricity, roads and the internet. As of the end of 2019, poor areas had basically solved the problems of electricity and drinking water safety; the proportion of rural households in the natural village where they had telephone, cable TV, and broadband reached 100 percent, 99.1 percent and 97.3 percent respectively; 99.5 percent of the rural households were located in the natural villages where the main roads are hardened; 76.5 percent of the rural households in the natural village could easily take the bus; 86.4 percent of the rural households in the natural village could handle garbage processing in a centralized way. The living environment and development conditions in poor areas have been greatly improved.

The level of public services and social security is constantly improving. In poverty-stricken areas, the basic public service system is increasingly efficient, and the level of social security is steadily increasing. As of March 2019, 92.7 percent of counties across China had achieved balanced development of compulsory education, allowing more rural children to enjoy better and fairer education. The medical service system has been continuously improved. The construction of cultural facilities has advanced constantly. In 2019, the proportion of administrative villages with cultural activity facilities was 90.7 percent, 16.2 percentage points higher than that in 2012. The cultural life of people has been increasingly enriched.

China has chosen a poverty alleviation path that suits its national conditions and done a good job at top-level design. Since the 1980s, China's region-scale poor population has decreased significantly. But the marginal effect of poverty reduction has been declining, the poor people are more dispersed, and the problem of poverty has become more prominent. The old poverty alleviation path is no longer enough to meet the new requirements. In 2013, General Secretary Xi Jinping proposed "targeted poverty alleviation" in a timely manner. The key is to work according to China's ground reality, identify the targets of poverty alleviation, find out the causes of poverty, adapt measures to local conditions, categorize problems and implement policies accordingly, and carry out targeted assistance. Four core issues must be addressed: whom to support, who will act, what action should be taken and how to withdraw from the program when people shake off poverty. The "six targeted requirements"—targeted support receiver, targeted project arrangement, targeted use of funds, targeted delivery of measures to households, targeted arrangement of leaders based on village conditions—have been put forward, thus achieving an organic unity between targeted requirements and poverty alleviation.

Those who needed support have been identified in a targeted manner. In May 2014, China issued instructions on the establishment of archives and personal cards for poor households and villages, providing an institutional guarantee for accurate identification of poverty. In 2014, 800,000 people across the country were organized for poverty identification and establishment of archives and personal cards in rural areas. As a result, a unified national information system and big data management platform were built, which had identified 128,000 poor villages and 89.62 million poor people. In 2015 and 2016, the government mobilized nearly 2 million people to carry out a review of the work on the establishment of archives and personal cards. Big data comparisons and other methods were used to further accurately identify the poor, eliminating the wrongly identified and adding the ones missed. From 2017 to 2019, Chinese government implemented the dynamic management of registered poor people, increased poverty alleviation measures and the situation of poverty-returning and further standardized poverty alleviation information in a timely and accurate manner. This has laid a solid foundation for the implementation of policies and measures as well as assessment and evaluation.

"Who will act?" China adopted a management system of "overall planning by the central government, overall responsibility by the provinces, and implementation by the cities and counties", and established a pattern of poverty alleviation work

Chapter I **The Great Legend**
China's Poverty Alleviation and Building an All-Round Moderately
Prosperous Society to the World

by the five levels of Party secretaries including provincial, city, county, township and village. A system of sending cadres to be top leaders of poor villages to help relief has been set up. More than 3 million cadres have been selected from national organs at or above the county level and State-owned enterprises and institutions to assist in the delivery of the "last mile" in poverty alleviation. The coordination between eastern and western China in poverty alleviation has been deepening: 267 economically strong counties (cities, districts) in the east were paired with 406 poverty-stricken counties in the west. And 320 units at the central level were paired with 592 poverty-stricken counties. Moreover, social involvement featured such programs as "ten thousand enterprises helping ten thousand villages".

"What action should be taken?" China has built a demand-oriented action mechanism, conducted in-depth analysis of the causes of poverty, formulated relief plans village by village and household by household, and integrated special poverty reduction programs and poverty identification results with the demand for development. China has implemented a five-in-one program to help the poor: to promote the development of some by assisting in their production and employment; improve the living conditions of some by relocation; help some shake off poverty by ecological protection; bring some out of poverty by education; and secure the living needs of some by providing basic living allowances. China has launched 10 major poverty reduction initiatives in fields such as health, education, finance and transportation, and launched 10 projects to help the poor, including vocational education, microcredit and enterprise assistance, creating a large number of effective poverty alleviation models. The government has guided and supported the working poor in their efforts to create a better life with their own hands, encouraged the poor in strengthening their determination and education to stop the intergenerational transmission of poverty, and built a strong social security net to ensure that all needy people enjoy support and insurance.

"How should those who are no longer poor exit the program?" The government has ensured that no one needs to worry about food and clothing; and provided compulsory education, basic medical care and safe housing. The assessment results have been used for comprehensive appraisal and evaluation of the major leaders of the provincial Party committees and governments.

China's great achievements are of great significance not only for the country itself but also for the international cause of poverty reduction. It has given a strong boost to the global poverty reduction process. China is the first developing country to achieve the Millennium Development Goals, contributing over 70 percent to global poverty reduction. Upon the completion of the comprehensive poverty reduction targets this year, China will achieve the targets set in the 2030 Agenda for Sustainable Development 10 years ahead of schedule, which will directly contribute to the world's poverty reduction process and bring about rapid poverty reduction in neighboring regions. The proportion of poor people in East Asia and the Pacific dropped from 59 percent (1.1 billion) in 1981 to 9 percent in 2013, reducing the number of poor people by 1.04 billion. In this, China's contribution was 82 percent. The fastest rate of poverty reduction has been witnessed in East Asia and the Pacific.

China has shared its experience in poverty reduction with the rest of the world. China's government-led, planned and organized poverty alleviation and development, in particular the strategy of targeted poverty alleviation and eradication, has provided effective Chinese wisdom and solutions for global poverty reduction. In a letter of congratulation to the 2017 Global Poverty Reduction and Development Forum, UN Secretary-General Antonio Guterres said that "targeted alleviation measures are the only way to help the poorest in society and to achieve the major goals of the United Nations 2030 Agenda for Sustainable Development. China has lifted hundreds of millions of people out of poverty, and its experience can offer valuable lessons to other developing countries".

China has strengthened the confidence of the international community in poverty reduction. There are still 766 million poor people in the world, 84 percent of whom are in sub-Saharan Africa and South Asia. They are in extreme poverty and it's a daunting task to reduce poverty in those regions. The success of China's targeted poverty alleviation practice not only proves the effectiveness of its poverty alleviation path and strategy but also provides solutions around the world to manage poverty more effectively through poverty-reduction achievements and models that

Chapter I **The Great Legend**
China's Poverty Alleviation and Building an All-Round Moderately
Prosperous Society to the World

stand the test of history. It has given hope to many developing countries mired in poverty, and further strengthened their confidence in fighting poverty.

China has cooperated with other countries in poverty reduction within its capacity. It has always shouldered its responsibility as a major country, provided assistance to other developing countries within its capacity without political strings attached, and supported and helped developing countries, the least developed countries in particular, to eradicate poverty. China will strengthen cooperation with the international community to jointly implement the 2030 Sustainable Development Goals.

IV. Demography and Reform
Form an Ideal Mix[1]

In the 20th century, as nation-states adopted nuanced ways to prosper and attain growth and modernity, principles of sustainable growth were deliberated within the broader framework of a global debate on developmental economics and equitability. In the post-war global construction, the industrial revolution or scientific breakthroughs produced limited income growth in underdeveloped societies. As nations were gaining independence and setting off nation-building, this became increasingly daunting.

The patterns of growth cycles among developed, developing and low income countries and societies were inconsistent as a global index of growth and standards of development measures varied as per geographic and demographic conditions. While the growth patterns differed globally, poverty emerged as central to the scores of challenges every country ended up addressing. As the United Nations Development Programme's *2019 Global Multidimensional Poverty Index*, 1.3 billion people—23.1 percent—are multidimensionally poor across 101 countries.

----

① By Aravind Yelery, senior research fellow at HSBC Business School at Peking University.

Poverty leads to a state of existence, representing deprivation, vulnerability and incompetency. Poverty inflicts cascading effects on education, health, and income disparity, too. On the backdrop of pandemics, combined with hunger and disease, poverty strikes a significant blow to communities across continents.

China's economic transformation is one of the rarest global developments in the 20th century. Compared to other significant time-frame incidents and phenomena in the century, China's success in materializing the well-being of society through economic policy breakthroughs is considered historic. Transcending experiences of Chinese reforms and modernization have set examples for several developing countries to focus on their challenges differently than those prescribed by developed economies.

There are different adjectives and phenomena used to attribute China's rise in economic terms, and all of these terms explain transformations in various aspects. The West, fellow Asian neighbors, and far-flung African and Latin American countries witnessed the rise of China as a miracle, but not many followed it as a model to be developed. As China rose, it did share the benefits and allowed many countries to be part of the broader phenomenon they called the Asian century or Asian globalization. Along with the innovative state approach to allow market forces to become chief performers and architects of modern China, Chinese entrepreneurial substance played an equally significant role. The role played by the provinces, institutions and the people decided the shape and scale of sub-national and micro-economic benefits of reforms. All these variables, performing in tandem, made record high digit growth possible. One needs to know what were the core domains of these reforms which kept a balance between ideology, governance, reforms and their unprecedented returns.

Apart from the metrics of meteoric growth, China also ranks quite high in beating poverty in measurable ways. Why measurable? This is because China's performance is unique: on the one hand, China exerted near to gravitational economic force to navigate global growth, and on the other, it remarkably brought down the global median of the poverty rate.

The beginning of the 20th century witnessed a spike in the poverty rate in China.

Chapter I **The Great Legend**
China's Poverty Alleviation and Building an All–Round Moderately
Prosperous Society to the World

Continuous wars and internal chaos brought China to its worst phase in history. The loss through wars and failing of the imperial order led to the widening of the poverty ratio, and its social repercussions were wide-ranging. The ideologies, movements and protests during the first half of the century questioned the social inequalities and rising level of unemployment and poverty.

After the founding of the People's Republic of China PRC, poverty remained one of the critical issues which challenged the Communist Party of China, and become an alternative to social evils. The exploitation by Western powers and the devastation caused by wars and military conflicts coincided with social crises that challenged the Chinese government and people.

By the mid-20th century and at the time of the founding of the PRC, China's population reached about 540 million, about three times higher than the level in 1500. It was a near-impossible task for the new government to focus on reducing poverty with limited resources at hand. The already hard-pressed resources had to cater to the needs of a tremendous population increase.

As a result, in the unfolding years of China's experiment with economic reforms, the eradication of poverty became a priority. While poverty remained the chief target of Chinese policies, it turned out to be the stepping stone to augment deeper reforms keeping demography at the center. Chinese leaders were conscious of endangered public health, which was another dimension of poverty.

These encounters with reality shaped the leadership's concepts toward nation-building through progressive national health policies. If poverty eradication was one of the long-term goals, public health was a vital instrument in augmenting structural makeover of the economy.

Demography is an essential lever of any economy, and China was one of the economies of the 20th century which inherited this dividend from the past, and reforming public health was seen as value-added. The respite from poverty-ridden communities turned out to be the significant breakthrough enabling efforts to build up capacities to deal with other challenges affecting growth trajectories not only in urban pockets but also in the agrarian countryside. Over the past 70 years, China initiated efforts to ensure better public health and turned it into an engine of economic growth and national strength.

China has made outstanding contributions to the reduction of the world's poor. The figures show China's determination in poverty eradication for decades, which is persuasive. Since the opening-up of the economy and loosening other controls over the production and capital accumulation, poverty alleviation kept a steady trajectory, and it is noteworthy that the share of China's poverty alleviation programs bolstered the global numbers of poverty reduction. For example, from 1981 to 1990, China pulled 152 million people out of poverty, and during the same period the number of people who benefited from poverty reduction globally accounted for only 31 million.

The latter decade of the 1990s witnessed the number increasing at an incremental rate, reaching 237 million. The numbers reflect the success of the Chinese model of poverty alleviation. From 1999 to 2010, China's poverty alleviation efforts helped 289 million people, accounting for 54.9 percent of the world's total poverty reduction results.

From 1990 to 2010, China lifted 526 million people out of poverty, which was about 75.7 percent of the world's results. China's success in controlling poverty was in line with the plan set forth by the Millennium Development Goals, which included eight development goals since the United Nations Millennium Summit in 2000.

The poverty-stricken rural population in China was reduced to 30.46 million by the end of 2017, with the poverty incidence dropping to 3.1 percent. China is further pursuing the 2030 Agenda for Sustainable Development aggressively. This was one of the milestones the Chinese reforms have achieved, and it has come with more comprehensive social benefits.

So far, China has contributed to over 70 percent of the poverty reduced across the world, the only country which lifted a sizable amount of people out of poverty globally. Going by the standard of the $1.9 poverty line, from 1981 to 2013, China lifted 850 million people out of poverty, with the percentage of people living in extreme poverty falling from 88 percent to 1.85 percent.

China has moved from being one of the world's poorest countries to fulfilling the dream of total elimination of absolute poverty by 2020. Such poverty alleviation is inseparable from a series of reforms in China over the past 70 years. According to one of the UN reports, 76 percent of the achievements made in the global poverty reduction cause are from China. Besides implementing these programs at home, China is also helping other developing and emerging countries to learn about poverty alleviation programs. For example, the China International Poverty Alleviation Center conducts workshops and training for officials from developing countries in Asia, Africa and Oceania. It helps them to know of Chinese efforts in poverty alleviation programs that can be used as a reference.

Looking at history, the social and political struggle China underwent in the last century, and China's rise to become the second-largest economy of the world seem like a dream journey. The revolutionary measure in alleviating demography from poverty lines turned out to be astounding. These experiences were not derived from any book or theories of econometrics. Still, all of these series of gradual and continuing transitions were the result of events and experiments in the wake of structural adjustments. These domains reflect China's commitment to development and well-being of Chinese society, and the progressive character of the Party and ideology.

V. Decisiveness and Devotion as Key Factors in China's Poverty Alleviation[1]

If one felt asleep at the beginning of 1950s or 1960s and woke up in 2020, one certainly would be astonished by many changes that the world went through. One probably would even has his/her own list of the new world's miracles. I have no doubt that China would be among them.

---

[1] By Ivona Ladjevac, head of Regional Center Belt and Road Initiative, Institute of International Politics and Economics, Belgrade.

Like other countries, China went through turmoil in the 20th century. But, unlike the other countries, China made a tremendous leap forward, which incorporated decades of perseverance and an obstinate will to develop. That great leap secured China's transformation from being a poor developing country to a major economic power and influential actor on the global stage.

Before establishing the People's Republic of China (PRC) in 1949, China was recognized as one of the most underdeveloped countries in the world. Like all underdeveloped countries, China had numerous problems: low life expectancy at birth, high infant mortality rate, illiteracy, income disparity, rural-urban disparity, regional disparity, gender disparity, agricultural-industrial disparity, etc. It was not a surprise knowing that, immediately after the collapse of the feudal system, China entered into the new phase, completely unprepared. Institutions were undeveloped, people were uneducated and territory was vast and predominantly unfriendly.

With the founding of the PRC, the country entered a new era, an era of development. Equally significant was the first-generation leader Mao Zedong proposition of the concept of "common prosperity". The common prosperity concept was based on the intensive survey of national conditions, at the same time actively searching the way of poverty alleviation through the planned economic system, agricultural cooperation and industrial modernization.

Mao primarily focused on poverty alleviation, knowing that it was the only key towards prosperity. Also, he considered it as a necessary precondition for social construction of the new state. That is why he set priorities and defined major aspects: first, persisting on socialism as a guarantee of poverty alleviation; second, common prosperity as the goal of poverty alleviation; third, releasing and developing productive forces.

Practical experience justified his ideas. During the following years and decades, it was proved how important it was to develop the economy with ideological and political approaches, to mobilize the widest social forces to participate in poverty alleviation. In addition, Mao insisted on the goal of "achieving the common prosperity of all peasants". The only road to that goal was "gradually achieving

Chapter I **The Great Legend**
China's Poverty Alleviation and Building an All—Round Moderately
Prosperous Society to the World

socialist industrialization and socialist transformation of the handicraft industry
and capitalist industry and commerce that is (…) enabling all peasants to prosper
together". At the same time, releasing and developing the social productive forces
were seen as the fundamental measure for solving basic social conflicts and the
fundamental driving force for promoting social progress.

These ideas were considered reasonable due to the poor foundation of economic
development. Namely, 40 to 50 percent of the population upon the founding of
the PRC was under the situation of serious poverty. Anti-poverty was regarded
as a prerequisite for consolidating and developing the socialist system. Thus
the government established the planned economic system, implemented land
reforms, focused on developing industrialization, improved education and medical
care, guaranteed full employment in cities, and provided social welfare and a
social assistance system that had potential to promote the growth of the national
economy and improve people's living conditions.

Data shows that between 1952 and 1978, by implementing five consecutive
Five-Year plans, China's national economy reached average annual growth rate
of 7.3 percent while the total industrial output was 11.4 percent. Before, China
was incapable of building a car, an airplane or a tractor, but now the situation
had changed, China developed structures that included more than 500 industrial
categories. This achievement is even greater considering that China was
economically blocked by the West, and its funds, talents, resources and experience
were limited.

Progress was visible, but lots remained to be done, primarily because of the need
to focus more on poverty alleviation that was a heavy burden for the Chinese
government. It is true that the government pushed hard to achieve balance
between development in urban and rural areas, but extreme poverty required more
complex measures that would lead to development of self-supporting capabilities.
Also, rural areas were even more demanding, natural conditions were severe, and
natural disasters and epidemics were frequent. Thus, in spite of strong will and
vigor, low levels of technology and productivity, the complexity of poverty factors
and insufficient economic support were all factors that decreased perspective of

improving self-development capabilities of the poor. It was the time to seek new solutions.

There is no doubt that the initial phase of Chinese development started with the proclamation of the PRC, but after it followed the new phase: the phase of the reform and opening-up which started in 1978.

The Third Plenary Session of the 11th Central Committee of the Communist Party of China held in December 1978 stands as a historic turning point for the development of modern China. It also opened up a new era of poverty alleviation.

In this new phase, the criteria for judging the success of China's reforms shifted from the nation's political ideology to a pragmatic stance to judge by results. In other words, under the premise of upholding the values of common prosperity, the CPC acknowledged China's unique political and institutional advantages, and continued to expand and innovate poverty alleviation measures. But this time, measures were not only strictly performed for rural areas, they were planned to be promoted in the whole country. The idea was to boost economic and social development not only of the poverty-stricken areas, but also in the entire country.

At that time, China was led by Deng Xiaoping, a prudent and "far-sighted realist" who asserted that "it does not matter if a cat is black or white, as long as it catches mice". Practically speaking, the saying meant bravely introducing something completely new. Namely, Deng advocated the idea that, in the field of economics, the Chinese government should allow regions, enterprises, workers and peasants to gain more income and live a better life through hard work. He thought that if some people's standard of living is raised first, this will inevitably be an impressive example to their "neighbors". He assumed that people in other regions and units would want to learn from them. In Deng's opinion, this was the way that could push the entire national economy to develop continuously. Deng pointed out that "the nature of socialism is to release and develop the productive forces, eliminate

Chapter I **The Great Legend**
China's Poverty Alleviation and Building an All–Round Moderately
Prosperous Society to the World

the exploitation and polarization, and ultimately achieve common prosperity"[①].

In 1983, the Central Committee of the CPC delivered the "Several Issues in Current Rural Economic Policies", which pointed out the importance of the Third Plenary Session of the 11th Central Committee that made possible numerous changes in China's rural areas. The most far-reaching impact had been the introduction of the agricultural production responsibility system together with the contracted responsibility system. Local governments made institutional changes based on the conditions in the field and implemented a two-level operation system based on contracted household operations and the combination of centralization and decentralization in the collective rural economy. This system greatly mobilized the enthusiasm of the majority of peasants and secured food and clothes for hundreds of millions of poor people.

Among the rural areas that were the focus of the poverty alleviation program, special attention was given to vast rural areas of the central and western regions. An example of planned, organized and large-scale development-oriented poverty alleviation was the "Three-West" agricultural construction project launched in 1982. This project fundamentally solved the poverty problem in Hexi and Dingxi of Gansu province and Xihaigu of the Ningxia Hui autonomous region.

In 1986, the Chinese government began to implement planned, organized and large-scale rural poverty alleviation and established development-oriented policies. On the one hand, government turned its focus towards improving the production and living infrastructure in poverty stricken areas and enhancing regional overall economic and social development capabilities; on the other hand, the government actively improved the health and cultural quality of the poverty stricken population, and changed the previous poverty alleviation methods. The government also set up specialized agencies to determine the poverty standards and key areas to be supported, arrange special funds and prepare special and necessary policies. These efforts have born visible results. The per capita net

---

① In *Selected Works of Deng Xiaoping*, Vol 3. People's Pnblishing House, PP.373.

income of peasants in poverty stricken counties increased from 206 yuan in 1986 to 483.7 yuan in 1993. The number of poverty-stricken people in rural areas decreased from 125 million to 80 million with an average annual reduction of 6.4 million. In other words, the proportion of poverty-stricken peasants fell from 14.8 percent to 8.7 percent.

Although the results were significant, the battle against poverty had to be continued. Thus, in 1994, the Central Committee of the CPC and the State Council promulgated a national poverty alleviation plan (1994 – 2000) to continuously and deeply promote poverty alleviation and development. In this period, the Central Committee, led by Jiang Zemin, further improved the ideological contents and work system of poverty alleviation through integrating poverty alleviation and development into national development strategies and profoundly addressed the specific issues such as the standards, contents and subjects of poverty alleviation. Top priorities were set to solve the problem of food and clothing for the remaining poverty stricken population, to consolidate the achievements of poverty alleviation, to build a well-off society based on adequate food and clothing, and to comprehensively promote the economic and social development of poverty stricken areas.

By the numbers, this seven-year plan led to decreasing of poverty stricken population in 2020 to 30 million while the incidence of poverty in rural areas dropped from 30.7 percent to around 3 percent. The number of poverty stricken people in the key counties under the national poverty alleviation program decreased from 58.58 million in 1994 to 17.1 million in 2000.

By the end of 2000, the proportions of administrative villages in poverty stricken areas with power supply reached 95.5 percent, with highways 89 percent, with postal services 69 percent and telecommunication services 67.7 percent. The economic and social development speed of poverty stricken counties also accelerated greatly. In the period of 1994 – 2000, the agricultural added values of the key counties with national support increased by 54 percent, with an average annual growth rate of 7.5 percent; the industrial added values increased by 99.3 percent, with an average growth rate of 12.2 percent; the per capita net income of peasants increased from 648 yuan to 1337 yuan, with an average annual growth rate of 12.8 percent.

In the period that succeeded, the Central Committee of the CPC led by Hu Jintao put forward higher requirements for poverty alleviation and development, and put the importance and goals of poverty alleviation and development in a broader and deeper historical context. Hu emphasized that poverty alleviation and development were an important embodiment of the "people oriented" concept and a fundamental requirement of the scientific outlook on development. It was necessary to "seek and promote development from people's fundamental interests constantly to meet people's economic, political and cultural rights and benefits, and let the development achievements benefit all the people".

Under the strategic background of developing the western regions, all local governments further coordinated urban and rural economic development. According to the principle of industrial support for agriculture and urban support for the countryside, the governments comprehensively promoted rural economic and social development which benefited most poverty-stricken peasants in rural areas. On the basis of the regulation abolished on January 1, 2006 on "Agricultural Taxation of the People's Republic of China, peasants finally were exempt from paying various taxes. Subsequently, the government introduced numerous subsidies. Among them were subsidies for seeds, agricultural machinery and equipment, materials, etc. At the same time, government introduced other preferential policies, such the agricultural tax exemption pilot program and rural compulsory education. In addition to these policies and measures, the national government gradually established and improved the rural social security system, promoted the construction of infrastructure including rural drinking water, electricity, roads and biogas. The national government also invested more financial resources in the fields of "agriculture, rural areas and peasants" as well the poverty alleviation and development. The expenditure of the central government increased from 214.42 billion yuan in 2003 to 857.97 billion yuan in 2010, with an annual increase of 21.9 percent.

During the first decade of the 21st century, the Chinese government set the poverty alleviation target as the population below the poverty alleviation standard. The national government confirmed 592 key counties in the national poverty alleviation and development program. In order to solve the outstanding problem, the government implemented the model of promoting poverty alleviation and development in whole villages, and also implemented the poverty alleviation programs meeting local characteristics in some areas with special difficulties through education development, industrialization, employment instead of outright grants, relocation and financial support.

In the process of poverty alleviation, the local governments also paid great attention to the development of human rights. The national government provided special support for the 22 ethnic groups with a population of less than 100,000, issued the "Development Plan for Supporting Ethnic Minorities (2005 — 2010)" and invested the supporting funds of 3,751 million yuan for ethnic minorities and their communities to accelerate the pace of their development. The government also designed special program for poverty alleviation of women by implementing "China's Women Development Program (2001 — 2010)", which gave priority to alleviating women's poverty and reducing number of poverty-stricken women.

The direction of the next decade was determined at the 18th National Congress of the CPC. President Xi Jinping has set poverty alleviation and development at the core of the overall development strategy. Along with that, the government put its efforts in achieving the extremely important strategic mission: building an all-round moderately prosperous society. This mission needed to be integrated into the "Five-in-One" plan and the "Four-Comprehensive" strategic layout for decision-making. The "Five-in-One" plan establishes a relationship of mutual support with overall socialist modernization, including the construction of economic, political, cultural, social and ecological systems, while the "Four-Comprehensive" plan included building a moderately prosperous society, deepening reforms, advancing the rule of law, and strictly governing the CPC. Subsequently, the idea of eliminating poverty, improving people's livelihoods and achieving common prosperity has been an important part of the Thought on Socialism with Chinese Characteristics for a New Era proposed by Xi.

Chapter I **The Great Legend**
China's Poverty Alleviation and Building an All-Round Moderately
Prosperous Society to the World

Both for the Party and for the people, Xi's Thought on Socialism with Chinese Characteristics for a New Era has become a dominant guiding principle. In its origin, it has been spiritually inspired by Confucianism. It has Mao's revolutionary determination, and it has a Deng-like reformist approach. Being such, it is knitted with 14 main principles that call for complete and deep reforms and new developing ideas, including absolute authority of the Party over the people's army, harmonious living between man and nature, and "one country, two systems" and the reunification with the motherland, etc.

Related to poverty alleviation, a long-term mechanism has been introduced to solve its practical problems. For that purpose, the "Measures for the Implementation of the Responsibility System for Poverty Alleviation" was issued, enhancing the poverty alleviation management system of "central coordination, provincial responsibility and local implementation". Apart from that, the policy, the investment, the monitoring and the assessment systems for poverty alleviation were established.

Under the strong leadership both of the CPC Central Committee and the State Council, the overall coordination of the State Council Leading Group of Poverty Alleviation and Development, followed by active cooperation of local governments and participation of the society, the implemented measures have bared the fruit.

According to the World Bank, calculated on the international poverty standard of expenditure of $1.9 per capita per day, China in the past 40 years has succeeded in reducing the number of poverty-stricken people by more than 700 million. In those terms, China has made "unprecedented achievements" in rapid economic growth and poverty alleviation. Even more, China has the prestigious status of being the first developing country in the world that has achieved the poverty alleviation goal set by the United Nations 2030 Agenda for Sustainable Development. By reaching that goal 10 years in advance, China has proved to be the leader in poverty alleviation on a global scale.

Available data for 2019 assures that living standard of the people in the rural areas still has an ascending trend. For example, in the first three quarters of 2019, the per capita disposable income of rural residents in poverty-stricken areas was 8163 yuan, which means an increase of 10.8 percent in comparison with the same period of 2018.

China's outstanding experience in poverty alleviation may be the example for other countries, especially knowing that China is willing to make a contribution in building a community with a shared future for mankind. As President Xi wisely observed, the world system has been seriously disrupted and endangered by rising hegemonism. That is why building partnerships to promote open, innovative and inclusive development that benefits all is a must. Ordinary people and the quality of their lives will define our future.

The Chinese proverb says: "Be not afraid of growing slowly, be afraid only of standing still."

Chapter I **The Great Legend**
China's Poverty Alleviation and Building an All–Round Moderately
Prosperous Society to the World

03

Bringing Hope to Developing Countries' Poverty Alleviation

I. Poverty Alleviation in China[①]

Previously, Chinese people suffering from poverty and harboring expectations for a better life often greeted each other with "Have you eaten yet?". It attests to the hard life of hundreds of millions in the past when they could not enjoy even basic living standards.

After 40 years of reform and opening-up, Chinese are using different expressions in greetings, such as "you've gained weight" or "you look thinner than before". The changes show that basic living standards have been met and the focus is on improving the quality of life.

A Chinese proverb says, "a well cannot be dug by a single shovel", which is similar to the Western one, "Rome was not built in a day". I was born in Harbin, Northeast China, in 1961. My mother often told me that she could not afford to eat eggs or drink milk when she was pregnant. In the 1970s, my parents, who were railway engineers, sent 15 yuan ($2.1) to my paternal and maternal grandparents respectively every month from their salary, which was 56 yuan each, because rural life was even harder.

The close relations between urban and rural households are typical of a traditional

---

① By Yin Shuguang, former deputy editor-in-chief of Hong Kong newspaper Wen Wei Po and researcher at China Foundation for International and Strategic Studies.

agricultural society and show benevolence highlighted in Confucianism. Such a fine tradition has made the Chinese people diligent, patient and optimistic.

China ushered in a historic turning point in 1978 when the late leader Deng Xiaoping initiated reform and opening-up. Since the college entrance examination system was restored in 1977, I got a change to be admitted to a key middle school in Heilongjiang province. All I thought about then was working hard to enter college. The Japanese feature film *Manhunt* became a hit in China in the same year, which surprised people with the scenes of skyscrapers in Tokyo and traffic flows. Opening up became a common aspiration in China.

I could not imagine owning a car or traveling to Tokyo at that time. Since China implemented a planned economic system, most daily necessities in limited volumes could only be purchased through coupons. My family of four lived in a 12-square-meter room, in which the only major home appliances were a sewing machine and a radio.

Deng is known as the chief architect of China's reform and opening-up. Around 40 years ago, he made bold and thrilling proposals including "Socialism does not necessarily mean poverty"; "Development is the top priority"; and "Let some people get rich first".

In 1987, the 13th National Congress of the Communist Party of China proposed that "China is still and will long remain in the primary stage of socialism". As the key part of Deng Xiaoping Theory, it laid the theoretical foundation for reform and opening-up and unified the thoughts and actions of the CPC. The theory promoted the establishment of a socialist market economic system with Chinese characteristics and provided a solid institutional and industrial guarantee for achieving the goal of alleviating poverty and building a moderately prosperous society by 2020.

In November 2013, President Xi Jinping proposed "Targeted Poverty Alleviation" to make China's extensive poverty alleviation work better defined. Xi goes to China's rural areas to instruct on poverty reduction many times every year and

Chapter I **The Great Legend**
China's Poverty Alleviation and Building an All-Round Moderately
Prosperous Society to the World

developed evaluation standards for local officials' work, stressing on long-lasting and practical efforts. In light of this, China's remarkable progress in poverty alleviation has not been achieved by accident.

Reform and opening-up has helped around 800 million Chinese people shake off poverty, reducing the poverty rate by 94 percent. As of 2019, the number of people suffering from extreme poverty in China had fallen to 5.51 million, accounting for only 0.4 percent of the total population of 1.4 billion. China became the first developing country to achieve the poverty reduction goal of the Millennium Development Goals of the United Nations.

"China has lifted around 800 million people out of poverty, which is the greatest poverty reduction feat in history," UN Secretary-General Antonio Guterres said while visiting during the 70th anniversary of the founding of the People's Republic of China in 2019.

Since the beginning of this year, the emergence of the novel coronavirus pandemic has led to a severe global economic recession and has affected the Chinese economy in an unprecedented manner. However, the Chinese government has confronted the difficulties and aims to achieve the priority goal of eradicating absolute poverty this year by supporting 5.51 million of its people.

China has made remarkable achievements in combating poverty. In February 2017, Guterres lauded China in a speech at the Munich Security Conference saying it "has become the country making the greatest contribution to global poverty alleviation". China's achievements on poverty reduction can be attributed to the following efforts:

First, the reform and opening-up policy played a key role in poverty reduction. China's poverty reduction has been in line with the progress of the policy over the past 40 years, which has expanded from coastal areas and large cities to underdeveloped areas in the central and western regions, rural areas and third- and fourth-tier cities. The gradual expansion has made it possible for China to complete the goal of targeted poverty alleviation this year and help people suffering from absolute poverty lead a better life.

Second, the government has developed feasible policies and mechanisms. It has introduced "Five-Year Plans" covering goals on poverty reduction and established the State Council Leading Group Office of Poverty Alleviation and Development with a vice premier as its head. China's provincial, city, county and township administrative departments all have officials working on poverty alleviation.

Third, the central government sets aside a large amount of funds for poverty alleviation in budgets every year.

Fourth, China's constitution stipulates that the country adopt a unified system, which allows the government to launch policies nationwide and provide strength and experience for effective implementation of poverty reduction measures.

Fifth, it has settled on eight key areas for poverty alleviation: infrastructure, relocation, education, sanitary improvement, financial support, industrial development, tourism and the internet. The major fields in line with China's national conditions and characteristics have been integrated with new economic revolutions such as the booming digital economy, which have driven poverty reduction through technology.

In the second half of 2013, Xi proposed the Belt and Road Initiative, which provides new opportunities for international cooperation in poverty reduction. The initiative has been progressing smoothly worldwide and driving cooperation between China and countries along the route, helping local people get employment, and have access to cleaner drinking water, and allowing more children to receive education.

I went to Tajikistan in 1995 during its civil war. Before going there, a local friend asked me to buy a bag of flour and sugar. When arriving in Dushanbe, the capital, I learned that its per capita income was only $5 at the time and understood what poverty meant.

Chapter I **The Great Legend**
China's Poverty Alleviation and Building an All—Round Moderately
Prosperous Society to the World

Peace and development should be the eternal theme of the international community and international poverty reduction cooperation needs to be strengthened.

The expectation of building a fair society and shaking off poverty is shared by people around the world, which is one of the signs of the progress of human civilization. The world wars in the 20th century and civil wars in many countries have made people realize the importance of peace and development.

The United Nations Millennium Development Goals and the 2030 Agenda for Sustainable Development have listed eradicating poverty and famine as the world's primary goals and top agenda items.

There is a long way to go for global poverty reduction. As long as the governments and people of all countries work jointly, international poverty alleviation will see greater achievements.

II. A Good Reference Point for Developing Countries[1]

China is the first developing country to have achieved the Millennium Development Goals of the United Nations, making significant contributions to global poverty alleviation. Since the implementation of the reform and opening-up policy in 1978, it has helped more than 700 million of its people shake off poverty, contributing more than 70 percent to global poverty reduction over the past 40 years. As it implements the strategy of targeted poverty alleviation, China has announced the goal of helping all poor people and counties under the current definition shake off poverty and eliminate absolute poverty by the end of 2020. In light of its achievements, China's macro policies and practices are of great value for many developing countries.

---

[1] By Wu Peng, director of the International Development Department of the China Foundation for Poverty Alleviation.

China has vast experience in poverty alleviation from various perspectives, of which macro policies can be narrowed down to four aspects.

First, the government has been advancing reform and opening-up and maintaining rapid economic growth, making policy and laying an economic foundation.

Second, it has formulated a slew of policies supporting the poor, which include land systems clarifying farmers' rights of land use and income distribution, effective employment policies, compulsory education ensuring that all school-age children receive education, basic medical insurance in urban areas, cooperative medical scheme in rural areas, and social security systems based on social insurance, assistance and welfare, special assistance benefits for entitled groups and social mutual assistance.

Third, the government has implemented special plans to boost the self-development of poverty-stricken regions and the poor. It has launched a seven-year priority poverty alleviation program (1994—2000), the Outline for Poverty Reduction and Development of China's Rural Areas (2001—2010) and the Outline for Development-Oriented Poverty Alleviation for China's Rural Areas (2011—2020), as well as plans for supporting specific groups including women, children, the disabled and ethnic minorities.

Fourth, the government has mobilized the participation of all social sectors and given full play to the advantages of China's systems. Through pooling efforts of the government, social communities and the market, China has developed a social system with cross-regional and cross-sector participation of all social communities.

China's poverty alleviation practices also have four aspects.

First, the government has established and improved central and local departments, implementing an accountability system for clarifying responsibilities, tasks and power of provincial governments and delivering funds.

Chapter I **The Great Legend**
China's Poverty Alleviation and Building an All-Round Moderately
Prosperous Society to the World

Second, it has fixed the poverty line according to domestic conditions and adopted multi-dimensional assessment standards, which include ensuring food and clothing and providing compulsory education, basic medical treatment and housing.

Third, the government has implemented targeted poverty alleviation by providing support for needy groups, boosting suitable projects, making full use of capital, dispatching personnel familiar with local conditions and ensuring effects to help the poor get access to the benefits of various policies.

Fourth, it has been keeping abreast with the times in exploring new modes of poverty alleviation, mainly through collaboration between eastern and western regions, promoting fixed-point poverty alleviation and improving skills training, relocation, industrial development, education, technologies, ecological protection, social security, tourism, paper mulberry planting, installation of photovoltaic panels, income from assets, financial support and e-commerce.

Many developing countries are keen on drawing on China's poverty alleviation experience, which has won global recognition, but they need to make policies in line with domestic conditions instead of copying China's practices given the differences in political systems and phases of development. China's practices can be a good reference point for other developing countries.

First, the Chinese government has formulated medium- and long-term plans to achieve its goals. The plans have proposed clear requirements on targets, beneficiaries and priorities, fundamental principles, contents and approaches, policy guarantees which include capital input as well as organization and guidance in line with China's economic and social development in different phases. Other developing countries can draw on China's experience by formulating medium- and long-term plans, reaching consensus, pooling resources, reducing communication and decision-making costs at all levels and improving work efficiency to achieve their goals. Moreover, the plans need to be followed through. While some developing countries have outlined detailed roadmaps for poverty alleviation, the plans have either been shelved due to financial constraints or dropped due to the election of different leaders.

Second, China has developed a complete system of poverty alleviation departments at all levels. Based on the administrative system, the government has established the State Council Leading Group Office of Poverty Alleviation and Development for overall planning of poverty alleviation and development across the country, and provincial, municipal, county and township level departments for efficient implementation. However, lower-level administrative departments in some developing countries are often managed by tribal chiefs or community leaders and have limited capabilities to launch poverty alleviation plans. Since China's practices show that a complete institutional system plays a key role in meeting its goals, governments in other developing countries can establish similar systems based on domestic conditions and cooperate with local communities to implement plans more effectively.

Third, China has provided references for identifying and registering poor households through procedures such as public appraisal, on site surveys, public notices, random checks and information registration. After identifying the poor, departments are held accountable and targeted measures are fixed to ensure implementation. While some developing countries receive a large amount of aid from international development organizations every year, much of the money is consumed before reaching the poor. The reason is that international development organizations tend to spend much on selecting beneficiaries by hiring part-time workers to identify poor households through questionnaire surveys and community consultations to ensure equity, largely consuming resources. The number of surveyed people is often more than twice that of those receiving aid. If these governments can draw on China's experience on identifying and registering the poor, poverty alleviation organizations can provide targeted support for the identified groups and benefit them more with the saved costs.

Fourth, China's down-to-earth poverty alleviation modes can also provide good reference. Since China is the world's largest developing country, its economic and social situation before shaking off poverty was similar to that of many other developing countries. Therefore, its methods and modes have already proved successful in many cases, one of which is the water cellar project implemented by the China Foundation for Poverty Alleviation in Ethiopia. During a drought in

Ethiopia in 2011, working staff of the foundation found through field surveys that local poor rural households mainly got access to drinking water by transporting water on trucks or digging wells, both of which entailed high costs.

To cope with the problem, the staff tried building water cellars commonly seen in arid regions in China, collecting rainwater during the rainy season, storing it in cellars and extracting the water during the dry season to provide drinking water to poor households. The low-cost project has been embraced by poor rural households in Ethiopia, with its third phase implemented and the construction of 120 water cellars complete.

China has brought hope to the international community for eradicating poverty. Its experience can provide a good reference for other developing countries. Both the Chinese government and social communities are willing to share the experience with countries in need to help them achieve the goals of the United Nations 2030 Agenda for Sustainable Development in the shortest possible time.

III. Poverty Reduction and Economic Development Advance Side by Side[1]

Since the founding of the People's Republic of China, the country has made remarkable economic and social achievements, and achieved great progress in poverty alleviation. Since the reform and opening-up, over 700 million people, more than the total population of Latin America, have been lifted out of poverty in China.

In the process, China has accumulated experience in poverty alleviation and is ready to share with other poor countries. However, some Western countries are prejudiced in their view that China achieved all this by seizing special

---

[1] By Zhang Chi, assistant researcher at the Institute of Economics, Chinese Academy of Social Sciences.

opportunities. In their opinion, China took advantage of the transfer of the world production system to become a global factory. Also, they believe China utilized cheaper labor force to make its economy develop rapidly and its success is just an accidental phenomenon.

These scholars look at economic development in a mechanical way and misunderstand the logical relationship between economic development and poverty alleviation. Each era has its own opportunities for development, and economic growth does not necessarily lead to large-scale poverty reduction. Instead, it may lead to polarization and an increase in the relatively poor population.

Economic development is just part of China's success in poverty reduction. The concept of poverty reduction and the role the government plays are also crucial. Developed countries boast relatively mature economic and social models. The proportion of the poor population is decided and a sound comprehensive aid system is established between the government, private sector and enterprises. China's experience in poverty reduction may have little reference for developed countries, but it can be of great positive significance for a majority of developing countries. These countries should pay attention to the following points when it comes to poverty reduction.

First, they should unify the methods and goals for poverty alleviation. The ultimate goal of reducing poverty is to ensure basic living conditions for the people and improve their quality of life. Before China's reform and opening-up, poverty reduction was mainly achieved by improving people's overall living conditions. Although per capita income was relatively low by world standards, the people's quality of life had improved.

The "Targeted Poverty Alleviation" work carried out by the Communist Party of China since the 18th National Congress emphasized on establishment of a long-term poverty alleviation mechanism to prevent returning to a state of poverty. Poverty alleviation cannot be solely achieved by offering material support like money, food or medicine. It is also necessary to build appropriate infrastructure to improve quality of life and living capacity.

Chapter I **The Great Legend**
China's Poverty Alleviation and Building an All-Round Moderately
Prosperous Society to the World

Second, they should address poverty problems in the development process. We should increase investment in poverty reduction work in the development process, so that the impoverished can enjoy the dividend of growth. Also, polarization should be checked and social income distribution level should be rationally adjusted.

Third, a balance should be struck between the leading role played by the government and the people's initiative. Due to the positive external significance of poverty alleviation work, the government is sparing no effort to promote the work. To reduce poverty at the national level, it is necessary to make overall plans, coordinate the interests and relationships of all parties, and comprehensively utilize various resources. The government has advantages in these areas. Poverty reduction undertakings need a lot of financial support, and it is beneficial to use funds with the endorsement of government credit.

Smooth progress of poverty alleviation work requires a country to develop a detailed plan through the government, from the top to the bottom, and establish an effective monitoring feedback mechanism. Countries should also fully respect people's initiative, correctly respond to people's innovation and exploration in the cause of poverty alleviation, and rationalize and legalize related experience with the help of the government. Only through this can we promote positive interactions, mobilize people's enthusiasm and ensure the success of poverty reduction undertakings.

China's experience in poverty alleviation is worth promoting for the benefit of other countries.

Developing countries should be able to reduce poverty through aid projects, which China has actively participated in, especially in Africa. With the help of China, many railways, highways, hospitals and other infrastructure have been built, which has greatly improved the living conditions of locals.

Developed countries often just offer material support to African countries. But China, by helping African countries promote their industries and improve their economic level, aims to help Africa fundamentally solve poverty problems. Through aid projects, China has brought advanced technologies and ideas to developing countries and established a bond of friendship with them. It is a direct way to promote China's poverty reduction experience.

China's poverty alleviation experience can be disseminated through the Belt and Road Initiative, the Asian Investment Bank and etc. China has undergone dramatic changes in growth and is aware of the real needs of poverty alleviation in developing countries. However, it becomes difficult for China to promote its valuable ideas among international organizations, which are often led by Western countries. But many new international institutions led by China, such as the Forum on China-Africa Cooperation and the Shanghai Cooperation Organization, can become platforms for China's voice to be heard. For instance, specialized poverty alleviation institutions can be established in these international organizations with the Chinese playing a vital role; a sub-forum on poverty reduction can be set up in international conferences to highlight Chinese experience and give more developing countries the opportunity to learn from China.

China's achievements in recent decades have attracted officials from many developing countries to have a careful study. Systematic training can help these officials learn more about China's programs.

IV. Lessons and Inspiration for Pakistan[1]

China's unique struggle against poverty, lifting nearly 800 million people out of their abject state, is among a few remarkable marvels of the 21st century. China achieved this fate by carefully navigating through the challenges to become a prosperous and flourishing economic behemoth. Courageous and visionary leadership, coherenct policies, forceful approaches and efficient methods for

---

[1] By Muhammad Asif Noor, director of Institute of Peace and Diplomatic Studies in Pakistan.

Chapter I **The Great Legend**
China's Poverty Alleviation and Building an All-Round Moderately
Prosperous Society to the World

identifying challenges, revolutionizing traditional operating systems to use advanced technologies, bolstering the agrarian relief program and reform process, these are the critical contours of the entire process of the Chinese poverty alleviation program.

China has not merely strengthened its own overall economy but has helped reduce 70 percent of global poverty. China is Pakistan's strategic ally, a linchpin in its foreign policy, a companion in the time of crisis, and Chinese development has helped Pakistan massively.

China has moved on to become a regional and global economic giant, launching mammoth projects and the Belt and Road Initiative, offering the China-Pakistan Economic Corridor as a crucial link. Through CPEC, China is providing Pakistan extensive support in establishing connectivity projects involving long-term advances. With the CPEC going ahead at full steam, there is a strong impetus to the China dream of shared prosperity.

The central question is that if China has made such extraordinary progress, then what are the implications and lessons for Pakistan. Pakistan, with a population of 2.2 billion people and situated in a significant geographical position, is a developing country. Overall development with a focus on poverty alleviation has consistently remained an influencing doctrine of Pakistan's entire socioeconomic drive for more than seven decades.

However, regardless of all these committed efforts and policy-level reforms, convictions remain ineffectual as a result of a profusion of complex structural and administrative challenges. Various latest foreign and national development reports paint a gloomy picture of Pakistan's poverty level. For instance, according to the latest UNDP Human Development Index, Pakistan is at the 150th position among 189 countries.

Prime Minister Imran Khan, soon after assuming office, vowed to work for the people and eradicate poverty by effectively utilizing the methods used by China to support its populace. Apart from various government-led programs, the CPEC has entered its second phase where, along with a focus on connectivity, energy, agriculture and industrial development, one important component is socio-economic development and poverty alleviation.

President Xi Jinping has not only guided China to achieve its goals but also has inspired the Pakistani leadership with his visionary approach for China. President Xi is providing China a global economic development drive, and the CPEC as a key component of the BRI, is changing the entire landscape to help Pakistan in poverty alleviation.

Another important benefit for Pakistan is that, through the CPEC, China has provided assistance to Pakistan in developing a strong network of railways, highways and communications projects, helping Pakistan build its capacity to support its marginalized communities. This has increased linkages from farms and smaller industrial units to the national and regional level. Pakistan, through Gwadar, is providing the shortest, secure and low-cost route for China's trade to reach global markets. It is also important to note that this is not only assisting China but also providing Pakistan an opportunity to go beyond by utilizing effectively these developed networks to reach and connect at the regional and global level in business, trade and economic matters.

Pakistan is being able to access to all the latest development in research, knowledge and technology in diverse sectors. Be it agriculture, water and resources management, e-commerce, industrial development and cooperation, strategic asset building, energy, Pakistan is continuously seeking and receiving assistance from China.

For instance, Pakistan was facing a severe energy crisis in the years before inception of the CPEC, but now we can meet our demand. Connectivity linkages are helping industry, acting as lifelines to Pakistan's economic base. Furthermore, China provided a rapid response and support to deal with the recent locust attacks in different regions of Pakistan with innovative solutions. Pakistan's e-commerce and business are thriving by creating linkages with leading e-commerce companies in China.

Chapter I **The Great Legend**
China's Poverty Alleviation and Building an All–Round Moderately
Prosperous Society to the World

Pakistan is an ally of China but also a beneficiary as a result of China's continuous reforms and sustainable policies related to socioeconomic development. Pakistan trying to inculcate the development experience by transforming its entire national ethos is one big key factor.

For any development process to be successful, there is a need for a blueprint to be home grown apart from long-term plans. What is also important for Pakistan is that China's development model is with Chinese characteristics and the country has adjusted to emerging changes. They didn't remain chained to the old school of thought during the entire period of development. Pakistan needs to learn these important lessons from China and adhere to the policy of commitment and consistence with an indigenous model based on local realities with a pragmatic outlook that best fits our needs. Development has to be a long-term, committed process and should be regardless of who is in power.

And finally, Pakistan, as a result of China's reform and opening-up, and the launching of the CPEC, is also following austerity and trying to eradicate corruption from all levels of society, especially in the process of implementing development projects. Pakistan is also putting emphasis on the transformation of the civil services and providing ample support, including promotions to reward efficient and honest work.

When we look at China's development experience, we observe that the destiny of a nation lies in the hands to those who are honest and committed to the task, and show leadership in the face of adversity. It is such men and women who made the commitment to their land that are now seeing the fruits of prosperity—with China standing in 2020 achieving the goal of prosperity and its people enjoying the fruits of development.

V. Africa Needs Informed Leadership to Fight Poverty[1]

In the last 20 years, perceptions of Africa have changed dramatically—from a "hopeless" to a "hopeful" continent. This change was underpinned by a movement from negative and stagnating economic growth rates of the 1970s and 1980s to positive and relatively stable growth in the subsequent years. However, Africa's image as a continent of wars, famine and abject poverty remains unchanged, albeit with minor spatial improvements in peoples' welfare. This paradox of "Africa rising", in terms of revamped growth amidst entrenched poverty, has been a preoccupation of many decades for politicians, academicians, researchers, policy makers and development partners searching for policies, strategies, programs and projects to tackle poverty.

A confluence of policies have been formulated at the global, regional and country levels, and in some cases implemented, but the speed of poverty alleviation in the continent has been persistently slow when compared to other developing regions in the globe. This gloomy picture, coupled with projections which show that the world's poor will in the future increasingly be concentrated in Africa, calls for urgent and concerted efforts to address the pandemic of poverty.

Indeed, there are many causes of poverty in Africa, including conflict, environmental degradation and high population growth.

However, the fundamental reason is that revamped growth has neither been inclusive nor ushered in structural transformation of economies. The delayed transformation is evidenced by the dominance of a low-productivity agricultural sector, the source of livelihood for the majority of the population on the one hand, and de-industrialization of economies on the other.

---

[1] By Humphrey P.B. Moshi, professor of economics of the University of Dar es Salaam, director of the Center for Chinese Studies, and chairman of Tanzania's Fair Competition Commission.

Chapter I **The Great Legend**
China's Poverty Alleviation and Building an All–Round Moderately
Prosperous Society to the World

This state of affairs is contradictory, in both theory and practice, which underscores the symbiotic relationship between the two sectors in the sense that the development of the agriculture sector, in terms of enhancing productivity, is the surest way for alleviating poverty and promoting industrialization. Indeed, the development experiences of Asian countries, especially China, are a clear testimony to this phenomenon. Their successful industrialization experiences, which not only led to higher productivity in the agricultural sector but also reduced poverty and inequalities quite dramatically, need emulation and adaptation by African countries. To the extent that China is Africa's second-largest trade partner and there are a variety of cooperation arrangements among them, African countries are eager to see the cooperation become a powerful force for the realization of structural transformation and poverty alleviation. In its fight against poverty, Africa has a lot to learn from China's socioeconomic model, which was able to reduce poverty significantly within a reasonably short time.

In the process of building a moderately prosperous society in all respects, China has accumulated rich experience in poverty reduction, including maintaining sustained and steady economic growth, continuously introducing social policies that are conducive to the development of poor regions and poor people, incorporation of poverty alleviation and development into China's overall development strategy, and making development fundamental to reduce poverty. Other important experiences include giving full play to poverty alleviation targets, prioritizing the development of agriculture and comprehensively promoting economic and social development in rural areas, giving priority to the building of infrastructure such as roads, water supply, electricity, gas and housing in poor regions, and stimulating social participation to let the government, society and market play their roles.

During the 40-plus years of reforms in China, the country has adopted a socio-economic development model which was, and continues to be, inclusive in nature. And it has lifted 800 million people out of abject poverty.

Indeed, despite COVID-19 challenges, the Central Poverty Alleviation Work Meeting in March 2020 made it clear that the poverty alleviation target of ensuring the remaining 5.51 million rural people, 52 counties and 1,113 villages are lifted out of poverty by the end of 2020, remains unchanged.

This unprecedented performance provides yet another lesson to the African continent, which is a home to over 400 million who are still in abject poverty. To effectively eradicate poverty, African leaders should adopt some key aspects of the Chinese model of development while being cognizant of local context, but also enhance cooperation with China in all spheres of the economy.

In his 29-article book, *Up and Out of Poverty*, President Xi Jinping outlines "the hows" of transforming a poverty stricken area (Ningde prefecture) into a prosperous region though change of mindset, economic development and management, and leadership. We are not advocating for their adoption but for adaptation to reflect the realities or characteristics of the continent. We have identified three critical areas which appear to be relevant to the African context, but are conspicuously missing in contemporary poverty reduction endeavors. These identified areas should be the critical ingredients for informing policymakers, at various levels, in charting the way to ending poverty in Africa.

The first and foremost is the need to change mindsets on the condition of poverty. That is, "poverty alleviation requires a change of attitude and mentality wearing away at the poverty mentality". In other words, poverty is not destiny; it can be confronted and ultimately overcome. This is both an inspiration and motivation to do something about it, given that all developed countries were, at one point in the past, embroiled in poverty.

The second is the need to use the available resources to fight poverty. In most cases, in a poverty ridden area the most abundant resources are in agriculture in terms of crops, forestry, livestock and marine products. The economics of developing resources to ensure their effective and efficient utilization is the main conduit for lifting a country from poverty. This is the "economic chorus" according to Xi. Likewise, industrialization of such areas should be resource-based by processing products emanating from the agricultural sector. This aspect underscores the close linkage between agriculture and industry. It is advised that in drafting a sound industrial policy, focus should be on "leveraging agriculture to develop industry,

Chapter I **The Great Legend**
China's Poverty Alleviation and Building an All–Round Moderately
Prosperous Society to the World

while also using the developing industrial sector to support agriculture".

Mobilization of the people and effective leadership are critical ingredients for addressing poverty. Xi stresses that "(leaders) at all levels become deeply involved with the people in real situations, always coming from the people and going to the people". Xi goes further to outline the qualities of effective leadership which can drive development: being credible, discipline, diligent, non-corrupt and humble. These attributes are necessary if leadership are to enjoy peoples' trust and support. Furthermore, leadership must be a role model by being selfless, doing practical things rationally, and promoting scientific thinking and reasoning.

VI. China's Wisdom in Helping Uruguay's Poverty Reduction①

The year 2020 is a milestone for the great rejuvenation of the Chinese nation, as the country eradicates absolute poverty in this year, and completes the building of a moderately prosperous society in all respects and achieves its first centenary goal. Over the 70 years since the founding of the People's Republic of China, especially since the launch of reform and opening-up, over 700 million people in China have been lifted out of poverty, accounting for more than 70 percent of the global total in the same period.

The original aspiration and the mission of Communist Party of China was to seek happiness for the Chinese people and the rejuvenation of the Chinese nation. The CPC Central Committee with General Secretary Xi Jinping at its core has put forward the governance philosophy of poverty alleviation, which is that all Chinese people should strive for common prosperity. Xi has stressed that "no one should be left behind on the road to prosperity". This is China's solemn commitment to poverty alleviation, and it is also a guide to future poverty alleviation work.

---

① By Wang Gang, Chinese ambassador to Uruguay.

In recent years, with poverty alleviation work entering a critical period, China has made targeted poverty alleviation its basic strategy, emphasizing fine-tuned management and accurate allocation of resources.

The great efforts made by the CPC and the Chinese government for the ambitious goal of completing the building of a moderately prosperous society in all respects will be achieved this year. China's strategic thinking and scientific plan for targeted poverty alleviation mean that no one will be left behind. The most essential change is people's mindsets, and they acted on their own initiative to combat poverty.

In today's world, unbalanced and inadequate development is still prevalent, the gap between the North and the South is still huge, and poverty and hunger are still serious. Poverty and its associated problems of hunger, disease and social conflict continue to plague many developing countries. Presideht Xi has put forward the vision of building a community with a shared future for mankind, to solve the problems of unbalanced development, the governance dilemma, the digital divide and the resources gap.

Adhering to the concept of poverty reduction through joint efforts, common governance and shared benefits, and the concept of development-oriented poverty alleviation, China has combined green development with targeted poverty alleviation, and combined its own poverty alleviation with international poverty alleviation.

While promoting poverty alleviation at home, China has been a strong advocate of global poverty reduction. Over the past 70 years, China has provided more than 400 billion yuan ($57.3 billion) in aid to nearly 170 countries and international organizations, implemented more than 5,000 foreign aid projects, sent more than 600,000 aid workers, trained more than 12 million people for developing countries, and helped more than 120 developing countries meet the Millennium Development Goals.

On November 1, 2018, the foundation was laid for a new school in Montevideo, the capital of Uruguay, which was being built with China's aid, and it will be completed soon. The new building, two blocks from the old one, will have nine classrooms and a "Confucius classroom". Maria Sum, the principal, said the school's hardware has improved greatly thanks to China's help, and the curriculum has become more extensive, with Confucius Institute teachers giving regular classes. The school has organized teachers and students to visit China two years in a row, and the experience of studying in China has inspired the children's enthusiasm and motivation for learning. Fernando Lugris, Uruguayan ambassador to China, told reporters that the Chinese aid had given the children hope that "when they see the new school building in the Casavaya district, they will believe that a better future awaits them".

Under the framework of the Belt and Road Initiative, China stands ready to uphold justice and pursue shared interests, and to work with other countries, including Uruguay, to pool their wisdom to jointly tackle the challenge of poverty and make unremitting efforts to build a community of a shared future for mankind.

The Journey

CHAPTER

II

Experience and Innovation of China's
Targeted Poverty Alleviation

扫码获取
★ 脱贫故事分享
★ 脱贫攻坚解读
　 与回顾

01

High-Quality Employment and Income Increase

I. Economic Growth Is a Key Driver[1]

Since the beginning of the economic reforms in the late 1970s, around 800 million people have been lifted out of poverty in China, and the country is preparing to achieve the Sustainable Development Goals of the United Nations 10 years in advance to eliminate extreme poverty by 2020. This historical success has accounted for more than 70 percent of global poverty reduction.

This is mainly because of overall economic growth which has changed the world economy and partially due to specific policies targeted to combat poverty, experimented and implemented in the last decades, especially after the launch of the "targeted poverty alleviation" strategy primarily aimed at eliminating extreme poverty in rural areas.

This unprecedented achievement is the result of rapid economic growth following the economic reforms that began in 1978 and the subsequent progressive opening of China to international markets both in the form of international trade and openness to foreign investment. The story of fighting poverty in China has been the success story of the Chinese economy as a whole, a story that has encountered many difficulties.

China's economic development has required managing the migration of a large

---

[1] By Giovanni Tria, Italian former minister of Economy and Finances.

number of people from the countryside to the cities, from agricultural production to manufacturing, and then to services.

These big changes have also led to the emergence of economic inequalities, inevitable in periods of rapid growth. China had to deal with territorial inequalities between rapidly developing coastal provinces and relatively-laggard inland provinces, and with social and economic inequalities within provinces and cities with a higher rate of growth, as a growing number of people came out of extreme poverty and many of them became middle class. So the successful reduction of poverty is also a success in taking these inequalities into account and keeping them under control.

The success in poverty alleviation is also because of the ability to maintain a balance between the development of a market economy with a growing private sector and the planned economy with administrative decentralization and the central government. The capacity of maintaining this balance has been very important to ensure both rapid economic growth and lifting a huge number of people from poverty. This is especially true when the crucial issue was to ensure the growth of human capital, and strengthening health and education in a transition period characterized by massive internal migration, in which these two fundamental factors of economic growth and emancipation from poverty have been increasingly based on private savings.

The fight against poverty in China has been a development strategy for a country whose size required the search for a continuous balance between rapid and inclusive growth. Today, it requires specific inclusive policies for some sections of the population and the development of areas left behind.

However, understanding to what extent China has contributed to alleviating poverty globally, we should also consider both the direct impact of Chinese economic growth as a driver of growth in other emerging and developing countries and how the Chinese success presents a lesson that has changed how we look today at development policies even in international development cooperation institutions.

Regarding the direct impact of Chinese economic growth on the global economy and, in particular, on the growth of other developing and emerging economies in Asia and Africa, we should consider how China has been at the center of a complex growing network of global supply chains which have contributed to a number of low-income developing economies that have gradually hosted low value-added production following the increase of wages in China and the transformation of the Chinese economy.

China, in fact, has gone from growth sustained by exports and investment to growth increasingly sustained by domestic consumption, from manufacturing to an increasingly service-oriented system through an extensive use of manufacturing outsourcing and, finally, from innovation imported through a foreign direct investment to endogenous innovation. This is the way China has climbed the value-added ladder along international supply chains, driving and transferring technology within a dense network of production chains and international trade which has played an important role in the process of inclusion in international trade, foreign investment flows and technological transfer to many low-income developing countries.

China has allowed many developing countries to exploit their comparative advantages following the Chinese development model based on opening up to international markets and foreign investment. From this point of view, China has also had an overall influence on traditional development cooperation and aid policies to combat poverty.

At the same time, China also played an effective growing role in South-South development cooperation at a time when traditional North-South aid has not been as effective as it could be. Essentially Western donors and official aid programs of multilateral development institutions failed in helping low-income countries to overcome bottlenecks in terms of infrastructure that hinder industrialization and economic development.

This failure was due to a decrease in resources allocated by advanced countries to development aid. The difficulties of public budgets of most advanced countries, especially after the financial crisis, had a role in this phenomenon along with a sort of disillusionment of the effects of many development projects, most intended to alleviate situations of extreme poverty rather than transform economies and put them on the road of balanced and inclusive growth as a basis for eradicating poverty on a large scale. In this sense, the Chinese way to development has been a lesson and South-South cooperation has developed into a combination of instruments such as trade, aid, and public and private investment.

China's approach to development has been accused of leading to debt-trap diplomacy in granting development loans to already indebted countries. However, the question is debatable because Chinese aid to poor countries has partially compensated for a fall in intervention by advanced countries and development banks, and because it is important to not only look at the debt-GDP ratio but also consider whether the loans allow debt aimed to finance infrastructural investments needed to increase growth in the medium to long term with effective reduction of poverty.

The debate on the effectiveness of China's development policies in Africa and Asia is open among analysts and policymakers, but certainly China's domestic experience and its way of cooperating with developing and emerging countries over the past two decades changed both development economics and the way multilateral development banks design their policies and programs.

In this context, Italy's collaboration with China on the goal of poverty alleviation has a 40-year history.

Italian development cooperation in China has been active since the Chinese government decided to open its doors in 1978. Italy was among the first countries that offered assistance to China in the early days of its development, and for a long period was among the main donors, through both grants and aid credit lines programs. The type of assistance has changed as the Chinese economy evolved, passing from food aid, programs and projects to support education and training, and specific projects for poverty alleviation in rural areas.

Italian assistance programs for the protection and enhancement of Chinese cultural heritage have also become important for two reasons. First, they linked the two countries with the most cultural heritage in the world. Second, these programs helped the development of poor areas by creating remunerative activities related to tourism and also because the reference to the heritage and historical culture of a country is an important factor of collective mobilization.

However, the most important contribution that Italy has made to reducing poverty in China is through bilateral trade, technical and scientific cooperation, and the flows of Italian private investments in sectors in which the Italian industry is particularly strong. In other words, just as the Chinese success in the fight against poverty has been the result of unprecedented economic growth, so has the Italian contribution through commercial relations and economic cooperation based on the complementarities between the two economies which were gradually strengthened over the past decades.

Today, building on this positive experience in China and on the experience of economic cooperation with lower-income countries separately developed by Italy and China, the two countries can cooperate to develop joint programs and projects to eradicate poverty in the rest of the world. They can cooperate in designing sustainable investment programs through multilateral development banks in which they already share strategic missions and on the basis of agreements signed for economic cooperation in third countries and in the framework of the Belt and Road Initiative.

There is a growing consensus on the idea that global poverty alleviation will be crucially conditioned by economic cooperation to support the economic growth of a hyper-connected world inhabited by almost 8 billion people, in which the fate of all countries, especially the poorest, depends on the ability to exploit the economic comparative advantages of each economy through its integration into the global economy. At the same time, this cooperative action by countries that have already come out of the poverty trap is in the global interest. The fight against poverty worldwide is in fact one of the global public goods, together with the fight against climate change and the defense of health, which can only be a success in a cooperative globalized world.

II. Reducing Inequality Leads to Poverty Alleviation[1]

The framework of "poverty-growth-inequality triangle" describes intricate relationships between the three factors. The progress that BRICS countries have made in reducing poverty can be explained under this framework, disentangling the contributions of growth and changes in income inequality that lead to poverty alleviation.

According to our research, among BRICS members, China was the poorest in terms of the poverty rate before 2004; thereafter, India has been the poorest. Conversely, Russia has had the lowest poverty rate. South Africa and Brazil are at the middle level.

Taking into account the population scale and changes in the poverty rate, China has been the most successful country in fighting poverty. According to the Asian Development Bank, the target of reducing extreme poverty included in the United Nations Millennium Development Goals would not have been realized if China was excluded from consideration. Endorsed by 192 heads of state among UN members, MGDs call for halving the poverty rate between 1990 and 2015, during which China's contribution to global poverty reduction reached 63.9 percent. Contrasting this with its contributions to the global growth of around 30 percent, it is more than appropriate to mark China's achievement in eliminating extreme poverty as a miracle.

The progress made by BRICS countries can be attributed to policies promoting economic development and particularly supporting the poor. According to Country Diagnostics: China Toward More Inclusive and Sustainable Development, a report issued by the World Bank in 2018, poverty reduction in China was unprecedented in speed and scale and this is related to government

---

[1] By Wan Guanghua, professor and director of the Institute of World Economy at Fudan University.

policies. In addition India introduced anti-poverty measures such as providing employment in rural areas and steering fiscal policies towards inclusive growth. Brazil helped its people escape from poverty through economic development. In Russia, the government focused its reform strategies on reviving the economy, thereby reducing poverty. Finally, the Black Economic Empowerment and the "National Development Plan 2030 of South Africa" also took socioeconomic development as an essential goal.

To eradicate poverty, BRICS countries emphasized both social assistance and economic development. Governments provide various supports to improve people's welfare and, at the same time, explore channels to help them create wealth. China has implemented an all-round model. For example, poverty-stricken areas can develop local industries to stimulate economic growth and increase income. Surplus rural laborers are encouraged to migrate and work in cities. Professionals in agriculture, e-commerce and other areas have been dispatched to poor areas to offer guidance and technical support.

All social sectors, such as private enterprises, social organizations and individuals, have been mobilized to participate in implementing poverty alleviation and development programs. Thus, China has hewed a poverty alleviation and development path with Chinese characteristics featuring multiple entities.

Besides, China has made targeted poverty alleviation the primary policy based on information of people in need since 2013. The people and authorities in charge were clearly identified, and their responsibilities were clarified. Also, different regions follow different development approaches due to diverse natural and geographical conditions that are specific to them. Although other countries also attach importance to targeted approaches for poverty reduction, such as Russia's social assistance program, they still lack practical and concrete policies.

What role has economic growth and income distribution played in poverty reduction in BRICS countries, especially in China?

Our research found that BRICS members' poverty reduction achievements can be mostly attributed to growth, while income distribution only played a supporting role. Moreover, some of them experienced widening gaps between the rich and poor for many years, instead of improvement in income distribution. Therefore, it has become a common challenge for BRICS and the international community to curb inequality and strive for inclusive growth. Fortunately, inequality reduction was listed as an important goal under the 2030 Agenda for Sustainable Development Goals (SDGs) of the United Nations.

Of course, economic growth is critical for reducing poverty. However, that is no reason for ignoring income distribution as it directly relates to poverty and indirectly affects growth. By and large, the chief reason underlying the relatively less remarkable achievements in poverty reduction in Brazil, Russia and South Africa is their worsening income inequality. For example, South Africa has the highest level of inequality among BRICS, followed by Brazil, whose Gini index is between 45 and 55 percent.

In addition, inequality rose in all BRICS countries except Brazil. The Gini index for South Africa rose from 58.4 percent in 1975 to 60.2 percent in 2015; and India from 38.1 percent in 1973 to 47.2 percent in 2012. China has seen rising inequality since the reform and opening-up, with the Gini index increasing from 28.4 to 43.3 percent over 30 years. Although income distribution has been improving, China's Gini index is still at a high level of space 41.1 percent in 2015. After the dissolution of the Soviet Union, Russia faced a dramatic rise in Gini index between 1990 and 1995, but then gradually improved. The index fell from 37.4 percent to 33.3 in the next 10 years. In Brazil, the Gini index dropped from 50.3 percent in 1970 to 46.5 percent in 2017.

Income distribution in these countries hampers progress in poverty reduction.

As representatives of emerging and transition economies, BRICS countries usually have their problems such as income distribution and poverty overlooked compared to their rising economic power. This perception should be changed not just because of the poverty and inequality goals being included in the SDGs of the UN, but also because economic growth is highly influenced by poverty and inequality. For instance, many Latin American countries, including Brazil, face stagnation or the so-called middle-income trap due to their large income gaps. And, income disparity breeds crime that undermine foreign investment flows into South Africa.

Thanks to the reform and opening-up, China's economy has become the fastest-growing in the world which led to dramatic poverty alleviation. However, there are some socioeconomic problems caused by the rising income disparity, among which the most pressing one is the weakness in domestic consumption. Domestic consumption cannot rise when the rich do not increase their spending, while others lack purchasing power. In other words, excessive savings and high-income inequality, as well as corresponding sluggish domestic demand, can undoubtedly drag down China's growth amid the anti-globalization wave.

Of course, economic growth can help lift people out of poverty, providing more income and a better environment. Better income distribution can also enhance these positive impacts. Income distribution can be improved via fiscal policies of taxation and government transfers. As a matter of fact, poverty in many regions or countries can be eliminated by improving income distribution. Taking India as an example, in 2019 the proportion of the population living below the poverty line of $1.9 per capita per day was 10.7 percent. If income could be equalized, this 10.7 percent of the poor would have been out of poverty. In fact, the same can be said even if higher poverty lines of $3.2 or even $5.5 are used. This is because India's GDP per capita has exceeded $2,000, implying more than $5.5/person/day when GDP is adjusted by the so-called purchasing power parity.

For China, the government needs to raise domestic demand and boost household consumption. This will help China continue its progress in poverty reduction when economic growth faces a downward trend. What is more vital is to tackle the increasing wealth gap in the country that offsets the benign impacts of growth on poverty eradication and harms growth sustainability.

In other BRICS countries, it is necessary to control consumption and increase savings to generate investment, which is essential for promoting economic development and poverty reduction. And China's experience with government, social forces and even international cooperation leading to poverty elimination sets a good example for other nations.

02

Changes in Rural Revitalization, Integrated Urban-Rural Development and Population Structure

I. Rural Revitalization—A Key to Ending Poverty[①]

At the press conference at the annual session of the National People's Congress on May 28, 2020, Premier Li Keqiang indicated that China still has 600 million people whose income is less than 1,000 yuan ($140) per month. Before COVID-19, China had around 5 million poor people based on the official national poverty line, which is equivalent to the World Bank definition of extreme poverty, which is less than $1.90 per person per day measured in purchasing power parity. Because of the pandemic, people above that line may fall back into poverty. But the Chinese government reconfirmed its commitment to end extreme poverty in 2020 through various policy and spending programs including expansion of the coverage of subsistence allowance and unemployment benefits. While there is no doubt that this goal will be achieved, the question is how to sustain the end of extreme poverty and make further progress in revitalizing rural areas to achieve various targets beyond income-based extreme poverty such as education, health, housing, rural living conditions and the environment by 2035. Learning from other countries' lessons and experience is important.

[①] By Fan Shenggen, professor and director of Acadcmy of Global Food Economics and Policy at China Agricultural University, former director general of the International Food Policy Research Institute.

From 1971 to 1979, South Korea implemented *Saemaul Undong* (New Village Movement), a community-based integrated program that brought rural development to the forefront of the national political agenda. The program aimed to close the growing income and living-quality gap between rural and rapidly-developing urban areas. The program first focused on village-level self-help projects, then quickly expanded into a full array of investments in irrigation, agricultural inputs (especially modern seeds), electrification and transportation. Mothers' clubs helped women initiate income-generating projects and participate in decision making. As a result, farm household income increased five-fold from 1970 to 1979, reaching parity with urban households. The lessons from this model could inform countries whose national leadership is committed to linking national programs with local participation and mobilization.

During its rapid industrialization and urbanization from the 1950s to 1980s, Japan experienced a sharp decline in population, abandoned farmland and degraded natural resources in rural areas. Since the 1990s, the country has launched several programs to revitalize or invigorate rural areas. In addition to investing in rural infrastructure and improving living conditions for local residents and migrants, one feature of these programs is to promote inclusive rural-urban linkages to connect local farmers with urban consumers through farmers' markets and cooperatives. Rural populations in Japan are skewing older, like in China, as young people migrate to urban areas. In 2000, Japan implemented a mandatory social long-term care insurance program providing elderly people in rural areas affordable home- and community-based services such as home help, adult day care and visiting nurses.

In Thailand, developing niche products and empowering rural areas have been key to poverty reduction. The government's "One Tambon One Product" (OTOP) program, which supports the production and marketing of items from Thailand's 7,255 *tambons*, or sub-districts, sparked local entrepreneurship and provided alternative incomes for poor farmers. Thailand has also promoted rural-based initiatives including organic rice farming, handicraft production and rural tourism to increase local employment and sustainable livelihoods. Thailand's experience in community-based development emphasizes strengthening communities so they can withstand external economic shocks, such as the 1997 Asian financial crisis and the 2009 global downturn, and provide a stable base for improving the quality of life for community members. A key element of this approach is active and informed participation from the people so that development is based on their own needs and aspirations.

The European Union has traditionally used agricultural subsidies to protect farmers but began to reform its agricultural subsidy policy in 2000, to provide direct income support and payment for environmental services to farmers. A special fund is used for developing rural areas including investing in rural infrastructure. The new EU farm policy has introduced better-targeted and more equitable safety nets that reward farmers for climate-friendly and sustainable practices.

At the beginning of the 20th century, agricultural and rural areas in the United States were prosperous. However, in the 1960s and 1970s, a large portion of the rural population moved to the cities. Recently, there has been a new trend that people are leaving cities. They live in places two or three hours away from the city center so that they can enjoy both greater living space as well as fresh air in suburban or rural areas and have access to quality healthcare, entertainment options and other amenities available in the cities. The US recently unveiled a $1.5 trillion infrastructure investment plan of which a substantial portion will be used to improve rural infrastructure, including transportation, hydropower and broadband connectivity. New technologies and work modalities, such as e-commerce and telecommuting working from home, have also shown potential to revitalize rural areas, creating business and development opportunities as well as keeping rural towns connected.

China has successfully controlled COVID-19 and is in full economic recovery. Ending poverty is not just a short term goal for 2020, but should also be a key launch pad for long term elimination of poverty beyond income, including health, education, living conditions and rural environment. These are also key goals of rural revitalization. Based on the successful experiences and lessons from other countries and China's own characteristics, China should consider the following strategies to end poverty measured in multiple dimensions both in the short and long run through rural revitalization.

First, productive sectors including agriculture and food and post-production value chains in rural areas must be revitalized while protecting returning migrants by using part of the stimulus package. During the National People's Congress session in 2020, Premier Li announced a fiscal stimulus package of almost 3.6 trillion yuan to lead China's economy recovery following the COVID-19 disruption. Many rural migrants could not return to their urban jobs due to closures or slowdown in manufacturing, construction and services sectors. Therefore, unemployment benefits should be distributed to unemployed migrants to build rural roads, telecommunications, irrigation and other productive assets. Part of the package could be used to help returned migrants to start new businesses to regenerate economic activities and employment in rural areas. The strategy of "one village one product" and promotion of heritage and agricultural tourism in South Korea, Japan and Thailand could provide important lessons for China in this regard. Social protection policies used by South Korea, Japan and Thailand during the Asian financial crisis in 1997 and the global financial crisis in 2008 to revitalize rural productive sectors are useful experience for China to design the revitalization of the productive sector.

Second, rural education, health and nutrition of rural residents, particularly children and women, must be re-emphasized or prioritized. Future human capital, including education and health, is a foundation for achieving poverty reduction, improving wellbeing of rural residents and modernization of rural areas in the long run. These investments include, first and foremost, improving primary and secondary education. Better educational systems have a strong positive impact on many indicators of human development, including income, wages and labor productivity. Policy should also be redesigned to focus on improvement of nutrition instead of grain sufficiency for rural residents. Providing nutritious and healthy diets for children and women is an essential part of overall improvement of human capital development. The Thai experience is particularly relevant here. Community leaders and experts identified basic minimum indicators of nutrition, health and education that translated into goals reflecting local priorities that could be monitored for progress. In addition, volunteers at the community level play a critical role in achieving these indicators in Thailand.

Third, improving the environment is key to rural revitalization. In the past, due to overuse of fertilizers and pesticides, and overexploitation of both surface and underground water, rural natural resources and environment were severely degraded. Rural areas can contribute to rural and urban environmental quality through sustainable practices such as conservation agriculture, rainwater harvesting and payment for ecosystem services, which provide community members with incentives to manage ecosystem resources and protect biodiversity. Adopting community-based management systems for water and forests also offer opportunities for shared prosperity, environmental sustainability and social cohesion. Access to clean drinking water and sanitation including building more toilets and garbage disposal should also be part of the revitalization effort. As a result, rural living conditions could be improved for attracting people to stay or even come back from urban centers. China could follow the successful reform of the EU's Common Agricultural Policy by converting agricultural subsidies to investment in rural infrastructure and in improving the environment. More support should be used to promote research and development, production and value chain development of nutritious foods such as vegetables, fruits, beans and fisheries.

Fourth, empowering and motivating rural villages and communities have proved to be one of the most successful strategies in revitalizing rural areas in South Korea, Japan, and Thailand. Devolution of governance is vital to taking development to the people. A decentralized system of governance that is participatory, transparent and accountable, and balances fiscal powers with assigned functions will be able to respond to local contexts, needs and aspirations.

Finally, strengthening rural-urban linkages—including physical, economic, social and political connections—are crucial for revitalizing rural areas and ending poverty sustainably in both rural and urban areas. Urban growth increases food demand and spurs dietary changes in urban areas—new demand can create opportunities for rural producers to improve their livelihoods. Broken value chains and poor coordination weaken rural-urban links and hold back progress on food security and nutrition. Investment in rural infrastructure and intermediate towns—

quality rural and feeder roads, electricity, storage facilities, communications and information—can build connections and create hubs of economic activity bernefitting smallholders and cities. The rising satellite towns within one to two hours commuting distance and working from home using IT in the US is a good example for China to consider. Integrated rural-urban food systems by using technologies such as modern greenhouses and ITC platforms, benefiting both farmers and urban consumers in the Netherlands, is another example that China could also learn from.

II. Focus on Rural Areas Is the Key[1]

China's goal to eliminate absolute poverty by 2020 through the use of an array of policies will be a great achievement for humanity and sets an example for the rest of the world.

In 1949, at the early period of the founding of the People's Republic of China, the government redistributed land to peasants, and thus beginning to improve the conditions of the more than 90 percent of the population engaged in the agricultural sector.

But the most spectacular results were achieved from 1978 onwards when China adopted its policy of reform and opening-up. It is reported that China has been able to lift around 800 million people out of poverty since 1978, something that has no precedent in the world history.

China at the beginning of 1979 adopted measures to achieve the Four Modernizations: modernization of industry, agriculture, defense, and science and technology. The modernization of agriculture is very important since most of the poor lived in rural areas and were employed in the agricultural sector. The

---

[1] By Carlos Aquino, professor and coordinator of the Center of Asian Studies at Peru National University of San Marcos.

modernization of the agricultural sector was based on several elements.

Peasants were allowed to cultivate their own plot of land and to sell the surplus in the market. The decollectivization of land brought incentives for peasants to work harder and thus production increased, as did their income.

The government began an effort to improve infrastructure, such as roads, to help modernize the rural sector and to bring produce and products quicker and less expensively to the markets. Also, several financial institutions lent money to the agricultural sector and helped peasants buy necessary tools to improve productivity. China has several financial institutions operating in rural areas, and among them the biggest is the Agriculture Bank of China.

To alleviate poverty in rural areas, the government abolished agriculture taxes starting from 2006. Historically, taxes from the agriculture sector were the main source of income for the government, and so the elimination meant that a type of tax collected for over 2,000 years was coming to an end.

Rural markets experienced great development and this allowed farmers to sell produce not only from their land but also from raising their animals, or from producing goods for the markets.

Also, in 2005 the government decided to begin abolishing school fees in rural areas as well as many other minor taxes, so life for peasants began improving a lot.

Together with the modernization of the agricultural sector and rise in the income of peasants, another measure helping to eliminate poverty in China was the modernization of industry. This is necessary, among others, for two reasons: first, because the modernization of agriculture led to an increase in the productivity of peasants and made many of them redundant, which made them leave the fields to look for jobs in the urban areas; and second, because incomes are higher in the industrial sector.

So, a large number of peasants left rural areas for jobs and the manufacturing sector was able to absorb them. In this regard, policies implemented by the Chinese government were successful as it allowed a large number of workers to be employed in the manufacturing sector that produced goods to the outside world, which led to China becoming the factory of the world.

Since 1978, China implemented policies to attract foreign capital, which in joint ventures with Chinese companies began producing inexpensive goods for foreign markets. But China also invested in education, and in science and technology, and began producing more sophisticated goods with more added value, and the income of workers rose fast.

Another policy the government adopted was a set of specific measures directed at groups with special characteristics or specific needs. China is a huge country with a complicated landscape and some people who traditionally lived in poverty.

A significant number of people live in almost inaccessible areas, high in the mountains, or in places with no roads. Some of the ethnic minorities, according to official statistics, were very poor before the founding of the PRC. The Chinese government gave special treatment to them so they could improve their situation.

For example, ethnic minorities, who comprise around 8.5 percent of the population, have traditionally enjoyed special treatment, from a more lenient childbirth policy than the Han majoring to preferential financial policies to help them develop and get rid of poverty. These policies include developing agriculture and animal husbandry in local areas, and the construction of highways and rural industries.

The Chinese government has formulated many policies that will help it to achieve the goal of eliminating absolute poverty. Several of them can be also of great use to many countries, especially to developing countries. In summary:

First, a policy is needed to help raise output in the agriculture sector and the income of farmers. For this, it is important to provide finance to help poor peasants acquire necessary tools. In many countries, peasants have no access to finance or are charged high interest rates, which condemn them to continue living in poverty.

Second, the provision of physical infrastructure, such as irrigation works and roads, will not only increase productivity but also bring agriculture produce closer to markets. Not only do farmers benefit, but also consumers have access to cheaper food.

Third, redundant and poor peasants go to the cities, and if no jobs are found, they constitute the poor in urban areas. The development of the industrial and manufacturing sector then is essential to employ them.

Fourth, education is one of the most important government provisions, so people can acquire skills needed to get better, high paying jobs. Only in this way will people rise above poverty.

Fifth, in many countries there are people who need special attention such as those living in remote areas, people with special needs such as the infirm, or from a disadvantaged or discriminated sector. For them, governments have to provide special measures, like subsides, to help them overcome disadvantages.

The COVID-19 pandemic has been a severe setback for all countries, and in many of them, many more people will fall into poverty. China, which was the first country to recognize the virus, was able to control it faster and at lower cost in the numbers of dead and in cost to the economy. For example, according to the IMF economic forecast in June 2020, the world economy will experience negative annual economic growth in 2020, at -4.9 percent, with the advanced economies at -8.0 percent and the emerging markets and developing economies -3 to 0 percent. But China will achieve annual economic growth of 1.0 percent.

The Chinese government will do its utmost to steer the economy to grow at a higher rate. The elimination of absolute poverty in China is at stake, but let's not forget that China has been the engine of the world economy from the beginning of this century. So, the world expects China to achieve its goal, and the lessons from its success could help the rest, and its development will be a boon for the world.

III. Poverty Alleviation via Rural Industrialization[1]

The year 2010 was a turning point in the global manufacturing landscape. China overtook the US as the world's largest manufacturing nation.[2] China accounted for 19.8 percent of the world's manufacturing output, compared to the 19.4 percent by the US. Since 2010, China has kept this new leadership position by progressively improving its productivity and enhancing its intensive technology innovation.

China's automobile industry is taking a global lead in production in the 21st century. In the first decade, China sold fewer than 2 million vehicles. In the years preceding 2020, China experienced years of double-digit growth, reaching 18 million vehicles (passenger cars and commercial vehicles) in 2010, and almost 28 million vehicles in 2018. Today, China's vehicle production is more than double the size of the US, around 2.9 times the size of Japan, and far bigger than any European country's auto sector.

---

[1] By Hua Wang, deputy president at Emlyon Business School, professor of Innovation Management and Managerial Economics.

[2] Peter Marsh, China Noses Ahead as Top Goods Producer, March 14, 2011, https://www.cnbc.com/id/42065544.

Table Top 10 countries in Vehicle Production, 2000-2019

(Unit: vehicle)

Country	2018	2010	2000
China	27,809,196	18,264,761	2,069,069
United States	11,314,705	7,743,093	12,799,857
Japan	9,728,528	9,628,920	10,140,796
India	5,174,645	3,557,073	801360
Germany	5,120,409	5,905,985	5,526,615
Mexico	4,100,525	2,342,282	1,935,527
South Korea	4,028,834	4,271,741	3,114,998
Brazil	2,879,809	3,381,728	1,681,517
Spain	2,819,565	2,387,900	3,032,874
France	2,270,000	2,229,421	3,348,361
World	95,634,593	77,629,127	58,374,162

Source: https://en.wikipedia.org/wiki/List_of_countries_by_motor_vehicle_production

The rise of the Chinese automobile industry is mainly driven by the policy of reform and opening-up in the late 1970s and 1980s, followed by the progressive growth of foreign direct investment in the 1990s. Global players established Sino-foreign joint ventures, bringing their global suppliers to China. In about three decades, from the 1980s to the 2000s, China progressively established the complete value chain of the automobile industry within its borders.

In parallel to the impressive growth of the Chinese automobile industry, there is the coexistence of another, rural-based automobile industry, producing millions of cars in the years following the 1990s. The development of this automobile industry in rural areas is a unique phenomenon within China's industrialization. This sector of the auto industry does not rely on direct technology transfer, nor investment from foreign companies. It is based on the needs of rural customers and creates important employment for converted workers in the rural regions, an important facet of industrialization and poverty alleviation.

Between the 1980s and 2000s, China's rural market was virtually ignored, save for the emerging niche market for farm vehicles (FVs). An FV is a new vehicle type, with three or four wheels. Most three–wheelers are made with single-cylinder diesel engines originally designed for stationary agricultural machinery. It is then adapted to satisfy the multiple purposes of farmers (for both agricultural activities and as tools for transporting people and goods) at an affordable price (on average less than half the price of conventional light trucks/vans). Production volume peaked in 1999 when 3 million FVs were produced, three times that of conventional passenger cars in the same year. The vehicle population reached about 22 million in 2010.

In contrast to traditional Chinese automobiles, where there has been significant support from the central government, FVs have developed in a grassroots fashion, not receiving the same support from the central government (Sperling et al., 2005)[1]. Prior to the mid-1980s, FVs were classified as a type of farm machinery. Their production was managed by the Ministry of Agriculture and benefitted from advantageous taxation regulations compared to conventional vehicles.

In the early stage of FV's development, hundreds of small enterprises in rural areas rushed into the business, some with the support of local governments. The tightening on industrial regulations and technology standards have accelerated industrial consolidation. The number of enterprises meeting the new norms of FVs dropped from 204 in 2001 to 120 in 2002. Market concentration accelerated. The market share of the top 10 enterprises to produce three wheelers increased from 59.5 percent to 65 percent and from 93 percent to 96 percent for top 10 four-wheeler producers.

---

[1] Daniel Sperling, Zhenhong Lin, Peter Hamilton, 2005, Rural vehicles in China: appropriate policy for appropriate technology, Transport Policy, 12(2), March 2005, Pages 105-119.

Figure 1

Chinese Farm Vehicle Production, 1985-2009[1]

(Unit : Vehicle)

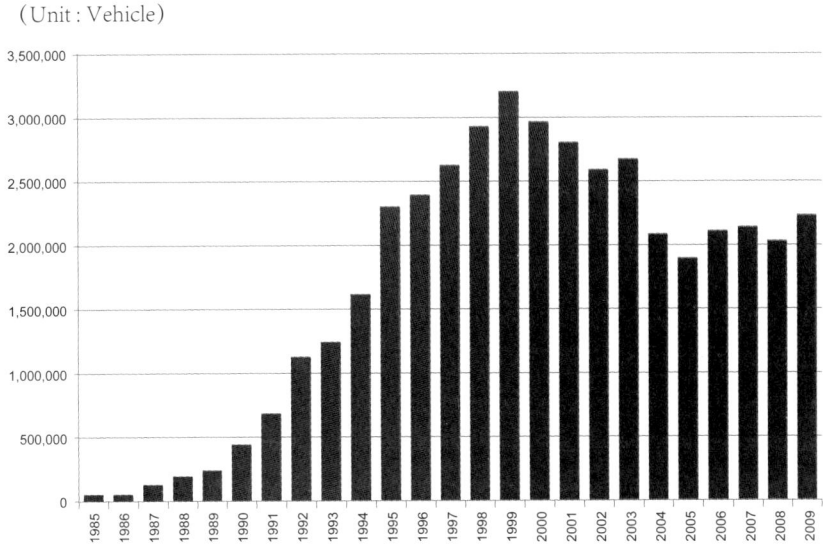

In the late 2000s, an increase in incomes of people living in towns and cities close to rural areas generated new mobility needs. A type of low-speed electric vehicles (LSEVs) for passengers started production in 2007, by companies in various industries (Wang & Kimble, 2012a)[2]. The typical LSEV has a simple structure, a top speed of 40 to 70 km/h, a cruising distance of 80 km, 100 km or 150 km, and costs between 20,000 yuan to 40,000 yuan ($3,100 to $6,200). The LSEV is an interesting Chinese case of frugal innovation, tapping the marketing potential of the bottom of the pyramid (BOP). Unlike CFV consumers, LSEV consumers are mainly located in third-tier or fourth-tier cities, and small towns and villages.

The value proposition of LSEVs to low-income consumers in rural areas was clear. Priced at an average of 25,000 yuan, they are much cheaper than a traditionally

---

[1] Wang, H., Kimble, C., 2012a. The Low Speed Electric Vehicle–China's Unique Sustainable Automotive Technology, in: Sustainable Automotive Technologies 2012. Springer, pp. 207–214.

[2] Wang, H., Kimble, C., 2012b. Business Model Innovation and the Development of the Electric Vehicle Industry in China, in: The Greening of the Automotive Industry. Palgrave Macmillan.

compact car, which is priced at least 40,000 yuan. The running costs of LSEVs are also lower than small gasoline-powered cars. To travel 100 km, the cost of electricity is around 6 yuan, whereas the cost of gasoline would be 49 yuan, about 8 times higher. In addition, the charging solution of LSEVs is much simpler than refueling. Households in rural areas have private parking spaces to charge the lead-acid battery from an ordinary 220-volt outlet, eliminating the need to drive several kilometers to underdeveloped petrol station networks. In short, similar to FVs, LSEVs are a consumer-driven product, not state-driven.

FVs and LSEVs both have annual market sizes of over 1 million, illustrating the fascinating existence of the dual economy structure. This dual economy is composed of distinctive agricultural and industrial sectors (Lewis 1954)[1]. Despite the impressive economic growth of China after the opening-up period in the late 1970s, the per capita annual income of rural households in 2018 was 14,617 yuan, with less than a third of those living in urban areas (39,250 yuan). According to the China Statistical Yearbook of 2019, China still has 552 million people living in rural areas, representing 39.4 percent of the Chinese population. Their low purchasing power and inelastic needs of transportation, both for production and consumption purposes, were a strong foundation for low-cost vehicles, a huge untapped market for conventional carmakers.

On the other side of the coin, the industrialization and massive production of low-cost and low-priced vehicles in China's rural areas provide a rich field of observation for new growth theories when compared to industrialized automobile clusters. This is a wave of creating indigenous automobile segments. There is no direct involvement of foreign direct investment, nor official central government support. It is a form of industrialization based on the demand of low-income people and domestic inter-industry technological spillover from matured automobile or mechanical industries. People in rural areas and small cities are both producers and consumers of those products, thus creating a new circle of industrialization, urbanization and positive contribution to the dynamic evolution

---

① Lewis, A., 1954. Economic development with unlimited supplies of labor. *The Manchester School*, 22(2), pp.139–191.

of the dual-economy structure. In the long run, there is the possibility of moving towards economic convergence via an increase in income level, human capital, technological intensity and more skilled workers in rural areas (Banerjee and Newman, 1993; Mesnard, 2001; Rapoport, 2002, Yuki, 2007).[1]

Figure 2

Income per capita of Chinese Urban and Rural Area, 1990-2018

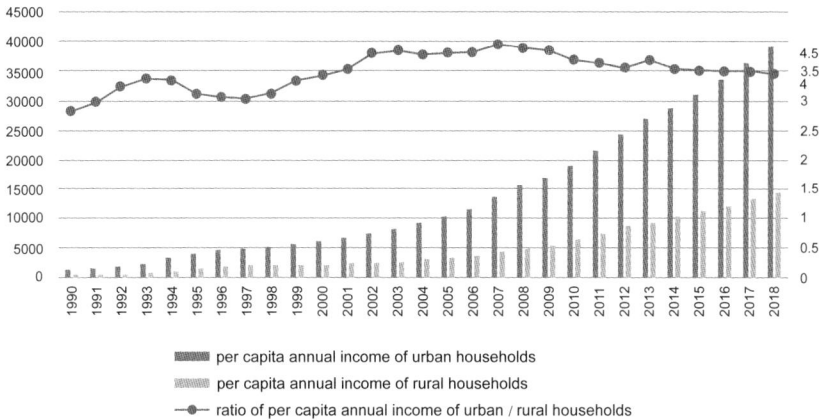

per capita annual income of urban households

per capita annual income of rural households

—●— ratio of per capita annual income of urban / rural households

Source: http://www.stats.gov.cn/tjsj/ndsj/

In a transitional economy, marked by a dual-economic structure, and in particular in a nation with a huge population, there exists two automobile industries. One is for the middle-class population mainly living in big cities, while the other is for the population in rural areas, towns and villages. The FVs and LSEVs, because of their low price, low running costs and ease of use, offer a clear value option to low-income consumers.

---

[1] Banerjee, A. V. and Newman, A. F. (1993). Occupational choice and the process of development. The Journal of Political Economy, 101 (2), 274-298.

Mesnard, A. (2001). Migration temporaire et mobilite intergenerationnelle. Louvain Economic Review, 67 (1), 59-88.

Rapoport, H. (2002). Migration, credit constraints and self-employment: a simple model of occupational choice, inequality and growth. Economics Bulletin, 15 (7), 1-5.

Yuki, K. (2007). Urbanization, informal sector, and development. Journal of Development Economics, 84, 76-103.

The market in China is large enough to experiment with many different types of technologies and to incorporate those technologies into many different product types. FVs and LSEVs are products with mature technology. Driven by big market needs, hundreds of carmakers rushed into their production. Fierce competition pushed the industry towards consolidation and the generation of economies of scale and mass production—a typical hallmark of industrialization.

This industrialization, different from the classic Chinese automobile industry, is mainly driven by market demand from rural areas and is organized by privately-owned local companies, without technology and financial support from multinational companies. It is an illustration of indigenous development of industry.

FVs and LSEVs have generated millions of employment opportunities and have contributed to poverty alleviation. These jobs cover the sub-industries of components suppliers, producers, dealers and after-sales service providers. There is also the phenomenon of geographic proximity. Those industrial clusters of FVs and LSEVs are located in provinces with big rural populations. Industries are absorbing labor through proximity.

Interestingly, China's LSEV industry is also in the early stage of exploring overseas markets. Foreign institutional buyers (e.g. governments, police departments, hospitals, post offices and airports) have bought LSEVs as a "green solution" while also cutting costs. Private consumers in the US, for example, have also bought LSEVs as a second or third car. The sales of LSEVs to the US have increased from 5,000 vehicles in 2008 to around 20,000 in 2010 (Wang and Kimble, 2010c)[1].

In summary, development of FVs and LSEVs are interesting cases in illustrating poverty alleviation via rural industrialization in China. The central government

---

[1] Wang, H., Kimble, C., Leapfrogging to Electric Vehicles: Patterns and Scenarios for China's Automobile Industry. International Journal of Automotive Technology and Management 11(4), 312–325 (2011).

should further balance between high-tech driven industrialization, and the "low-tech" (frugal technology) industrialization for the 40 percent of the population living in rural areas. A dual industrial policy for the dual economy might be more efficient in alleviating poverty that will further accentuate solid industrialization. This industrial development and institution setting from China might have important implications for developing countries, especially those with large populations.

03

Offering Education Satisfied by People

I. Tap the Educational Dividend[①]

It is widely believed that the rapid growth of the Chinese economy in its reform period has benefited from the country's demographic dividend. In 1980-2010, China's working-age population aged between 15 and 59 grew at an annual rate of 1.8 percent. That helped China form what ancient Confucians considered the ideal population pattern in which the producers are many and the consumers few. It guaranteed adequate labor, improved human capital, high returns on capital investment, and resources reallocation (productivity), and therefore, unprecedented high growth. In the same period, the average annual growth rate of gross domestic product was 10.1 percent.

Since 2010, the working-age population has declined, and the population dependency ratio has increased. As a result, economic growth has slowed. At this juncture, some scholars suggest that China can and should take advantage of its second demographic dividend. Before accepting the advice, however, we should first clarify what the second demographic dividend is and where we can find it.

Conventional wisdom regards the second demographic dividend as the favorable condition for high savings resulting from the decline of the dependency ratio. According to this view, in an aging society, if people recognize the necessity of saving for the rainy day as motivation and if there exists a fully funded pension

---

① By Cai Fang, vice-president of the Chinese Academy of Social Sciences (CASS), chairman of the National Institute for Global Strategy of CASA.

system as a mechanism, a high savings rate can still be achieved. This explains how a second demographic dividend is created.

But it is not a low dependency ratio alone that will help China spur its economic growth after the window of working-age-population opportunity closes. By allowing capital investment to be coordinated with labor input, China was insulated from a diminishing return on capital during that high growth period. That is what the demographic dividend is all about. Therefore, finding ways to prevent a diminishing return on capital in an era without an unlimited supply of labor is the real challenge facing China in gaining another demographic dividend.

The first demographic dividend was basically a transitory advantage and it did not last as the driving force for economic growth. In a later stage of economic development, economic growth can no longer rely on the total size of the population and its age structure. Instead, future economic growth has to rely on sources that can be cultured and thus sustained. Economic theories and development experiences show that total factor productivity (TFP) and human capital are the most important, sustainable drivers of growth, and they are mutually conditional and supportive of one another.

By nature, TFP is an allocative efficiency, or gains from efficiently allocating production factors given their constant quantity. Since how well production factors are allocated depends on workers' skills and entrepreneurship, to increase TFP requires the improvement of human capital, which is a more demographic advantage. A large body of empirical studies shows that human capital, measured as years of schooling that workers attain on average, not only makes a direct and significant contribution to economic growth, but also makes an indirect contribution to economic growth by simultaneously improving TFP.

In addition to improving human capital through learning-by-doing, education is the major contributor of the overall accumulation of human capital. In addition, the foundation laid by various levels and types of education determines the effectiveness of learning-by-doing. Educational development is first embodied in the quantitative expansion of education, which is often measured as years of schooling. Educational development also has its qualitative dimension, the improvement of quality. However, that needs to be based on the expansion of quantity. When the quality of education is set, the increase of years of schooling implies an overall enhancement of human capital, whereas the reverse is not necessarily true. The externality that characterizes education is the reason why quality of education should be improved through expansion of quantity.

Quality is a form of efficiency. In economic activities, efficiency improvement requires full competition and creative destruction—that is, letting efficient enterprises enter the market and inefficient ones exit. However, different from material production, education is not only a means to supply production factors, but also to meet the goal of people's all-round development. For this reason, there can only be creation but not destruction in the process of education development. Incontrovertibly, schools cannot be bankrupted, nor students' learning process be interrupted.

Cultivating skills and talents requires expansion of education scale. That is, the efforts of increasing years of schooling for new entrants to the labor market are equivalent to the enhancement of both quantity and quality of education. The experience of China and other countries show that once the universality of nine-year compulsory education is completed, the window of opportunity for further increasing the years of schooling opens in pre- and post-compulsory education stages, which, in China's case, is preschool education and senior high school.

First, prolonging compulsory education to include both preschool and senior high school will be economically and socially beneficial. First, education that meets the demand of economic growth and social development in an era of rapid technological advancement has a high social rate of return. Studies show that the social rate of return for preschool education is the highest among all stages of education.

Second, the compulsory education stages are essential to block the intergenerational transmission of poverty. Surveys show that the existing gap in preschool education results in unequal starting point between rural and urban children, and that the lower enrollment of rural juveniles for senior high school and thus university is the root cause of social immobility.

Third, the government paying for those stages of education can relieve households' financial burden and reduce the costs of opportunity, therefore helping increase young parents' willingness to bear children, which is vital in a time of low fertility.

II. Universal Education Is a Key Tool[1]

Poverty is the greatest challenge to human development, and intellectual poverty is the root cause of poverty. "We must put intellectual poverty reduction as a priority in poverty alleviation," said Chinese President Xi Jinping at the National Conference on Poverty Alleviation and Development in 2016, "Education is the key to dealing with the inter generational transmission of poverty". The year 2020 marks the completion of building a moderately prosperous society in all respects and eradicating extreme poverty, and it also marks the basic modernization of education.

In fact, poverty reduction through education began in 1949 when the People's Republic of China was founded. At that time, China's per capita GDP was only $49; more than 80 percent of the country's population was illiterate, and the figure reached 95 percent in rural areas. Chairman Mao Zedong once sighed: "China is poor and blank—poor means lack of wealth, and blank means lack of education."[2] He vowed to lift people out of the trap of illiteracy, which he and his fellow revolutionaries took as a historical mission.

On Dec 23, 1949, when wars were still being fought in some areas, the first National Conference on Education was held, heralding a 70-year endeavor to

---

[1] By Gao Shuguo, deputy secretary-general and researcher of the Chinese Education Society.

[2] *Collection of the Works of Mao Zedong*, Vol 5, People's Publishing House, 1996. P 345.

reduce education poverty. It was unprecedented in terms of the priority, policy and mobilization scale. A series of policies were unveiled. The All-China Federation of Trade Unions issued the Interim Provisions on the Use of Trade Unions' Cultural and Educational Expenditure in 1949, which clearly stipulated that education expenses should account for 60 percent of trade unions' cultural and educational expenditure. In 1950, then-premier Zhou Enlai signed the Directive on Part-time Education for Employees, which clearly stated that improving workers' literacy was the main goal of training during their time off. In the same year, the Government Administration Council issued the "Instructions on the Farmer's Sparetime Education". It, for the first time, proposed the target and standards of eliminating illiteracy—setting an example for global poverty alleviation through education.

Since 1951, a literacy campaign, led by the government and with the participation of grassroots organizations, has been in full swing throughout the country. At the end of 1953, nearly 4.08 million people had cast off illiteracy. By 1981, 140 million people had acquired literacy, including 10 million workers and 130 million farmers. The illiteracy rate for workers was merely 5 percent, and about 25 percent for working-age people in rural areas.

From 1978 to 2000, the average schooling years rose from 5 to 7.79 years, and the illiterate population dropped from 240 million to 99.6 million people. Between 2000 and 2010, the number of illiterate people aged above 15 dropped by 39.77 million, and the rate of illiteracy for the first time fell from 5 percent to 4.88 percent. China has achieved a crucial victory in reducing poverty through education, and it is the only developing country among the six most populous countries to fully achieve the United Nations goal of education for all.

Since the 18th Communist Party of China (CPC) National Congress in 2012, China has continued to push forward the work of targeted poverty alleviation. On December 29, 2012, during a visit to Fuping county, Hebei province, General Secretary of the CPC Central Committee Xi Jinping stressed that it is China's stated goal to ensure adequate food and clothing, and guarantee access to compulsory education, basic medical services and safe housing for impoverished rural residents by 2020. Education has since become a key indicator of poverty alleviation, signaling a major battle against poverty.

There are many reasons for the backward education in poor areas, including economic, political, cultural and traditional factors as well as individual reasons. The gap in the levels and opportunities for education caused a vicious circle in the poor areas: government's insufficient budget in education led to low level and fewer opportunities of education, which caused lower labor quality and hampered local economic development and eventually took a heavy toll on investment in education. Therefore, governments at all levels have increased investment in education for poor areas and for impoverished families. Education is seen as an important means for social equity and an approach to nurture people's self-motivation to fight against poverty.

In 2018, the Chinese government kicked off a special project on poverty alleviation through an education project, covering 680 poor counties. In February 2018, a three-year implementation program (2018−2020) was carried out for poverty alleviation through education in severely impoverished areas, in which the Chinese government vows to largely increase the overall level of education in the severely impoverished areas and provide basic public education services to every impoverished family in record. The program also stipulates that all funds are provided from admission to graduation for poor students at all educational stages, to ensure children from poor families access school. No student is allowed to be left out of school because of the financial difficulties of their family.

To tackle college students' financial difficulties, the Ministry of Education and the People's Bank of China have, through years of efforts, established a multifaceted policy package, including scholarships, student loans, work-study assistance and tuition fee reduction. The student support policy covers all stages of education, public and private schools and students in financial difficulties. The total number of funded students nationwide reached 520 million with the total amount of funds spent at 886.4 billion yuan.

From 1978 to 2019, the number of rural poor in the country reduced to 5.51 million, and the poverty incidence in rural areas dropped from 30.7 percent to 0.6 percent. Between 2010 and 2020, the average years of schooling in rural areas increased faster than in urban areas. The average years of schooling in China rose from 5.2 years in 1982 to 9.35 years in 2018. It is estimated that by 2035, the proportion of the number of people receiving higher education will exceed 25 percent, and the average years of schooling will rise to about 11.5 years.

We should further address the high dropout rate in nine-year compulsory education in some rural and poor areas, and monitor the areas with high dropout rates to ensure the rate be lower than 5 percent by 2020. The Ministry of Education is also trying to lift the rate of high school education to 90 percent by 2020.

Education is an important means to combat poverty. It could stop the intergenerational transmission of intellectual poverty and transform the overburdened population into human resources. In the past 70 years, the government has successfully handled illiteracy eradication and formed a set of effective ideas, models and methods.

First, leadership. The CPC and the central government have defined poverty alleviation through education as basic national policy. The highest leadership has personally designed, organized and initiated the engagement, thus forming a scientific leadership system for casting off illiteracy.

Second, institutional advantage. The socialist system is a great advantage for the success of China's education and poverty alleviation. The Party and government give full play to the advantages in terms of theory, politics, organization, system and close ties with the people. All their measures taken are in the interests of the people.

Third, social mobilization, which is an important strategic capability of the Chinese government. In the last seven decades, under the leadership of the CPC Central Committee and the State Council, China has mobilized all forces that can be mobilized to win a people's war against poverty through education. Social participation and division of labor are the mechanism for the smooth operation of

China's poverty reduction through education.

Fourth, cooperation mechanisms. The government has closely cooperated with international organizations, learned from the successful experiences of various countries in eradicating illiteracy, accepted the guidance and assistance of UNESCO and other international organizations, actively supported and participated in the efforts of international organizations, and fulfilled the global literacy responsibility as a large responsible country.

While the Chinese people have been eradicating economic poverty, they have basically eliminated intellectual poverty, too. China created the thought, theory and mode of poverty alleviation through education, making great contributions and providing an example for mankind to eliminate poverty.

04

Achievement and Prospect of Green Poverty Alleviation

I. Energy-Driven Program Delivers Double Dividends[①]

After the 18th National Congress of the Communist Party of China, the Party and the government were determined to alleviate poverty with firm resolve and confidence, and stepped up efforts in various fronts. As a result, all people in rural areas will have been lifted above the current poverty line by 2020.

To achieve this target, various departments and agencies came up with their plans, covering education, medical treatment and health, transportation, employment and training. The old poverty alleviation program depending on the development of agriculture and resources turned to one that focuses on alternative livelihoods and development guarantees.

Of all the measures, energy programs have become a major way of simultaneously reducing carbon emissions and poverty. People still living in poverty are mostly located in western China and some mountainous regions, where geographic remoteness and poor communication make development difficult. However, these regions are often endowed with abundant solar and water resources, adding to the prominence of energy-driven poverty alleviation.

---

① By Lin Boqiang, head of the China Institute for Studies in Energy Policy at Xiamen University.

Energy-driven poverty alleviation refers to the efforts of various parties, mainly energy companies, helping disadvantaged regions eradicate poverty with the guidance of governments. Current practices include distribution of photovoltaic (PV), hydropower and biomass energy.

On the one hand, China's PV industry is developing at a fast pace and its competitiveness is also increasing. On the other hand, the lack of electricity, abundant sunshine and low cost of distributed energy in rural areas constitute the right ingredients for PV power generation. It's in line with the green economy philosophy and could help improve the environment and maximize the utilization of new energies. Low-cost small hydropower and biomass energy programs also boost industries in rural areas and increase farmers' incomes.

Energy-driven poverty alleviation can help upgrade rural power grids and thus facilitate PV and hydropower programs. In 2018 alone, China invested 40.5 billion yuan in upgrading power grids in poor rural areas and enhancing the capability and quality of the power supply as well as promoting the use of electric agricultural machines and boosting local economic development.

At the same time, energy-driven poverty alleviation helps environmental protection. By replacing firewood with new energy, farmers have seen their income increase and kitchen sanitation improve. They no longer need to chop wood so that the forests are preserved. In short, positive environmental and economic benefits are generated in this process.

In spite of the achievements made, there are still issues to be dealt with in energy-driven poverty alleviation.

Some energy-driven poverty alleviation projects are not built up to standards in the first place and are then poorly managed and maintained. Village power stations in some remote poverty-stricken areas are constructed and run by villagers themselves. Their lack of expertise and experience often leads to malfunctioning. Problems have also emerged such as the lack of unified standards in site selection, design, installation and construction, outdated energy management practices and technologies as well as improper operations. As a result, some equipment can't meet set goals and some even become a burden.

Some households' lack of drive could also limit efficiency. If the model of energy-driven poverty alleviation is to offer money and materials, those who are being helped may become dependent on such giving and unable to have a right outlook on wealth or learn new skills. If those who are being helped are mainly the elderly and disabled, their education and physical condition could also limit the efficacy of poverty alleviation efforts. Wind, solar, small hydropower and other renewable energy programs often need large investment at the initial stage and a long time to recover input. But disadvantaged households usually do not have enough money for investment and are desperate for quick returns. It's impossible to change their way of living and perception of environmental protection in a short time. Isolated cultural atmosphere and the outflow of young labor in some localities even mean inadequate human resources for clean energy development. These are all hindrances to clean energy promotion.

If governments run the whole show of energy-driven poverty alleviation programs, the lack of other stakeholders' participation will lead to rigid mechanisms and unsatisfactory gains. For instance, in some ethnic minority regions where clean energy systems are mostly government-planned programs, there are such issues as inadequate training and guidance, lack of equipment maintenance and poor benefits.

Inaction results from lack of local governments' regulation. Some local governments only provide financial aid and preferential policies but ignore the vital link of regulation. In some other localities, governments, eager to seek instant success, even support some improper programs.

To eliminate poverty by 2020 and accelerate the building of a moderately prosperous society in all respects, China introduced the following new policies on energy-driven poverty alleviation in 2019:

Pilot programs of PV-driven poverty alleviation in 50,000 poor villages with favorable sunshine conditions; and 2.8 million poor households have seen an annual income increase of 3,000 yuan. Not long ago, the Ministry of Finance's 113.6 billion yuan of poverty alleviation funds in advance and a 5.675 billion yuan renewable energy subsidy for 2020, which will help mitigate the negative impact of lagging subsidies. This is really great news for PV-driven poverty alleviation and PV programs in rural areas.

Based on successful experience, 2 million kilowatts of installed capacity of small hydropower stations have been built in rural areas, which could bring benefits to 1 million households in 10,000 poor villages.

Thanks to unremitting efforts, remarkable achievements have been made in energy-driven poverty alleviation. But due to various constraints, the energy foundation in China's rural areas is still weak, service levels are low and the development of clean energies lag behind. Targeted poverty alleviation has now entered a crucial stage, where we should make good plans, focus on industries' roles in poverty eradication, speed up the transformation of working models, and enhance the "self-generation capability" of those being helped. We should devote ourselves wholeheartedly in the work of fixed point poverty alleviation, accelerate grid upgrades in such areas, develop new energy programs in line with local conditions, form greater synergy with relevant industries, give better play to "PV plus" and strive to create more opportunities for economic development through energy-driven poverty alleviation.

II. Leveraging China's Green Soft Power[1]

China has been trumpeting its commitment to building a green Belt and Road Initiative, a theme emphasized at the Second Belt and Road Forum for International Cooperation held in Beijing. And the central government has issued a number of implementation policies, including the Guiding Opinions on Promoting

---

[1] By Hu Min, Diego Mendero. Hu Min, director of the Green Development Program. Diego Merdro, strategic advisor of the Green Development Program.

a Green Belt and Road Initiative and the Belt and Road Initiative Ecological Environmental Protection Cooperation Plan, aiming at ensuring the initiative is clean and green.

The challenge is a familiar one—how to balance development and environmental protection. Much like in China 20 years ago, for many countries involved in the Belt and Road Initiative, improving access to electricity, a critical precondition for employment, poverty alleviation and public health, is the top policy priority. This development need can overwhelm efforts to mitigate long-term climate change risks.

We have seen some efforts by China to promote clean energy in the Belt and Road Initiative, and the Asian Infrastructure Investment Bank has participated in several clean energy projects, including Egypt's Benban Solar Park, one of the world's largest projects of this kind. In Argentina, the China Development Bank and China Export-Import Bank have provided 85 percent of the financing for the Cauchari solar power plant, the largest in Latin America.

However, the set of policies to regulate the environmental impact of China's development finance is large, complex and less stringent than domestic policies. A World Bank report states: "China has a growing collection of guidelines but they still lack essential details concerning implementation, monitoring, and enforcement."

But China's policies are only half of the equation. The environment, energy and climate policies in partner Belt and Road countries are equally important, in determining the environmental impact of the projects that China invests in.

One recommendation from the World Resources Institute is that Chinese investment should be linked to the National Determined Contribution (NDC) of the Belt and Road partners under the Paris Agreement. This, however, is only a partial solution. In Indonesia, for example, the NDC goal accommodates an energy development plan that allows the proportion of coal-fired power grow around five times its current size by 2050. In the end, it is the laws and regulations in partner countries—what kinds of appliances can be used, what kinds of cars can be driven, what kinds of buildings can be built, what kind of energy can be used—that will affect local energy consumption and emissions patterns.

So what can China do to help? Setting stringent environmental guidelines for its overseas investments—a "hard power" approach—is important. But it is even more important that China provide financial and technical support to its Belt and Road partners by sharing its experiences and the lessons it has learned in implementing clean energy, environment and climate policies. We can think of this as China's green soft power.

Although China itself is still trying to win its war on pollution, in the past few decades it has established a comprehensive system of laws, regulations and strategic plans for environmental protection and clean energy, some of which are considered world-class. For example, China has established stricter power plant pollution emissions requirements than the United States and the European Union. And China's Stage 6 light duty vehicle standard is one of the most stringent emission standards in the world, according to International Center of Clean Transportation.

Developing countries participating in the Belt and Road Initiative can draw on China's experiences, since China's environmental protection and carbon mitigation practices as a developing economy may be more relevant to them than those of the developed economies. To take one example, China's issue of overcapacity in coal-fired power plants might also soon appear in other Central Asian Belt and Road countries. China can share the lessons it has learned in this area with its Belt and Road partners.

Policymakers should map out the gap in policies between China and other Belt and Road countries, sector by sector, and identify the ones with the largest greenhouse gases mitigation or environmental impact potential. Policy dialogues should be centered on the most effective policies. Ecological protection standards related to mining, minimum efficiency levels for energy intensive industrial products, and green standards related to infrastructure development can all be adapted to Belt and Road countries.

China is good at using strategic communications in support of its comprehensive plans for clean energy, energy conservation and emission reductions. The majority of Chinese Belt and Road-related investment in Jordan, one of the top three investment destinations in recent years, is flowing into shale oil development projects that meet local requirements for energy supply diversification. However, Jordan also has abundant solar and wind energy resources, and cheap desert land. According to a Greenpeace report, it's technically feasible for these resources to supply six times the current total electricity demand by 2050. With the right support for long-term planning and strategic communications, Jordan could make bolder moves toward renewable power generation.

To accomplish all this, joint policy research and technical cooperation should lead the way. The strategic framework for much of this is already in place. Now is the time for concrete action. "Environmental Policy and Standard Coordination and Convergence" is one of the 25 key projects in China's Belt and Road Initiative Ecological and Environmental Cooperation Plan. On April 25, at the second Belt and Road Forum for International Cooperation in Beijing, the National Development and Reform Commission, Energy Foundation China, the United Nations Economic and Social Commission for Asia and the Pacific and the UN Industrial Development Organization jointly launched a Belt and Road Initiative Green Cooling Initiative. One of the actions it calls for is to promote collaboration and dialogue on environmental standards. This is a step in the right direction.

05

Digital Technoloay and E-commerce Breaks down the Barriers of Communication and Marketing Channels in Poor Areas

I. Digital Technology Is a Big Enabler[1]

Digital technology is being increasingly adopted in economic and social activities and is profoundly transforming production patterns and people's lifestyles in modern society. However, it is essential for developing countries to have a more inclusive digital economy to prevent the rich-poor gap from widening. In China, e-commerce, digitally inclusive finance, and poverty alleviation programs supported by big data have had a positive impact on poverty reduction.

First, e-commerce promotes income growth capacity building of the poor. China has the world's fastest-growing e-commerce market, where more than 40 percent of global e-commerce transactions take place. Many poor people, too, have benefited from the booming e-commerce industry. For example, the National Rural E-commerce Comprehensive Demonstration Project has helped nearly 3 million registered impoverished households realize income growth. In 2019, online retail sales in 832 poverty-stricken counties reached 107.6 billion yuan ($15.7 billion) totally.

E-commerce platforms have greatly reduced the threshold for small and micro businesses to enter large markets. Rural residents who were marginalized in terms

---

① By Jiang Xiheng, vice-president at the China Center for International Knowledge on Development.

of their geographic location, access to information, and development capabilities, can now display their agricultural products and handicrafts online and find buyers, thereby increasing sales and revenue. Also, e-commerce drives the development of whole industrial chains, creating job opportunities and providing diverse options for rural labor. Online retailing has created over 28 million jobs in rural China. In addition, rural e-commerce also benefits the most disadvantaged groups such as women with children and the elderly. The ratio of male to female entrepreneurs on the Alibaba e-commerce platform is close to 1:1, compared to 3:1 for the entire business sector.

More importantly, e-commerce can also promote the transformation of mindsets and provides learning opportunities, thus stimulating the entrepreneurial potential of the poor. Between April 2015 and March 2017, 1.12 million people from 765 national-level poverty-stricken counties joined 559 courses offered by Taobao University online.

Second, digital technology promotes inclusive finance. The difficulty and high investment costs of financing have always been proved to be a bottleneck for the survival and growth of small and micro-enterprises. Many countries have explored different ways of providing them inclusive finance loans, but the high cost and credit gap remain the two major barriers for poor people to get loans. However, the G20 High-Level Principles for Digital Financial Inclusion endorsed by the G20 in 2016 marked the beginning of the digital era of inclusive finance, creating new ways of problem solving.

In China, traditional financial institutions utilize digital technologies to improve the availability and convenience of financial services for marginalized groups. Financial agencies also support non-cash payments for bulk purchase of agricultural products such as grains, and the issuance of pensions, medical insurance, and agricultural subsidies.

Since its establishment in 2015, China's first cloud computing-based commercial bank, MYbank, has provided contactless loans to more than 4 million customers in 146 poverty-stricken counties. In 2017, JD.com launched digital agricultural loans. In two years, this project had collaborated with more than 100 cooperatives in Shandong, Hebei and Henan provinces, and other places, providing loans of roughly 1 billion yuan with zero overdue repayments and defaults.

Third, big data, too, supports targeted poverty alleviation by improving accuracy and ensuring the fairness of poverty identification. In 2014, the Ministry of Civil Affairs began promoting the establishment of information verification platforms based on big data in different regions.

As of October 2019, big data platforms had covered 96.8 percent of provincial-level areas and 91.9 percent of city-level areas. The use of big data networks to pre-screen poor families is now the mainstream norm. Meanwhile, comprehensive analyses of impoverished areas through big data helps formulate targeted assistance. With the combination of geographical information such as climate and land forms, and social information such as family composition, personal capabilities, economic and financial conditions, big data helps to systematically analyze the reasons for poverty at the county, village, and household levels, providing stronger support for poverty alleviation.

However, the application of big data still needs improvement. Only 5.9 percent of China's cities have used databases for professional data development, and only 1.8 percent have submitted reports to higher authorities based on big data analysis.

Real-time data sharing and the dynamic comparison of various databases on poverty alleviation, education, industry and commerce, civil affairs, health and other areas can improve the efficiency of using public resources. It can also track and monitor the progress and efficiency of poverty alleviation in different regions and organizations.

Multi-dimensional data assists government agencies in choosing the most appropriate poverty alleviation projects and setting reasonable standards. For example, in Shanghai, big data is widely used to set the annual poverty standard. Research based on big data, such as "the minimum living standard based on checked data", provide recommendations to government agencies such as the

Ministry of Civil Affairs on national social policies.

Finally, big data contributes to improving the efficiency of using poverty alleviation resources and promoting evidence-based decision-making. Digital technology has been playing a positive role in China's poverty reduction. Nevertheless, some conditions enabling this should be noted:

There is extensive coverage of traditional and digital infrastructures in China's rural areas, including the majority of impoverished areas. As of March 2020, China's internet coverage rate reached 64.5 percent. More than 98 percent of administrative villages have fiber optic and 4G connections, and the proportion of poverty-stricken villages with broadband access reached 99 percent, which guaranteed internet access for the vast majority of people via computers or mobile phones. Besides, thanks to traditional infrastructure such as power grids and roads, people in most residential areas in China enjoy stable electricity power supply and transportation facilities.

The government and digital platform enterprises have established partnership for development. Governments at all levels have an open and encouraging attitude toward the development of the digital economy and actively cooperate with digital companies to better identify and help the poor.

The inclusive business models adopted by digital platform companies have made important contributions. Through e-commerce, financial services and philanthropic programs, digital platforms have helped empower women, young people, the disabled, and small businesses in impoverished areas. With digital platforms, these groups have access to broader markets, low-cost development opportunities, and escape poverty through entrepreneurship or employment.

II. Modern Rural Economy Booster[①]

Since 2014, the Ministries of Commerce and Finance and the State Council Leading Group Office of Poverty Alleviation and Development, among other departments, have implemented comprehensive pilot projects to bring e-commerce to rural areas in 1,231 county-level initiatives, covering all 832 counties with income levels below the national poverty line. The total online retail sales volume in the 832 counties reached 180.4 billion yuan ($25.9 billion) in 2018, a 49.3 percent increase from the previous year, and rural e-commerce has created more than 30 million jobs. Over 10 million people have benefited from these projects, of whom 3 million have seen their incomes increase. In Huanxian County of Gansu Province, for instance, e-commerce has helped the average household income increase from 750 yuan in 2015 to 1,100 yuan in 2016, 1,560 yuan in 2017, and 2,450 yuan in 2018.

Success in rural e-commerce comes from the strong support of large e-commerce companies. Over 800 "Taobao villages", clusters of rural online entrepreneurs who have opened shops on Taobao, Alibaba's e-commerce platform, have sprung up across different counties whose income levels fall below the provincial poverty line. For instance, 12 impoverished villages in Caoxian county, Shandong Province, have eradicated poverty by creating Taobao villages. Over 20,000 people, or one out of every five who rose out of poverty in Caoxian county did so as a direct result of leveraging e-commerce. Pinduoduo, an e-commerce platform that allows users to participate in group-buying deals, has 140,000 online businesses started by people living in places with income levels below the national poverty line, generating annual sales of 16.2 billion yuan and creating over 300 local jobs. Also, national industry associations have played a role in poverty reduction through e-commerce. In 2017, the Ministry of Commerce launched a platform to manage all information related to poverty reduction through e-commerce.

---

① By Hong Yong, deputy researcher of E-Commerce Research Institute at Chinese Academy of International Trade and Economic Cooperation of the Ministry of Commerce.

Despite rapid growth in recent years, rural e-commerce has barely transitioned out of its initial phase, and there is much room for growth.

First, rural e-commerce needs to be better focused and more effective. Some of the pilot projects bringing e-commerce to rural areas suffer from issues such as the poor targeting of lower income families, suboptimal allocation of capital, and lack of focus in the measures undertaken. For example, rural e-commerce suffers from imbalanced development due to different natural conditions, levels of economic development and logistical costs in different places. Nevertheless, the pilot project special fund failed to fully consider these differences and opted for equal allocation of capital. Some of the county-level e-commerce regulatory authorities lacked overall project planning, were afraid to use the fund or lacked the skills required. As a result, funding disbursement was slower than expected.

Second, window-dressing and bureaucracy are still rampant. Some of the county-level e-commerce public service centers are hardly used except for showing off to authorities. A few of the warehouses in logistics distribution centers sit idle, and some are located too far from each other to take advantage of network effects. Some regions pursue a high coverage rate of village-level service centers single-mindedly, encouraging major e-commerce platforms to set up these centers only to end up with a demand shortfall.

Third, the talent shortage in rural e-commerce needs to be addressed. There are different degrees of scarcity of professionals with expertise in areas such as rural e-commerce marketing, operations and design, and in particular, highly-trained professionals. Most of the resident population in rural areas are retirees, and the young children they care for (whose parents have left to work in the cities), who are not keen on learning to use the internet. As e-commerce training takes away time that could be used on farming, some of the residents have been reluctant to participate. The participants are diverse groups of individuals with very different needs and learning styles, but the content and methodology of training represent a "one size fits all" approach. The training courses are heavy on theory and offer few opportunities for hands-on learning. Some e-commerce training centers only teach basic platform operation skills such as setting up an online store, publishing notifications and accepting orders, but fail to provide comprehensive coaching on specialized skills such as product design, promotion, operation, graphic design, customer relationship management and warehouse management. As the course is of little relevance, students are uninterested in applying their knowledge to online entrepreneurship.

To facilitate rural revitalization and poverty reduction effectively, it is vital to foster industries with competitive advantage, find new ways to develop county-level e-business, and promote multi-channel rural e-commerce through various approaches. First, integrate online retail and wholesale platforms, including leading commodity business-to-business trading platforms operated by companies such as yimutian.com, zhongnongwang.com and agr580.com, agricultural product wholesale platforms such as 1688.com and meicai.cn, verticals in perishable products such as benlai.com and yiguo.com, as well as other e-commerce platforms for agricultural products. Second, integrate rural e-commerce into the cross-border value chain so that the products can be sold abroad, generating a global market presence and providing off-season products in different parts of the world. This also provides an opportunity for differentiation, product upgrading and market transformation. Third, leverage social media, such as WeChat, Weibo, Toutiao, TikTok and Kuaishou to enable rural e-commerce. Some internet celebrities in rural areas have managed to generate traffic to their online stories. Creating channels for e-commerce platforms and underprivileged counties to work together is also important. For example, companies on e-commerce platforms can assist aspiring entrepreneurs in rural areas with product development, branding and training, through which the two can establish a long-term partnership.

III. E-commerce Has Great Potential in Poor Areas[①]

By combining leading internet technologies with the poorest areas and population, e-commerce has created a host of innovative measures to help poverty reduction and rural revitalization. Data shows that by the end of 2019, online retail sales of goods from poverty-stricken counties had reached 239.2 billion yuan, growing 33 percent on a year-on-year basis. About 5 million farmers have been employed and their income increased.

First, we should improve e-commerce infrastructure, including transportation, internet, electricity, logistics, warehousing, etc. By the end of June 2020, all townships and villages, where conditions permit, have been connected by tarmac or cement roads, 98 percent of poor villages had access to optical fiber (increasing from 70 percent in 2017), 96.6 percent townships and villages had set up express delivery service stations, and e-commerce service centers were in place in all 823 national-level poor counties. In a word, all counties, townships and villages in poor areas have been covered by e-commerce management and logistics networks.

Second, we need to develop specialty products to boost poverty reduction. Poor regions should develop their own products based on realities on the ground, like black fungus in Zhashui county of Shaanxi province, apples in Lixian county of Gansu province and honey in Ximeng county of Yunnan province. Inspection and testing of the quality and safety of agricultural products should be stepped up; standards should be formulated on origin certification, quality, tracing, refrigeration, preservation, classification, packaging and cold-chain logistics; certification for novel, special, quality and branded products should be promoted to ensure that e-commerce poverty alleviation meets standards, reaches considerable size and has its own brands.

---

① By Zhang Wenguang, president of School of Government, director of Research Center for Rural Areas at Beijing Normal University.

Third, we should improve support systems. Primary-level poverty alleviation officials should mobilize and encourage the poor to engage in e-commerce by letting them understand how to share the dividends of technological advancements. Banks and payment platforms should facilitate micro-credit and modes of payment; relevant associations and social organizations should provide poor households with standardized services in goods collection, tiered packaging, branding, marketing, logistics and after-sales service to ensure steady long-term progress.

Fourth, we should build platforms for company-to-company cooperation. The State Council Leading Group Office of Poverty Alleviation and Development has already united producers in poor areas with a large number of e-commerce platforms, including JD.com, Suning, Alibaba and Pinduoduo. During the June 18 2020 online shopping festival, the transaction value of agricultural products within the first hour was 17 times higher than the same period in the previous year at JD.com. There were more than 1.2 million sellers from poor counties on Tmall of Taobao. Xiangyun county of Yunnan province sold out overstocked potatoes during COVID-19 by using the express service of China Post.

Fifth, we should empower entrepreneurs in rural areas. Over 10 million people are estimated to have received e-commerce know-how and skills training nationwide by the end of 2020 and more than 1 million young high-caliber e-commerce professionals will be ready to work in rural areas, which means that each poor village will have at least one specialized person. We should encourage college graduates who come from rural areas to return home after graduation, and support youth, women and physically challenged people in rural areas engage in e-commerce employment or business start-ups. We have trained 1.22 million women with relevant skills and set up 636 such demonstration centers.

Last, we should build the architecture for poverty alleviation within which government, society and market join forces to create synergy. Through east-west collaboration, the market and technology advantages of the eastern regions could complement the labor, land and natural resources of the west. Through programs

like Project Hope and Guangcai Program, we can mobilize more resources from
all sectors of society to help win the battle against poverty. Through targeted
poverty alleviation, we have enhanced support to poverty-stricken areas. For
example, centrally-administered State-owned enterprises in the poverty alleviation
campaign in the first half of this year purchased 927 million yuan worth of over
1,800 kinds of agricultural products from 178 counties hard hit by COVID-19,
thus reducing the disease's impact on these areas.

Poverty alleviation through e-commerce has, on the one hand, promoted the
development of poor rural areas and boosted the income of poor residents, and on
the other, opened up new prospects for industrial and overall development in rural
areas.

E-commerce has helped overcome remote locations, poor transportation conditions
and other hurdles and given agricultural products in remote areas access to city
market. This has brought about tangible results in industrial development and
income increase in poor areas. In particular, e-commerce has solved many urgent
problems and helped sell overstocked agricultural products during COVID-19,
and sales of such products registered a new record high during this year's June
18 online shopping festival. The digital economy in rural areas, represented by
e-commerce poverty alleviation, has become a new driving force in resolving
issues related to agriculture, rural areas and farmers and in achieving the target of
poverty eradication.

At the same time, it has boosted industrial development in rural areas. By
integrating production, supply, sales and purchases, e-commerce has mobilized all
forces in society to join the battle against poverty. On the one hand, e-commerce
gives products from poor areas direct access to domestic and international
supply and industrial chains; on the other hand, it changes the traditional way
of production and sales, empowers leading companies, cooperatives and self-
employed entrepreneurs and incorporates them into a more stable coalition, thus
laying a solid foundation for long-term industrial prosperity in rural areas.

What's more, e-commerce is injecting new impetus into rural development.
Targeted poverty alleviation underlines the importance of educational

improvement and technological advancement. E-commerce energizes indigenous strength in poor households by training millions of farmers and attracting large numbers of migrant workers home. Digital technology is the new agricultural material, cellphone the new farming tool and live streaming the new farm work.

The world today is undergoing great changes rarely seen in a century. Chinese people should ride with the tide of the times, nurture opportunities in crises and open up new space in a changing landscape. Poverty alleviation through e-commerce is an innovative step that China takes to contribute wisdom and experience to the world's poverty reduction cause.

First, China has a strong leadership core. The Communist Party of China is the fundamental guarantee for the success of poverty eradication. Only with the leadership of the CPC was it possible for a large country with a population of 1.4 billion to lift 800 million people out of poverty in four decades. This is unprecedented in the human history and is a huge contribution to the world's poverty reduction efforts. The CPC, with its clear political strength, has rallied Chinese people of all ethnic groups, coordinated human and material resources in an effective manner, mobilized all possible strengths, explored new ways of surmounting difficulties and made exceptional achievements in a relatively short period of time.

Second, we should stay committed to the policy of e-commerce poverty alleviation. The actions we take need to be accurate and targeted. Authorities at various levels should adopt specific measures based on ground realities and focus on quality rather than pursuing merely quantity. Responsibilities need to be set clearly. The role of evaluation and assessment should be stressed and people in charge should take primary responsibility. Capital and project management systems and rules should be strictly followed to increase the efficiency of capital distribution and utilization. Results should also be accurate and precise. Relevant authorities should make use of the rural monitoring and managing system of the Ministry of Commerce to promote information and data sharing, generate unified statistics in various aspects and explore a mode of piloting, promotion and popularization.

Last, we should give full play to the strength of socialism with Chinese characteristics and pool all possible resources to deal with major issues. We should continue with efforts to improve infrastructure and public service in regions with deep-seated poverty, which will lay a solid foundation for poverty alleviation. All forces of society should be mobilized to join the endeavor. With east-west complementarity and multi-level collaboration, we should further integrate poverty reduction with educational improvement and coordinate development with the protection of basic needs. We should take a holistic perspective in improving top-level design, incorporate poverty alleviation into a comprehensive strategy, and blaze a new trail of poverty alleviation with Chinese characteristics.

IV. Taobao Villages Should Be an Inspiration for Africa[1]

Walk around any town or village in Kenya, and you'll see small shacks as well as beautifully kitted out shops with the name "Mpesa". Mpesa is Kenya's equivalent of China's WeChat Pay or Alipay or Wave Money and ApplePay in other countries. Created in 2007—a few years before mobile payment took off in China, Mpesa operates primarily on smart messaging service (SMS) as well as online, and has been credited with enabling an estimated 186,000 families, or as many as 2 percent of Kenyan households, to move out of poverty. There is also a huge gender impact. In households with access to mobile money, women are more likely to move out of agriculture into businesses, resulting in poverty reduction in female-headed households twice the country average.

China has its own online equivalent of Mpesa in respect of alleviating poverty— "Taobao villages". A joint 2019 World Bank and AliResearch report credited these villages with helping thousands of China's rural residents lift themselves out of poverty since 2015. Women seem to benefit the most. According to the Alibaba

---

[1] By Leah Lynch, deputy director at Development Reimagined.

Research Foundation, the ratio of women to men entrepreneurs in e-commerce is almost equal, compared to a ratio of 1:3 in traditional businesses. But what are these villages and how could this experience be relevant to Kenya, and more broadly the African continent?

The "Taobao Village", defined as "a village that generates 10 million yuan or more in e-commerce sales annually and has 100 or more active online shops on Taobao operated by local residents", is the brainchild of the e-commerce giant Alibaba, and aims to reduce poverty by creating online shops for rural residents. Two years after the launch of the villages, China's State Council Leading Group Office of Poverty Alleviation and Development and a host of top government bodies jointly released guidelines that called for construction of 60,000 "e-commerce poverty relief stations", as well as a quadrupling of e-commerce sales for villages in impoverished rural counties by 2020.

Alibaba's program effectively acted as a pilot for others to emulate and scale up as mandated by government. As part of the China's targeted poverty alleviation campaign, local governments sponsored e-commerce and clothing-production training classes, provided low-cost loans, and encouraged successful entrepreneurs to prioritize hiring locals who remained below the poverty threshold. Young entrepreneurs also played a pivotal role in growing e-commerce in rural China. Recent government-backed policies encouraged over 130,000 new graduates to return to their hometowns or villages (what would be known in Kenya as "shags") and—amongst other projects—set up online shops and services to help their friends and families.

E-commerce or digital trade has been a powerful leapfrogging tool to boost trade, create employment, raise incomes and reduce poverty in China. And it could be so in Africa as well. Yet, despite some African countries leading in mobile payments, Africa still lags behind in terms of e-commerce sales. Unlike in China, where the e-commerce market is dominated by two big tech giants, in Africa the sector has multiple players with many start-ups (around 264 operational across at least 23 countries). Jumia, Africa's biggest and best funded e-commerce platform is still yet to turn a profit and sales are still very unevenly distributed with Kenya, South

Africa, and Nigeria accounting for over half of consumers in Africa in 2017.

Yet, there is still potential in e-commerce.

Africa has the fastest growing youth population in the world, who all need jobs, and fast. According to the African Development Bank, of the continent's nearly 420 million youth aged 15-35, one-third are unemployed. And there is already familiarity with mobile phones—the most popular tool for online shopping. The World Bank report said there are 650 million mobile users in Africa, surpassing the number in the United States or Europe. In some African countries, more people have access to a mobile phone than to clean water, a bank account or electricity. Africa also has a growing middle class, 330 million people, concentrated in Egypt, Nigeria, South Africa, Algeria and Morocco who want to spend, spend, spend. Finally, there is the increasing number of Made in Africa brands and goods being produced across the continent, in the larger markets as well as emerging markets such as Rwanda, Senegal and Ethiopia. From fashion to skincare, African products are becoming well respected and desirable.

This all points to a huge opportunity for growth in the African digital trade sector and with the COVID-19 pandemic providing a key opportunity for inclusive e-commerce and related digital solutions, tools and services to thrive, there is a real opportunity.

But having lived and worked in both China and Africa, I know it isn't so easy to replicate China's model across Africa.

Here is the first challenge. Africa, made up of over 50 countries, is unique. There is a diverse range of policies, market sizes, consumer profiles, languages, and other contextual differences making economies of scale difficult to achieve in terms of coordination and logistics.

The fact is all too often the focus in Africa is on building technology and platforms. That's the easy part. The key is building the physical infrastructure around it—roads, rail, airports, internet portals and more. It's why in Africa, companies often find it very hard to compete with cheap goods from overseas where infrastructure is considerably stronger.

But with better logistics, it's possible to imagine an incredibly vibrant and differentiated ecosystem of sellers across Africa. If funding and loans are channeled into training the vast number of small and midium-size enterprises in cities and towns on how to utilize e-commerce and market their products— the results could be very similar to Taobao Villages. African villages could build their own e-commerce hubs. Africa has a huge, increasingly educated young population, and government-backed schemes encouraging young entrepreneurs to build e-commerce hubs in the rural areas could harness this talent.

The second challenge is that fundamental "ways of working" are holding e-commerce back from flourishing across the continent.

For example, in China, 54 percent of the population use mobile money for e-commerce purchases. Yet, due to lack of trust in products and delivery, 90 percent of customers across African countries use cash on delivery – not mobile payments. In rural locations this is particularly complex and costly for companies if a delivery driver makes the trip only for the customers not to pay. There also remains the persistent challenge of lack of systematic addresses and postal systems. This makes it very time consuming (and costly) for delivery drivers to locate costumers, particularly in rural areas.

Part of the challenge in Africa is that while customers are familiar with mobile money such as Mpesa, these systems have been developed to support inclusion as opposed to building trust and convenience like in China. Only 10-15 percent of the population has access to a bank account. Most African online retail stores and services therefore effectively limit their customer base by requiring that their customers have a bank account or a payment service that is linked to one.

With these two challenges—logistics and ways of working – do my colleagues and I think it's nevertheless possible for e-commerce to have a role in African poverty reduction, as it has in China?

The answer is an emphatic yes, especially with a focus on addressing these two challenges. I also think China (and others) can be helpful partners in doing so in two specific ways.

First, enable, don't compete against local e-commerce companies. Alibaba has been expressing interest in the African market by encouraging local entrepreneurs, and selling some initial African products on its platform in China, such as Rwandan coffee beans. During the COVID-19 pandemic Alibaba developed a new partnership with Ethiopian Airlines for cross-border logistics for the donation of medical equipment. These relationships could enable Alibaba to grow quickly on the continent. But this could also decimate home-grown e-commerce companies. Partners such as Alibaba, Amazon and others should therefore invest in existing African e-commerce platforms and empower them to expand their reach as opposed to capturing the market themselves.

Second, listen to the needs of African governments and private sector organizations. China's success was spurred by investments in e-commerce companies, allowing the private sector to grow and expand. Although equity funding in African tech start-ups has increased rapidly—reaching $1.16 billion in 2018, overall foreign direct investment flows into Africa are limited, just 3.5 percent of the global total. In the wake of COVID19, the growth of digital trade in Africa offers a unique opportunity for investment—based on a growing middle-class consumer market. The actions African governments have taken to stem COVID19's spread across the continent have demonstrated their willingness to act fast to save their populations. With this knowledge, it's time to invest in Africa, not pull out. And e-commerce is a perfect opportunity, as it can also—as Taobao villages did—create jobs and reduce poverty.

I hope that soon, walking around Kenya's cities and villages, we will see the emergence of a new set of signs beyond Mpesa.

Joint Effort

**Mutual Relations between China's Poverty
Alleviation and Global Development**

扫码获取

★ 脱贫故事分享
★ 脱贫攻坚解读
　与回顾

01

China Injects Sustainable Power to Global Poverty Alleviation

I. Ensure Fundamental Human Rights First[①]

Many of the people who write about human rights are Western writers who were born and grew up in affluent societies. So they have no understanding of the more fundamental needs of poor people. Instead, for example, they emphasize the importance of the right to vote. So what is the importance of the right to vote if we do not have enough to eat?

So this is why all people who promote human rights should emphasize that before we enjoy all human rights, we must first have the ability to exercise five fundamental human rights. One, the right to live in safety. Two, the right to have enough to eat. Three, the right to have basic medical care. Four, the right to receive education. And five, the right to attain a job with income to feed the family. But if you don't enjoy these five rights, we cannot enjoy all other human rights.

And these five rights are fundamental. This is why the recent story of China is very important for the rest of the world to understand. In the past 40 years, China has delivered these five basic rights to its people faster and more comprehensively than any other country has done in human history.

And the reason why this accomplishment is even more remarkable is that the

---

① By Kishore Mahbubani, professor at the National University of Singapore, former Singaporean ambassador to the United Nations.

Chinese people suffered a great deal in the century of humiliation from the Opium War in 1840 to the founding of the People's Republic of China in 1949. At that time, the majority of the Chinese people were threatened by foreign invasions, civil war, famine and starvation, lack of medical care, lack of access to modern education, and massive unemployment. It's important to understand the very difficult conditions the Chinese endured before recent development to understand how far they have come.

And it is also true, therefore, that in the longest part of Chinese history, for thousands of years, the living conditions of Chinese people in the rural areas did not improve. The vast majority of Chinese peasants lived very hard lives, struggling to stay afloat. They had barely enough to eat, nor access to education or healthcare. Their life expectancy was also very low. So there are some statistics that reflect how remarkable China's development has been. As recently as in 1980, the percentage of the Chinese people in the rural areas experienced poverty was close to 100 percent. By 2016, 36 years later, rural poverty rate had been reduced to 4.5%, declining by 95.5 percent.

And if you look at the overall picture, the figures are equally striking. In 1980, over 90 percent of the total population, 981 million were living below $3.20 a day. By 2016, the number had fallen to 5.4 percent. That's a remarkable reduction.

This Chinese story of unprecedented human development is important for the world to understand for one important reason: even in 2020, there are still hundreds of millions living below the poverty line in Asia, Africa and Latin America. The respective numbers are 53.9 percent for South Asia, 12.5 percent for East Asia, 68.1 percent for Sub-Saharan Africa and 10.4 percent for Latin America.

This makes up a total of 2 billion people, or 26.4 percent of the world's population, who live in extreme poverty. So the most important thing we need to do for them is to rescue them from poverty.

Until recently, many economists thought that eliminating poverty was impossible. But the story of China tells us that in poverty reduction, a mission impossible can become a mission possible.

This is why we need to spread the story about China to every corner of the world. But the big question remains: why did China succeed? The answer is that China implemented correct policies, both domestically and internationally, to achieve these poverty reduction goals.

On the domestic front, when I was dean of the Lee Kuan Yew School of Public Policy at the National University of Singapore, I taught students at the school that for countries to succeed, they should follow the magical MPH formula.

Now, MPH does not stand for miles per hour. It stands for "Meritocracy, Pragmatism and Honesty". And the one thing that China has been able to do is to improve the quality of governance by implementing meritocracy.

M stands for Meritocracy. Meritocracy means that the Chinese government was able to select the best people to work and serve in many agencies of government. And when you have good governance, you can have the right policies to improve people's lives.

P stands for pragmatism. And the best definition of pragmatism actually come from the late Chinese leader, Deng Xiaoping, who said "it doesn't matter if the cat is black or white; if it catches mice, it is a good cat". China has this unique ability to select the best policies from the world, learn from the best practices and implement them in a pragmatic fashion. So pragmatism is another thing we need to learn from China if we want to solve many of the problems in the world.

H stands for honesty. At the end of the day, as history teaches us, the countries that succeed are the ones that are able to fight corruption and ensure that the resources of the country are used to help the people rather than be put in private pockets.

On the international front, China has implementing the right policies by integrating itself into the liberal rules-based international order. If the whole world can replicate China's experience in poverty reduction, we would then have achieved the greatest improvement in the human condition since human history began.

II. Targeted Measures a Pointer for Others[1]

Poverty eradication is the core goal of the United Nations 2030 Sustainable Development Goals (SDGs) and the biggest development challenge as well. In 2019, the Nobel Prize in economics was awarded to three development economists for their theoretical contributions in reducing global poverty through field experiments. China has created the largest poverty alleviation miracle in human history. During 1981-2015, there has been a reduction of 874 million people in absolute poverty in China ($1.90 per person per day), accounting for 74.5 percent of the world's absolute poverty reduction (1,173 million people) in the same period. China has made a great contribution to world poverty reduction. China's poverty eradication strategies, especially the practices and theories of the Targeted Poverty Alleviation, have critical implications for the world.

In 2020, China will put an end to thousands of years of absolute poverty, build a moderately prosperous society in all respects, and take the lead in achieving the poverty alleviation goal in the SDGs 10 years in advance.

The path of poverty alleviation in China has contributed Chinese wisdom to global poverty governance. In 2013, President Xi Jinping put forward the theory of Targeted Poverty Alleviation for the first time, which became the fundamental strategy for tackling poverty. Targeted Poverty Alleviation mainly includes "six targets": targeted objects, targeted projects, targeted use of funds, targeted measures for each household, targeted village-based poverty relief cadres, as well as targeted poverty alleviation results. At the same time, Targeted Poverty Alleviation requires the implementation of "five groups of poverty alleviation": poverty alleviation groups through production development, relocation, ecological compensation, education and social security. Targeted Poverty Alleviation is an effective strategy for China to reduce the remaining poorest population, and also a major innovation in the theory and practice of poverty alleviation.

---

[1] By Hu Angang, dean of the Institute for Contemporary China Studies, professor of the School of Public Policy and Management at Tsinghua University.

China's Targeted Poverty Alleviation still faces key challenges. First, the causes of poverty are complicated and it is difficult to get rid of it. Second, there are problems such as "waiting for help" and fear of difficulty of the poor in the process of poverty alleviation. Subjective factors might impede the progress of poverty alleviation. Third, even if elimination of absolute poverty is completely achieved, there will still be relative poverty and return to poverty. The ability of the poor to be "self-hematopoietic" needs to be cultivated. To eliminate absolute poverty is the "last bastion" of poverty alleviation, which is directly related to the quality and effectiveness of poverty alleviation. In the face of various subjective and objective causes of poverty, China must further implement the Targeted Poverty Alleviation strategies.

China should continue Targeted Poverty Alleviation and further refine the measures. Successful poverty alleviation requires "favorable time, favorable place and harmonious people", in which the most important aspect is the power of people. There are a few points that should not be neglected:

First, it is better to teach one how to fish than to give the fish. Poverty alleviation cannot always rely on "giving money". It is necessary to change outmoded production methods and business operations, and promote new technologies, new projects and new ideas.

Second, poverty alleviation should ensure the bottom line for the poor. There should be a more comprehensive insurance mechanism to enhance the fault tolerance rate of the poor, reduce their risk aversion, and let them dare to try.

Third, a "hand-in-hand" approach in needed to help the poor. There are all kinds of unforeseen problems in the process of poverty alleviation. It is critical to provide sufficient guidance and timely solutions to ensure successful poverty alleviation.

Fourth, "poverty alleviation through aspiration". Poverty alleviation requires aspirations and confidence. There should be a deeper understanding of the difficulties and emotions of the poor from their own perspectives.

Fifth, it is essential to introduce scientific measures, such as a commitment mechanism, supervision and reminder system to help the poor. These measures have been proved effective in helping them pursue long-term interests, resist immediate temptation, increase the participation rate and reduce the withdrawal of poverty alleviation projects.

As a large country with a population of 1.4 billion, China is the most important experimental field for global poverty reduction. Starting as a poverty-stricken country, China has become the world's largest economy (by purchasing power parity) and is about to build a moderately prosperous society in all respects. The success of Chinese poverty alleviation provides example, experience and strategies for global poverty governance.

02

International Cooperation and Exchanges on Poverty Alleviation

I. Belt and Road Initiative Drives Africa to Shake off Poverty[1]

Shaking off poverty is the primary goal of the Sustainable Development Agenda of the United Nations. Today there are around 700 million people suffering from extreme poverty in the world, of whom more than half live in sub-Saharan Africa. Sixteen of the 20 poorest countries in the world are in Africa. Western countries have long provided assistance and debt relief to African countries, but the number of extremely poor people in sub-Saharan Africa rose from 290 million in 1990 to 414 million in 2010. According to *Dead Aid: Why Aid Is Not Working and How There is Another Way for Africa*, assistance and debt relief show the "benevolence" of Western countries while failing to improve the ability of African countries to address poverty.

Similar to Africa, China once had a large number of poor people, mostly in rural areas, where construction of infrastructure including dams, irrigation and roads has greatly boosted incomes. China built about 42,000 kilometers of rural roads every year on average from 1994 to 2000, promoting the free flow of local agricultural products and surplus labor. Economic development zones attracted many labor-intensive industries, created a large number of employment opportunities and brought the demographic dividend into full play. Since the reform and opening-

---

[1] By Shen Chen, assistant research fellow of the Institute of World Economics and Politics at the Chinese Academy of Social Sciences.

up, China has lifted more than 800 million people out of poverty. According to the World Bank benchmarks, its poverty rate fell from 90 percent in 1981 to 1.7 percent in 2018, contributing to more than 70 percent of global poverty reduction.

China's experience in poverty alleviation has attracted wide attention from the international community, including African countries. In 2016, the Afrobarometer released a survey on how Africans view China's influence, which showed that its model for national development was acknowledged by 24 percent of respondents. About two-third of Africans viewed China's influence as "somewhat positive" or "very positive". Against such a backdrop, the Belt and Road Initiative proposed by Chinese President Xi Jinping has seen proactive support in and participation by African countries. As of June 2020, a total of 43 African countries had signed cooperation agreements on the initiative.

The COVID-19 epidemic has led to big increases in prevention and control costs and health expenditure of African countries. The countries are also trying to revive economic growth and ensuring employment to prevent local people from returning to poverty or becoming poorer. In light of this, Xi proposed at the Extraordinary China-Africa Summit on Solidarity against COVID-19 that China and Africa should "strengthen Belt and Road cooperation and accelerate the follow-up to the Forum on China-Africa Cooperation Beijing Summit. Greater priority needs to be given to cooperation on public health, economic reopening and people's livelihood". The initiative can drive China-Africa cooperation on economic and trade financing, industrial transfer and technological exchanges and promote transformation and upgrading of cooperation.

Weak infrastructure is the largest hurdle to Africa's development. Power shortages are problem in Africa, and a multinational which once donated thousands of laptop computers to African countries found that they could not be charged. With industrial enterprises depending on stable electricity supply, power shortages cause severe damage to industrialization in Africa. Meanwhile, African countries with weak railway transport depend largely on road transport, which makes intercity transport quite expensive. The lack of intercity transportation capacity has greatly restricted the production of local enterprises, with production volumes failing to reach the expected level. The fee collection modes of electronic communication devices in Africa also remain to be improved.

Improving African infrastructure has been the focus of China-Africa cooperation. In the 1960s and 1970s, China spent $450 million on building the 1,860-km Tanzania-Zambia railway. After that initiative, China paid great attention to the construction of railways, highways, aviation, ports, power and telecommunication in Africa and promoted inter-connectivity of different African regions. According to the US-based Brookings Institution, China's average annual investment in infrastructure in Africa totaled about $10 billion, accounting for one-third of the total foreign funds. In October 2016, the railway from Addis Ababa, the capital of Ethiopia, to Djibouti opened to traffic. The railway connecting Nairobi, the capital of Kenya, and Mombasa, the largest port in East Africa, opened in May 2017. The railways are "flagship projects" under the initiative in Africa, which have allowed countries to see more sophisticated infrastructure including railways, roads and ports, creating a large number of jobs and driving investment in industrial zones, tourism and real estate along the railways.

For a long time, Western media outlets have viewed China-Africa economic cooperation to be an exchange of infrastructure for natural resources through policy banks. From their perspective, China's policy banks sign guarantee agreements with African countries and the latter use local natural resources to gain lower-interest loans and use the loans to build infrastructure, while China met its demand for resources and energy through the cooperation mode. Today, the financing options for China-Africa economic cooperation have greatly increased and the role of policy banks has weakened. Chinese State-owned and private enterprises have become major investors in Africa, in which the latter have turned into key driving forces for economic cooperation.

In 2017, McKinsey released a research report entitled The Next Factory of the World: How Chinese Investment Is Reshaping Africa, which detailed previously-ignored private investment from China. According to the research team, more than 10,000 Chinese companies operated in Africa in 2017, mainly in Nigeria, Zambia, Tanzania and Ethiopia. About one-third of the private enterprises were in the manufacturing industry and mostly small and micro enterprises. According to research findings of the Heritage Foundation, China's investment in Africa has become diversified. In addition to conventional projects including mineral resources and infrastructure, Chinese investment has also gone into industries including real estate, banking, finance, insurance, logistics and retail. Since the implementation of the initiative, China's contribution to Africa's GDP growth has exceeded 5 percent every year. In addition, many Chinese merchants and technicians who know Africa well have settled there and become key forces for driving sustainable development of the economy and trade as well as technology transfer in many fields.

As a people-centered philosophy, inclusive development entails balanced development between humans, humans and nature, as well as humans and society, and needs to be evaluated by multiple criteria including human development, green development, social welfare and happiness indexes. As President Xi said, "the world needs to lead economic globalization and ensure justice and equity to make economic globalization more dynamic, inclusive and sustainable and enable people around the world to feel happier and more engaged and satisfied". At the Belt and Road Forum for International Cooperation held in May 2017, Xi further announced that China would provide 2 billion yuan ($292 million) of emergency food aid to developing countries involved in the initiative, increase funding to the South-South Cooperation Assistance Fund by $1 billion, and launch 100 "happy home" projects, 100 poverty alleviation projects and 100 healthcare and rehabilitation projects in countries involved in the initiative. While developed countries have reduced or suspended assistance to African countries, China and other developing countries support each other in solidarity, which helps address the urgent needs of developing regions such as Africa.

Inclusive development focuses on reducing poverty and promoting social equity. In addition to humanitarian assistance for meeting basic living needs of the poor, inclusive development is mostly achieved through trade, finance and technical training. Since 2015, China has provided Africa with 30,000 government scholarships and trained 200,000 technicians to help improve the quality of the local workforce. In 2019, the World Bank released the report Belt and Road

Economics: Opportunities and Risks of Transport Corridors, proposing that the full implementation of the initiative can help 32 million people shake off moderate poverty and increase the trade volume of the global market and countries involved in the initiative by 6.2 percent and 9.7 percent respectively. The growth of foreign direct investment in developing countries involved in the initiative will reach 7.6 percent. Promoting inclusive trade, finance and education through improving the capacity of African countries for self-reliance, which can help enhance production capacity and promote industrialization and exports while avoiding long-term reliance on foreign assistance.

As Tony Blair, the then British prime minister, said when setting up the Commission for Africa in 2004, "Africa has always appeared to be a desolate land. I have said on many occasions that I believe Africa is a scar on the conscience of the world." However, it has 40 percent of the world's natural resource reserves, 60 percent of uncultivated land and a billion-strong growing labor force. There is no reason for Africa to remain poor, for Africans can create wealth through their own efforts. As the initiative and the Extraordinary China-Africa Summit on Solidarity against COVID-19 suggest, Africa needs not sympathy and assistance but global solidarity and cooperation.

II. Indonesia Is Riding the Belt and Road Wave[1]

China and Indonesia are complementary partners in the Belt and Road Initiative (BRI) and the former is willing to integrate the BRI with the Global Maritime Fulcrum, which will promote the development of Indonesia's Regional Comprehensive Economic Corridor.

At the Belt and Road Forum in April 2019, Indonesia and China signed 23 memorandums of understanding on investment and trade cooperation worth a total

[1] By Paulus Rudolf Yuniarto, senior researcher at the Research Center for Area Studies of Indonesian Institute of Sciences, visiting scholar at Fudan University Research Institute.

of $64 billion. For Indonesia, the funding will focus on developing projects in four economic corridors: North Sumatra is a logistic hub in the Malacca Strait area, North Kalimantan is well-known for its world-class hydropower resources, and North Sulawesi and Bali for Chinese tourists.

Indonesia and China are reported to have drafted a framework agreement for cooperation in Kuala Tanjung, North Sumatra, as the first project. Indonesia's State-owned port operation Pelindo I signed a head of agreement for the development of Kuala Tanjung Port with representatives from the Port of Rotterdam Authority in the Netherlands and the Zhejiang Provincial Seaport Investment & Operation Group Co Ltd in China on Nov 14, 2019.

In addition to the four, there are also other cooperation projects, such as the Jakarta-Bandung high-speed railway, mid-size power plants in several locations in Java, a mine mouth in Central Kalimantan, a special economic zone in Jonggol-West Java, an integrated industrial zone in Ketapang, replanting oil palms in Sumatra, and the Meikarta Integrated Industrial Area in Bekasi-West Java.

China has facilitated large-scale infrastructure construction, and energy and transport projects, as well as the relocation of manufacturing industries. Indonesia expects to gain benefits, such as technology transfer and training, and also to capitalize on demographic advantages, such as labor force and tourism, for economic growth through this cooperation platform.

However, there have been public doubts of the long-term benefit of China-Indonesia cooperation under the BRI, besides the so-called debt trap issue, and how this collaboration can improve people's welfare in terms of the poverty alleviation.

According to the Indonesian Central Statistics Agency's 2019 survey, 9.82 percent, or close to 26 million, of Indonesians are considered poor. The number is actually higher because the government's poverty line is low, and it assumed that poverty statistics is not in sync with reality. In addition, the COVID-19 outbreak has had a severe impact on Indonesia's economy through fewer exports, delays in foreign direct investment and lower tourism revenue. The economic shock means more people are vulnerable to falling into poverty. GDP growth is estimated to deteriorate to 2.1 percent in the baseline scenario and 3.5 percent in the lower-case scenario in 2020. The baseline refers to a scenario of economic growth decline with a speedy recovery, and the lower case scenario is defined as deeper contraction followed by a slow recovery.

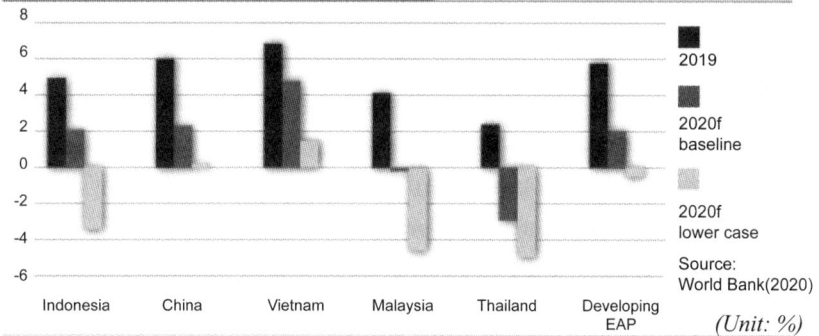

Economic Growth Forecast

| 2019 |
| 2020f baseline |
| 2020f lower case |

Source: World Bank(2020)

(Unit: %)

The Indonesian government, through its "National Medium-Term Development Plan 2020", has made the eradication of poverty a top priority. The government has liberally been distributing cash and non-cash benefits like village funds for local development and issuing health benefit cards and food discounts to eradicate poverty in remote and urban areas. But poverty remains a challenge. Poverty alleviation spans a broad range of areas, such as poverty trends, social assistance, social insurance, community-based programs and generating more and better jobs. More than that, this effort needs to be in tandem with the international community to support poverty alleviation programs. In this regard, the BRI could support the poverty alleviation program in Indonesia and Indonesia can benefit from the BRI cooperation.

For underdeveloped countries, investment in infrastructure and poverty alleviation are two of the most pressing public policy issues and they are linked in multiple ways. The BRI concept links infrastructure investment with sustainable creation of jobs. The proposal has been extended to cover non-infrastructure investments as well, including the digital economy, cultural ties and people-to-people exchanges. The BRI is also designed to address the massive and urgent need to create trade, jobs, tourism, migration, and education across the region. Consequently, the initiative will try to achieve exchanges of people, ideas, capital and networks, and socio-cultural exchanges on a global scale. Practically, this initiative has significant potential in terms of economic benefits including participation in the establishment of infrastructure links that connect the flow of goods and human resources between China and the BRI partner countries.

With the Asian Infrastructure Investment Bank as the main financial institution—there are other banks involved too—China is building sophisticated transportation systems, dams, ports, communication systems, proper sanitation and clean water facilitices, roads, bridges, airports and hydroelectric plants that are now the foundation of the BRI investment model. Many of these projects will have a strong impact on local communities, creating new opportunities locally, regionally and possibly even globally. It is all these aspects and the uniqueness of the BRI that should be utilized adequately by policymakers and stakeholders for local and national economic development.

For Indonesia, investment in infrastructure is needed, and at the same time, China offers what Indonesia needs. Infrastructure development is crucial for the Indonesian economy in three ways. First, development in transportation and logistics infrastructure, energy infrastructure, water management infrastructure (for irrigation and public consumption), as well as information and communication technology infrastructure, will contribute to the growth of its competitiveness. Second, infrastructure development is needed to address the current supply crisis in Indonesia. Third, infrastructure problems in many sectors act as obstacles in attracting FDI and boosting industrial growth.

Moreover, the benefits Indonesia gets from the BRI include Chinese technology transfer (skills and training) and infrastructure investment. The archipelago can also capitalize on demographic advantages. BRI projects will contribute to reducing poverty to below 9 percent in three provinces (except Bali) where the BRI projects are in place, according to Coordinating Minister for Maritime Affairs Luhut Pandjaitan. Potential problem such as debt traps must be avoided. In BRI cooperation, Indonesia should not use the government-to-government route, but business-to-business, to alleviate debt risks in the state budget.

China has lifted over 800 million people out of poverty by 2017, according to a World Bank study. China is the first developing country to reach the poverty reduction target of the Millennium Development Goals. Results of anti-poverty policies between 1978 and 2006, when the poverty standards were raised constantly (from 100 yuan/person in 1978 to 693 yuan/person in 2005), show that the rural population in poverty decreased from 250 million to 21.5 million, with proportion of people in poverty declined from 30.7 percent to 1.6 percent. This also testifies to China accomplishing the poverty reduction task within the context of MDGs. China has contributed to 70 percent of global poverty reduction by offering help to more than 120 countries for the achievement of the MDGs. It is "a great achievement of China" in the history of mankind.

(Unit: %)

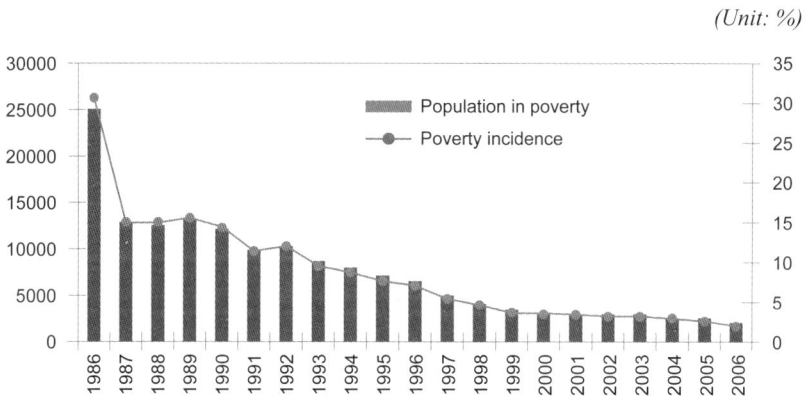

Source: Development Research Center of the State Council, 2006.

Based on this success story, the BRI partner countries, including Indonesia, can learn from China. China's experience in poverty alleviation is worth emulating in other countries. Besides infrastructure, we have the opportunity to learn how the Chinese government developed its poverty alleviation strategy. According to China's State Council Leading Group Office of Poverty Alleviation and Development, there are four factors behind China's success story: reform and opening-up or institutional innovation; economic growth and infrastructure development; integrated urban-rural development; and development-oriented poverty reduction and self-reliance. These programs contain key lessons for countries considering poverty reduction strategies.

The Chinese government has a strategy that suit its national situation. Poverty alleviation means not only offering support such as money, food or medicine, but also building appropriate infrastructure to improve people's quality of life and earning capacity. In addition to the State Council Leading Group Office of Poverty Alleviation and Development, provinces, municipalities and autonomous regions, prefectural (city) and county governments have also set up corresponding organs in their regions.

The implementation of these strategies and policies has significant impacts: accelerating the development of underdeveloped areas, changing the trajectory of the center of economic gravity, and reducing China's poor population significantly.

The BRI is a harbinger of a new round of opportunities for underdeveloped countries, particularly in terms of infrastructure development—building roads, railways, bridges and ports across the region. The initiative has not only opened the floodgates of infrastructure investments, both state-owned and private, but also facilitated the movement of labor and tourism, and cooperation in education and poverty alleviation. Therefore, the BRI should generate more collaborative relations among peoples, human mobility, and social-cultural basins, where it is not only economic flows, but also the human interaction that shapes deep connectivity and shared prosperity between China and other countries.

III. Sino-Africa Poverty Alleviation Cooperation and Experience Sharing[①]

Africa—a continent of over 50 nations—has had very poor poverty alleviation

---

① By Ehizuelen Michael Mitchell Omoruyi, researcher of the Institute of African Studies at Zhejiang Normal University, China.

experiences in recent decades, unlike China. Although China shares a lot of similarities with numerous African nations, China had been in a worse condition for a long time, and even worser in some areas. China's fight against poverty was as daunting as the one faced by Malawi.

But since the reform and opening-up, China has experienced an average annual GDP growth of about 10 percent until 2014, raising per capita GDP almost 49-fold. China's share in the global economy rose from 2.7 percent to 16 percent; the nation's per capita GDP rose from $155 in 1978 to over $10, 000 in 2019. In 1981, China's poverty rate was 88.3 percent based on the headcount ratio at $1.90 a day; in 2010, this poverty rate was 11.2 percent (Liu, 2020)[1]. The World Bank estimates that the number of extremely poor people globally—those who live on $1.90 a day or less—has fallen from 1.85 billion in 1990 to around 736 willion in 2015. During the same period, China has helped 602.7 million people escape poverty, accounting for 54 percent globally. This is a quarter of a million people per day, or 200 persons per minute (World Bank, 2017)[2].

China has contributed more than any other nation to global poverty reduction. In the past four decades, China has pulled over 700 million people out of poverty, even larger than the population of Europe, which was 741 million in 2016. In addition, in 2018, the average annual income of rural residents in impoverished areas rose to 10, 371 yuan ($1,530) with an inflation-adjusted year-on-year growth of 8.3 percent. What the world achieved in the space of 200 years—the reversal from over fewer that one in five people living above $1.25 to fewer that one in five living below that threshold—China managed in little more than 20 years (Chandy, 2015)[3]. This remarkable accomplishment was due in large part to speedy economic growth over this period. China's development experience shows the

---

[1] Liu, X.(2020). A Critique of Precision Precision Poverty Alleviation: Does China Approach Adequate Policy Tools? Journal of Business and Adminstration Studies Vol. 14, No.1.

[2] World Bank. (2017). "From Local to Global: China's Role in Global Poverty Reduction and the Future of Development." The World Bank, Washington, DC.

[3] Chandy, L., Kato, H., and Kharas, H. (Eds) (2015). The Last Mile in Ending Extreme Poverty. Brookings Institution Press.

significance of making sure that growth is broad-based across sectors and regions and inclusive of poor people.

In terms of requirements and relevance for other developing economies, especially African nations where several nations still rely on development assistance, the key aspects of China's development successes include how China cooperated with the international donors, how it developed its agricultural sector and rural regions, how it expanded its infrastructure and how it created an attracted environment for businesses to flourish and create employment. With that said, China's accomplishment in alleviating poverty may also partially be attributed to the geographically targeted poverty reduction program first introduced in 1986, when 331 counties were identified as the key targets in the national development-oriented poverty-reduction program (Zhang et al, 2003)[1]. In 2001, with the decrease of the rural poor, it was judged that the county was no longer the suitable targeting unit; thereafter, the village took the place of the county as the basic unit of targeting, making the targeting more precise.

After President Xi Jinping initiated the targeted poverty alleviation in 2013, China had attained brilliant accomplishments. However, the Chinese leadership was fully aware that the fight remains tough; as such, as of the end of 2015, there were still over 60 million rural inhabitants living under the poverty line: 129,000 poverty-stricken villages, 14 contiguous extremely poor areas and 832 poverty-stricken counties. As an ambitious leader, President Xi decided to go one step further to eradicate the absolute poverty in China completely in all respects by 2020 by enforcing a radical form of a targeted poverty reduction program, in which the individual household is the targeted unit.

The Chinese government set a new ambitious target to lift no less than 10 million people out of poverty yearly from 2016 and intended to lift a total of 43.35 million rural residents out of poverty by 2020. Since the central government and local

---

[1] Zhang, L., Huang, J., and Rozelle, S. (2003). China's War on Poverty: Assessing Trageting and the Growth Impacts of Poverty Programs. Journal of Chinese Economic and Business Studies,1(3), 301-317.

governments are faced with a large urban-rural gap and regional disparities, the completion of the 2020 poverty alleviation goal is not the end of the poverty fight, but it indicates that the nation's poverty alleviation work will enter a novel stage characterized by transformational secondary poverty and relative poverty.

The main achievement of the five generations of Chinese leadership in alleviating poverty is rooted in a solid targeted, all-round and coordinated poverty reduction strategy coupled with the nation's leadership capacity, potential determination, self-reliance and public engagement with Chinese characteristics. It was the particular ability of the government to increasingly recognize constructive aspects of the numerous theories and ideologies that have been tried elsewhere. The Chinese government was able to espouse these theories and ideologies in their policy plans, and these can be sustained at the national level down to counties and provinces, with economic, ecological, and socioeconomic diversity. China's remarkable poverty alleviation success came as a result of the Chinese poverty alleviation framework which can be credited mainly to the Chinese people's selfless services, strong leadership and dedication through the nation's industrial policies, high rate of economic expansion, pro-poor macroeconomic policies, government poverty alleviation policies as well as targeted programs. All these can be summarized under three main components: (1) economic growth policies for the poor; (2) a rural social safety net; and (3) development-oriented poverty alleviation strategies and programs (Liu Jian et al., 2009)[1], thereby revealing that Chinese government policies in this area are effective.

China devised a policy of pairing the well-developed eastern provinces with those in the west; this system is generally known as "*duikou zhiyuan*", which literally means "pairing assistance." Changsheng (2018:34)[2] asserts that the developed provinces are expected to commit resources to assist the underdeveloped provinces which they are paired with.

---

[1] Liu J., X. Li and F. Liu. (2009). A Study on Povety Reduction in Rural China. Beijing: China Finance and Economics Press.

[2] Changsheng, Z. (2018) (ed) "The Evolution of China's Poverty Alleviation and Development Policy (2001-2015). Springer, PP. 34.

The above east-west pairing-off poverty alleviation system was established to narrow the development gap between the eastern and western regions. Under the principle of advantage complementation, mutual benefits, long-term partnership and common development, the two sides of the pairing-off poverty alleviation have carried out multi-layer poverty alleviation partnership in several forms in the field of government assistance, enterprise cooperation, social assistance, industrial development, cadre exchange, personnel training and labor transfer. Former Chinese leader Deng Xiaoping pronounced that in the reform and opening-up process, the regions which become prosperous first should help those still in poverty. The purpose of this targeted strategy was to ensure that everyone in China achieve common prosperity.

Following the footsteps of his predecessors, President Xi highlighted the significance of targeting individuals in designing anti-poverty programs in 2013. The Chinese president affirms that targeting poverty should be more accurate to allow limited finance to attain the greatest effects. Since President Xi's statement, the Chinese poverty reduction policies have focused on providing opportunities by building assets for the poor and transferring assets to the poor, largely circumventing pure "handouts". Poverty alleviation programs have sought to raise the income-generating capacity of poor rural households. In rural regions, the Chinese government has innovated a poverty alleviation mechanism that enables the government to provide snowballing support to basic public services, human capital development, and significant investments in agriculture, enterprises, and infrastructure.

In 2015, the Chinese government further re-emphasized the task of wiping out poverty in the rural regions and rehabilitating the entire impoverished regions by 2020, meaning there will be strategic plans and policy measures of narrowing development gap by finding a solution to clothing, shelter and food problems, alleviating poverty, improving the environment by solving the climate change problem and enhancing capacity. If China can achieve its 2020 goal by eliminating poverty and narrowing the development gap in China, then this would be another milestone for China's reform and opening-up, and China will be the first nation to attain Goal 1 of the United Nations 2030 Agenda for Sustainable Development,

10 years ahead of the deadline, which is eradicating "poverty in all its forms". As such, China's 13th Five-Year Plan (2016—2020) for Economic and Social Development demonstrated concrete requirements and measures. This is the first time the Chinese leadership has made poverty reduction a significant part of a Five-Year Plan, and assisting poverty-stricken communities to shake off poverty has been listed as an obligatory index.

In 2016, the World Bank report affirmed that China's State-sponsored programs were raising poor people earnings, implementating early childhood development, providing of quality education and healthcare, giving cash transfers to poor families, constructing rural infrastructure and giving of subsidies to rebuild homes, and these were all effective in reducing poverty. Also, according to Ehizuelen (2019)[1], the Chinese government has dispensed in advance part of its 2019 poverty eradication fund to local governments. The poverty reduction fund already allocated to 28 provinces, autonomous regions and municipalities, totaled $13 billion, accounting for 86 percent recorded in 2018. Part of the allocated funds of $13 billion will be used to support regions in deep poverty, including Xinjiang, Tibet, parts of Yunnan, Gansu and Sichuan. The fund deployed under the poverty eradication campaign covers numerous areas, including improving people's lives, funding for rural infrastructure, agricultural subsidies, and discounted loans (Ehizuelen, 2019). Also, a projected 13 million urban employment opportunities will be created yearly, keeping the record of the unemployment rate at a low level of 4 percent over the current years (Hu, 2018)[2].

The broad objective for such assistance is to encourage self-development and empowerment of poor populations. The longing of the Chinese people for a better life is strong; the Chinese leadership will maintain a proactive policy stance in 2019 with a higher deficit-to-GDP ratio to leave policy space to address the

[1] Ehizuelen, M.M.O. (2019). China's Last Lap in Eradicating Poverty by 2020. China Daily, March 14, 2019. Retrieved 17 April 2020 from global.chinadaily.com.cn/a/2019/14/WS5C89b8da3106c65c34ee93a.html.

[2] Hu, B. (2018). China's Economic Transformation. DOC Research Institute. Retrieved July 6, 2019 from https://doc-research.org/2018/01/chinas-economic-transformation/.

poverty issue. Multi-sector approaches, targeted strategies, good leadership, constant innovation, such as using e-commerce to connect farmers to the markets, have been the core enablers of poverty alleviation in China. China's achievements in poverty alleviation in the past four decades have been possible as a result of the Chinese government's strong leadership and the mobilization of impressive levels of resources and innovation. Notably, in order to move millions of Chinese people out of poverty, the Chinese leaders made the decision to move away from the comfort zone of easy revolutionary rhetoric, took economic modernization as a central task, launched reform and opening-up, and traveled the difficult terrain of "crossing the river by feeling the stones" .

All these spectacular wins imply that China is marching toward winning the last lap against poverty regardless of COVID-19. It is hoped that suitable attention on the part of Chinese people will surely assist the "Middle Kingdom" to actualize the "two centenary goals" and China's dream of national rejuvenation. This kind of development model should be a driving factor for Africa's integration. No wonder development economic experts affirm that China's rapid economic transformation and its impressive development trajectory may provide a lesson for Africa, where China's presence has grown immensely over the same period.

While combating poverty at home, China is also actively assisting other developing nations, such as the African nations which hope to learn from China's experience to help the over 400 million impoverished people in Africa exit poverty. At the Forum on China-Africa Cooperation (FOCAC) Summit held in Beijing in September 2018, President Xi reaffirmed his nation's support for poverty alleviation in Africa under the three-year plan when he pledged the sum of $60 billion to support for the continent of Africa, in a quest to alleviate poverty by 2030 globally and the African agenda that intends to create the "Africa we want" by 2063. Studies show that poverty and unemployment are major problems in Africa; countless African nations could not meet Millennium Development Goals targeted on poverty reduction (Asante, 2017)[1]. In this sense, the $60 billion is

---

[1] Asante, R. (2017). "China's Security and Economic Engagement in West Africa: Constructive or Destructive?" China Quarterly of International Strategic Studies, Vol. 3, No. 4 pp. 575-596.

crucial to Africa's sustainable development.

Africa and China have agreed to implement the China-Africa poverty reduction plan dubbed the "Happy Life" project, which involves around 200 poverty reduction programs focusing on women and children in Africa. Such programs include the Assistance Fund for South-South Cooperation, which would facilitate the implementation of the 2030 Agenda for Sustainable Development in Africa, the 2015 Johannesburg Action Plan development which includes knowledge sharing strategies on how to eradicate poverty. On top of that, China reaffirms the continuous organization of the China-Africa Poverty Reduction and Development Conference and to endorse it as an official sub-forum under the framework of FOCAC. This initiative has permitted China and Africa to jointly explore poverty alleviation policies and strategies, while gradually creating a multilevel intergovernmental and intersociety dialogue platform for alleviating poverty. With that said, it is in this context we look at the potential for African nations drawing possible poverty alleviation lessons from China.

In terms of agriculture-led growth and diversification of rural family incomes, some lessons from the rapid development of agriculture for poverty alleviation in China can be drawn for African nations. Firstly, the Chinese poverty alleviation programs have a strong focus on rural regions and agricultural advancement, as the government's poverty alleviation efforts have concentrated extensively on the rural areas. Nevertheless, we should be cautious in drawing on the experiences of China's growth and poverty alleviation strategies more broadly, given the two different contexts.

China has been a unified nation in spite of the nation's cultural diversity and massive territory, while Africa is a continent of over 50 nations with diversified social, economic and environmental conditions. China has had more favorable socio-political and demographic conditions than Africa. But the lesson to be learned is how China succeeded in improving the living standards of its rural population. Also, African nations need to learn how smallholder-based agriculture in China has been developed, and simultaneously learn lessons on the range of difficulties related with Chinese agricultural development, like the emergence of an unequal society with a robust urban-rural divide, unclear land rights for farmers and highly intensive farming, leading to pollution and the degradation of natural resources.

Secondly, the sustained high economic growth, a necessary condition for poverty alleviation, has remained a challenge for African nations. The Chinese industrial and service sectors, growth were truly based on the fundamental agricultural reforms initiated over four decades ago. Africa can learn from these Chinese government policies on how China attracts and regulates foreign investment to support industrialization and technological development.

Thirdly, speedy economic growth and active macroeconomic, industrial and social policies propelled China into the ranks of the super-middle-income nation status, making it a global economic powerhouse today, and African nations aspire to upper-middle-income nation status in the near future. The Chinese transformation over this period wielded increasing influence over the development path of African nations, either via bilateral trade and financial flows or indirectly via growth spillovers and terms of trade effects.

Although all these example of China's experience sound positive, nevertheless, there are four limitations in learning from China's success against poverty reduction.

Firstly, until the late 1970s, most economic resources in China were under state control, and through reforms, they were equally distributed in rural areas. It empowered the poor. The power and political structure in Africa is totally dissimilar, comprising of civil and military bureaucracies, political and religious forces, landed rural elites, and a strong caste system. Throughout China's reforms, the Chinese leadership has targeted the poverty-stricken areas, whereas it is hard to distribute economic resources, like land, in poor regions of Africa, where few families control the land.

Secondly, compared with China, Africa tends to have weaker state institutions, and this has an adverse effect on both the implementation of anti-poverty programs and the provision of key social services and infrastructure to African people.

Thirdly, population growth in Africa is soaring. The high dependency ratio, because of high fertility, seems to be a binding constraint for economic growth and poverty reduction.

Fourth, the poor legal system and social situation, linked with extremism and terrorism in Africa, could be a serious constraint to designing poverty alleviation policies and implementing them.

In summary, the lessons from China have significant implications for African nations. The government-led and development-oriented poverty alleviation programs have contributed immensely to alleviating poverty in China by improving infrastructure, and hence, improving the production conditions in poor areas of China. The government poverty alleviation programs have also offered micro-loans and training to the poor, which tend to raise their incomes and improve their capacities.

With that said, it is important and advisable for both parties to learn from each other. For that reason, Africa needs to draw selectively upon China's poverty alleviation experiences based on each African nations' own characteristics of history, culture and economics. That means, during the localization process of the foreign experiences on poverty alleviation, African nations should form their own poverty reduction mode with African characteristics. For China, during the process of poverty reduction cooperation, the guiding ideology should be the construction of a community with a shared future for mankind, and the principle should be based on equality, inclusiveness and diversity of cooperation with respect for the autonomy of African poverty alleviation strategies, mobilizing various forces to carry out comprehensive poverty alleviation measures.

On the other hand, both parties should try and deepen their collaboration by concentrating on transferring their various developmental experiences based on their capacities, which in terms of the logic, should center on "what I did" rather than "what you need to do (to catch up with each other and learn from each other)". Furthermore, China and Africa should try and strengthen their collaboration by inducing Chinese scholars to learn more about poverty and development in Africa and to disseminate the information in China. Experience sharing and augmented training and capacity building activities can be deepened by conducting joint research and exchange via augmented fund input on poverty alleviation in China and Africa.

The Way Forward

Challenges and Sustainable Development of
China's Poverty Alleviation

扫码获取

★ 脱贫故事分享
★ 脱贫攻坚解读
　与回顾

01

Challenges in the Next Hundred Year

I. Now to Win the Fight against Indigence[1]

Global poverty has been falling for decades: in the 1960s, around 50 percent of the world population was living in extreme poverty (defined as living on less than $1.90 per day); today, that number is around 10 percent (Chart 1). China has been at the forefront of this achievement and is responsible for over 70 percent of the fall in poverty levels worldwide over the past 40 years.

Chart 1: Share of the World Population Living in Absolute Poverty, 1820—2015

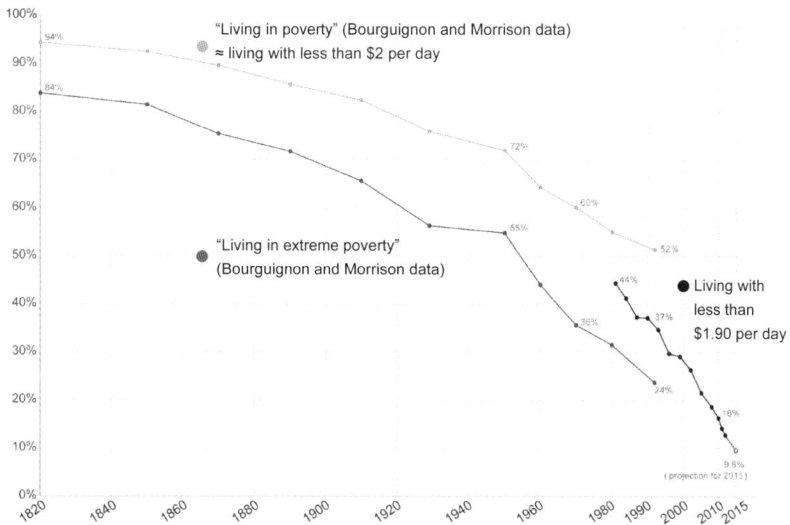

---

[1] By Ian Goldin, professor of Globalization and Development at the University of Oxford and former vice-president of the World Bank.

Data source: 1820—1992 Bourguignon and Morrison (2002)—Inequality among World Citizens, in The American Economic Review; 1981—2015 World Bank (Povcal Net). The interactive data visualization is available at OurWorldData.org. Licensed under CC-BY-SA by the author Max Roser.

Chinese poverty reduction is a success story of historical significance. Over the past 40 years, the Chinese government has embarked on a well-organized campaign to reduce poverty and turn the nation into a middle-income country within a generation.

From the announcement of targeted economic reforms in 1978, the number of extremely poor Chinese went from 60 percent of the population in the 1990s to less than 2 percent in 2014, according to the World Bank, with over 700 million people being lifted out of extreme poverty in 40 years (Charts 2 and 3). This has been achieved through a concerted modernization of the economy.

Chart 2: China and World Poverty Headcount (International Standards)

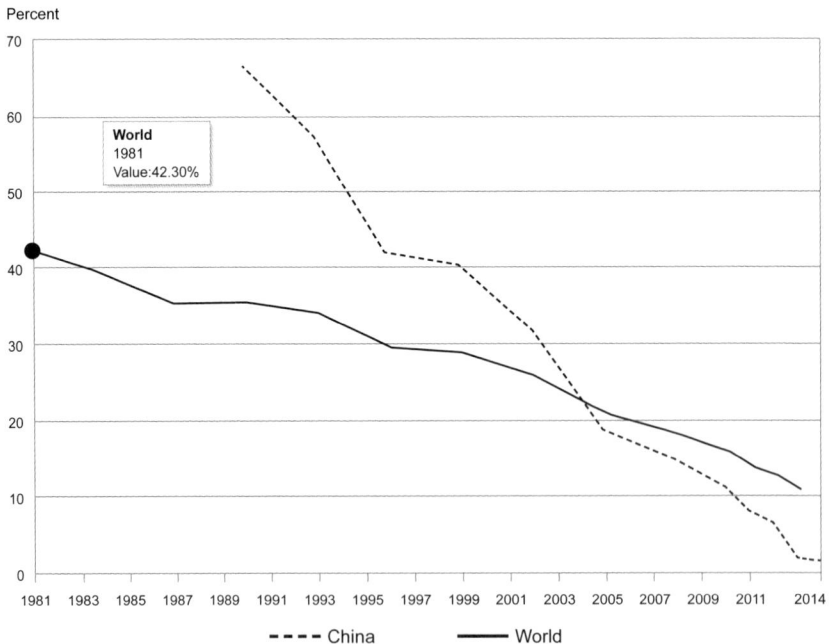

Source: the World Bank.

354

Chart 3: China Poverty Headcount (National Standards) 2010—2017

Percent

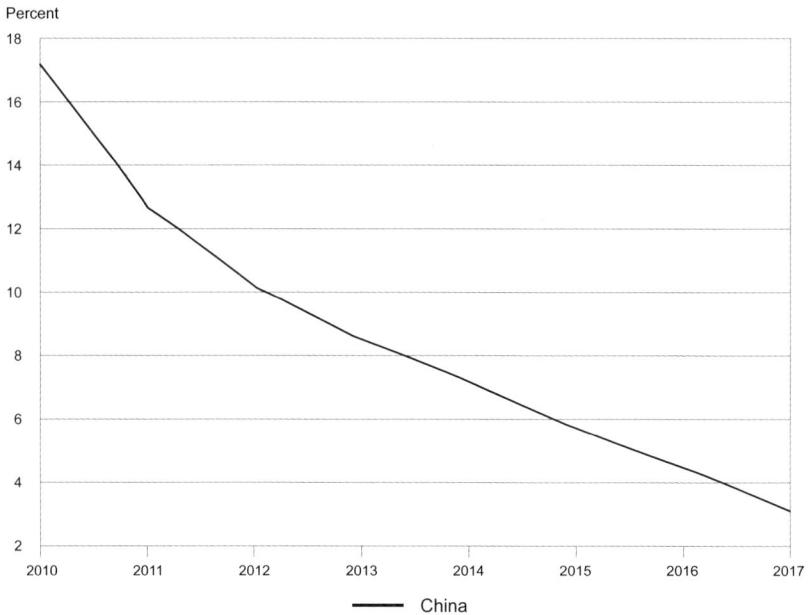

— China

Source: the World Bank.

Agriculture has reduced in significance as a share of employment from over 75 percent 40 years ago to under 25 percent today, with manufacturing and then services overtaking agriculture to account for the largest share of employment. This has been associated with a process of urbanization and a commitment to universal education and health services as well as access to clean water and electricity. Whereas barely 20 percent of the population lived in urban areas 40 years ago, now over 60 percent of the population of 1.4 billion people are urban (Chart 4). Urban wealth has also increased more than five times since 2000 (Chart 5). Along with urbanization has come dramatic increases by 12 years in life expectancy to 77 years. Average incomes increased by over 40 times and when adjusted by purchasing power by over 60 times.

Chart 4: Urban and Rural Population in China, 2006—2016

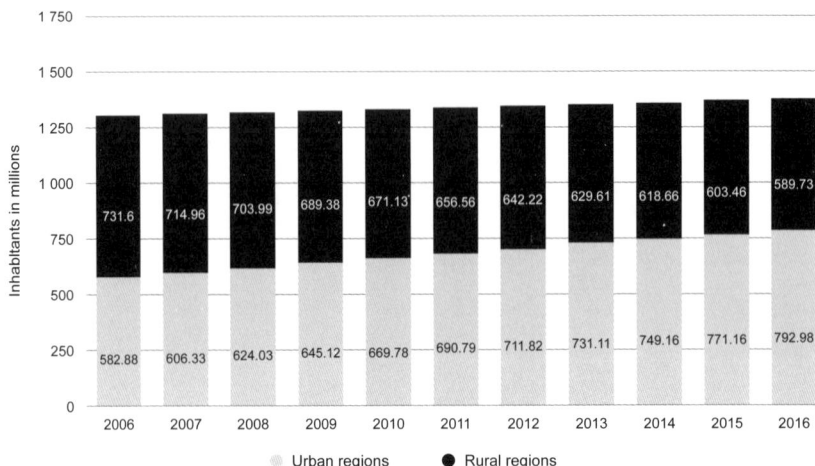

Source:Chinese National Buren of Statistics

Chart 5: Rural and Urban Income in China, 1990, 2000, 2010—2016

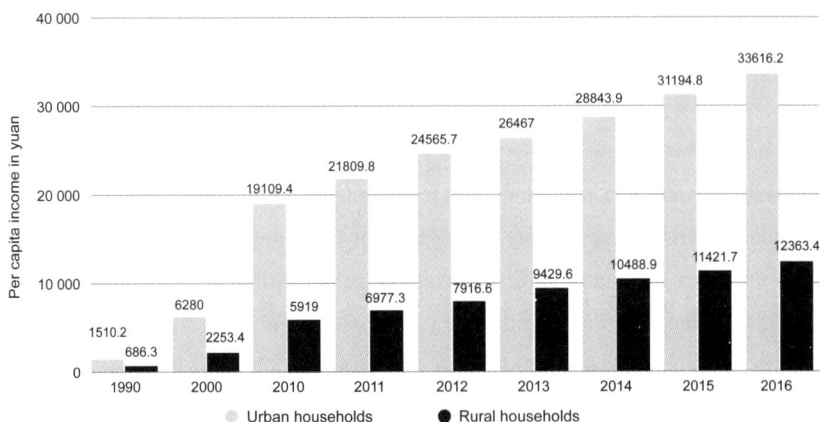

Source:Chinese National Buren of Statistics

The ambition of the Chinese government, as announced by President Xi Jinping at the Global Poverty Reduction Forum in 2015, is to eradicate extreme poverty in China by 2020. Considering China's extraordinary economic success, this objective appears to be in reach.

How has China achieved such a remarkable feat and what lessons can developing countries learn from China's poverty reduction?

The key to the Chinese success is that, together with strong economic growth, development policies specifically aimed at poverty reduction have been firmly in place since the market reforms were initiated 40 years ago. The Organization for Economic Co-operation and Development identifies development-oriented leadership and the building of a national consensus as the main factors that have allowed for the near-elimination of poverty. This has entailed a rigorous implementation of development and social policies, a uniform system for measuring policy performance, and the concerted effort of the private and public sectors, motivated by a unifying national commitment to shared goals. Defining precise developmental goals, and generating a collective impetus toward their achievement for the entire population, including both the public and the private sectors, has played a crucial role in the Chinese poverty reduction strategy, setting an example for developing countries in their struggle against poverty.

The achievement of such ambitious goals would not have been possible without a coherent and effective policy implementation mechanism. The Chinese case is unique in the way development policies were trialed and, if successful, scaled up and rolled out nationwide; or withdrawn, if ineffective, in a dynamic learning process that proved extremely effective. Policy trial and experimentation has been common since the beginning of the Chinese poverty reduction effort: the effectiveness of policies, rolled out in local areas first, has been assessed empirically, and implemented on a national scale thanks to careful monitoring and the rotation of civil servants around the vast country.

The introduction of land ownership which spurred agricultural productivity in the late 1970s is, for example, the result of a successful village-wide experiment of "household land responsibility". Market policies, gradually liberalizing capital flows, trade reforms, and financial exchanges, have been tested first in Special Economic Zones since their inception, and the Free Trade Zones and Economic and Technological Development Zones represent the success of Chinese sectoral and experimental policymaking.

The development of cities like Changsha in Central China are a case in point for this unique growth strategy. Coming from a very low base and a relatively isolated and poor region, the city has experienced prodigious growth in recent decades: its GDP per capita increased fourfold from 2000 to 2012, and its industrial profile changed from heavy industry and manufacturing to high-value-added, capital intensive industries such as auto motive and media/communication. This was achieved through a mixture of national intervention—particularly the Rise of Central China plan—and effective decentralization. Investment in R&D and labor training initiatives, together with policies to promote internal competition between different cities and provinces have ensured the development of cutting edge industries and rapid economic growth, accompanied by improvements in health, education and infrastructure in a growing number of rapidly advancing cities and regions. At the local level, a system of "leading groups" helped coordinate the activities of firms' managers, the local administration, and national agencies to achieve growth effectively. Programs have been implemented for the development of local human capital, combined with the attraction of talent and the drawing on lessons from the rest of the country as well as from international organizations, other countries and international experts.

In this, as in other areas of development, carefully planned experiments with close monitoring of the results, adjustments to improve outcomes through trial and error and then scaling of the lessons to a widening number of areas and people has been at the heart of the Chinese poverty reduction strategy. The combination of the depth and breadth of commitment to the objectives and the process of combining an understanding of the best global and national practices with learning by doing and adapting to local circumstances is the most important lesson from China.

Funding for policy implementation has been sought both from public investment in infrastructure and technological innovation, and through the responsible use of international resources and investments, which facilitated the learning, transformation and adaptation of best practices internationally. This remarkable openness to examining global experiences and being open to adapting and implementing changes in consultation with local communities is another vital lesson of the Chinese experience.

An early result from the initial institutional effort toward poverty reduction has been mass job creation, as private and public investments, and the construction of a network of transport and communication infrastructure created new jobs, and shifted workers toward the productive sectors of manufacturing and services. Today, over 80 percent of employment and around 60 percent of investment comes from the private sector (Chart 6).

Chart 6: Investment by the Private Sector as Share of
Total Investment, 2006—2016

Percent

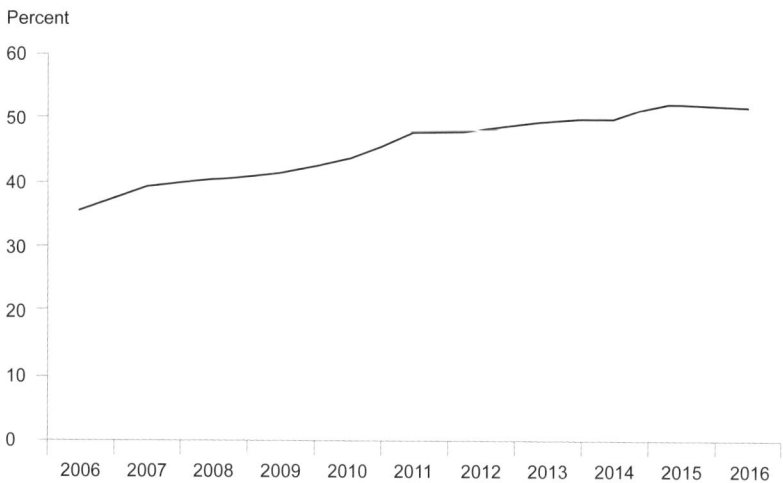

Source:*Chinese National Buren of Statistics*

This would not have been possible without the creation of an impressive network of educational, social and research institutions, and widespread transport and communication links. With an increasingly far-reaching and solid structure in place, the Chinese government has created the springboard for poor citizens to lift themselves out of poverty, inspiring a sense of responsibility and allowing access to educational and technological resources. Self-reliance has been a key theme in this process, at the individual, community and the city and institutional level. Competition for places in the top educational and civil service institutions is intense and based on merit, leading to high levels of preparation and competence at the national level, an unprecedented feat for a developing country.

The Chinese growth phenomenon, impressive as it is, does have its risks:

particularly, the environmental sustainability of such rapid growth. This has resulted in a need to reduce the intensity of water and energy use and overcome pollution and the reliance on fossil fuels. These challenges are recognized by the government, and are part of the 2020 ambition to eliminate extreme poverty. Eager to maintain social stability, and reap the benefits that come with sustainable growth, the Chinese administration has embraced the pursuit of a wide range of environmental policies. President Xi has declared his intention to transform China into an "ecological civilization". Chinese leadership in climate change has seen a remarkable acceleration in renewable energy use, with China in a short time becoming the biggest manufacturer and user of solar and wind energy. As a result of these and other efforts, China has managed to achieve a reduction of 46 percent in carbon intensity of GDP over 2005—2017, ahead of its ambition to achieve a 45 percent reduction by 2020.

Reforestation has also been a priority, and since 1978, over 66 billion trees have been planted by Chinese citizens, including in the arid northwest where planting is well-advanced to create a "Green Great wall" to stop advancing desertification. Another notable example of a large-scale mass reforestation effort has recently been initiated which aims at planting over 400,000 hectares of trees in Hebei province—one of the most polluted in the country. Environmental concerns are a primary motivation behind this effort; however, concerns about public health and economic considerations are also important. Respiratory and cardiovascular diseases are recognized as a major source of ill health in China and Hubei province's residents are among those that have been seriously affected by pollution.

Growing environmental concerns are one side effect of China's rapid economic growth. Another has been rising inequality. The inevitable consequence of rapid income growth from a very poor society that was one of the most egalitarian in the world is that some people have escaped poverty and got richer more rapidly than others. The country's Gini coefficient recently has hovered just above 0.4 (Chart 7), which is high by world standards. The higher the Gini coefficient, the more unequal the society, and although on this metric the United States, Brazil and Mexico are more unequal than China, much of Asia and Europe now has lower inequality than China.

Chart 7: China Gini Coefficient 2003—2016

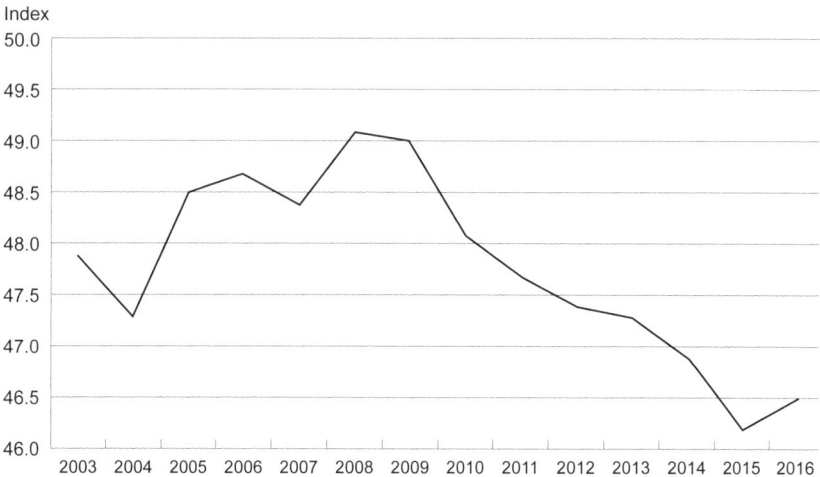

Index

Source: National Bureau of Statistics

In part, growing inequality is the result of income gains for the poor having been achieved through job creation in the industrial sector, which has spurred internal migration toward urban areas, as well as through the implementation of welfare policies and improvement of public services. The urban share of wealth was 80 percent in 2015, up from 30 percent in 1975. The increase in inequality that the country has been experiencing has a strong geographic dimension, as it reflects the divide between urban and rural areas, with urban areas enjoying more rapid increases in income than rural areas.

There is, however, evidence that this trend might be reversing in recent years, thanks to targeted interventions in isolated rural areas, the introduction of minimum wage regulation, and a commitment to tackling corruption. The Chinese government has prioritized improving purchasing power at the bottom of the income distribution, not least to help the shift of the economy from investment-driven to consumption-driven. The pledge of publication of official guidelines on how to reduce inequality represents an important step in this direction. This provides further weight to the case of China as an emergent global leader in social policy.

Not only has China established itself as a global economic power, but it has also accepted its role in international governance. Beyond the commitment to global environmental standards and its leadership in combating climate change, it is also playing a growing role in overcoming poverty worldwide. Chinese investments have targeted the Asian and African continents, providing aid, and, more importantly, contributing to the development of better infrastructure for transport, communication, and market development. Its leadership role in establishing the Asia Infrastructure Investment Bank, the New Development Bank, and the Belt and Road Initiative similarly reflects these broader international commitments to shared development.

Naturally, the Chinese experience is not an example of a one size-fits-all solution to poverty. Every country's journey toward poverty reduction starts from unique conditions and at a unique point in time, encountering different obstacles and opportunities. The Chinese model is not a template, but it can inspire large-scale decisions and policies to be referenced and adapted to other countries' contexts. A notable example is the early and continuous focus on rural productivity—which accomplishes the double aim of alleviating hunger and elevating the incomes of poor rural workers. The Chinese growth policy has always been informed by a deep understanding in the role of human capital growth and infrastructure in spurring economic prosperity, providing a clear lesson to other developing countries: the provision of affordable education and health care, with generous subsidies to the poorest households helps ensure the improvement of social mobility.

Over the past 40 years, China has demonstrated that the scourge of poverty can be defeated. The Chinese experience offers vital lessons which demonstrate that with the necessary will, the global targets of the Sustainable Development Goals can be achieved. As China continues to focus on the elimination of extreme poverty domestically and further improves the lives of its citizens, its domestic achievements in poverty reduction will be increasingly strengthened by an emphasis on environmental sustainability and a focus on those at the bottom of the income distribution. Building on its unique achievements over the past 40 years, China's growing commitment to help eradicate global poverty is a source of inspiration for all those committed to the Sustainable Development Goals.

II. Cooperation Is the Best Way Ahead[①]

Has any anti-poverty initiative in history ever lifted more people from abject poverty than the national economic development program China launched four decades ago by opening up its economy to the world? The answer is no.

Imagine what we could call a "Pyramid of Poverty". In 1978, nine out of every 10 in China's population of 1 billion people were struggling to survive on an income below the "extreme poverty line" as set by the World Bank at just under $1.9 a day.

Today, the pyramid has been flipped on its head. People who previously spent most of their life hungry, have doubled their calorie intake. Most of previous generations' waking hours were spent attempting to provide enough food for themselves and their children to survive. Today, families can eat together, stay together and play together.

Since 1978, China has seen more than four decades of rapid economic growth. According to the "Rule of 72"—divide 72 by the annual growth rate to determine when an economy or investment will double—the Chinese economy has almost doubled every seven years. Some individual Chinese citizens have experienced a 50-fold increase in their standard of living. It could be argued that 40 years of miracle growth have created a greater increase in human well-being for more individuals than occurred in the previous more than 4,000 years of China's history.

In 2004, then World Bank president Robert Zoellick declared that "China's efforts alone" put the world on track to achieve this goal. In Zoellick's words: "Between 1981 and 2004, China succeeded in lifting more than half a billion people out of extreme poverty. This is certainly the greatest leap to overcome poverty in history."

---

① By Graham Allison, professor and the first director of the Harvard Kennedy School, director of Harvard's Belfer Center.

In 2017, then World Bank President Jim Yong Kim highlighted what he called "one of the great stories of history". China, he said, had lifted 800 million people out of the miseries of extreme poverty and thereby extended the average life span of its citizens by more than a decade.

China's success in adopting its distinctive version of a Party-led market economy, which has overtaken the US to become the largest economy in the world (in terms of purchasing power parity).

The Chinese people are rightfully proud of what their individual efforts and the leadership of their government have done. But they also recognize the fact that this was possible only because of the stable international economic and security order. That order enabled all the Asian miracles—and none more than modern China itself.

In our interconnected world, it instead goes beyond to a number of "mini-MADs"— challenges threatening mutually assured "defeat", if not "destruction", for both countries that neither can overcome alone. The novel coronavirus is an iconic example. Viruses carry no passports and respect no borders. When an outbreak becomes a pandemic infecting citizens around the world, since no nation can hermetically seal its borders, every country is at risk. The inescapable fact is that all 7.7 billion people alive today inhabit one small planet Earth. As President Kennedy noted in explaining the necessity for coexistence with the Soviet Union in facing mutual, existential nuclear danger: "We all breathe the same air. We all cherish our children's future. And we are all mortal."

Pandemics are one "mini-MAD". Preserving a biosphere in which citizens can breathe the air, managing financial crises to avoid great depressions (and their political consequences), and preventing the spread of the means and motives for mega-terrorism are others. For each of these, intense cooperation and partnership will not simply produce mutual benefits. In these arenas, neither state can ensure its most vital interest in survival without serious cooperation from the other.

Sustainable Development of China's Poverty Alleviation

I. Last Mile "Connectivity" Helps Reach Goals[1]

After thoroughly studying the entire course of China's reform and opening-up, one can conclude that in the past four decades China has not only created an economic growth miracle but also created one of social stability. The primary reason for the double miracles is that the enlarged pie has been widely shared by ordinary Chinese, which increases people's happiness and sense of gain as the country makes economic progress.

The practice and result of poverty alleviation are the best manifestation of such a shared development. Back in 1981 when China's population accounted for 22.4 percent of the world population, its people were living on less than $1.9 (in purchasing power parity terms at 2011 prices) of the World Bank criterion of absolute poverty, and its people made up 46.4 percent of the world's poor. In 2018, while China's population accounted for 18.4 percent of the world total, there were hardly any people in China who lived on or below the same criterion of absolute poverty. The success story of one-fifth of humanity is certain to show the world China's wisdom and solutions in poverty alleviation.

Making the pie bigger is the prerequisite for fairly distributing it. In 1978-2018, the annual growth of China's GDP in real terms was 9.4 percent, not only the

---

[1] By Cai Fang, vice-president of the Chinese Academy of Social Sciences (CASS), deputy director and chief expert of National High-Level Think Tank at CASS.

highest in the world during this period, but also unseen in any other period of the economic history of the world. Such growth allowed China to rapidly catch up with developed countries in standard of living.

According to the World Bank income categorization based on per capita GDP, China was among the poorest in the low income group in 1978 when reform and opening-up was launched. Benefitting from its demographic dividend and taking advantage of globalization during that period, China crossed the threshold of lower-middle income in 1993 and the threshold of upper-middle income in 2009. In 2018, China's per capita GDP reached $9,771, which is close to the threshold of high income.

China did not stop there with the belief of trickle-down economics that assumes the outcomes of economic growth, technological advancement and globalization would be automatically shared by all the people. What followed presents the China experience of the nature of sharing. First, its economic growth pattern in the period can be characterized by a resources reallocation process in which employment expansion, income increase and productivity improvement were simultaneously achieved. Secondly, social security programs were established and perfected as the labor market development demanded stronger social protection. Last but not the least, from the very early stages, the government initiated a State plan of rural poverty alleviation with specific goals at each stage of its implementation.

All these characteristics of economic development make China an outstanding role model and the greatest contributor to world poverty reduction. According to World Bank data, during 1981—2015, the number of the world's poor reduced from 1.89 billion to 753.0 million, while the number of the Chinese poor reduced from 877.8 million to 9.6 million.

That is, China has physically contributed 76.18 percent to the world's poverty reduction in the period, in addition to enriching the experience of fighting poverty. After 2015, China continued its rural poverty alleviation efforts with a criterion higher than the World Bank standard. In 2018, the number of the Chinese rural poor was 16.6 million and the poverty rate was as low as 1.7 percent.

China's success in poverty reduction sets a brand new, living example in applying the people-centered philosophy to development, which does not exist in conventional textbooks. In countries implementing poverty alleviation strategies, there is a phenomenon of diminishing returns in poverty reduction efforts. Some scholars and practitioners even consider it the law of poverty reduction. As poverty alleviation succeeds, and as a result, the number of the poor reduces to a relatively smaller fraction of the population, policy effects tend to fade. This is because that in the later stages of poverty alleviation, the remaining poor usually have particular disadvantageous features—disadvantaged demographic characteristics such as handicaps, illness, old age, poor education and unfavorable geographic conditions of residence, production and ecology prevent them from completely getting rid of absolute poverty.

In many countries, as a result, poverty reduction efforts get stuck in the last mile. In physical investment, if an investor encounters the phenomenon of diminishing returns to capital, it is rational to stop further injecting money in the same project. The fundamental difference between an investment project and a poverty reduction program is that the latter deals with people who are the ultimate goal of development. Upholding the people-centered development philosophy and determining to break the "law" of diminishing returns of poverty reduction, the central government has solemnly pledged that, by 2020, China will eliminate the phenomenon of poverty in the rural areas.

While the goal will be definitely reached as planned and predicted, China has already started to deploy further tasks to sustain its poverty reduction efforts, which include normalizing the policy and mechanism of poverty alleviation to consolidate what has already been achieved, paying close attention to and coping with new causes of poverty, tackling risks that may cause shock-induced poverty, formulating higher criteria to implement the new strategy of poverty alleviation, and solving relative poverty.

II. People-Centered Approach Yields High Returns[1]

China's people-driven and people-centered model has ensured its drastic decline in the population of rural areas living in absolute poverty. If calculated by the absolute poverty line set by the Chinese government in 1986, subsistence issues had been solved by the end of the 20th century, and absolute rural poverty had been eradicated by the beginning of the 21st century.

Since the 1986 poverty line was, in fact, a low-level destitution standard, the Chinese government in 2012 raised the absolute poverty line for rural areas in line with socioeconomic realities on the ground and decided to eliminate absolute poverty in rural areas by 2020. From 2012 on till now, the basic conditions for poverty reduction and rural development have greatly changed and are hugely different from those in the earlier era after reform and opening-up.

To start with, for a long time after reform and opening-up, poverty-stricken people closely linked with economic growth as the main participants in agricultural development and township enterprises were farmers. But as we entered the 21st century, it became very difficult for these groups to increase income in major industries. Meanwhile, widening urban-rural and wealth gaps added to the difficulty to the old poverty reduction model. What's more, the urban-rural disparity in basic public services was becoming more apparent.

Against such a backdrop, normal measures were not enough to eradicate the remnants of absolute poverty. What we needed to do to realize the target of eliminating absolute poverty by 2020 were unconventional actions that reduce the constraints of current systems.

Therefore, the targeted poverty reduction and alleviation campaign was initiated in 2012 with the goal of eradicating absolute poverty by 2020. The main agenda

---

[1] By Li Xiaoyun, chair professor of humanities at China Agricultural University, member of the Advisory Committee of the State Council Leading Group office of Poverty Alleviation and Development.

of the campaign included efforts to make sure that rural residents' per capita disposable income reached a minimum of 2,300 yuan, and efforts to address prominent issues to ensure rural poor people did not have to worry about food or clothing, and had access to compulsory education, basic medical services and safe housing. By the end of 2019, the number of rural residents living in absolute poverty had fallen to 5.51 million, and 97 percent of registered poverty-stricken households had access to basic necessities. Judging from the current trend, we're capable of winning the critical battle against poverty by 2020. Even though the COVID-19 pandemic has had a huge adverse impact, it will not change the fundamental aims of the poverty eradication campaign.

The serious challenge we face now is to consolidate the achievements in poverty alleviation. The current achievements are in part because of special policy initiatives and ensuring the supply of resources. Although we have made some institutional innovations, such as education-driven poverty alleviation and health-themed poverty alleviation, the campaign is still a temporary approach that does not involve enough systematic and institutional arrangements.

There are about 30 million people who have been lifted out of poverty but are very likely to fall back into poverty if exposed to risks. After COVID-19, some of these people have fallen back into poverty and the number is increasing. Therefore, we should focus on consolidating the achievements made.

To prevent people from falling back into poverty, we need to establish a long-term mechanism that includes both emergency aid to vulnerable groups and daily actions incorporated into socioeconomic development.

First, we should put in place an integrated urban-rural system for employment. As more poor people get employed in non-agricultural industries, such a system could effectively prevent them falling back into poverty.

Second, we need to reform current poverty alleviation policies in line with empowerment. Reducing poverty by building local industries was largely a government effort, but a long-term mechanism needs sustainable empowerment and market development arrangements.

Third, government departments, State-owned enterprises, government-affiliated institutions and first secretaries of the Communist Party of China village committees, serving as village-stationed providers of support, have greatly eased human resources shortages in poor areas, but we need to consider long-term sustainable human capital to consolidate the achievements made.

Fourth, while preventing people from falling back into poverty, we should also put in place effective mechanisms for stopping new poverty from emerging. Education and health are the two areas that need huge attention.

III. Digital Economy Can Provide Fresh Impetus for Global Growth[①]

Strengthening cooperation in the digital economy and transforming China's digital experience in accordance with local conditions is essential to boost economic recovery and social growth across the world.

It is no exaggeration to say that the digital growth has dramatically altered Chinese people's lifestyles and improved livelihoods nationwide. China's accomplishment in poverty alleviation is a classic example of the indispensable role the digital economy can play in driving and innovating for growth.

Take agriculture, for example. In the past, hundreds of millions of farmers in China faced difficulties linking local products with markets. However, e-commerce has done wonders in giving agricultural products access to bigger markets.
Rural e-commerce is now booming in China, showing that the dividends from the digital economy are not limited to developed countries or metropolises. As long as

---

① By Yu Zirong, vice-president of the Chinese Academy of International Trade and Economic Cooperation of the Ministry of Commerce.

the conditions are right, the digital economy can play a bigger role in promoting economic growth in developing countries or rural areas.

However, digital technology alone is not the sole contributor to rural e-commerce's success in China. The huge demand of the domestic market, an increasingly upgraded transportation and digital infrastructure, a sound business environment, an improvement in people's livelihoods, favorable e-commerce policies and positive actions by all the parties concerned have all played a role. In other words, the building of an all-round digital society cannot be accomplished overnight. To promote the localization of digital experience, we need to carry out plans step by step.

It is safe to say that the time is now ripe to promote global digital cooperation. The development of telecommunications infrastructure will boost the popularization of the internet in a cheaper, faster and more convenient manner. In 2019, the global smartphone penetration rate exceeded 80 percent, and the internet usage rate reached 86.8 percent in developed countries and 47 percent in developing ones, laying a solid foundation for global digital cooperation.

As for developing countries' willingness, most countries have begun to carry out plans to develop the digital economy. Southeast Asian countries, such as Vietnam, Thailand, the Philippines and Malaysia, have clearly listed digitization as the priority for growth, actively promoted the building of digital infrastructure, improved the regulatory legal framework, encouraged cashless payment systems and upgraded logistics and distribution. Kenya, Nigeria and South Africa enjoy huge room for cooperation in improving communication facilities, e-commerce, and digital capacity building.

The international community has successively introduced digital development cooperation plans. For instance, the World Bank has launched an e-agriculture project in Côte d'Ivoire with a view to promoting affordable broadband access to more than 1 million rural households. Crop production and price information can be disseminated in real time to boost smallholders' productivity. Also, the employment issue of women in poor areas can be resolved by offering them the chance to learn digital skills.

In recent years, China has injected impetus into international digital cooperation among developing countries in a variety of ways, including assisting the building of digital infrastructure, building digital trading platforms, conducting digital scientific research cooperation and promoting distance education.

China assisted Asian and African countries in building digital infrastructure in the past, providing new momentum for their economic and social development. China's aid to Tanzania's national broadband backbone network project reduced the country's telephone tariffs by 58 percent and internet tariffs by 75 percent. It is satisfying to witness remote rural areas enjoying the convenience of modern communications.

In the field of innovating digital trade environment, China helps small and medium-sized enterprises and disadvantaged groups to build cross-border e-commerce platforms, and offers favorable conditions and training in customs clearance, warehousing, logistics, and technological usage.

China has also laid the foundation for participating in digital international cooperation. But what can be done to improve it?

First, China should identify demonstration projects in accordance with the recipient countries' national policies by focusing on livelihood-related projects that have great potential and economic power. Medical care, education and agriculture are all in need of digital transformation and management.

Second, China should actively encourage pioneering companies to go overseas, and give full play to the technical and management advantages of the private sector, especially supporting leading digital companies to play the key role in restoring social life and helping restart work in the post-pandemic era.

Third, relying on China-assisted vocational and technical schools, human resource development cooperation projects, scholarship projects and digital enterprise training platforms, China can actively help developing countries understand and accept the new concepts and methods in digital management and operation.

Fourth, China should strengthen dialogue and cooperation with multilateral mechanisms, such as the United Nations, G20, BRICS as well as related digital scientific research institutions, so as to promote China's digital technology, standards and services, reach a consensus on digital development, and join hands to contribute to the post-pandemic recovery.

To sum up, digital growth cooperation offers developing countries a proven way to promote their economic and social development.

IV. Industrial Development with Distinctive Local Features[1]

Since the implementation of the targeted poverty alleviation strategy, China has made remarkable achievements, with the number of poverty-stricken people dropping from 98.99 million at the end of 2012 to 5.51 million at the end of 2019; and the poverty incidence dropping from 10.2 percent to 0.6 percent. By the end of 2020, severely impoverished areas will also be lifted as a whole from absolute poverty.

Developing industries with distinctive local features are key to poverty alleviation.

By fostering sustainable industries adapted to rural areas, poor households can not only increase their income, but also improve their human capital and eventually get out of poverty.

Statistics from the State Council Leading Group Office of Poverty Alleviation and Development show that, of the 4.754 million households that were lifted out

---

[1] By Zhu Haibo, associate professor of Agricultural Information Institute of the Chinese Academy of Agricultural Sciences.

of poverty in 2018, 3.528 million benefited from industrial support measures, accounting for 74.2 percent. According to the Ministry of Agriculture and Rural Affairs, by September 2019, 92 percent of the country's poor households had participated in the development of industries with distinctive features and advantages, and 67 percent of those who had been lifted out of poverty were mainly through industrial assistance. Although poverty alleviation through development of industries with distinctive local features has shown good results, there is no denying that industrial development in rural areas is still at the primary stage and relies heavily on government subsidies. The market competitiveness of the industry is still very weak, the reasons including the low levels of organization and low technological levels of industrial development, the poor ability of small farmers, the gap between production and marketing, and lack of branding.

Poverty alleviation in sustainable industries is influenced by multiple factors, including the choice of industries based on resource endowment, a good environment for development, the level of entrepreneurship, government support and guidance, and a fair and incentive-linked mechanism. What is also important is that severely impoverished areas are remote and far from the market, so the market mechanism is not well established and there is scarcity of capital. Therefore, the government plays a crucial role but at the same time, it should bear in mind its main job is to build up the competitiveness market players to tap the power of the market.

First, in promoting poverty alleviation through sustainable industries, the government should not only be proactive, but also needs to clarify the boundaries. On the one hand, industrial development in severely impoverished areas lacks external support, such as capital, technology and leading enterprises. The government should give full play to its resource mobilization ability. At the same time, we should make full use of poverty alleviation funds allocated by the central government, explore potential industries, cultivate capable market players and promote industrial development.

For example, our research team went to Weixi county in Diqing Tibetan autonomous prefecture of Yunnan province in December 2018 and July 2019 for field research. Weixi is a deeply impoverished area, and it is one of the few places in China which has authentic medicinal produce. Since 2017, under the guidance and support of the Weixi County government, Weihong Company has been focusing on Chinese herbal medicine planting and processing and uses the "company + professional cooperative + base + farmer" mode. It promotes the development of village collective economy in deep poverty-stricken counties and increases the income of impoverished households. The company signed a joint stock partnership agreement with Pule, Zhazi, Aluo, Anibi and Kangpu villages in Kangpu Township. Five villages have invested 2.3 million yuan into the company, and each of them can receive a 20,000—40,000 yuan bonus every year. At the same time, by planting Chinese herbal medicine, the company helped 552 households increase their income, which includes 209 poor households, and the average household income increased exceeded 5,000 yuan.

On the other hand, the role of government should have boundaries. In terms of industrial development, the government is not omnipotent. The government should play its role on the basis of respecting market rules and exerting limited liability, and mainly provide public services such as logistics infrastructure, technology promotion, technical training, quality supervision, public brand creation and maintenance with external characteristics to reduce transaction costs. At the micro level, enterprises, social service organizations, cooperatives and farmers should become independent operating entities facing the market, participating in competition, making decisions on their own and bearing risks on their own, to give full play to the benign role of the government.

Second, we should create characteristic industries relying on leading enterprises and branding to realize added value. The development of regional industry in poverty-stricken area must first identify the market potential and comparative local advantage. Only based on a natural endowment structure, including the characteristics of its natural environment, agricultural and forestry products and human capital, can poverty-stricken counties produce competitive products. This way, they can build up a stronger industry chain with resource integration, deep processing and industry service. For example, Weining county is one of the poorest counties in Bijie, Guizhou province. Thanks to its soil conditions and the cold climate in the mountains, it produces sugar-sweetened apples, potatoes, yellow *dangshen* (a traditional Chinese herb) and other agricultural products.

During field research in December 2018 and July 2019, it was found that with the help of Guizhou's digital development strategy and "Internet+", Weining applied the development mode of "e-commerce + modern mountain agricultural park in university + specialized cooperation with farmers + planting and breeding farmers" and vigorously promoted e-commerce of agricultural products. Starting in 2016, Yimin E-Commerce Company takes advantage of the local government's beneficial policies on e-commerce, enjoys low operating costs and focuses on the market, and has the company developed rapidly. Weining's sales of apples and potatoes alone reached 5 million yuan in 2019.

For the extension of the industrial chain, we should give importance to the scales, standardization and quality production of upstream products, and promote the organization of smallholders through cooperative organizations of village communities. We should pay attention to cold-chain storage for agricultural products sold in other seasons to avoid the phenomenon of "high yield but not good harvest" caused by seasonal oversupply. We should attach importance to brand building based on an industrial chain of high-quality agricultural products to create premium brand.

Third, the development of industrial poverty alleviation in poverty-stricken areas can't rely only on poor households. Locals should improve support to foster industrial development, focus on potential characteristic industries, and rely on leading companies and cooperatives. Additionally, the government should promote the competitiveness of the industrial chain, and provide support policies including credit, land use and development compensation.

In addition, in the process of promoting industrial cooperation, division of work and large-scale production, it is necessary to actively cooperate with poor households, launch skills training and provide jobs. Poor households can truly be integrated into industrial development, benefitting from industrial development and improving their own ability.

For example, during the research conducted in December 2019, it was found that Chenguang Biotechnology Group in Shache county, Kashgar city, Xinjiang Uyghur autonomous region, actively encouraged poor households to plant marigolds. At the beginning, local farmers were skeptical and their enthusiasm was not high. After research and discussion, the government of Shache county realized the prospect of this industry and urged government officials and technological personnel of enterprises to actively launch publicity work. At the same time, government officials and technological personnel also provided training programs to farmers for planting marigolds. The local government also promoted enterprises, cooperatives and farmers to form an industrial development consortium. Now, the marigold is "rich flower" for local farmers.

03

China's Poverty Alleviation Success
Contributing to Global Poverty Governance

I. Asian Countries Can Draw on China's Experience[1]

Asian countries feature different resource endowments, leading to sharp distinctions in terms of economies and development policies. Therefore, the effects of poverty alleviation and the wealth gap also vary in these countries.

With the novel coronavirus pandemic severely impacting the global economy, as well as frequent armed conflicts in some regions and prevailing trade protectionism, Asian countries can only achieve overall poverty alleviation and safeguard prosperity and stability of the region by furthering multilateral cooperation and mutual learning.

Poverty levels in Asia have been falling. According to the Sustainable Development Report 2019, the current headcount ratio of extreme poverty in Asian countries is 1.85 percent, well below 2 percent, when measured against the poverty line of $1.90 per person per day. It means in general, absolute poverty had been eradicated and the situation is changing for the better.

However, a large number of people in some countries still live in absolute poverty. The numbers of extremely poor people in three Asian countries—India, Indonesia and Bangladesh—are still more than 10 million, standing at 38.9 million, 11.83

---

① By Sun Jingying, researcher of the Institute of World Economics and Politics and National Institute for Global Strategy at the Chinese Academy of Social Sciences.

million and 11.81 million respectively.

According to the Asian Poverty Reduction Report issued at the Boao Forum for Asia, poverty in Asia is concentrated in a few countries, compared with nearly even distribution in Africa. The wealth gap between Asian countries is also different from that in African countries. This is because poverty in Asian countries has existed along with development while inequality in Africa is caused by underdevelopment. In addition, poverty in Asian countries is caused by income gaps. The main problems in the region include youth unemployment, malnutrition and shortage of infrastructure and public services, especially shortage of medical services.

China's poverty alleviation experience can be narrowed down to a two-phase approach, providing good reference points for other Asian countries. In the first phase, it saw overall poverty alleviation along with rapid economic growth with the launch of reform and opening-up. However, economic growth cannot reduce poverty caused by the income gap. So, in the second phase, the government implemented targeted poverty alleviation programs to help the people shake off poverty and eliminate extreme poverty.

In the first phase, the reform and opening-up policy created a favorable environment for poverty alleviation: exports, investments and domestic demand drove economic growth. Industrialization promoted the development of labor-intensive sectors and provided the poor with a large number of accessible jobs, achieving overall poverty alleviation. During the process, China formulated practical economic policies in line with real conditions, such as introducing foreign-funded enterprises and allowing the private sector to develop independently. The boom of labor-intensive industries expanded the scale of employment in the secondary industry, helping the rural poor earn higher incomes by working in cities, thus reducing poverty in rural areas. China also promoted industrial transformation and upgrading and steadily improved industrial economic efficiency. From 1979 to 2018, for example, the labor productivity of China's manufacturing increased from 2,734.2 yuan to 157,514.4 yuan per person, increasing 56.6 times. It created consistent driving forces for advancing economic growth and increasing residents' income.

Targeted poverty alleviation led by the government was initiated in 2013. It's the core of the second phase. The battle focuses on improving social equity as China's economic and social structures has become unfavorable for poverty alleviation. In line with China's economic and social growth, targeted poverty alleviation measures have integrated financial assistance with self-development of the poor, developing a new system of poverty alleviation.

Therefore, the key take-away for other Asian countries from China's poverty alleviation experience includes boosting economic growth when the poor population is large, and targeted poverty alleviation that plays a key role once the proportion of the poor population is reduced to less than 20 percent of the total. It should be noted that targeted poverty alleviation measures are based on the earlier poverty alleviation measures instead of replacing then with new ones. Since countries can see the best effects of poverty alleviation during the phase of economic growth, driving economic development and allowing the majority of workers to get involved in the economy is the most practical approach with the least burden on governments in the process of large-scale poverty alleviation.

In light of this, Asian countries need to seize the opportunities in the current era to further promote the integration of the industrial, supply and value chains, and achieve regional economic integration based on the multilateral framework for common prosperity, which shows great potential for cooperation in many fields including utilization of productive factors, industrial development and inter-generational transfer of technologies.

The foundation for Asian countries' development in the 21st century lies in solidarity and stability, for which major global and regional powers have to bear key responsibility. Stable and predictable bilateral relations between major countries can ensure the multilateral cooperation in political, economic and social fields, and help achieve common development in Asia. Political and social stability, consistent development strategies and the government's determination to ensure the economic and social system is fair and just are important for alleviating poverty. China's experience is being used as reference by Cambodia, Indonesia, Malaysia and Vietnam to reduce poverty. And to achieve overall poverty alleviation, Asian countries need to work jointly to maintain domestic and regional stability.

II. What the Rest of BRICS Can Learn from China's Experience[1]

This year, I suspect, will go down as remarkable in the history of mankind as a result of the unanticipated COVID-19 pandemic, the loss of life that hit so many countries unprepared, and the associated collapse of economic activity. The United Nations has reported that this shock has already been so big that it will reverse some of the progress on the eradication of poverty. Let's hope it is temporary because almost definitely one of the greatest achievements of my professional lifetime, extending back to 1983, has been the dramatic reduction in global poverty. And it is really important that the world recognizes this more frequently during these more challenging days as it truly has been a superb consequence of world economic development.

Although a number of parts of the world have shared in the dramatic reduction in poverty, including many parts of Latin America, parts of the Soviet Union and Eastern Europe, small parts of Africa, and other vast swathes of North and parts of Southeast Asia, China has been at the center of this remarkable improvement. So not only has China lifted hundreds of millions of people out of basic poverty, but it has also succeeded for probably around half the same number, achieving the living standards of a major G7 economy.

I would like to think I did have some awareness of this potential, being the author of the original BRICs report in 2001, when I first wrote a paper entitled The

----

[1] By Jim O'Neill, coiner of the term "BRIC", former commercial secretary to the UK Treasury and chair of Chatham House.

World Needs Better Economic BRICs, in which I laid out a scenario where Brazil, Russia, India and China would likely have a bigger share of the global economy. And in subsequent years, together with my then colleagues at Goldman Sachs, we suggested that by the late 2030s, these four nations could collectively become as large in nominal US dollars as the combined size of G7, the most advanced countries. As part of this, we also suggested that sometime before all four became as large as the G7, China itself could become as big as the United States.

As I look to the future during this COVID-19 pandemic, which is still gripping most of the world, the question is, what can other BRICS countries learn from China in its remarkable success from lifting so many people from poverty? It is also something that is even more applicable perhaps for most African nations, especially those in sub-Saharan Africa that, sadly, is where most of the world's poverty is now prevalent.

Ultimately, economic growth is driven by two forces, the size of a country's labor force and its productivity. The biggest determinant of a country's labor force is that nation's demographic trends, so those with high birth rates and life expectancies, typically enjoy the best labor force dynamics, and the only other factor that can really influence the size of a labor force significantly is immigration. Countries with large populations, especially if they are young, typically can grow more than others. In this regard, China and India have a huge advantage over the other BRICS nations, because of course, they are the only ones with populations way in excess of 1 billion.

This brings me to the second determinant of economic growth, productivity, and while China doesn't especially enjoy a natural advantage over the other BRICS countries, it has probably experienced stronger productivity growth in recent decades. This is something other countries can learn from, and indeed, I believe it is important that each of us try to learn from others, especially things that can be helpful.

Trying to improve productivity is, unfortunately, not only difficult, but not a known science. Economists like myself believe that certain successful policies are likely to improve productivity, but we don't know for sure. We can only make educated guesses! But there is quite a bit of anecdotal evidence from the most successful countries in terms of reported productivity and their typically higher levels of prosperity that we can all look to. Usually, there are things like education, life expectancy, healthcare, the quality and availability of infrastructure, both human and physical, and perhaps in modern times, various forms of technology that would all appear crucial. In addition, stability or strength in the quality of governance institutions, and the stability of the macro economy, including the amount of international trade and investment a nation pursues, and its level of national debt, all seem important. On many of these indicators, China also typically scores better than the other BRICS countries.

During my time as chief economist of Goldman Sachs, alongside the BRICs idea, I also presided over the creation of an index called the Growth Environment Score, which attempted to measure 18 variables that we selected, as being statistically significant for sustainable growth and positive productivity change. Most of those highlighted above were among the components.

We used to publish annual GES index scores for around 180 countries every year, although they stopped publishing them in 2014. But here are some important illustrations that are pertinent to this discussion.

The overall index consisting of the 18 different variables were benchmarked and measured in a score that could be no higher than 10, so it could be anywhere from 0 to 10, with 10 being the best.

In the 2014 index, Singapore scored the highest of all countries at 8.10, and Eritrea, scored a very low 2.50, the lowest of 183 countries. Singapore's success, is itself relevant, as it often seems a country that China has tried to learn so much from. Importantly in my view, South Korea scored third, with a score of 7.83, which for a while surprised me, but when I look at its remarkable success at raising its living standards, it is not to be ignored. Looking at the components, South Korea seems to score especially high marks for its education and use of technologies. I often say to leaders or the policy advisors to leaders of many countries that wish to improve their productivity, South Korea is a country that can be learned from, especially as it has more than 50 million people, and it is not especially well-endowed with natural resources.

As far as the BRICS are concerned, China scored highest, with a score of 6.03. So China could still learn from other countries, including Singapore and South Korea, as I am sure it will do. The larger Western nations typically score between the highs of Singapore and China, although interestingly, in 2014, China's GES score went above Italy for the first time.

As for the other BRICS countries, Russia scored next at 5.51, Brazil just below with 5.43, South Africa at 5.29, and India, notably lower, around 4.22, which in terms of the league table, was more than 100 places below China, at 151 versus China at 49.

In this regard, a glance at the index components shows many things that the other BRICS countries can learn from China, notably its education achievements, its use of technology, as well as many indicators about macroeconomic stability, especially the degree to which China engages in international trade and investment. For China itself to achieve its longer-term ambition of even greater shared wealth for all its own citizens, it needs to do better on some of these scores, and in others, such as aspects of governance and the rule of law, it has quite a bit of progress to make. But it is definitely the case that all of the other BRICS countries have more to learn from China if they wish to achieve the same kind of success, perhaps especially for India as it tries to satisfy its burgeoning population.

III. Lessons Latin America Can Learn from China's Poverty Alleviation[1]

Although it can be stated that there is much heterogeneity among the 18 Latin American countries, still in the better-off ones, poverty and extreme poverty hasn't been eradicated, and more worrisome, have increased in the past years. The most updated figures show that in 2018, 30.1 percent (185 million people) were below the poverty line in Latin America, and 10.7 percent (66 million people) were under the extreme poverty line.[2]

Traditionally, Chile and Uruguay have been the better positioned countries in Latin America in the battle against poverty. Both in 2018 show less than 11 percent of their population living in poverty, and less than 2 percent in extreme poverty. The panorama is quite different in the rest of the region, being the most dramatic situations, more than 40 percent of their population living in poverty and 19 percent in extreme poverty.

---

[1] By Andreas Pierotic, minister counselor and head of the Economic & Trade Department of the Embassy of Chile in China from 2014 to 2019, trade negotiator for the government of Chile, China desk in the General Directorate for International Economic Relations of the Ministry of Foreign Affairs of Chile.

[2] The United Nation's Economic Commission for Latin America and the Caribbean is the most authoritative organization following up the region's poverty alleviation statistics through its annual reports. See Economic Commission for Latin America and the Caribbean, Social Panorama of Latin America 2019, Santiago, 2019, p. 92 https://repositorio.cepal.org/bitstream/handle/11362/44989/1/S1901132_en.pdf

Table 1[①]: Latin America (15 countries): Poverty and extreme poverty rates

	ECLAC estimates				
	Extreme poverty				
	2015	2016	2017	2018	
Argentina[b]	...	2.9	2.8	3.6	
Bolivia (Plurinational State of)	14.6	...	16.4	14.7	
Chile	4.0	5.0	5.5	5.4	
Brazil[c]	1.8	...	1.4	...	
Colombia	11.3	12.0	10.9	10.8	
Costa Rica	4.6	4.2	3.3	4.0	
Dominican Republic[d]	9.2	7.2	6.4	5.0	
Ecuador	7.0	7.5	7.0	6.5	
El Salvador	10.4	10.7	8.3	7.6	
Honduras	19.0	18.8	...	19.4	
Mexico[e]	...	11.7	...	10.6	
Panama	8.0	8.5	7.6	6.2	
Paraguay	7.3	7.9	6.0	6.5	
Peru	5.4	5.2	5.0	3.7	
Uruguay	0.2	0.2	0.1	0.1	

Source: Economic Commission for Latin America and the Caribbean (ECLAC), on the basis of Household Survey Data Bank (BADEHOG) and official figures on poverty and extreme poverty.
a Countries for which ECLAC poverty estimates are available from 2015 onward.
b ECLAC estimates refer to the fourth quarter of each year. The official estimates refer to the second half of each year.
c From 2016 onward, the ECLAC estimates refer to the Permanent National Household Survey (PNAD-Continua) and are not comparable with those of previous years. The

---

① ECLAC uses a harmonized and common mathematical methodology to asses every Latin American country. It classifies between poor and extreme poor by assesing a person's income or its household income below the "poverty line" or the "extreme poverty line". These lines represent the level of income than enables each household to meet the basic needs of all its members, considering food prices in each country and non-food needs. Ibid, p 91.

	Total poverty				Variation 2017-2018	
	2015	2016	2017	2018	EP	P
	…	21.5	18.7	24.4	0.8	5.6
	34.7	…	35.2	33.2	-1.7	-1.9
	18.8	19.8	20.3	19.4	-0.1	-0.9
	13.7	…	10.7	…	…	…
	30.6	30.9	29.8	29.9	-0.2	0.1
	17.4	16.5	15.4	16.2	0.7	0.8
	29.7	27.3	25.0	22.0	-1.5	-3.0
	23.9	24.3	23.6	24.2	0.5	0.5
	42.6	40.5	37.8	34.5	0.8	-3.3
	55.2	53.2	…	55.8	…	…
	…	43.7	…	41.5	-1.0	-2.3
	17.9	17.0	16.7	14.5	-1.4	-2.2
	23.4	24.0	21.6	19.5	0.5	-2.1
	19.0	19.1	18.9	16.8	-1.3	-2.1
	4.2	3.5	2.7	2.9	0.0	0.3

reported official data refer to estimates from the Brazilian Institute of Geography and Statistics (IBGE) (2019), based on the lines used by the World Bank for low- and medium-high-income countries.

d The ECLAC figures are based on the national labour force survey and refer to September of each year until 2015. From 2016 onward they are based on the continuous national labour force survey and are annual.

e The official poverty measurement is multidimensional. Therefore, the estimates published by the National Council for the Evaluation of Social Development Policy (CONEVAL) are used as an unofficial national reference, namely "population below the minimum welfare threshold", which is taken as a measure of "extreme poverty", and "population below the welfare threshold", which serves as a proxy for "total poverty".

Latin America hasn't been successful, considering the region as a whole, in sustainably and speedily lowering poverty and extreme poverty prevalence in the past 20 years, nor is it expected that there will be sharp drops in the upcoming years that allow the region to eradicate extreme poverty and halving all poverty by 2030, as proposed in the agenda of the Sustainable Development Goals.[1]

On the contrary, total population in poverty in 2018 in Latin America increased 2.3 percent compared to 2014, that is, around 21 million people. For the same period, the extreme poverty increase was even higher: 2.9 percent, that is, around 20 million people. Thus, the region has witnessed an overall increase of poverty since 2015, especially in extreme poverty.[2] This draws a rather pessimistic picture for Latin America's governments to reach the SDG on time.

The United Nation's Economic Commission for Latin America and the Caribbean's most optimistic projected scenario for the region to accomplish these goals requires Latin American GDP per capita to grow 2 percent from 2019 to 2030, and to reduce in the same period income distribution inequality of 1.5 percent per year and attain an annual Gini reduction of 1.5 percent,[3] all of which is highly improbable to attain.

Irregularity and weakness of the decrease in poverty levels is the current landscape of Latin America's fight against poverty and extreme poverty. Having in sight a sharp decrease forecast regarding economic growth this year for the region (-4 percent, or even

---

[1] ECLAC explains that for Latin America, the target of total poverty by 2030 is 14.5% (as the indicator stood in 29.1% in 2019). For extreme poverty, the target is 3%. "Extreme poverty equal to zero is not used as a scenario because of certain methodological limitations of income measurements based on household surveys, which mean that even in a scenario in which extreme poverty is eradicated, measurements would continue to indicate an extreme poverty rate greater than zero". Ibid, p 115 and 116.

[2] Ibid, p 93.

[3] Ibid, p 115 and 116.

more cannot be ruled out),[1] and a slow recovery expected not before 2022—2023 due to the COVID-19 impact,[2] it's urgent that Latin America's poverty alleviation policies are reinforced and governments look more carefully to successful stories in this field, such as China's.

Figure 1: Poverty and extreme poverty in Latin America (percentage)

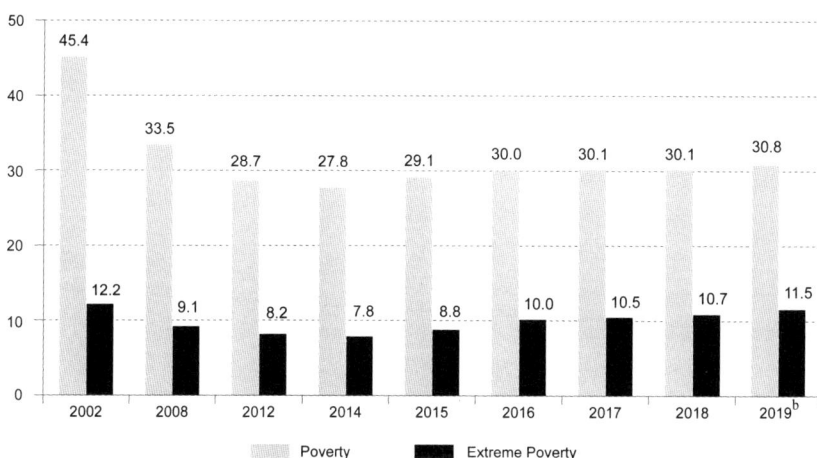

Source: Economic Comission for Latin America and the Caribbean (ECLACI, on the basis of Household Survey Data Bank (BADEHOG).

a Weighted average for the fllowing countries: Argentina, Bolivarian Republic of Venezuela, Brazil, Chile, Colombia, Costa Rica, Dominican Republic, Ecuador, El Salvador, Guatemala, Honduras, Mexico, Nicaragua, Panama, Paraguay, Peru, Plurinational State of Bolivia and Uruguay.

b The values are projections.

---

[1] See Economic Commission for Latin America and the Caribbean, Latin America & the Caribbean and the Covid-19 Pandemic: Economic and Social Effects, April 3, 2020 https://repositorio.cepal.org/bitstream/handle/11362/45351/1/S2000263_en.pdf

[2] Goldman Sachs reported by Reuters, May 20, 2020 https://www.reuters.com/article/us-latam-economy-goldman-sachs/latin-americas-economy-to-shrink-record-7-6-this-year-goldman-sachs-idUSKBN22V2QB.

Table 2: Latin America (15 countries):
Classification of countries by poverty and extreme poverty rates, 2018[a]

		Poverty					
		Under 15%	**15% to 20%**	**20% to 25%**	**25% to 30%**	**30% to 35%**	**Over 35%**
Extreme poverty	**Under 5%**	Uruguay Chile	Costa Rica Peru	Argentina			
	5% to 10%	Panama	Brazil Paraguay	Ecuador Dominican Republic		El Salvador	
	10% to 15%				Colombia	Bolivia (Plurinational State of)	Mexico
	Over 15%						Honduras

Source: Economic Commission for Latin America and the Caribbean (ECLAC), on the basis of Household Survey Data Bank (BADEHOG).
a Includes only countries with available information for 2017 or 2018. Data refer to 2018 except in the case of Chile (2017).

China and Latin America have common poverty alleviation goals, but do not share historical and cultural roots, nor geographical and ethnic proximity. These factors make it a hard task to extract transplantable experiences from China to be implemented in Latin America with perspectives of success.

As such, I have ruled out both micro or specific poverty alleviation policies and macroeconomic and social development policies that have indirectly and directly influenced China's virtuous cycle of spectacular economic growth and poverty alleviation. These micro and macro policies have shown great results in China, but given Latin America's political, economic and social structural differences with China, could not be replicated there.

Yet, I firmly believe after observing China's governmental institutional building these past 20 years, that is, precisely vis-à-vis institutional building, there is an unexplored connecting node that could allow Latin America countries to learn valuable lessons that may be even adjustable to their local context and conditions.

Consequently, I have done the exercise to specifically extract, in the sphere of poverty alleviation institutional building, the four main precise successful lessons from China that should be taken in account by any Latin American government that aims to work sustainably to reach its poverty and extreme poverty eradication goals by 2030.

a) Stable specialized poverty alleviation bureaucracy

Latin American governments have not attached importance to establishing and nurturing specialized poverty alleviation profession within the state's institutional framework. Thus, responsibility regarding poverty alleviation in some cases is spread in several independent sectorial ministries (usually health, housing and education), unaccountable local elected officials, or in specialized agencies whose top officials aren't decoupled from the 4-5 year presidential term thinking. Therefore, poverty alleviation bureaucracies in Latin America do not withhold a state policy character, as China does, rather than a current, and therefore disposable, governmental policy status.

China's experience here is valuable for Latin America. In great measure, its success relies on a consolidated poverty governance system, which is dominated by the State Council Leading Group Office of Poverty Alleviation and Development established in 1986. The Leading Office was set to serve specifically for formulating principles, policies and plans in impoverished regions in a planned and organized manner. It controls top down specialized offices at the province, prefecture, county and town levels. It is the core of long-term policies implementation and works side by side sharing political responsibility for meeting poverty alleviation goals with Party secretaries at the levels of province, city, county, town and village across China.[1]

---

[1] See Hu Fuguo, *Understanding China: Poverty Alleviation*, Foreign Languages Press, 2019. p. 87 and 100.

No matter the changes of leadership in China, the poverty alleviation bureaucracy has shown to be firmly institutionalized as the holder of the responsibility for one of China's highest permanent interests. This is one of the greatest and baseline lessons that Latin America should learn from China: they must not only centralize, but carve out the poverty alleviation bureaucracy from the common practice of other institutions, so its officials and professionals are isolated as much as possible from the changing political environment that the countries of our region—because of the nature of our political systems—experience every four or five years.

b) Long term but adaptable poverty alleviation policies

A direct consequence in Latin American countries lack of strong and stable specialized poverty alleviation bureaucracies is the impossibility of drafting long-term policies on this topic. As seen through the lens of China's experience, important areas of work are consubstantial to the capacity of a country to be able to support and sustain policies in time. Infrastructure, housing and healthcare facilities construction or industrial and agricultural development are clear examples of naturally long-term poverty alleviation policies that delivered results in China, that entail not only extended vision and execution, but the power of allocating enduring budgets.

This is such a simple lesson, however with such profound influence and impact, that must be examined by Latin American countries. If there is one feature that all the region's countries share, it is precisely their failure in allocating long-term budgets that finance enduring poverty alleviation policies.

Secondly, adaptability is a key element of poverty alleviation policies. According to what I have seen in China, long-term policies in the field always behold the possibility of adjustment according to new contextual conditions. China's policymakers never rule-out *ex ante* the necessity to review their long-term policies according to new findings, acquired knowledge, foreign experience or even failure, among others. In our time, information and knowledge are shared and incorporated speedily. China's bureaucracy has shown clear understanding of this characteristic of our era, incorporating it as a natural part of its policy review processes. As such, Latin America should not forget that designing long-term poverty alleviation policies does not mean to petrify them.

c) Designing targeted poverty alleviation policies

Latin American countries have a long history of failed policies that have been based in useless projects that have cost not only money, but precious time. The path in the region to fulfill the SDGs has left a long trail of well-financed, but miscarried poverty alleviation programs. Contrasted with China, it's relatively easy to conclude that among the important reasons for Latin America's current outcome are the lack of precise designing of the policies that sustained them, as well as a faulty identification of the impoverished population at the base.

This probably is the most difficult issue that policymakers face. China, indeed, has also encountered challenging issues in this regard that have required President Xi Jinping to personally address them, formulating in 2015 the need of commitment of poverty alleviation policymakers with the "six precisions": precision in selecting beneficiaries, in project arrangement, in the utilization of funds, in tailoring measures to households, in sending the right personnel to poverty-stricken villages and in poverty elimination outcomes; and requested also their commitment with lifting people out of poverty in "five batches" : through industrial development, through relocation, through ecological compensation, through education and through the social safety net.[1]

For sure, this specific policy setup for China's poverty-related bureaucracy may not be completely suitable for Latin America's specific circumstances, but it sheds light upon both the difficulties and cruciality of solving policy precision related issues. Specifically, Latin America could particularly benefit from China's experience developing mechanisms to precise the selection of the beneficiaries of poverty alleviation policies and tailoring the measures for those selected.

---

[1]   Ibid, p. 89.

Generally speaking, Latin America has commonly missed accuracy in identifying the poor, especially due to the high prevalence in our countries of the informal economy, a problem also seen in China, with the important difference that China boasts an improved technological and on-the-ground citizenship identification and registry system. This is the first major step that Latin American policymakers should take in order to assure not leaving anyone behind. Registering people accurately is the basic requirement to have cutting-edge information on the actual income of households. Nevertheless, Latin America's governments should also understand that registering should be dynamic because poverty is dynamic as well; population may fall into poverty because of accidents, health issues, natural disasters, etc. Additionally, the identification and measurement should not only consider income because poverty is multidimensional, involving access to education, health, housing, among others.[1] So, perfecting the identification system is the first step that most Latin American countries should endeavor to do.

On the other hand, China used to have a "free flooding" system[2] to implement poverty alleviation, which means that the policies in China weren't always targeted nor tailored to individual context conditions, but generally applied with scarce effectiveness. This is still happening in Latin America. The region mostly hasn't been able to implement a "precision drip dropping" system as in China, due not only to the lack of the implementation of precise information systems of impoverished households just remarked, but also to the lack of professional poverty alleviation agencies with long-term goals and accountability.

d) Accountability in poverty alleviation goals

Finally, Latin America has been struck by the lack of enforceable accountability systems aimed at high-ranking poverty alleviation officials. As explained previously, the region's agencies dealing with poverty haven't been carved out of the bureaucracy system and are subject to the the the outcomes of electoral politics.

---

[1] Ibid., p 109.

[2] Ibid., p 130.

As such, high-ranking officials in charge of policy design and execution on the topic are usually neither well versed in poverty alleviation nor accountable to administrative bodies, given the fact that they are not career officials, but politicians for which administrative sanctions bare no significant consequence for their professional future, given also that their career path is not devoted lifelong to the public sector.

On the other hand, the accountability of poverty alleviation officials is weakened by the diffusion of responsibility among an array of ministries, agencies, municipalities and other local authorities. Therefore, the design of public administrations in Latin America only promotes the dilution of responsibility, the absence of accountability of officials, and consequently, nurtures poor performance in the battle against poverty.

China, conversely, has understood that making officials responsible for their work on poverty alleviation issues is central to conquer the ambitious set goals. Accordingly, it has enforced a system in which designing and executing suitable policies is expected from its officials, which are all career public official. Critical for their professional upward pathway is the assessment of the effects of the policies carried out by them. Thus, the State Council Leading Group Office of Poverty Alleviation and Development has been given the authority to conduct inspections and evaluations annually[1] throughout China's hierarchy, from top (provincial) to town level officials, rewarding accomplishments and punishing irregularities. It relies on advances in technology (standardized statistical cross-evaluation systems between provinces, app-wide data collection system and big data evaluation platforms) and on third-party organizations, such as research institutions and social organizations, to verify the results: the effects of the policies implemented by the supervised officials, the accuracy of the identification and exit of the impoverished population, accuracy of the budgeting, the satisfaction of the beneficiaries, and the level of completion of the general goals (eg. stable access to adequate food and clothing, compulsory education, basic medical services and housing).

---

[1] Ibid., p 141.

Strong responsibility in all levels of officials involved in poverty alleviation explains an important part of China's success. The concepts of career professionals, responsibility, accountability, inspection and results evaluation must be carefully considered and adapted to its own institutional reality by Latin America's poverty alleviation governmental organizations.

IV. China's Poverty Experience to Madagascar[①]

I have worked in Madagascar for four years. Many are curious and ask me how China could lift 800 million people out of poverty in just a few decades. What is the secret of the miracle? In activities enhancing communication between China and Madagascar held by the Chinese embassy in Madagascar, *Up and Out of Poverty* is always welcomed by local people. The book is a compilation of President Xi Jinping's major works while he worked in Ningde in East China's Fujian Province, which includes ideas and processes for China's development. These Chinese experiences have achieved increasing recognition and emphasis in global poverty eradiation.

There has been a historic transformation of China since the founding of the People's Republic of China in 1949. It has grown into a flourishing country with comprehensive strength. Industrialization has been realized in a few decades, which typically took several hundred years in developed countries. Economic development has empowered Chinese people, increasing their sense of fulfillment and happiness. From 1949 to 2018, per capita annual income rose from nearly $70 to $9,470, and life expectancy has risen from 35 to 77 years. Education levels have also been greatly lifted, from over 80 percent of the population being illiterate to 94.2 percent having completed nine-year compulsory education by 2018. Not only has China made the remarkable achievement of large-scale poverty reduction, it has also shaped the biggest middle-class group in the world, consisting of over

---

① By Yang Xiaorong, former Chinese ambassador to Madagascar.

400 million people. Adhering to a people-oriented development concept, rapid development and massive poverty reduction are taking place in China, and the fruits of reform and development are being shared by the poor.

China's experience of poverty alleviation shows the world that the path determines development, which should be designed according to local features and situation. Thanks to the strong leadership and institutional advantages of the Communist Party of China and hard-working Chinese people, China is successfully exploring a path of socialism with Chinese characteristics leading to outstanding results in poverty elimination.

Having seen a similar fate in the past, China shares the common goal of getting rid of poverty with Madagascar and other African countries. China's achievements in fighting poverty can provide some encouragement and lessons for African countries, including Madagascar.

Firm confidence serves as a prerequisite. As the largest developing country in the world, China's development was based on a weak foundation, but through tenacious efforts it has grown into the second-largest economy in the world and successfully lifted the largest population in the world out of poverty. It is also the first developing country to achieve the United Nations Millennium Development Goals.

Africa has many developing countries with great potential for economic take-off. They enjoy abundant natural resources and intelligent people. Therefore, the miracle in China definitely can be recreated in Africa as well. A Madagascan friend told me that African countries should be confident seeing China's economic development because per capita GDP of many African countries was no less than that of China before the reform and opening-up in 1978. Aided by efficient exchanges with China, it is expected that African countries can achieve prosperous and powerful economies.

China and Madagascar should communicate well on development. As an old Chinese saying goes, "teaching one to fish is better than giving a fish".

Madagascar is actively carrying out its national initiative for revitalization, where China's experience during economic development and eradicating poverty can be helpful. For instance, Madagascar is giving great priority to development and the industrialization and modernization of agriculture. China always regards development as the fundamental approach to eliminate poverty, reducing poverty through industrial development. Madagascar is one of the countries with the greatest biodiversity in the world. China is also experienced in getting rid of poverty by making full use of local ecological advantages. To develop the country, Madagascar needs more professional experts and equipment. China can provide both equipment and training. So far, China has invited hundreds of Madagascans to participate in economic and technological cooperation and training programs.

China always attaches great importance to aid to Africa. In response to the poor infrastructure in Madagascar, the Chinese government built a highway in Madagascar in the 1980s, functioning as the economic lifeline connecting the capital Antananarivo and the largest economic city Tananarive. Chinese workers made selfless contributions and overcame various difficulties; five of them even lost their lives. In recent years, China has aided the construction of roads to the airport as well as "egg roads", which has effectively settled the problems of transporting eggs from poultry areas, boosting the development of the local economies and people's livelihoods.

What is worth highlighting is that as the largest developing country in the world, China helping African countries is part of South-South Cooperation, revealing their true brotherhood.

The year 2020 is a milestone year for China as it will see a decisive victory in fighting poverty and realization of the goal to build a moderately prosperous society in all respects. While striving to shake off poverty, China will also actively promote global cooperation in this field, promoting mutual benefit for common development.

V. Relevance and Lessons of China's Poverty Alleviation for Bangladesh and Beyond[1]

The success of China's poverty alleviation mainly comes from three stages of institutional reforms, bringing encouraging results in poverty alleviation. The first stage of institutional reform took place in the Chinese land system. The structure of collective farming was replaced with the "household contract responsibility system" which highly motivated individual farmers who were now able to enjoy fruits of their own labor. The second stage was in the market of agricultural products. Gradual liberalization restructured the market for agricultural products, resulting in a sudden increase in agricultural products price. By 1984, the farmers' wages became quite close to the factory workers'. The third stage was implemented by absorbing surplus agricultural labor. The rural economic structure was optimized due to the increase of township and village enterprises (Khan 8 Riskin, 2001)[2].

However, China was a very versatile country and every region had its own problems with the reform activities. Thus, the Chinese government established the State Council Leading Group on Economic Development in Poor Areas in May 16, 1986, which was renamed as the "State Council Leading Group on Poverty Alleviation and Development" in 1993. Core responsibilities of the Leading Group included observing poverty conditions in China's various underdeveloped regions, finding out solutions for severe development problems in poor areas. The State Council Poverty Alleviation Office is the regular office department for the Leading

---

[1] By Niaz Ahmed Khan and Alvy Al Srijohn. Niaz Ahmed Khan, professor and former chairman of Department of Development Studies at University of Dhaka, senior academic adviser of BRAC Institute of Governance and Development, chairman of Bangladesh Tropical Forest Conservation (Arannayak) Foundation and former country representative-Bangladesh of IUCN-International Union for Conservation of Nature.

Alvy Al Srijohn, lecturer in Development Studies at the National Institute of Textile Engineering & Research (NITER), Dhaka, Bangladesh.

[2] Khan, A. R., & Riskin, C. (2001). *Inequality and Poverty in China in the Age of Globalization.* Oxford University Press.

Group and it has similar but smaller subordinate offices in provinces, autonomous regions, municipalities, prefectures and counties (Xiaoyun and Remenyi, 2008)[1].

In face of the problems of inequality and development gap, in April 2001, the Chinese government created a program named the "China Rural Poverty Alleviation and Development Program (2001-2010)", identifying 148,000 poor villages and designing village-wide poverty reduction plans. Another innovative initiative taken by the Chinese government was "Three Rural Issues", positively taking measures in solving problems in agriculture, rural areas and farmers, for example, reducing agricultural taxes, subsidizing the compulsory education schooling fees of rural students, initiating a rural cooperative healthcare nation-wide.

It is evident that China has perceived the concept of poverty from a "problem" perspective. The Chinese government has put great emphasis on poverty conditions and formulated evidence-based detailed policies, plans and programs to fight poverty. In addition, it should be noted that the Chinese government has successfully kept economic development running while at the same time trying to close the income gap created by the increasing inequality. It appears that China's policy makers were aware from the very beginning that achieving high economic growth does not mean anything unless the national income is being distributed based on equality and equity (Yan, 2016)[2].

Bangladesh and other South Asian countries may benefit from the relevant Chinese experience of poverty alleviation by way of eliciting and internalizing some crucial and proven lessons including the following. It may, however, be noted at this point that these lessons and suggestions are not meant to be universal or infallible; they are essentially indicative. The aim is to explore and furnish a range of ideas drawing on the Chinese experience, which other countries may consider and implement after careful consideration of their respective (particular) contexts,

---

[1] Xiaoyun, L., & Remenyi, J. (2008). Making poverty mapping and monitoring participatory. Development in Practice, 18(4-5), 599-610.

[2] Yan, K. (2016). Poverty Alleviation in China. Springer-Verlag Berlin.

condition and realities of the field.

The Chinese government was aware of the problem of inequality from the very beginning. They planned ahead and prepared countermeasures to deal with inequality and other problems associated with it. The Chinese case amply brings home the importance of carefully thinking about and planning for encountering the problems of socioeconomic inequality from the very beginning of any development effort and agenda.

China has taken many specially geared policies and functional measures to protect and safeguard the interests of vulnerable groups (for example, rural farmers and factory workers) in line with the principle of reducing disparity. Special efforts were made, for example, to strike a balance between the income levels of farmers and factory workers, as well as cushioning these vulnerable groups from such shocks as natural disasters and sudden market failures. These measures later helped China to lessen the inequality between rural and urban areas. Rising inequality and iniquity pose a formidable challenge for Bangladesh and casts a dark shadow on the country's otherwise impressive progress in poverty reduction (see, for example, Matin 2017)[1]. One analyst posits this pertaining question regarding Bangladesh:

The economic trend shows that Bangladesh is now the 31st largest economy in the world in terms of purchasing power parity and will become the 28th by 2030. It is expected that Bangladesh will be the 23rd largest economy in the world by 2050 as a developed nation. Indeed, it indicates that the country is heading through a stunning growth. However, this growth progression may become meaningless if eventually we turn out to be a country having "growth without equity".

In exploring possible answers to the above question, the Chinese practices may provide useful insights. China has used its vast manpower to produce innovative

---

[1] Matin, K.A. (2017) 'Economic Growth and Inequality in Bangladesh', Paper presented at the 20th Biennial Conference on Economic an Ethics of the Bangladesh Economic Association. held during December 21-23, 2017 in Dhaka.

and low-cost products, and thereby, gaining a competitive edge in the export-oriented industries.

China is a rare example of achieving the highest rate of economic and scientific excellence despite having very poor infrastructure and resource to begin with. As a country, China can be an encouraging illustration, of what is popularly dubbed as "making the impossible possible" for Bangladesh and other South Asian countries. In the context of the "Look East" outlook of many nations in the South Asian region (including Bangladesh), coupled with China's rising influence and prominence in the global order, China offers an interesting and encouraging case to be examined and explored for mutual learning and benefit sharing.

听脱贫历程
懂脱贫攻坚

【脱贫故事分享】

以生动事例展现脱贫攻坚工作上的努力与经验

另外，还可添加"智能阅读向导"

帮你回顾和理解脱贫攻坚一路走来的历程

☑ 中国脱贫攻坚图鉴

☑ 解读脱贫攻坚展现出来的伟大精神

▶▶▶ ◀◀◀

微信扫码